THE MAKING OF REVERSE DISCRIMINATION

THE MAKING OF REVERSE DISCRIMINATION

How DeFunis *and* Bakke *Bleached Racism from Equal Protection*

ELLEN MESSER-DAVIDOW

UNIVERSITY PRESS OF KANSAS

Published by the University Press of Kansas (Lawrence, Kansas 66045), which was organized by the Kansas Board of Regents and is operated and funded by Emporia State University, Fort Hays State University, Kansas State University, Pittsburg State University, the University of Kansas, and Wichita State University

Library of Congress Cataloging-in-Publication Data

Names: Messer-Davidow, Ellen, 1941– author.
Title: The making of reverse discrimination : how Defunis and Bakke bleached racism from equal protection / Ellen Messer-Davidow.
Description: Lawrence : University Press of Kansas, 2021 | Includes bibliographical references and index.
Identifiers: LCCN 2020044296
ISBN 9780700632206 (cloth)
ISBN 9780700632213 (paperback)
ISBN 9780700632220 (epub)
Subjects: LCSH: Affirmative action programs in education—Law and legislation—United States—History. | Discrimination in higher education—Law and legislation—United States—History. | Universities and colleges—Admission—Law and legislation—United States—History. | Race discrimination—Law and legislation—United States—History. | Minorities—Education (Higher)—United States. | DeFunis, Marco—Trials, litigation, etc. | Odegaard, Charles E., 1911–1999—Trials, litigation, etc. | Bakke, Allan Paul—Trials, litigation, etc. | University of California (System). Regents—Trials, litigation, etc.
Classification: LCC KF4155 .M47 2021 | DDC 344.73/0798—dc23
LC record available at https://lccn.loc.gov/2020044296.

British Library Cataloguing-in-Publication Data is available.

Printed in the United States of America

10 9 8 7 6 5 4 3 2 1

The paper used in this publication is acid free and meets the minimum requirements of the American National Standard for Permanence of Paper for Printed Library Materials Z39.48-1992.

CONTENTS

ACKNOWLEDGMENTS

As always, many people made this book possible.

The University of Minnesota supported my research and writing with a Graduate School Grant-in-Aid of Research and a College of Liberal Arts Research Grant for research travel, material, and assistants. Doctoral students in the Department of English provided invaluable assistance, retrieving books and briefs, reading drafts, fixing citations, and participating in many pleasurable conversations about their work and mine. I am grateful to Heather McNeff, Santi Clark, David Lemke, Aleisha Smith, and especially Zoe Rodine, who reviewed all chapters, checked citations, and drafted the bibliography.

Brilliant colleagues provided important advice on draft chapters: Robert M. O'Neil (who patiently offered advice on all things related to *DeFunis v. Odegaard*), Andrew Elfenbein (who read the full typescript), and Timothy Brennan (who asked incisive questions about purposes and strategies).

I am grateful to the officials who sat for interviews lasting two hours or more, excerpted in this book: Julian Bond (NAACP), Roger Clegg (Center for Equal Opportunity), Diane Gross (Lawyers Committee for Civil Rights Under the Law), Wade Henderson (Leadership Conference on Civil Rights), Curt Levey (Center for Individual Rights), Kevin Nguyen (American Civil Rights Institute), and Theodore Shaw (NAACP Legal Defense and Education Fund). Also interviewed were two major participants in *DeFunis*—Robert M. O'Neil and Craig Sternberg (who kindly furnished a copy of the trial transcript).

Special thanks go to associates of the University Press of Kansas—two readers who wrote detailed reports that I could use as a page-by-page checklist, and David Congdon, acquisitions editor for political science and law, who provided insightful comments on the originally submitted typescript and chapter revisions. It was the best editorial experience I have ever had!

Finally, I want to acknowledge three distinguished scholars who have inspired me (as well as hundreds of other scholars in diverse fields). Warren Bennis (1925–2014) introduced me to the theory and activities of academic institutions back in the 1970s when he was the University of Cincinnati president. By phone and email, Annette Kolodny (1941–2019) provided constant encouragement throughout my work on this book and indeed throughout our forty-year friendship. Stanley Fish (1938–), in our South Florida conversations, patiently listened to my muddled arguments about racial discrimination cases and responded by explaining the law.

INTRODUCTION: WHAT IS "REVERSE DISCRIMINATION"?

> On what "table," according to what grid of identities, similitudes, analogies, have we become accustomed to sort out so many different and similar things?
>
> —Michel Foucault, *The Order of Things: An Archaeology of the Human Sciences* (1970)

Every book tells a story, but not every book tells the backstory of why it came to be written and where it sits in the crowded field of writings on its topic. This book examines *DeFunis v. Odegaard* (1974) and *Regents of the University of California v. Bakke* (1978), the first cases on "reverse discrimination" in professional school admissions to reach the United States Supreme Court. The disputes generated a voluminous literature consisting of litigant and amicus briefs, court opinions, media feature stories, scholarly articles, law review forums, and monographs on the cases themselves or, more generally, on the constitutionality of race-conscious remedies for racism. Yet as I read the literature, I found myself interested in the "not-said"—undisclosed facts, deracialized principles, and disappearing interests—and hoped to discover what had bleached racism from the principle of equal protection described in these cases.

MAKING THE JOURNEY

My journey began in the early 1990s when, or so it seemed to the television-viewing public, the clamoring figure of "Political Correctness" burst onto the national stage. To many of my academic colleagues, the PC debate appeared to be another skirmish in the by then forty-year-old war over democratization—this one a surgical strike against higher education launched by Reagan administration apparatchiks and conservative intellectuals. The clarion call to defend Western culture was sounded by National Endowment for the Humanities (NEH) chair William J. Bennett in *To Reclaim a Legacy* (1984) and amplified by his successor, NEH chair Lynne V. Cheney, in *The Humanities and the American Promise* (1987), *Humanities in America* (1988), *50 Hours* (1989), *Tyrannical Machines* (1990), and *Telling the Truth* (1993). By the early 1990s, conservative best sellers like E. D. Hirsch Jr.'s *Cultural Literacy* (1987), Allan Bloom's *The Closing of the American Mind* (1987), Charles Sykes's *Profscam* (1988), Roger Kimball's *Tenured Radicals* (1990), and Dinesh D'Souza's *Illiberal Education* (1991) were appearing at the rate of two per year, and scores of articles in the *New Republic*, *Commentary*, and *Academic Questions* were denouncing progressive research, multicultural teaching, student groups, speech policies, and affirmative-action programs.

While many of my colleagues were vigorously refuting the PC claims, I was asking a different question: how had conservatives produced and distributed this massive discourse? Touring the movement's shadowy infrastructure, I interviewed officials associated with think tanks, training institutes, advocacy groups, law centers, and media outlets, afterwards writing a series of articles that described their funding and activities.[1] Along the way, I noticed proliferating attempts to ban affirmative action—voter referenda in California, Texas, Washington, and Michigan; an executive order in Florida; and lawsuits in several states. The initiatives worried me because, since its inception in the early 1970s, affirmative action had helped people of color and white women enter the white male-dominated precincts of education, business, and politics, to name a few. In 2001 and 2002, just as *Gratz v. Bollinger* (2003) and *Grutter v. Bollinger* (2003), the widely publicized reverse-discrimination cases against the University of Michigan, were climbing the judicial ladder, I began to explore these initiatives, again conducting interviews at conservative and progressive organizations engaged in the struggle.

At the time, I assumed that the tools I borrowed from sociology of social movements and the new knowledge studies, which had been so useful in analyzing conservatism and writing *Disciplining Feminism: From Social Activism to Academic Discourse* (2002), could be redeployed in a project on affirmative-action law. But as I read the reverse-discrimination cases and followed their citations into the thickets of racial discrimination discourse, I soon found that those methods illuminated very little about the internal workings of the discourse itself. With daunting intertextuality, each opinion bundled together innumerable references to facts, precedents, constitutional commands, statutory provisions, agency regulations, and procedural codes. Since many of the references pointed to earlier texts, I read regressively, hoping to piece together the twists and turns of judicial thought as it traveled from past to present.

Even within the *DeFunis* and *Bakke* briefs, the details of each case reconfigured themselves like bits of glass in a rotating kaleidoscope. By using rhetoric to refract points of fact and law, the adversaries constructed different versions of "racial discrimination" that in turn extruded contradictions onto the surface of each text's story. While I expected a dispute to produce contradictions, I was surprised to find that the texts constituting each case had discursive incommensurabilities. The pro-minority briefs offered abundant historical, sociological, statistical, and experiential facts about systemic racism that, they argued, justified race-conscious remedies; yet the courts mostly dismissed these facts as irrelevant to the narrowly framed dispute between a white applicant and a predominantly white university that appeared in plaintiff and defendant briefs. As an academic scholar, I couldn't understand why court opinions sought to detach the factual filaments of minority exclusion from the nodes of equality principles.

Seeking explanations for the flimsy web of racial jurisprudence, I delved more deeply into law scholarship, following their citations to cases on public schools, employment, government contracting, housing, and voting, but this excursion prompted more questions. Why didn't law scholars follow each case from beginning to end? Historians would. Why didn't they set each case in its social surrounds? Sociologists would. Why didn't they interrogate the construction of the facts and the logic of presumably fact-based precedential reasoning? Critical analysts would. Why didn't they notice that a narrative's frame, syntax, and lexicon made some things appear and others disappear? Literary scholars would. In short, why didn't law scholars problematize the mechanisms that ordered legal-judicial discourse and shaped its objects of analysis?

Lost in this tangled web, I felt pressured to start writing. For cases, as noted above, I chose *DeFunis v. Odegaard* and *Regents of the University of California v. Bakke* because they were the first to reach the Supreme Court challenging race-conscious admissions to professional schools. For material, I cast a wide net, researching each case's precipitating circumstances, reading briefs and opinions as it journeyed through the courts, and examining the societal forces that buffeted the litigation. For my object of analysis, I chose to dissect precisely what had been eluding me: the order of the discourse. How had its mechanisms narrowed each story to a single white male applicant and a single university program? How had they enabled the plaintiffs' supporters to assemble "reverse discrimination" as a new object of legal analysis? How had the mechanisms helped the courts dismiss the historical, sociological, statistical, and experiential facts of "systemic racism"?

SUMMARIZING THE CASES

Conventional stories of the two cases that I will examine in this book usually begin with a nod to the early 1970s, the period when universities were instituting affirmative action, and then provide a vignette of the plaintiff's journey before launching into their disquisition of a chosen issue. We learn from the vignette of *DeFunis v. Odegaard* that Marco DeFunis, twice rejected by the University of Washington (UW) Law School but accepted by other law schools, alleged that the UW admissions program had discriminated against him by withholding the resident preference to which he was entitled; during the trial, this nonracial claim was recharacterized as racial discrimination. The trial judge held the program to be unconstitutional and ordered DeFunis's enrollment, the Washington State Supreme Court justices reversed the ruling but affirmed the order of admission, and the US Supreme Court justices mooted the case because DeFunis was soon to graduate.

The constitutional issues the Court dodged in this case quickly returned in *Regents of the University of California v. Bakke*. From this vignette, we learn that Allan Bakke, twice rejected by eleven medical schools, alleged that the University of California Davis (UCD) Medical School maintained a racial quota. By allocating eighty-four places to regular admission and sixteen places to special admission, it prevented him, on grounds of race, from competing for all one hundred places in the entering class. The trial judge held the admissions program to be unconstitutional, the California Supreme Court justices affirmed the ruling and ordered his enrollment, and the US Supreme Court justices fractured on the issues, leaving Justice Powell to craft the compromise that race could be one of several factors considered in the individualized review of applicants.

What we do *not* learn from these conventional stories is that *DeFunis* and *Bakke*, although originating in West Coast states, had incubated in New York City racial conflicts over public schools, jobs, and cultural institutions. The organizations embroiled in this conflict—such as the B'nai B'rith Anti-Defamation League, American Jewish Congress, Sons of Italy, United Federation of Teachers, and Chamber of Commerce—circulated a histrionic quota discourse that mustered Jewish and white-ethnic groups nationwide. Broadening their attack on affirmative action, the organizations filed complaints against fifty-two universities and submitted amicus briefs in *DeFunis* and *Bakke* as well as several employment cases. Thus, well before the Supreme Court agreed to hear *Bakke*, these organizations had mobilized at the local and federal levels to resist the equalization of material opportunities and legal rights.

As soon as the *Bakke* litigants decided to appeal the California Supreme Court ruling, civil rights groups leapt into action, submitting preliminary briefs that urged the US Supreme Court to vacate the state court judgment and remand for a trial that would disclose minority interests. Once the Court agreed to hear the case, Black leaders organized protests and flooded the White House with communications; Black cabinet members pressured the president; the Congressional Black Caucus objected that the solicitor general's motion to participate in oral argument did not represent the views of the legislature; and 240 organizations and individuals submitted 57 amicus briefs. As media coverage fueled the uproar, the justices uncharacteristically made their displeasure known to the solicitor general, who told the attorney general that they "felt the newspaper accounts subjected them to improper public pressure when they were about to hear oral argument."[2] After deliberating for nine months, they issued six opinions that in turn loosed a deluge of commentary on racial discrimination in law and life, beginning with 514 law review articles in the first year alone.[3]

Most of the voluminous literature on *DeFunis* and *Bakke* has focused on the Court's far-from-definitive answers to important constitutional questions and only briefly summarized the facts that appeared in the official case records. In this respect, it has replicated the factual deficiencies created by the participants in *DeFunis* and *Bakke,* who sidelined the maneuvers of the white plaintiffs, ignored the interests of applicants of color, and bleached the color from equal protection. The case facts, as I will demonstrate in this book, deserve more scrutiny than they received because they presumably grounded the courts' judgments of law. Thus the disposition of facts—how they functioned conceptually in relation to legal principles, procedurally in court hearings, and linguistically in representing social circumstances—became one of my central themes. By restoring the facts from the social surrounds and the court hearings, my chapters reveal how participants used the mechanisms of language and law to construct the white-centered narratives that served as the template for the dozens of anti–affirmative action projects that followed.[4]

Chapter 1 depicts the racialized conflict over New York schools, unions, and cultural institutions during the 1960s and 1970s. On one side, communities of color demanded better opportunities for education and employment; on the other side, Jewish organizations, white-ethnic organizations, and a Jewish-dominated teachers' union mobilized their resources to resist change. Crunched in the conflict, officials on the board of education temporized, heads of cultural institutions folded, and students sat at home during a year of school shutdowns. Chapter 2 analyzes two law review articles that became the paradigms for briefs and opinions in the two reverse-discrimination cases I will examine. Lino Graglia's "Special Admission of the 'Culturally Deprived' to Law School" (1970) used the rhetoric of invidiousness to style race-conscious admissions programs as quotas that gave "preferences" to "less qualified" minority applicants. Robert M. O'Neil's "Preferential Admissions: Equalizing Access of Minority Groups to Higher Education" (1971) used the treatise genre to mold social facts and legal principles into a strong rationale for the constitutionality of the programs.

Chapter 3 restores to *DeFunis* the facts omitted from the deficient record assembled at trial, summarized on appeal, and encapsulated in law review articles. It describes the pervasive racism in Seattle housing, education, and employment; Black protests in the community and on the UW campus; the sanitized history of university outreach; and the family's maneuvers to secure special treatment of DeFunis. This more complete story makes it possible to see the fragility of the plaintiff's discrimination claim.

Chapter 4 tracks the coloring of the case from the originally filed complaint through the trial. In his complaint, DeFunis attorney Josef Diamond alleged that the law school admissions committee discriminated against his client by wrongly denying him a state-resident preference. During the trial, he used racialized language to transform this race-neutral claim into the concept of reverse discrimination, which in turn enabled the judge to "find" an equal protection violation. Chapter 5 follows *DeFunis* to the Washington State Supreme Court. After reviewing theories of fact construction, I examine how the brief and opinion writers used time and action framing to narrow the story, malleable language to characterize the facts, abstract principles to give them a legal effect, and specious reasoning to link them to the admissions dispute.

Chapter 6 provides a close reading of Justice Douglas's dissent, the only substantive opinion when the Supreme Court mooted the case. Relying on psycho-biographical interpretation, scholars have attributed the text's contradictions to Douglas's personal ambivalence about race-conscious remedies. Instead, I demonstrate that the text's contradictions are discourse effects of his attempt to reconcile the social-scientific and experiential facts of discrimination with the abstract principle of equal protection. Douglas did not have an ambivalence problem; rather, the social and legal discourses had an incommensurability problem.

Chapter 7 restores the facts omitted from and distorted during the *Bakke* trial. Although disadvantaged by the medical school's preferences for well-connected, spousal, and younger applicants, the thirty-two-year-old Bakke fixated on the minority admissions program and designed his litigation with the highly inappropriate assistance of a medical school staffer.

Chapter 8 exposes what happened during the truncated discovery and waived trial. After Bakke lawyer Reynold Colvin and UCD lawyer Donald Reidhaar agreed to forego witness testimony, the trial consisted of only their opening statements, their briefs, and UCD admissions data. Colvin depicted the admissions program as a racial quota scheme that displaced highly qualified white applicants, Reidhaar justified the program as a remedy for vaguely defined "societal discrimination," and no one represented the interests of minority applicants, whose absence enabled the judge to "find" racial discrimination against Bakke.

Chapter 9 examines the reasoning during the California Supreme Court phase, which concluded with a ruling for Bakke. By rejecting the amici's facts about systemic racism in education, medical practice, and healthcare access; by interpreting equal protection as an individual rather than group right; and by declining petitions for a retrial that would disclose minority interests, the court reproduced the pattern of litigation without minority representation.

Chapter 10 examines the language and logic in Supreme Court briefs, oral argument, and conference memoranda. Here I show how the participants constru(ct)ed "societal discrimination," "education pipeline discrimination," "racial quota," and "statistical discrimination" as objects located outside or within the "truth" of racial discrimination jurisprudence. By cocooning the disputed medical school places in the twisted strands of legal discourse, the participants obscured the location of *Bakke* within the field of struggle over the distribution of society's material and symbolic resources.

Finally, the concluding chapter focuses on how the conservative movement installed the new racism during the post-*Bakke* struggle to dismantle affirmative action. I argue that it accomplished this task by strategically reorienting its organizations, deploying several forms of coordination among the organizations and with government entities, and channeling plentiful flows of financial, human, and informational resources to projects that diminished the access of communities of color to material and symbolic goods.

DISCIPLINING THE LAW

Only after drafting the fuller stories of *DeFunis* and *Bakke* did I think again about methods and theories. Searching law reviews for explanations of legal discourse, I found many discussions of the interpretive schools—formalism, realism, critical legal studies, critical race and feminist theories—but no incisive analyses of legal studies as an institutionalized discipline consisting of mechanisms for producing and circulating knowledge. Could the tools of "the new knowledge studies" be adapted to my present inquiry?

During the early 1980s, the Society for Critical Exchange (SCE), headquartered at Miami University in Ohio, set out to develop a new analysis of literary studies as a discipline. Scholars who attended its meetings read histories of modern disciplines, studies of professionalization, and Michel Foucault's work on power/knowledge formations. From the late 1980s forward, an SCE offshoot, the Group for Research into the Institutionalization and Professionalization of Literary Studies (GRIP), broadened this scope in an effort to piece together a multidisciplinary field. David Shumway (an original SCE member) and I organized three international conferences that drew scholars from usually nonconversant fields, such as accounting, architecture, economics, education, geography, gerontology, philosophy, and political science. Then we circulated their work in coedited journal issues and, later with David Sylvan, in a co-edited book series published by the University Press of Virginia.[5]

Thinking about legal studies, I realized that its scholars had not engaged with the concept of boundary-work, the growth of specializations, and other features of disciplinarity.[6] In his landmark article, "Boundary-Work and the Demarcation of Science from Non-Science: Strains and Interests in Professional Ideologies of Scientists" (1983), Thomas F. Gieryn wrote that "the intellectual eco-system has with time been carved up into 'separate' institutional and professional niches through continuing processes of boundary-work designed to achieve an apparent differentiation of goals, methods, capabilities and substantive expertise."[7] As his wording suggests, scholars often describe disciplines as intellectualized and institutionalized territories whose residents engage in boundary-work to differentiate their inquiry from its neighbors, win institutional homes and resources, expand into new territories, and regulate in-flows and out-flows of knowledge. A discipline with permeable boundaries welcomes cross-traffic with other fields that in turn diversifies its objects, methods, and knowledge, while one with relatively impermeable boundaries limits this traffic to unify the core. Notwithstanding such fringe hybrids as "law and literature" or the metastasizing hybrid of "law and economics," the law seemed, to me at least, to have nearly impermeable boundaries.

What mediates the reciprocal constitution of boundary and core are well-disciplined practitioners. As Tony Becher explains in *Academic Tribes and Territories*:

> When the patriotic feelings within a discipline run high, deviations from the common cultural norms will be penalized and attempts to modify them from the outside will be rejected. Any systematic questioning of the disciplinary ideology will be seen as heresy and may be punished by expulsion; any infiltration of alien values and practices will be dealt with, either by direct resistance or by incorporation into the prevailing framework of thinking.[8]

Despite their best efforts to police their boundaries and unify their core, practitioners will experience the fracturing and fractiousness that inevitably result from growth. As their field becomes more crowded with scholars or scientists who develop its knowledge, specialisms that form around theories, methods, or topics diversify the once coherent core.[9] In an exceptionally insightful article, "Neoliberalism and the Crisis of Legal Theory," Corinne Blalock apprehends this dynamic at work in legal studies. Mainstream scholars, she explains, faulted critical legal studies (CLS) for presenting negative critiques without positive alternatives, but incorporated some of its insights; feminist, race, and leftist "crits" splintered off; and, as neoliberalism became the hegemonic paradigm in politics and law, they retreated into specialist camps taking their theories with them.[10]

With respect to boundary-work, the participants in and commentators on *DeFunis* and *Bakke* demonstrated that they were disciplined practitioners. From the trial phase through the final rulings, the litigants' attorneys, many of the amici, and most of the judges used boundary-work to frame the cases as disputes between a single white plaintiff and a predominantly white university and to evict minority information whenever it was introduced. Afterwards, scholars who wrote about the cases stayed within bounds by analyzing high court opinions rather than also attending to the documentary and social surrounds. Editorial personnel reinforced boundaries by featuring mainstream articles in major law reviews while leaving transgressive ones to seek homes in peripheral ones. All of this boundary-work did not occur in an ideological vacuum; it reflected the hegemonic theory of possessive individualism.

INDIVIDUALIZING THE SOCIAL FORMATION

The theory emerged in John Locke's *Two Treatises of Government* (1689), a work that refuted Sir Robert Filmer's patriarchal theory of society consisting of hierarchically arranged male-headed households within the monarch-headed state. After using scriptures to undercut Filmer's own scriptural arguments, Locke offered a new model of society that made the individual the basic unit to which natural traits, duties, and rights were attached. Originally subsisting in a state of nature but capable of freely consenting to a governing authority, this rational individual had certain proprietary rights: he owned his body, his labor, and the fruits of his labor, a principle that C. B. Macpherson famously called "possessive individualism." During the eighteenth century, the rights component provided a foundation for the political and juridical principles inscribed in the United States' founding documents; a century later, the proprietary component was used to rationalize capitalist accumulation, as Karl Marx and Rosa Luxemburg explained.[11]

Lockean individualism cycled through various schools of conservative, reformist, and liberal thought in Europe and America before congealing into what became the neoliberal project, which emphasized the proprietary component. Initially fashioned at the Colloque Walter Lippmann in Paris, neoliberal thought was developed at the Mont Pelerin Society, founded in 1947 by intellectuals and journalists from Western Europe, the United Kingdom, and the United States, including such luminaries as Friedrich Hayek, Ludwig von Mises, Karl Popper, and Milton Friedman. After World War II, adherents used think tanks, universities, and media to spread the discourse, which became hegemonic during the Reagan and Thatcher era. As a form of market fundamentalism, it seeks to privatize public services, deregulate business, reduce trade barriers, manage money flows and interest rates, financialize debt, and minimize government through spending cuts for social and cultural programs. These policies gained a global reach when the International Monetary Fund (IMF) and World Bank required countries seeking development loans to institute neoliberal structural adjustments.[12]

Today individualism is the commonsensical method for interpreting words, actions, and events. People presuppose that the individual or the personified unit conveys a message emanating from its motivation and intention: journalists gloss tweets as symptoms of the president's psychological state, teenagers interpret mom's eye-rolling as an adult put-down, and financial analysts blame the nervous market for plunging stock prices. Individualist interpretations are rampant in legal circles: we see them behind the claim that the Fourteenth Amendment protects the individual, not the group, from racial discrimination; the demand for evidence of the perpetrator's intent; and the personification of collective entities such as Congress and corporations. In the now infamous *Citizens United v. F.E.C.* (2010), the majority justices transformed Citizens United, a wealthy political action committee (PAC) that distributed a film opposing a candidate for electoral office, into a "person" entitled to speech protections. Jolted by the case, law scholars hastened to provide genealogies of "person" and "corporation" to reveal how the transformations occurred.[13] While their work provides fascinating examples of linguistic fluidity, it does not problematize individualism.

DEFAMILIARIZING THE COMMONSENSICAL

To gain a critical purchase on legal texts, I had to choose additional tools that would allow me to defamiliarize the commonsensical. Three varieties of social constructionist theory offered the most promising toolkits. The first is sociologist Anthony Giddens's structuration theory. Explicated in *The Constitution of Society* (1984) and other works, it endeavors to model the social order without replicating the binaries—actor/structure, subjectivity/objectivity, and meaning/action—that have plagued the social sciences. Giddens models society as rule-bound human actions that, when distanciated over space and time, constitute the social structures that in turn regulate human actions.

Among the many important features of this model, one is that action and structure are co-constitutive: "The repetitiveness of activities which are undertaken in like manner day after day is the material grounding of what I call the recursive nature of social life. By its recursive nature I mean that the structural properties of social activity . . . are constantly recreated out of the very resources which constitute them."[14] Another is their rule-bound nature: actors' practices and structural processes are ordered by formal rules, such as laws, that are usually textual and enforced by strong sanctions and by informal rules, such as customs, that are primarily tacit and enforced by weak sanctions.[15] To apprehend and perform the informal routines, people monitor social activities at the level of tacit awareness. This practical apprehension of routines builds on the work of ethnomethodologist Harold Garfinkel, who studied how people perform such activities as standing in queues and taking turns in conversations, and the work of sociologist Erving Goffman, who studied (among other things) how people interpret meanings conveyed by facial expressions, body positions, and gestures.

When textually regulated and tacitly routinized activities are distanciated in space and time, they become structural elements that order further action; and when these structural elements are regionalized (or, one might say, calcified) by institutional and organizations ensembles, they stabilize the social system. Emphasizing the importance of space-time distanciation, Giddens writes,

> Human societies . . . would plainly not exist without human agency. But it is not the case that actors create social systems; they reproduce or transform them, remaking what is already made in the continuity of *praxis.* The span of time-space distanciation is relevant here. In general . . . it is true that the greater the time-space distanciation of social systems—the more their institutions bite into time and space—the more resistant they are to manipulation or change by any individual agent.[16]

Although structuration theory foregrounds the importance of institutions and organizations in stabilizing society, I want to call attention to two limitations. It does not offer a robust explanation of societal shifts, and it equates discourse with language. In "Althusser's Liberation of Marxian Theory," economists Stephen Resnick and Richard Wolff build on Althusser's concept of overdetermination to model how societal changes occur:

> Althusser insisted that no social entity was ever determined by one or a subset of other social entities. Rather each and every entity within society was always presumed to be determined by the effects of *all* the other entities at once. It was overdetermined by all those others. . . . Further, each social entity bears within itself the traces of all the other social entities that together comprise its overdetermination. . . . As such, each entity is the site of the different effectivities of all other social entities. An individual is the site, for example, of the effects of class, parents, jobs, religions, politics, literature, biology, etc.[17]

The multiple identities residing in a single entity (or the multiple effects residing at a single site) produce contradictions that constantly shift identities and relations. Thus in the everyday social world, the so-called unitary person presumed by individualist theory is overdetermined by the multiple discourses that converge on him in social settings. In the context of affirmative action, is the Jewish subject located in the discourse of Black anti-Semitism, which tells him to fear that it will roll back his people's hard-won educational gains, or is this subject located in the discourse of white progressivism, which reminds him of the Jewish-Black alliance in the struggle for educational opportunity? Since straddling the contradiction is untenable, the Jewish subject, like the white male plaintiffs in *DeFunis* and *Bakke*, must choose to reside in one discourse.

Every discourse is potholed with contradictions that, although it seems counterintuitive, speed rather than stall its motility. Foucault explains why:

> Such a contradiction, far from being an appearance or accident of discourse . . . constitutes the very law of its existence; it is on the basis of such a contradiction that discourse emerges, and it is in order both to translate it and to overcome it that discourse begins to speak; it is in order to escape that contradiction . . . that discourse endlessly pursues itself and endlessly begins again; it is because contradiction is always anterior to the discourse, and because it can never therefore entirely escape it, that discourse changes, undergoes transformation and escapes . . . from its own continuity.[18]

But what precisely is this endlessly shape-shifting apparition called discourse?

Discourse is not just language, even when language is broadly defined to include nonlinguistic symbolic systems. As evidenced by what we see in medical visits, football games, and courtship practices, discourse encompasses actors and actions, material objects and symbolic elements, bound together by particular relations. In "Post-Marxism without Apologies," Ernesto Laclau and Chantal Mouffe famously exemplified discourse in response to Alexander Geras's complaint that their book, *Hegemony and Socialist Strategy: Toward a Radical Democratic Politics* (1985), ignored real-world materiality. In one example, Laclau and Mouffe describe two bricklayers who are building a wall; one worker asks the other to hand him a brick, which he then cements into the unfinished wall. The authors note that the actors (bricklayers), the statement, the actions (passing and cementing), and the material objects (bricks, cement, and trowel) are part of the total operation of building a brick wall. "This totality[,] which includes within itself the linguistic and the non-linguistic, is what we call *discourse.*"

In another example, they demonstrate that the relations imposed on an ensemble of elements determine the nature of the discourse:

> If I kick a spherical object in the street or if I kick a ball in a football match, the *physical* fact is the same, but its *meaning* is different. The object is a football only to the extent that it establishes a system of relations with other objects, and these relations are not given by the mere referential materiality of the objects, but are, rather, socially constructed. This systematic set of relations is what we call discourse.[19]

In other words, the discourse bestows identities on and relations among the actors, actions, and objects.

This concept of discourse is consistent with Giddens's theory of social order. Dropping a letter into a red pillar box in London and playing football on a Newcastle street are ordinary routinized discourses, while the Royal Mail (the UK's postal system) and the Premier League (its system of football clubs) are institutionally regulated discourses that span space and time. The rules of any discourse, as we know from Michel Foucault's *The Archaeology of Knowledge and the Discourse on Language*, determine who may speak and act, with what authority, from which social or institutional locations, about which objects, and with which interpretive methods.[20] Almost anyone can drop a letter into a red pillar box, but only those who meet the requirements of the Royal Mail can carry out its postal activities. Similarly, almost anyone can join a ball game on a Newcastle street, but only those who meet the requirements to play for Newcastle United, which in turn must meet the requirements of the Premier League, can play in championship games.

As different as the various discourses are, they do not float like bubbles through infinite social space; rather, they mingle and modulate within historically and culturally specific epistemological fields that Michael Foucault calls "epistemes." It is no coincidence that his book, *The Order of Things: An Archaeology of the Human Sciences*, bore the French title *Les mots et les choses* (Words and things), because he uses the term "episteme" to denote the underlying epistemic order that determines the relations of word to word, thing to thing, and word to world. Thus different discourses of the same episteme generally deploy its logic of similarity and difference, attraction and repulsion, simultaneity and succession, correspondence and cause, when they go about constru(ct)ing what they presume to be autonomously existing natural and social phenomena.[21]

What did all this theorizing tell me about *DeFunis* and *Bakke*? First, legal-judicial discourse, like all discourses, consists of rules that determine the identities and relations of actors and objects, actions and processes, institutions and sites, variously constellated by meaning-making practices. Second, the underlying order of mainstream equal protection discourse resembles that of the long eighteenth century, which, as suggested earlier, stretches from Locke's possessive individualism through natural history's grand taxonomic projects to the Founders' not entirely democratic principles. The logic imposes the grammatical relations of word to word, the similarities or differences of thing to thing, and the unmediated correspondence of word to thing. The logic demands standardization and stasis in the face of complexity.

In the conclusion of this book, I analyze the field of law as a power/knowledge formation that sends stasis and change thrumming through the capillaries of society. But in the ten chapters on *DeFunis* and *Bakke*, I provide microanalyses of their social surrounds and the discursive mechanisms that prioritized the interests of the unitary individual over those of minority populations, rejected social-scientific and experiential evidence of systemic racism, and bleached racism from equal protection. To put it concretely, I will argue the adversarial structure of litigation, which required participants to tell competing stories about a complex social situation, loosed a flood of language that divergently characterized facts, precedents, and principles, thereby producing contradictions that fueled the discourse of reverse discrimination.

Now it is time to exit the galaxy of theory and examine the empirical ground—the social and linguistic practices that facilitated the law's shape-shifting discourse of racial discrimination.

PART I

THE CATALYSTS

1

FRENEMIES

> There were many culprits in this controversy. . . . This is a strange way for "friends" to act.
>
> —Ad Hoc Committee of Concerned Black People, "Are Jews Free from White Racism? A Black Position on 'Anti-Semitism'" (1969)

When *DeFunis v. Odegaard* entered the halls of the United States Supreme Court in the early months of 1973, it was surrounded by a crush of wrangling organizations that pressed their arguments in twenty-five amici curiae (friends of the court) briefs. According to Washington attorney general Slade Gorton and senior assistant attorney general James B. Wilson, who defended the University of Washington, the "friends" displayed some curious rifts.[1] Siding with DeFunis were the B'nai B'rith Anti-Defamation League (ADL), the Jewish Rights Council, and the American Jewish Congress, but siding with the university in a collective brief written by Marian Wright Edelman and Joseph Rauh Jr. were three more Jewish groups—the National Council of Jewish Women, the Union of American Hebrew Congregations (UAHC), and the UAHC's Commission on Social Action. Also siding with DeFunis was AFL-CIO, but siding with the university in the collective brief were four AFL-CIO affiliates—the United Mine Workers; the United Auto Workers; the United Farm Workers; and the American Federation of State, County, and Municipal Employees. Gorton and Wilson speculated that the AFL-CIO hoped to use a ruling for Marco DeFunis to reappeal three affirmative-action rulings against white union members, but they did not comment on why the AFL-CIO now made common cause with its foes, the Chamber of Commerce and the National Association of Manufacturers, which historically advocated for the interests of employers over those of workers.[2]

In 1977 when the Supreme Court agreed to review *Regents of the University of California v. Bakke*, the justices were inundated by fifty-seven amicus briefs representing more than 240 organizations and individuals. Aligned with Allan Bakke were the Anti-Defamation League, American Jewish Committee, American Jewish Congress, Queens Jewish Community Rights Council, Chamber of Commerce, American Federation of Teachers, New York Council of Supervisors and Administrators, and several white-ethnic groups. Unsurprisingly aligned with the university were minority organizations, academic institutions and associations, and some government agencies. Internal dissension over affirmative action prevented two powerful umbrella organizations, the AFL-CIO and the Leadership Conference on Civil Rights, from submitting briefs.[3]

Despite the schisms, all of the amici had one thing in common: they hoped or feared that the Supreme Court's decisions in *DeFunis* and *Bakke* would ripple from higher education across other sectors of society—schools, businesses, civil service, unions, housing, and government contracting. If we want to know why the wrangling amici were so exquisitely attuned to this ripple effect, we must return to the late 1960s when they fueled the racial conflict in which *DeFunis* and *Bakke* brewed.

THE FRAYING JEWISH-BLACK ALLIANCE

In 1967, when the Black riots and police crackdowns that had devastated Watts two years earlier swept like a typhoon through dozens of American cities, President Lyndon B. Johnson appointed a National Advisory Commission on Civil Disorders. Dubbed the Kerner Commission after its chairman, Illinois governor Otto Kerner, the commission had plenty of turmoil to study because, according to the Brandeis University Civil Disorders Clearinghouse, the nation was wracked by

"233 disorders in 1967 alone, and 295 disorders in the first four months of 1968."[4] In March 1968, the commission issued a report just shy of 250 folio-size pages that exposed the systemic racism afflicting African Americans who lived in urban and rural dumps across the country. The graphic prose and grim photographs documented poverty, hunger, slum and shanty housing, street garbage, rodent infestations, high death rates, widespread unemployment, substandard schools, crime waves, and police brutality. Predicting that the rioting would worsen, the commission recommended several measures to alleviate these conditions, but the disorder amplified in 1968.[5] Massive crowds protested the murder of Dr. Martin Luther King Jr. in April, mourned the assassination of Senator Robert Kennedy in June, and demonstrated at the Democratic National Convention in August. An astonished nation watched the televised melee when Chicago mayor Richard Daley activated 20,000 police and national guards, who battered protesters, journalists, campaign staff, and sedate Chicagoans on their way home for dinner.

Contemplating anarchy, officials urged the newly inaugurated president Richard M. Nixon to revive the Philadelphia Plan, a race-conscious program designed to increase the numbers of racial minorities working on federal construction projects in the metro area. Seeing the conflict over affirmative action as an opportunity to split "two major Democratic Party constituencies—civil rights and organized labor—so that it would be impossible for Democrats to satisfy both constituencies at once," Nixon mobilized the administration in what became a year-long dispute among contractors, unions, advocacy organizations, federal agencies, and Congress members over whether the Philadelphia Plan should include race-conscious hiring procedures and numerical goals.[6]

Meanwhile Vice President Spiro Agnew was castigating universities that used affirmative-action measures to integrate racial minorities into their white campuses. His attack did not signal a reversal of the administration's policy; rather, he was doing what his boss hired him to do. Nixon's choice of the Maryland governor as his running mate was a key element of his Janus-faced strategy to win the election by drawing white liberals away from Minnesota senator Hubert Humphrey and white conservatives away from Alabama governor George

Wallace. While Nixon spoke of school integration and employment opportunity to appease voters of color and their white supporters, Agnew fed the anxieties of Jewish and white-ethnic groups. From the 1968 campaign until his 1973 resignation, precipitated by a charge of tax evasion, he was the rhetorical point man in his boss's war against the Black Power and New Left movements, the liberal intelligentsia, the mainstream media, and other presumed enemies. Describing this role in a 1971 speech, he said, "Dividing the American people has been my main contribution to the national political scene since assuming the office of vice president. . . . I not only plead guilty to this charge, but I am somewhat flattered by it."[7]

Racialized rhetoric flooded into the media during 1968. At an April banquet held in Chicago, the ADL bestowed its human rights award on Governor Kerner for his leadership of the National Advisory Commission on Civil Disorders.[8] This gala proved to be the curtain call for the Jewish-Black alliance, for within months newspaper articles began exposing the fault lines where racial tensions reverberated. Covering a July meeting in San Francisco attended by 250 leaders of Jewish organizations, *New York Times* reporter Irving Spiegel described the seismic vibrations. In scores of cities—New York, Boston, Newark, Detroit, Cleveland, Chicago, St. Louis, and westward—African Americans had moved into neighborhoods traditionally populated by low-income Jewish and white-ethnic immigrants who, as they became financially secure, moved to white suburbs but retained their old neighborhood businesses. Reports that African Americans resented these businesses and vandalized them during community protests sent frissons of fear through Jewish and white-ethnic groups nationwide.[9]

Writing about this situation, *New York Times* reporter Bill Kovach quoted an American Jewish Committee official who refused to be named:

> When the Negro moved into the large city he moved into those areas most recently occupied by the Jews and many of the Jews still had vestiges of their holds there—as landlords and shopkeepers. In this conflict situation the symbol of white "oppression," the slumlords, the overcharging of shopkeepers, was the Jew. Because, historically,

> Jews had been more helpful in early stages of the conflict between Negroes and whites, they expected more from Jews and resented the fact they sometimes acted like other white men.

To undercut his source's psychologizing of African Americans, Kovach referenced an American Jewish Committee poll, which showed that Blacks were "less anti-Semitic than the rest of the population."[10] He did not comment on whether Jews harbored racist sentiments, perhaps unwilling to offend a large segment of the newspaper's readers.

Employment was another flashpoint. Historically barred from corporate offices, rarely elected to government positions, and only trickling into law and medicine, the second-generation of American Jews flowed into public service jobs where they found themselves working with ghetto dwellers who felt "the jobs should belong to blacks."[11] Mort Yarmon, director of public relations for the American Jewish Committee, told Kovach that

> for various historical reasons—among them the Civil Service and merit hiring that opened the professions to Jews when others were closed to them—the Jewish people have moved heavily into the social services and teaching fields, especially here in New York. These are exactly the two "pressure points" at which the Negro now makes his demand that "we be allowed to care for our own, to teach our own."

Putting it bluntly, Kovach wrote, "Present jobholders are fiercely protective of the merit system that allowed them into the professions despite prejudices. They see a threat to that system from the practice of compensatory hiring to benefit Negroes."[12] Oddly, Kovach did not notice the parallel between the civil service protections enjoyed by Jews and the civil rights protections promised to racial minorities.

Contemporaneous accounts show that many American Jews used the discourse of anti-Semitism to suture affirmative action to the horrors of the Holocaust and such homegrown haters as the Klan, the Coughlinites, the Birchers, and the McCarthyites.[13] Widely quoted in the media, Jewish leaders portrayed American Jews as a multiply victimized people who, after surviving virulent anti-Semitism to make good through talent and toil in America, were being revictimized by affirmative-action quotas that threatened to retrench their hard-won access to universities, professions, and upward mobility. But African Americans also felt chronically victimized: after being enslaved, lynched, segregated, and pauperized, they were embittered to find their former Jewish allies opposing their efforts to secure educational and employment opportunities.

NEW YORK, NEW YORK

Historians of identity-group turmoil have studied New York because its demography and economy made it the inevitable site of a racial storm. From the mid-nineteenth century on, Jewish and white-ethnic immigrants flowed to the city, providing a vast supply of low-skilled labor that supported its development as a major urban hub of industry, manufacture, finance, and culture. First-generation immigrants worked at grinding jobs to move their families out of the tenements and up the economic ladder; their children carved up the job territory, with the Irish predominating in the police force, Italians in sanitation, and Jews in the garment trade, public schools, and social services. When the white Protestant elites who ruled the city began modernizing its economy, "New York lost almost half of its jobs in the manufacturing sector" but gained "350,000 white-collar jobs" and 155,000 public sector jobs.[14] The implementation of competitive civil service exams by Mayor Robert F. Wagner Jr. helped those who were attending municipal colleges to move into professions and relocate their families in middle-class boroughs.[15]

During the postwar decades, low-skilled African Americans, Puerto Ricans, and Asians flowed to the metro area. In Brooklyn, African American residents ballooned from 4 percent of the total population in 1940 to 25 percent in 1970, turning Bedford-Stuyvesant, Ocean Hill, and Brownsville, once home to a mix of Jewish, Irish, and Italian families, into low-income Black neighborhoods. The people-of-color migrations solidified a Jewish-dominated directorate within the AFL-CIO that consisted of the International Ladies Garment Workers Union (ILGWU), the Jewish Labor Committee (JLC), and the United Federation of Teachers (UFT). But as Black, Puerto Rican, and Asian garment workers grew to outnumber Jewish ones, labor leaders responded by barring them from apprentice programs, union positions, subsidized apartments, and retirement homes available to white members. Such exclusionary practices, long deployed by unions across the country, were documented by NAACP labor director Herbert Hill and challenged by the NAACP through both litigation and direct action.[16]

Meanwhile, the UFT, established in 1960 and led by Albert Shanker, began to escalate the racial conflict over public schools. For a decade after the *Brown II* justices ordered school districts to desegregate "with all deliberate speed," New York maintained "a dual public school system" which divided 500,000 white students from 600,000 African American and Puerto Rican students.[17] According to Jerald E. Podair,

> In the "white" system, presided over by a cohort of experienced teachers, students read at or above the national average, and won a disproportionate number of National Merit and Westinghouse Science scholarships. In the "Black" system, pupils in crowded classrooms, receiving instruction from teachers who were learning on the job, read an average of two years behind the city's white students, and dropped out of school at a rate double that of the city as a whole.[18]

The New York City Board of Education had no members representing the Black communities of Bedford-Stuyvesant, Ocean Hill, and Brownsville. Most of the board's 4,000 staffers were Jewish, 99 percent of school principals were white, and 92 percent of the 57,000 teachers were white, with a 50 percent Jewish presence in both groups.[19] The board and the UFT, with help from white parents, stalled public school integration.

In 1963, Jewish, Irish, and Italian parents in the Queens neighborhood of Jackson Heights founded Parents and Taxpayers (PAT), which spawned chapters throughout the boroughs. PAT staged anti-integration protests throughout the metro area, demanded community control of the schools, and circulated outrageously racist statements. At an

NYC Board of Education meeting, one PAT member said, "I wouldn't live in Harlem for anything in the world. . . . I'd scrub floors. I'd take in laundry. I'd get any kind of job and I know I'd succeed because in the United States anybody can do anything if he tries hard enough. . . . If a Negro lives in Harlem it's because he doesn't want to work hard enough to get out of that environment." Another added, "It wasn't color holding them back. It was the kind of people they were. . . . They don't work hard or help their children in school or care about their families or keep their homes clean."[20]

The task of organizing a school boycott fell to Reverend Milton Galamison who, although vilified by the media, was a distinguished cleric. Soon after earning his theology degree at the prestigious Princeton Theological Institute, he served as pastor of the Siloam Presbyterian Church, a historic Brooklyn congregation attended by Black families. His leadership in the school wars catapulted him to further prominence.[21]

> On the opening day of the 1966 fall term, angry Harlem parents boycotted one school: Intermediate School 201. They demanded that the school be integrated or, failing this, that control be turned over to them. . . . The boycott marked the end of the school integration movement. Parent boycotts spread rapidly throughout the city, and the concept of community control spread with them. Officials cloistered in the sanctums of the city, state, and federal government bureaucracy and in the unions and foundations watched the unrest in the schools with mounting concern.[22]

Worried by the unrest, the NYC Board held a public hearing in December but allotted speaking time only to preapproved (and predominantly white) groups. When it refused to hear Lillian Wagner, the Black president of the Ocean Hill-Brownsville PTA, heated words ricocheted among Wagner, board members, and the audience until the board members marched out. Then sitting down in the vacated seats, several audience members anointed themselves as the People's Board of Education, elected Galamison as their president, and continued the hearing until the police arrived to remove them.[23]

In spring 1967 as Black and white neighborhoods alike embraced the concept of community-controlled schools, Mayor John V. Lindsay asked the state legislature for additional school funding but was ordered "to decentralize the city's public educational system down to the borough level."[24] Lindsay invited McGeorge Bundy, Ford Foundation president and former national security advisor to President John F. Kennedy, to head a decentralization task force that recommended creating small districts managed by a professional administrator and a local school board. When the UFT opposed this plan, the NYC Board cautiously decided to sponsor demonstration projects that would reveal the most "effective methods for achieving greater community involvement within different types and sizes of districts." After receiving project proposals, the board chose schools in Harlem, the lower East Side, and the previously spurned Ocean Hill-Brownsville.[25]

What began as incongruent visions of decentralization—the legislature seeing it as the physic for the board's bureaucratic paralysis, white parents seeing it as the antitoxin for integration, and Black communities seeing it as the cure for white-run schools that had failed their children—exploded into a racial conflict that spread beyond the New York boroughs. It would seep into *DeFunis* and *Bakke* and shape the participants' language.[26]

OUT OF BROOKLYN

In 1967 the Ocean Hill-Brownsville (OHB) community, with assistance from the Ford Foundation, submitted a demonstration project proposal that called for vesting its local board with powers traditionally exercised by the NYC Board, such as hiring principals, determining budgets, and approving teacher assignments, transfers, and suspensions.[27] Once chosen as the site of a demonstration project, the community held board elections and hired Rhody McCoy as the district administrator. Although the media portrayed him as a Black militant or an inept administrator, McCoy was an eighteen-year veteran of the NYC system who had served as assistant principal at "special" schools for students of color considered too disruptive to attend regular ones.[28] Working with Ford Foundation consultants, McCoy and the OHB Board began filling vacancies with minority principals, most of whom were not on the Board of Examiners' nearly all-white eligibility list. No one outside of their circle was pleased.

Teachers who served on the planning committee complained that the other members disregarded their suggestions. The NYC Board objected to the actions taken before it had formally approved the appointments of McCoy and board members. The UFT's Albert Shanker regarded the off-list principal selections as "the opening salvo in a battle that would eventually involve his teachers" and, preaching the virtues of merit hiring, joined the Council of Supervisory Associations in a lawsuit against McCoy and the OHB Board. On the first day of school in fall 1968, Shanker called a city-wide teachers' strike, but the OHB Black teachers and parents crossed the picket lines to teach classes.[29] Shanker responded by demanding a new city contract that contained three controversial provisions: (1) providing an enhanced integration scheme that would offer smaller classes and better services to lure white students to ghetto schools; (2) giving teachers the right to expel disruptive students; and (3) allocating $10 million for the UFT to spend on education programs as it saw fit.[30] Black communities regarded these provisions as a white power grab.

As the UFT's two-week strike was ending, hostilities erupted at a September 27 meeting of the NYC Board, where some 200 UFT members protested outside and an equal number of African Americans voiced their grievances inside. Stepping into the fracas, Shanker began criticizing the OHB project, but, according to a *New York Times* report,

> he was blocked by Negro women who kept shouting into the microphone such remarks as these: "We are sick and tired of Shanker and those teachers that are not black." "We kept those schools open. We didn't get one cent. We did it out of our own hearts." "Now Shanker is going to tell us we got T.B. We found those children can't read and write." The reference to tuberculosis was provoked because Mr. Shanker had warned parents . . . against sending their children to classes conducted by volunteers . . . [who] had not passed Board of Education physical examinations and might be suffering from transmissible diseases.[31]

Shanker's biographer, Richard D. Kahlenberg, placed most of the blame on Black communities,[32] but others argued that these communities were understandably riled by the UFT strike and the exodus of white teachers from the OHB and Harlem schools, thereby ensuring that students of color would be deprived of what their parents already knew to be a vastly inferior education.

Accelerating the conflict, McCoy and the OHB Board chairman mailed letters to eighteen Jewish teachers and one with a Jewish-sounding name, stating they would be transferred out of the OHB schools. Shanker pitched the action as anti-Semitic firings that violated the teachers' due process rights; in fact, the letter did violate policy, which specified that only the NYC Board could approve transfers.[33] Thus the fundamental question raised by the OHB letters was the one that had been hotly contested from the start: did the OHB Board have powers traditionally exercised by the NYC Board? Pressured by New York School Superintendent Bernard Donovan, McCoy submitted a formal complaint that charged the dismissed teachers with such failings as excessive blackboard writing, late arrival at school, and classroom pandemonium in which teachers cursed or hit students who wildly threw paint, chairs, and punches. Instead of ordering an investigation, Judge Francis E. Rivers rejected the charges and declared that teachers were entitled to due process.[34] Soon afterwards, the NYC Board, which now included Rev. Galamison and three more Lindsay appointees, announced a decentralization plan that "permitted local school boards to hire teachers directly, without reference to Board of Examiners lists, and to transfer teachers out of their districts involuntarily, as long as another district was willing to accept them."[35]

Insisting that these provisions violated the UFT contract, Shanker called a second strike in fall 1968; 54,000 of the city's 57,000 teachers walked out, only to return a few days later when the UFT reached a fragile agreement with the NYC Board. But when the OHB Board barred returning UFT teachers, Shanker resumed the strike, which lasted from September 13 to September 30; and when the New York ACLU condemned the UFT's actions, he called a third city-wide strike lasting from October 14 to November 17. In the end, an appeals court ruled that the decentralization plan was lawful, reinstated the OHB administrator and board, dismissed the OHB charges against teachers, and assured the UFT that future transfers would be arbitrated.[36] All parties got something—except the children of New York City, who were denied a half year of schooling.

MUDSLINGING AND MOBBING

Local media hyped the school wars throughout 1968 and 1969. The *New York Times* quoted Rabbi Marc Tannenbaum, the American Jewish Committee's Director of Interreligious Affairs, as saying the UFT was "'using the Jewish community' in what is essentially 'a labor-management problem.'"[37] The *New York Times* printed advertisements: one by prominent clergy and citizens claimed that the "academic retardation of inner city children is a national disaster" and the UFT was "threatening the rights of all citizens of New York City"[38]; another by OHB teachers defended the OHB Board against Shanker's charge of anti-Semitism.[39] Jonathan Kaufman later observed that the UFT used the discourse of Black anti-Semitism "to rally support for the strike. . . . The union was predominantly Jewish; black anti-Semitism was the perfect issue with which to strike back, to keep the teachers in line and to rally support in the Jewish community."[40] Indeed, when 500,000 copies of a leaflet describing Jews as bloodsuckers, money-changers, and Middle Eastern murderers were circulated, the OHB teachers maintained that the leaflets had simply appeared in their mailboxes, but Rhody McCoy said "the teachers were putting them in [mailboxes] themselves," and the New York ACLU claimed that Shanker himself had compiled the original leaflet. Kaufman concluded that "Shanker's decision to . . . focus on the question of black anti-Semitism was devastating. The leaflets uncorked the fears and uneasiness among Jews that had been building up in recent years."[41]

With each provocation, Jewish and white-ethnic organizations used the media to intensify racial anxieties. New York newspapers printed stories about "threats and intimidations against teachers in Ocean Hill-Brownsville and other black communities" that "vied for space" with coverage of the student protests at Columbia University and City University of New York, institutions that had educated generations of Jewish New Yorkers.[42] Writers for *Commentary* magazine, "one of the first journals of ideas to champion the UFT's cause," pilloried leftist and liberal intellectuals.[43] And New York University's appointment of John F. Hatchett as director of the Martin Luther King Afro-American Student Center ignited a firestorm of Jewish protest. Hatchett, a Harlem teacher, had previously written an article claiming "that Negro pupils were being 'mentally poisoned' by 'Jews who dominate and control the educational bureaucracy of the New York public school system,'" and, in response, the American Jewish Congress, the Catholic Interracial Council, and the Protestant Council had issued a joint statement condemning his views as "black Nazism."[44] When the NYU appointment was announced, the Jewish Defense League (JDL), a paramilitary group recently formed by Rabbi Meir Kahane, picketed with signs that compared African Americans to Nazis.[45] Anti-Defamation League president Dore Schary told the *New York Times*, "We fail to understand . . . how a university of N.Y.U.'s stature can continue to tolerate . . . the unbridled bigoted mouthings of a staff member who holds an ostensibly responsible position in a sensitive area." Rabbi Maurice N. Eisendrath, president of the Union of American Hebrew Congregations, said Hatchett was a "'base rabble-rouser' . . . 'obviously unfit to be associated with a reputable institution of higher learning.'" NYU speedily revoked the appointment.[46]

A week later, right after the UFT's third strike had begun, the mudslinging turned into mobbing. On the evening of October 15, Mayor Lindsay arrived to speak at the East Midwood Jewish Center in Brooklyn and found anarchy. Outside, "a crowd of 5,000 people . . . were chanting 'Lindsay must go'" and "'We want Shanker'"; inside, 1,700 people who "jammed both the synagogue and the auditorium beneath it" heckled Lindsay. When the disruption continued, Lindsay and his wife fled in their limousine, pursued by the surging crowd.[47] The next day, crowds turned on Republican senator Jacob K. Javits at campaign stops in Brooklyn. Whenever he mentioned the mayor's name, he met with "prolonged boos, lusty jeers, and shouts of 'Throw Lindsay the bum out.'" Although told that scapegoating was wrong, "The crowd booed. 'Dump Lindsay,' shouted the teachers. 'At least [Gov. George]

Wallace tells you he's a racist,'" yelled a man, while a woman shrieked, "'It's October 16, and my kids are still out of school.'" To their discredit, Republican leaders disavowed Javits, suggesting that he should join the Democratic Party, which, however, had aligned itself with Shanker in his battle against the OHB community.[48]

In December 1968, Julius Lester, a prolific creative and scholarly writer who had just published his first book, *Look Out, Whitey! Black Power's Gon' Get Your Mama!* (1968), set off another firestorm. As the host of a WBAI-FM radio program, he featured a Black schoolgirl who read anti-Semitic poems and a Black NYU student who commented, "As far as I am concerned more power to Hitler. He didn't make enough lampshades out of them." The American Jewish Congress demanded that the radio station fire Lester, Shanker complained to the Federal Communications Commission, and the Jewish Defense League filed a motion for a court hearing.[49] In January 1969, the Metropolitan Museum opened an exhibit, "Harlem on My Mind," which prompted more mudslinging. The Black community complained that the exhibit demeaned Harlem, while Jewish leaders complained that the catalog introduction, written by a sixteen-year-old Black girl, expressed contempt for Jews. Ignoring an ACLU warning that the Constitution protected even offensive speech, the Committee on Racial and Religious Prejudice, Anti-Defamation League, American Jewish Congress, and Jewish Defense League pressured museum director Thomas Hoving to withdraw the catalog. Telling the *New York Times* that the pressure has been "so great I don't think one person could withstand it," he removed the catalog from the museum and Random House removed it from bookstores. Later, Nathan Glazer admitted that the student had borrowed her statement from his *Beyond the Melting Pot* (1963). Both the distinguished Glazer and the demonized girl had surmised that Blacks might feel more American by sharing in the prejudice against Jews.[50]

In January 1969 and again in April, the ADL issued reports on Black anti-Semitism, and in May the militant Jewish Defense League, which never needed prodding to protect members of the faith against any presumed threat, overreached badly. As James Foreman spoke about Black reparations at Temple Emanu-El, a large Reform Jewish congregation in Manhattan, the JDL sent thirty men, clad in helmets and carrying weapons, to display their might at the temple doors. UAHC president Rabbi Maurice N. Eisendrath told the *New York Times*, "Jews . . . carrying baseball bats and chains, standing in phalanxes, like goon squads, in front of synagogues, are no less offensive and, in essence, no different from whites wearing robes and hoods, led by self-styled ministers of the gospel, standing in front of burning crosses. Neither Jews nor Christians nor America need such 'protectors.' If these be our friends, then God preserve us from our enemies."[51] Undeterred, the JDL placed an advertisement in a June issue of the *New York Times* that contained a photograph of armed Jewish men standing beside a synagogue door and a statement that violence might be necessary to defend the community. Only then did the ADL and other Jewish organizations condemn the JDL as a vigilante group.[52]

Some commentators speculated that Shanker had escalated the war of words to distract from the reality that school children were "collateral damage," but others noted that the strategy reaped union benefits. In 1968 alone, "there were 112 strikes of teachers and librarians, resulting in a total of 2,194,000 man days of work lost." This activism grew the national membership of the American Federation of Teachers (AFT) by "230 percent . . . as compared with a total 5 percent increase in membership in the ranks of organized labor."[53] It also helped Shanker: in 1974, he was elected as the AFT presidency, a position he held for over two decades.

FLAMING AND FEUDING

Admittedly, the flames of Jewish outrage were fanned by the Black Muslim churches, Black Panther Party, Student Non-violent Coordinating Committee, Students for a Democratic Society, and Young Socialist Alliance. A 1970 article by *New York Times* reporter Linda Charlton reprinted examples: a SNCC cartoon of Gamal Abdel Nasser and Cassius Clay held in a double noose by a fat hand bearing a Jewish star, and a Black Panther headline screaming in bold type "ZIONISM (KOSHER NATIONALISM) + IMPERIALISM = FASCISM." Such statements riled those who read the current conflicts through the lens of the Holocaust. Hebrew University professor Moshe Lazar told Charlton, "After Auschwitz and Buchenwald, overt anti-Semitism was no longer fashionable in most intellectual circles. . . . Now it is expressed in anti-Zionist propaganda"; and American Jewish Congress associate executive director Richard Cohen said, "We don't think there is any valid or real difference between anti-Israel sentiment and anti-Semitism. Anti-Zionism is a cover for anti-Semitism." Others revealed that racial politics had triggered generational feuds within the American Jewish family: Cohen speculated that the young Jewish leftists were motivated by "an insane kind of self-hatred" to rebel "against [their] parents"; this behavior, added Bertram H. Gold of the American Jewish Committee, was "traceable, in part, to their own lack of a sense of 'being Jewish.'"[54]

In media interviews, Jewish leaders neglected to mention that *Commentary*, the American Jewish Committee's nationally circulated magazine, had been amplifying the racist noise. Under the guidance of founder Elliott E. Cohen, the magazine had won an enviable reputation for spotting talented young authors who would later enter the literary canon.[55] When Cohen retired in 1960, his deputy editor took over. Norman Podhoretz grew up in the Brooklyn neighborhood of Brownsville when its residents were a mix of Jews, Italians, and African Americans. After attending Columbia and Cambridge Universities, he entered New York literary circles and became an important member of the emerging neoconservative camp. According to Nathan Abrams, he was determined to turn *Commentary* into "a source of anti-liberal and anti-black conservatism" that attacked presumed anti-Semites and anti-Zionists, Leftists, feminists, multiculturalists, environmentalists, gays, and African Americans.[56]

For a 1963 issue of *Commentary*, Podhoretz set the tone in his highly controversial autobiographical essay, "My Negro Problem—And Ours," which began by recounting his many run-ins with African American kids in the Brownsville schools and streets. As he tells it, "There were plenty of bad boys among the whites—this was, after all, a neighborhood with a long tradition of crime as a career open to aspiring talents—but the Negroes were *really* bad, bad in a way that beckoned to one, and made one feel inadequate." These bad boys, he revealed, aroused his desire and his dread: "But most important of all, they were *tough*; beautifully, enviably tough, not giving a damn for anyone or anything. . . . This is what I saw and envied and feared in the Negro." Shifting his narrative to the present, Podhoretz asked,

> Now that Brooklyn is behind me, do I fear them and envy them and hate them still? The answer is yes, but . . . certainly not in the same way. I now live on the upper west side of Manhattan, where there are many Negroes and many Puerto Ricans, and there are nights when I experience the old apprehensiveness. . . . I find that I am not afraid of Puerto Ricans, but I cannot restrain my nervousness whenever I pass a group of Negroes standing in front of a bar or sauntering down a street. . . . How, then, do I know that this hatred has never entirely disappeared? I know it from the insane rage that can stir in me at the thought of Negro anti-Semitism; I know it from the disgusting prurience that can stir in me at the sight of a mixed couple.[57]

This stew of libido and loathing marked the perturbed man at the helm of *Commentary*.

The journal devoted its January 1969 issue to Jewish-Black tensions. Sociologist Earl Raab's "The Black Revolution & the Jewish Question" addressed the Black Power movement, which "has already succeeded in reintroducing political anti-Semitism as a fashionable item in the American public arena—with what consequences no one can yet tell." Yet he prognosticated: "A good number of cities are soon destined to be numerically controlled or heavily dominated by their Negro populations. These are the cities in or around which most American Jews live, and in which their business and public lives are largely conducted. If the expressive black movement, with attendant political anti-Semitism, continues to grow, its effect on Jewish lives will be incalculable."[58] When interviewed by a *New York Times* reporter, Raab warned that "anti-Semitism [was] evolving as a political strategy of the black power movement in the big cities to force the 'white Anglo-Saxon Protestant Establishment' into concessions at the expense of Jewish interests."[59]

Commentary's April 1969 issue featured Nathan Glazer's "Blacks, Jews & the Intellectuals," which claimed that Black anti-Semitism

> has largely been the work of the black intelligentsia—to use an unfortunately indispensable word—abetted and assisted and advised by a white, predominantly Jewish, intelligentsia. When we attack black anti-Semitism, let us be perfectly clear that we are attacking the fruits of five years of growing rage and irrationality, centered among radical college students, but encouraged by a wide range of white intellectuals, many of them of Jewish origin.

After denouncing these groups for depicting "all the major institutions of society—the government, the army, the universities, business—as mad and cruel," he resorted to the McCarthyite tactic of naming over two dozen leftist collaborators, including Robert Brustein, Noam Chomsky, Barbara Epstein, Jules Feiffer, Edgar Friedenberg, Allen Ginsberg, Nat Hentoff, Norman Mailer, Marcus Raskin, and Susan Sontag.[60]

Throughout these tumultuous years, some leaders called for moderation. American Jewish Committee president Arthur J. Goldberg and American Jewish Congress vice president Murray Gordon told reporters that many of their colleagues were overreacting.[61] B'nai B'rith president Dore Schary cautioned, "'Let us be crystal clear—the statements of a few must not be attributed to an entire people. Negro anti-Semitism presents none of the dangers of fascism,'" adding that thousands of African Americans had worked to prevent interracial strife.[62] Appearing before the Kerner Commission a few weeks later, Schary "called . . . for public recognition that 'racism is the source' for most of the violence besetting America today. 'Racism fires the radical right, stimulates the radical left and induces black militancy, which in turn ignites white backlash.'"[63] At a national meeting of Hadassah women, Albert Vorspan, director of the UAHC Commission on Social Action, blamed Jewish organizations, particularly the ADL, for "stirring the Jewish community 'to the very brink of hysteria.'"[64]

AFFIRMATIVE-ACTION SKIRMISHES

Indeed, ADL president Seymour Graubard and executive director Benjamin Epstein led an aggressive campaign against affirmative action. In 1972, the same year the ADL submitted an amicus brief for the *DeFunis* hearing in the Washington State Supreme Court, it complained that the Albany campus of the State University of New York gave naked preferences to African Americans, Puerto Ricans, Native Americans, and women. When the campus president denied the allegation, the ADL upped the ante by filing complaints with the US Office for Civil Rights (OCR) that charged the Albany campus and fourteen other universities with reverse discrimination against whites. At the ADL's annual meeting, Epstein and others characterized university affirmative-action programs as imposing illegal racial, religious, and gender quotas, causing an uproar when the invited speaker, OCR director J. Stanley Pottinger, tried to explain that universities were using lawful numerical goals.[65] In March 1973, as *DeFunis* moved from the state court to the US Supreme Court, the ADL—joined by the American Jewish Committee, American Jewish Congress, Jewish Labor Committee, Jewish War Veterans, and Agudath Israel—submitted OCR complaints against fifty-two universities. A few months later, as Secretary of Health, Education, and Welfare Casper Weinberger spoke to 500 Jewish leaders at the ADL annual meeting in New York, he was heckled by audience members who claimed that affirmative action favored unqualified minorities in college admissions and employment.[66] In 1974, the year that the Supreme Court mooted *DeFunis*, the ADL teamed up with the Sons of Italy to complain that the City College of New York (CCNY) discriminated against three white men who had applied to its biomedical program. Receiving no satisfaction, the ADL and the Italian American Center for Urban Affairs filed parallel lawsuits against CCNY, later consolidated as a class action. In 1977 after the California Supreme Court ruled on *Bakke*, the ADL won a federal court judgment against CCNY's admissions program, which in fact had used racially discriminatory procedures. This latest initiative was guided by Larry M. Lavinsky, chair of the ADL's law committee and counsel for its briefs supporting Marco DeFunis and Allan Bakke.[67]

Next attacking affirmative action in employment, the ADL found itself tussling with the NAACP Legal Defense and Education Fund, known as "the LDF" in civil rights circles. In *Chance v. Board of Examiners* (1971), an LDF case challenging the test used for New York City school principals, the ADL and the New York Council of Jewish Organizations filed briefs arguing for continued use of the test, but the LDF prevailed in the Second Circuit Court of Appeals.[68] In *Kirkland v. New York State Department of Correctional Services* (1975), an LDF case challenging the test used to promote prison officers, the ADL again filed a brief supporting the defendants, this one a few months before urging the US Supreme Court to hear *DeFunis*.[69]

Jack Greenberg, who had joined the LDF in 1949 and worked on *Brown* with its famous team of Black lawyers, was Thurgood Marshall's handpicked successor to direct it (1961–1984). Knowing that Jewish organizations had provided early financial and legal support to the LDF and other civil rights organizations, he was deeply disturbed that they had turned against affirmative action.[70] Infuriated by the ADL's *Kirkland* brief, he phoned its officials to tell them they had made a bad mistake.

> The ADL's position bothered him not only on its merits—they were clearly wrong—but for what it portended for the future of black-Jewish relations. The longer the battle over affirmative action raged in the 1970s—with black groups on one side and Jewish groups like the ADL, the American Jewish Committee, and the American Jewish Congress on the other—the more Greenberg believed he was right. . . . Jewish groups opposing affirmative action were attacking the most successful, the best placed, the most articulate, the most influential, the most powerful segments of the black community.[71]

Undeterred, the opponents of affirmative action channeled the tempest that battered the boroughs of New York into *DeFunis*, where the discourse gained force and blasted into *Bakke*. Using the mechanisms of language and law, they shaped these cases as white-against-white disputes that sidelined minority interests.

2

JUST WORDS?

The seductive power of sweeping words crafted for particular situations is no doubt great.

—Amicus Brief for the National Council of Jewish Women et al., *DeFunis v. Odegaard*, US Supreme Court (1974), 24

In February 1970, under the glare of the media spotlight, Vice President Spiro Agnew told "2,000 cheering Illinois Republicans" at a Chicago fundraiser that affirmative-action supporters were "supercilious sophisticates" who by "some strange madness" had instituted racial quotas. "When next you are sick," he asked, "do you wish to be attended by a physician who entered medical school to fill a quota or because of his medical aptitude?"[1] Ratcheting up the rhetoric for Republicans at a Des Moines fundraiser in April of that same year, he described "this special black admissions business" as "a quota system" for admitting "Negroes or 'culturally underprivileged' youngsters" who were awarded "bargain-basement diplomas."[2] Agnew was using incendiary rhetoric to reach audiences beyond the loyalists who attended these fundraisers. But why? His objective could not have been to jump-start a conservative movement, because the 1964 Goldwater campaign had already activated a coalition of Christian fundamentalists, free-market advocates, intellectuals, and funders who were building an extensive organizational infrastructure. Nor could it have been to spark a race war, because for two decades white backlashes and police crackdowns had rumbled across the land whenever racial minorities participated in activism and litigation to secure education, employment, and voting rights. Rather, his rhetoric was a party-building strategy, calculated to recruit complacent whites, both the privileged class that inherited access to higher education and the lower classes that sought socioeconomic mobility, to the war against affirmative action.[3]

Sitting quietly outside of the mass media spectacle, law journals published two articles that would provide the paradigmatic narratives for *DeFunis v. Odegaard* and *Regents of the University of California v. Bakke* as they toured the courts from 1971 to 1978. Lino A. Graglia's "Special Admissions of the 'Culturally Deprived' to Law School," appearing in the December 1970 issue of the *University of Pennsylvania Law Review*, mounted a rhetorically provocative attack on race-conscious admissions, and Robert M. O'Neil's "Preferential Admissions: Equalizing the Access of Minority Groups to Higher Education," published in the March 1971 issue of the *Yale Law Journal*, provided a data-rich legal defense. From 1971, when *DeFunis* began its three-year journey to the Supreme Court, to 1978, when the Court issued six *Bakke* opinions, brief writers trudged along the routes charted by Graglia and O'Neil, augmenting the language and law of racial discrimination that appeared in these two articles.[4]

THE RHETORIC OF INVIDIOUSNESS

Why the *University of Pennsylvania Law Review* published Lino Graglia's article is a mystery, because it departed from the journal's usual subject matter and style. From 1967–1968 through 1979–1980, the journal featured sedate articles on constitutional and statutory law, judicial procedures, government regulations, and issues concerning employment, labor, housing, crime, securities, and licensing. Except for Graglia's article, followed by Derrick A. Bell's reply, it printed nothing on higher education until a 1979 article on *Bakke*. Even the short pieces it published displayed high-level scholarship; yet, in contrast to Jack Greenberg's erudite note on school integration, Graglia's fourteen-page indictment of race-conscious admissions contained no data or legal analysis.[5]

Making this very point, Derrick Bell complained that the article "eschew[ed] legal analysis for vague, unsupported suggestions that such programs may constitute 'reverse discrimination'" and was "outdated in its reportage, incorrect in its legal and educational conclusions, and misguided in its asserted moral concern for racial injustice." Nevertheless, he worried that intransigent law schools would celebrate "its publication in a respected law review" and its author "for his courage in having taken the unpopular side of a difficult question."[6] As it turned out, Bell underestimated the article's influence because DeFunis and Bakke supporters would weaponize its rhetoric in their own briefs.

To start with the title, as any reader would, "Special Admission of the 'Culturally Deprived' to Law School" relies on word substitution, disparaging understatement, and punctuation. The word "special" implies that minority applicants receive unmerited solicitude in the admissions process; the scare quotes around the phrase "culturally deprived" mock admissions officials who consider racial-minority applicants to be disadvantaged; and the phrase itself trivializes those victimized by the severe economic and educational effects of structural racism. The meanings implied by these linguistic gyrations signal the messages that Graglia goes on to convey throughout the article, among them that misguided admissions officials give preferences to unqualified minority applicants.

On the first page, Graglia asserts that the purpose of special admissions "is to increase Negro enrollment and . . . to a lesser degree, enrollment of certain ethnic groups such as Mexican-Americans or Puerto Ricans" (he uses "Negro" throughout the article).[7] Without citing any evidence, he claims that special admissions programs accept "nearly all Negro applicants" even if they "do not quite meet the minimum standards" and even if "they are of middle class backgrounds, have professional parents, or otherwise appear to have had average or above average opportunities."[8] To defuse any impression that he is stirring resentment, he assures readers that his "opposition to a policy so obviously well-intentioned . . . is no labor of love"; rather, he undertakes this task because "special admissions standards for Negroes will, I fear, disserve the cause of Negro equality, impair educational quality, and result in deviation of the schools from their educational function."[9] These opening statements preview his signature strategy of counterbalancing derogations of people of color (usually distilled to "Negroes") with professions of support for the abstract concept of equality.

Throughout his narrative, Graglia uses techniques of fictionalization to win reader assent to his claims, as in this passage on student activists of color: "Spokesmen for groups making demands on our universities should be recognized as literate, articulate, and intelligent human beings, not patronized as incompetents. Outrageous demands cannot, merely because they are such and often carry implied or explicit threats of violence, be treated as innocuous or inept misstatements of reasonable complaints. Intimidation and extortion are not inconceivable; they are all too real and immediate in our universities today."[10] Although mostly written in agentless-passive prose, this passage fictionalizes four parties—student leaders, university officials, the narrator, and the readers.[11] After briefly acknowledging that the student leaders are "literate, articulate, and intelligent," the narrator portrays them as campus thugs who make "outrageous demands" to extort concessions from cowed university officials (unnamed but implied). By contrast, the final compound sentence, which use the declarative mood to present the narrator's views, characterizes him as a reasonable and resolute man who comments on the alleged bad behavior.[12]

Through this fictionalization, the passage offers the fictionalized readers the loaded choice of identifying with disruptive students, spineless university officials, or the reasonable narrator. But the alignment of actual readers with these personae would have depended upon the views they brought to the text. Reflecting the makeup of the legal profession in 1970, the readers would have been predominantly white male law professors, students, and practitioners. For those harboring racist sentiments, the narrator's pejorative wording—"demands," "threats," "violence," "intimidation," and "extortion"—might have revived their anxieties about Black activism in their own communities. But for those shocked by recent displays of racism, the mention of violence and intimidation might have reminded them of the white mayhem during school integration in Little Rock (1957) and New Orleans (1960), lunch counter sit-ins (1960), Freedom Rides (1962), the Mississippi Freedom Summer (1964), or the Selma march (1965).[13]

In addition to student militancy, other invidious stereotypes roll through Graglia's narrative like drumbeats pounding the alleged racial minority inferiority into the readers' brains:

> Most major law schools which have enrolled substantial numbers of Negroes acknowledge that most Negro students, in general, have performed below the expectations suggested by their grade and test records. . . .
>
> Comparison of the performance of the specially admitted with other students is also difficult because most schools with a special admissions program provide additional tutorial assistance, lighter course loads, and other advantages to specially admitted students. . . .
>
> One of the most serious disservices done by lowered academic standards for Negroes in institutions of higher learning is to call into question the legitimacy of every Negro graduate.[14]

These statements depict the harms of "special admissions programs": by admitting unqualified "Negro" students, they incur costly tutoring services, lower academic standards, and create doubt about the competence of minority lawyers. In addition to blaming academic institutions for the fall-out from special admissions, the statements equate "the specially admitted" with "Negroes," thus masking the special admission of underqualified white athletes, veterans, and students with prominent parents, a widespread practice that O'Neil will criticize in his article.

More insidiously, the narrator himself questions the competence of minority attorneys when he cleverly undercuts the fact that minority lawyers serve as role models for students:

> I agree, but only insofar as the minority group lawyers are effective, able lawyers, the equals of their "majority group" peers. The abstract question whether Negroes can compete and succeed in this country has, I believe, been answered in the affirmative; there are few positions short of President and Vice President that Negroes have never attained. At the very highest level of the legal profession, the United States Supreme Court, Negroes are "represented"

> almost exactly in proportion to their share of the population. Ineffective minority group lawyers will disserve the cause of minority group equality and recognition. In the short run disserving the interests of their clients, they will in the long run reinforce stereotypes of incompetence. It will soon come to be believed that to get a *real* lawyer he had better be very white.[15]

Loaded with the rhetoric of invidiousness, this passage uses lexical equivalence to swivel between "Negroes" and "minority group" and pejoration to insinuate that minorities are not capable and effective lawyers. It racializes the performance standard, stating that minority lawyers must match the ability of their majority (white) peers, rather than saying that lawyers of all races should aspire to match the ability of exemplary lawyers of any race. In stating that the "question whether Negroes *can* compete and succeed" (my emphasis), the insertion of the little "can" edges toward the essentialist notion that successful Black lawyers have overcome some racial deficit in talent, ambition, or effort.

Two claims in this passage are particularly egregious. The narrator's veiled reference to Supreme Court Justice Thurgood Marshall implies that African Americans have obtained equality merely because Marshall was 11.1 percent of the nine-justice bench at a time when African Americans were about 12 percent of the total US population. Sadly, Marshall, the only African American to have reached this pinnacle by then, often found himself writing passionate dissents when the majority justices failed to provide minority plaintiffs with equal protection. In the concluding riff, the narrator argues that incompetent minority lawyers fail their clients, disserve their people's progress, and reinforce racist stereotypes. He adds, "It will soon come to be believed that to get a *real* lawyer he had better be very white." Ironically, this allusion to the whiteness of a "*real* lawyer," which comes at the end of the racially invidious riff, reveals Graglia's own bigotry. While anyone can be vexed at lawyerly incompetence, a bigot presumes that Black lawyers are incompetent and white ones are competent. Thus he would exceptionalize a talented Black lawyer by saying "really top-notch for a Black lawyer," and would singularize an incompetent white one by saying "oh well, he's a hack."[16] In short, close readers will recognize that white normativity infuses the passage; this same white normativity about intellectual and professional competence, I will argue in later chapters, infused the pro-plaintiff briefs and opinions in *DeFunis* and *Bakke*.

Graglia's use of invidious stereotypes in turn requires him to revivify his "reasonable man" persona. In this passage, he whips stereotyping and solicitude, minoritization and nationalism, into a bombastic froth:

> The basic principle underlying the new admissions policy is that because Negroes have been so long and so severely discriminated against in our society, merely ending this discrimination is not enough—discrimination in their favor is required. . . . Perhaps discrimination in favor of a minority can be distinguished from discrimination against a minority, but America consists of minorities and I fear the claims that could be made or conditions justified if this distinction should be generally accepted. . . . Societally approved racial discrimination, even as a temporary expedient to rectify past racial discrimination, dilutes the purity of that goal and undermines our most basic ideal that individual merit and individual need should be the only relevant considerations for societally distributed rewards and benefits.[17]

First, the narrator tinges with sarcasm a hyperbolic claim he falsely attributes to affirmative-action supporters—namely that African Americans, "so long and so severely discriminated against in our society," should be compensated by discrimination in their favor. Next he invokes the "nation of minorities" trope (which will reappear in the briefs of DeFunis and Bakke supporters), cuing readers to imagine the frightening spectacle of myriad racial, ethnic, religious, and economic groups complaining of past discrimination and clamoring for special treatment. Then he restores the "reasonable man" persona who uses elevated diction to describe the "purity" of the goal (eliminating discrimination) and the "basic ideal" of individual merit. The passage ends with the claim that individual merit and need should determine "societally distributed rewards and benefits," a phrase that, I will argue in later chapters, goes to the heart of the matter in *DeFunis* and *Bakke*.

Each of these individualized lawsuits to gain a place in a professional school program was a symptom of the larger struggle to continue the white monopoly over the nation's material and symbolic resources.

Graglia's rhetorical tactics—particularly the derogation of minority students, the exceptionalism of successful minority professionals, the "nation of minorities" trope with its agonistic identity-groups scenario, and the fierce battle over "societally distributed rewards and benefits"—will resurface powerfully in the *DeFunis* and *Bakke* briefs and opinions.[18] In the closing section, Graglia remarks, "Argument by parade of horribles is not the most persuasive, but the true horrible here, I believe, is that each of these proposals [race-conscious remedies] is being seriously urged today and some have been adopted."[19] If the author had taken his own advice on persuasion, he would have written, as Derrick Bell suggested, an article that grounded its arguments in fact and law.

THE TREATISE OF RACISM

In 1960 Yale University enrolled nine Black freshmen in an entering class of 1,212 students; ten years later, it enrolled eighty-three Black freshmen in a slightly larger class. This modest gain resulted from measures that, according to Jerome Karabel, responded to "the racial politics of the decade." Worried by social disorder, the Black Power movement, and the Kerner Commission report, Yale administrators initiated minority recruitment and scholarship programs that paradoxically transformed the small Black Student Alliance, formed in 1967, into a large activist organization that pressed the university on a host of racial issues.[20] Also responding to the turbulence, the *Yale Law Journal* published about one-third of its articles between 1967 and 1971 on such issues as the Vietnam War, public interest law, housing discrimination, voting rights violations, and school desegregation. Surprisingly, on higher education it printed only the anonymously authored "The Affirmative Duty to Integrate in Higher Education" (March 1970) and Robert M. O'Neil's "Preferential Admissions: Equalizing the Access of Minority Groups to Higher Education" (March 1971).[21] O'Neil's sixty-nine-page text resembles the treatise, an expository genre perfected in eighteenth-century Britain to explicate the principles and arguments of important fields such as moral philosophy or natural science. His methodical approach and respectful tone indicate that he, like those treatise writers, anticipated readers who had received a liberal education but needed a systematic review of the chosen topic.

Despite its many scholarly strengths, this widely read article made lexical choices that dampened its persuasiveness. Perhaps most problematic was O'Neil's use of "preferential admissions"—in this 1971 article and in another article, "Preferential Admissions: Equalizing Access to Legal Education," for a 1970 special issue of the *University of Toledo Law Review* on legal education and practice—to denote the race-conscious programs he defended.[22] In the same *Toledo Law Review* issue, Alfred W. Blumrosen had cautioned, "The choice of concept and expression may influence the success of any program." By using the phrase "preferential treatment," he argued, writers imply that the effort to integrate law schools is motivated by "white generosity and decency"; however, by describing the integration of minorities as a legal right, they could argue that it is a fundamental interest "requiring other interests and priorities to be set to one side while remedial obligations are attended to."[23]

O'Neill's use of "preferential admissions" in the titles of the *Toledo* and *Yale* articles would have immediately polarized his readers: those who took it to connote favoritism would have resented the discriminatory practice, while those who took it to connote a just remedy would have resented the word choice.[24] In the *Yale* article, O'Neil relegated his definition of "preferential admissions" to a footnote:

> At one extreme, a preference may mean no more than tipping the balance in favor of one student rather than another when all factors are roughly equal. . . . At the opposite extreme is the fixed quota—a guarantee that a certain percentage of the freshman class will consist of residents of the state, children of alumni, veterans, Catholics, pre-meds, or others. . . . There is a wide range of options between the fixed quota and the factor that merely tips the balance. . . . Preferences may sometimes be given by adding points to a standardized

> test score . . . when the raw score unfairly reflects the examinee's ability or potential. Or a test score may be disregarded altogether.[25]

Rather than using the language of legal obligation, O'Neil's wording—preferences, percentages, quotas, extra points, and disregarded scores—echoed the emotionally-cathected discourse that had inflamed public opinion.[26]

To be fair, the leaders and citizens who were embroiled in the nation's racial conflicts (see chapter 1) had rendered almost all terminology toxic, a problem O'Neil immediately acknowledges: "The preferential admission of minority students to college has become one of the most divisive issues in American higher education. It is also an explosive political issue, largely because the Vice President of the United States has determined to make it so."[27] Attempting to mollify his readers, he validates their diverse feelings about preferential admission:

> The very recent discovery of the critical underrepresentation of racial minorities on American campuses . . . has *profoundly disturbed* many in the academic community. Yet the prospect of preferentially admitting to college for the first time large numbers of students from radically different academic and cultural backgrounds *seems to threaten* basic educational values and convictions. Meanwhile, the pressure for expansion of minority enrollments collides directly with the *rising academic aspirations and expectations* of many lower middle class whites for whom college has for the first time in generations become a serious prospect.[28]

This narrative outreach—by affirming the emotions of fearful conservatives, underrepresented minority students, and aspiring lower-income white students—encourages both opponents and supporters of race-conscious admissions to journey through the long article.

In section 1, readers learn that college admissions has never been purely meritocratic. Although officials considered many factors—grades, test scores, personal essays, recommendations, extracurricular activities, work experience, and achievement in the face of physical disability and language barriers[29]—they traditionally preferred male applicants, state residents, athletes, and children of alumni, donors, leaders, and celebrities.[30] The question O'Neil asks, in language echoing Graglia's, is not whether preferential admission "defiles the purity of the admissions process," but "whether race or ethnic status should be permitted as a basis for dispensations . . . long accorded" on the basis of these other factors.[31]

Section 2 answers affirmative-action opponents who claim that the Constitution mandates color-blindness. Noting that the Supreme Court had not definitively ruled on race-conscious admissions, O'Neil diligently sifts through cases on schools, employment, housing, public facilities, and voting to conclude that the Court would have three options: it might forbid all race-conscious programs, approve those designed "to *help* . . . the persons for whose protection the Fourteenth Amendment was enacted," or subject programs to strict scrutiny review.[32] He believes strict scrutiny is the appropriate level of review, because racial classification is "more dangerous" than other classifications; it intensifies "differences among people" and weakens "government as an educative force."[33]

O'Neil's extensive legal analysis comes to rest on the core question: Can race-conscious admissions meet the strict scrutiny requirements, namely, that a narrowly tailored policy must serve a compelling governmental interest that cannot be served by a race-neutral or less burdensome alternative? After establishing the compelling need to integrate higher education, O'Neil addresses the narrow tailoring requirement. He recommends differentiating well-represented groups, such as Jewish and Asian Americans, from underrepresented groups that are "(a) victims of overt racial discrimination; (b) socio-economically disadvantaged; (c) unfairly appraised by standardized tests; and . . . (d) graduates of over-crowded, run-down and badly-staffed high schools." Under these criteria, most Black, Hispanic, and Native American applicants "present the strongest claims for special consideration."[34] He also recommends extending special consideration to relatively advantaged minority students, a highly controversial idea for those white readers who, if they had not witnessed the effects of negative stereotypes, peer hostility, and low academic expectations on minority students, might regard such actions as disagreeable atmospherics rather than actual discrimination.[35]

Next O'Neill rejects four commonly suggested alternatives. Expecting to expand the student bodies at historically Black colleges is unrealistic when "as many as 50 of the 128 black institutions . . . might have to close from lack of funds." Educating more minority students at two-year colleges prolongs their secondary school tracking into less demanding programs before abruptly inserting them "at the start of their junior year into virtually all-white student bodies."[36] Instituting open admissions at low-cost urban universities is unrealistic because few can afford to "throw their doors open to all who wish to attend."[37] Granting preferences to disadvantaged students of all races would not significantly increase minority enrollments at institutions with predominantly white applicant pools. Moreover, these alternatives are not really neutral because, by clustering minority students in historically Black colleges, two-year colleges, and certain urban universities, they entrench racial apartheid in the higher-education system.

In section 3, readers find themselves wading through heaps of data. Before the mid-1960s, O'Neil reports, no one surveyed minority enrollments because, as a College Entrance Examination Board official put it, "'we did not have . . . [many minority] students and did not know enough to worry about not having them.'"[38] Between 1967 and 1970, studies showed they made small gains: the proportion of white high-school graduates enrolled in college was six times greater than that of African Americans; 40 percent of the African American students attended historically Black colleges; and the number of Hispanic and Native American students was minuscule. All three groups disproportionately attended two-year colleges, took courses as nonmatriculated students at four-year institutions, and entered universities through race-conscious admissions programs.[39]

Next O'Neil presents appalling data on minorities in the legal professions. At a time when African Americans comprised 12 percent of the US population, they constituted 1 percent of the bar and far less in such states as Mississippi, with seventeen Black lawyers for nearly a million Black people, and Georgia, with thirty-four Black lawyers for 1.2 million Black people. The pattern was more acute for other groups: California had one Anglo lawyer for every 530 Anglos but one Chicano lawyer for every 9,482 Chicanos, while New Mexico and Arizona had no Native American lawyers for over 135,000 Native Americans.[40] Responding to the argument that white lawyers could serve minority communities, O'Neil cites studies showing that the few white lawyers serving minority communities were hampered by language barriers, ignorance of life conditions, and unfamiliarity with relevant laws.[41] Indeed, in an article for the 1970 *Toledo Law Review*, Thomas W. Christopher and Frederick M. Hart noted that Indian law—consisting of nearly 9,000 federal statutes and treaties, agency rulings, tribal charters, and jurisdictional conflicts among federal, state, and tribal governments—would "tax the imagination of the most competent lawyer."[42]

From the scarcity of minority lawyers, O'Neil backtracks to information on the segregated and inferior schooling, long hours at work, and unaffordable college costs that disadvantaged minority students who might qualify to apply to law schools. Next tackling the debate over standardized test bias, he reports that some critics claim they exclude "from college a disproportionate number of minority-group applicants, including many who would undoubtedly do satisfactory academic work," while others claim they exclude Black, Hispanic, Puerto Rican, and Native American students socialized into nonmajority languages and cultures but "are *more* qualified than whites who are admitted."[43] After reviewing the literature on testing produced by scholars, government agencies, and the Educational Testing Service (ETS), he makes two important points: validation studies show that the tests predict only for first-year grades and fail to predict for test-takers who are not comparable.[44] In the end, this review yields no firm conclusions as to "whether traditional admissions criteria [tests and grades] are *discriminatory* against minority applicants beyond the extent to which they are *exclusionary*."[45]

However, the authors who wrote about testing for the 1970 issue of the *Toledo Law Review* recognized that test scores reflected differences in past education that impacted test performance. They noted that minority students received little instruction in the test's dominant-culture language, reasoning, and content and little practice in such test-taking skills as selecting the right answer from multiple choices, writing an organized paragraph, and completing the test in the allotted time.[46] Clyde W. Summers, however, defended the LSAT's dominant-culture content and method:

> Legal problems cannot be understood except in the context of the culture in which they exist, legal institutions can be examined only from the perspective of the culture of which they are a part, and legal reasoning and legal concepts are inevitably linked with that culture. . . . It is not necessary that the student or lawyer be in the mainstream of that society or share its values; but it is necessary that he have a working knowledge of that society.[47]

But Sanford Jay Rosen made a crucial point about the dominant-culture context: "law school admissions criteria have operated within a hermetically sealed system," in which the bar examinations mirrored the law school curricula, which in turn mirrored the LSAT—even though none of these "are particularly good predictors of competence or success as a lawyer."[48] Arguing that curricular reform could disrupt the dominant-culture cycle, Haywood Burns referred to Racism and the Law, a new course at the New York University Law School that critically analyzed the law from slavery through the present. "Few would deny," he stated, "that law has been used in the building of a racist society. The way in which this process has taken place must be understood if we are to assess correctly the potential of law in eradicating racism in this society."[49]

The diverse opinions on test bias resulted from not only the skimpy testing literature but also the state of language research at that time. When O'Neil and others wrote about tests, structuralism was the reigning paradigm in anthropology, linguistics, and literature programs. Students journeyed from Ferdinand de Saussure's work on the Indo-European languages and the sign (consisting of signifier and signified) through the structuralisms of Claude Levi-Strauss, Edward Sapir, Benjamin Whorf, and Leonard Bloomfield to arrive at a full tutorial on Noam Chomsky's generative (or transformational) grammar. The itinerary did not include groundbreaking work in sociolinguistics, such as Basil Bernstein's analysis of how language codes differed in social and educational settings or William Labov's demonstration that Black English was a well-ordered dialect rather than a perversion of standard (white) English. Although both linguists soon published important books, Bernstein's *Class, Codes, and Controls* (4 vols., [1971–1975]) and Labov's *Language in the Inner City: Studies in the Black English Vernacular* (1972), their insights about class- and race-inflected language use did not enter mainstream legal thought in the years that followed. Thus when the pro-minority amici who participated in the *DeFunis* and *Bakke* appeals offered sophisticated critiques of how standardized tests disadvantaged minority students by using white-normed language, contents, reasoning, timing, and scoring, their information fell outside of the recognizable "truths" of the law (see chapters 5 and 9).

Additionally, readers who had been socialized into the law's atomistic mode of thinking might well have struggled with the third section of O'Neil's treatise. It contained an abundance of data on the economic, social, and educational conditions experienced by minority students, but it did not provide an organizing concept that illustrated how these conditions failed to prepare them for the law school application moment. By using the "education pipeline" concept, he could have delineated the racialized mechanisms that determined the flow of students all along the way from preschool to law school. By visualizing white and minority student flow, readers would be able to see that the dominant-culture LSAT was only one mechanism in the larger regime of educational discrimination; they would be able to see that a race-conscious admissions program, which contextualized minority test scores in background disadvantages, was a narrowly tailored interventions into the law school application moment of education pipeline discrimination.

The last section of O'Neil's article responds to Lino Graglia's portrayal of obstreperous minority student activists and spineless university officials. The few minority students on university campuses, O'Neil explains, find themselves alienated from the white culture and band together to demand safe spaces such as ethnic studies programs, separate dormitory quarters, and a critical mass of minority students and faculty. Instead of rigidly rejecting or nervously capitulating to their demands, administrators should try "to maintain enough difference, but not too much." "Perhaps only a long and often painful period of accommodation . . . will establish a viable entente—a degree of contact and familiarity that is collegial, but breeds neither contempt nor fear. In this way, the minority students may retain their identity and their individuality, yet share views and experiences with students who are eager to know them better and to live and work with them."[50] This sympathetic narrative of travelers who journey through identity-based conflicts to arrive at a mutual understanding stands in stark contrast to the abstract legal discourse in *DeFunis* and *Bakke* that would purge these cases of minority voices and viewpoints.

In this chapter I have emphasized words to show that they are pliable tools for constru(ct)ing facts and laws. The following chapters on *DeFunis* and *Bakke* will demonstrate two basic dynamics in the making of reverse discrimination. The first is that the plaintiffs' lawyers, amici, and friendly judges used pliable language to distort the facts, precedents, and principles included in the cases. The second is that the facts they omitted or expelled from the cases, together with the misrepresentations they included, produced the tiny portion of justice that the Supreme Court finally dispensed to aspiring minority students.

PART II

THE *DEFUNIS* CASE

3

THE STORIES THEY TELL

Special treatment, however, is what the DeFunis case is all about.

—Nina Totenberg, "Discriminating to End Discrimination," *New York Times* (14 April 1974)

In a 1998 article marking the twenty-fifth anniversary of the Supreme Court's announcement that it would hear *DeFunis v. Odegaard*, legal scholar Jim Chen reflected sardonically on the case:

> Over the past two decades, *DeFunis* has gotten lost in the constitutional cascade that followed *Bakke*. Legal scholars have obsessed over the affirmative action guidelines outlined in *Bakke* and ignored the Court's close call in *DeFunis*. Such are the perils of an academic tradition that favors grand theory over less glamorous questions of practice, procedures, and pragmatic consequences. Then again, to the extent that *Bakke* is "the Kama Sutra of educational affirmative action," why would—or *should*—scholars waste any time on the relatively pedestrian decision in *DeFunis*?[1]

Pitting himself against the tradition of favoring grand theory over case particulars and social consequences, Chen discusses three features that makes the case worthy of attention: the university's acknowledgment that it would not have accepted most of the minority admittees in the absence of race-conscious admissions, the relationship of the Court's mootness ruling to mootness doctrine, and the contradictory arguments for and against race-conscious admissions made by Justice William O. Douglas. But in restoring significance to *DeFunis*, he, like those he criticizes, fixates on what occurred during its final phase.

Furthermore, in comparing *DeFunis* to *Bakke*, Chen gauges "significance" in two ways: the quantity of texts that each case generated as an indicator of importance, and the Court's nondecision or decision on the legality of race-conscious admissions as an indicator of importance. *DeFunis* generated a large quantity of texts—litigant documents and an opinion in the trial court, seventeen amicus briefs and four opinions in the Washington State Supreme Court, over two-dozen amicus briefs and three opinions in the US Supreme Court, media coverage as it toured the courts, seven special issues of journals, some 150 articles on the case, and myriad citations in scholarly, journalistic, and government publications.[2] Given the *quantity* of attention the case received, I want to ask what diminished its importance. Was it diminished because, as Chen claims, the Court did not pronounce on the constitutional issues that scholars prefer to address? Or was it diminished by the mechanisms of legal-judicial discourse that selected and slanted the facts, precedents, and principles?

In the four chapters of this book on *DeFunis*, I will argue that its importance lies in the discursive practices that constru(ct)ed facts, precedents, and principles before, during, and after the trial. This chapter on the circumstances precipitating the litigation tells stories that were omitted from or distorted during the trial. Chapter 4 examines the trial language that colored the case and transformed the original nonracial complaint into the judge's holding of unconstitutional racial discrimination. Chapter 5 examines the mechanisms of language and law that enabled, but barely, the Washington State Supreme Court to affirm race-conscious admissions. Chapter 6 provides a close reading of Justice William O. Douglas's dissent, the only one addressing substantive matters. Although law scholars attributed his text's inconsistencies to his personal ambivalence about race-conscious measures, I will argue they were discourse effects that bubbled to the surface when he attempted to reconcile the incommensurable discourses of social science, lived experience, and law that divergently construed "racial discrimination."

Since much of the information I provide in these chapters—information about Seattle, the University of Washington, and the plaintiff—falls outside of the *DeFunis* story assembled in the courts and summarized in law review articles, legal scholars may object to my boundary transgressions. But that is exactly the message I am sending: we have to transgress the boundaries maintained by legal-judicial discourse in order to see why lawyers failed to tell the full story, why judges failed to recognize minority interests, and why scholars, for the most part, stayed within the resulting narrow precincts.

SEATTLE STORIES

In the early twentieth century, Seattle was a nonsegregated city of 77,000 whites, 2,990 Japanese, 400 Chinese, 400 Blacks, and less than two dozen Native Americans. As the minority populations grew, homeowners and lenders kept them out of white neighborhoods, education officials kept them out of white schools and universities, and union bosses kept them out of jobs in the aircraft, shipbuilding, lumber, and steel industries. By the early 1960s, the city was rigidly segregated: African Americans, the second largest minority group at about 5 percent of the total population, were ghettoized in the Central District and immured in poverty.[3] Nevertheless, they had built an anti-racist organizational infrastructure consisting of civil rights groups, churches, fraternal orders, and social clubs that advocated for improved conditions.[4]

In 1963, the Central Area Civil Rights Committee (CACRC), an interracial organization, began to coordinate the struggle, but the members were divided on how to deal with the "widespread opposition [to residential integration] among white homeowners, mortgage lending agencies, and realtors [who] insured that few blacks would live outside the Central District." Some favored "public education along with quiet attempts to locate 'pioneer' black families in white neighborhoods," while others felt that an open housing ordinance was "the most effective means of integrating the neighborhoods because it would provide legal penalties for those who chose to discriminate." As CACRC members publicly pressed for the ordinance and quietly located families of color in white neighborhoods, segregationists burned crosses on their lawns and shot out their windows; in response, civil rights groups mounted a 400-person march on city hall, a 24-hour occupation of the mayor's office, a 1,000-person march, and a 1,200-person rally. Spurred by the turmoil, the city council approved a housing ordinance but Seattle voters overwhelmingly rejected it, thus leaving Blacks ghettoized in the Central District.[5]

Residential segregation grounded Seattle's dual school system, which, according to a 1957 survey, crowded 81 percent of all Black students into "nine of the city's 112 schools." In 1963, the board approved a "Voluntary Racial Transfer Program (VRT)" that promised to "send an estimated 1,400 of the 7,000 black pupils . . . to various schools outside the Central District," but actually transferred only 238 Black students to white schools and only 7 white students to the nearly all-Black Garfield High School. Black parents objected that the VRT program placed the burden of transfers on their children and failed to improve Central District schools.[6] In 1966 when the system still consisted of over one hundred white schools and thirteen crowded Black schools, frustrated Black leaders held a two-day school boycott and sponsored freedom schools that (like the 1964 Mississippi Freedom Summer Schools) taught Black history, culture, and activism. On March 31 and April 1, nearly 4,000 students (about 30 percent were white) attended freedom schools held at Mount Zion Church and Temple De Hirsch. Angry school officials announced they would discipline participating students; the NAACP sued, asking the court to order the school district to submit a desegregation plan; school officials stalled; and the Black community embraced Black Power.[7]

The catalyst that balkanized the city into rival groups—temporizing school officials, cautious integrationists, Black Power activists, and backlashing whites—occurred in spring 1967 when the local chapter of the Student Non-violent Coordinating Committee (SNCC) decided to host a visit by Stokely Carmichael, SNCC chairman and Black Power leader. The chapter asked permission to rent the Garfield High School auditorium for his speech, the school district refused, an ACLU lawyer intervened on behalf of SNCC, and a court ordered the district to make the auditorium available. Speaking to the 4,000 people (20 percent were white) on April 19, Carmichael chastised integrationists, declaring, "What must be abolished is not the black community . . . but the dependent, colonial status forced upon it. . . . We are all born free. We are enslaved by institutionalized racism." Attacking the media for fueling white fears, he said, "No one is talking about the blacks taking over the country, but about taking over our own communities."[8] His visit inspired waves of Seattle activism orchestrated by SNCC, the Black Panther Party, the Nation of Islam, and the University of Washington's Black Student Union. Eventually the school board created a Central District committee to co-administer the schools, and the NAACP withdrew its lawsuit, but not until 1977 when threatened with new litigation did the board agree to the mandatory busing of minority and white students.[9]

Throughout the 1960s, the Black community fought employment discrimination, staging protests that targeted the retail, civil service, shipping, aircraft, and construction industries.[10] Although the aircraft and construction industries had "generated the 'biggest economic boom since the Alaska Gold Rush,'" a 1966 state report found that the "15 Building Trades unions, representing over 29,000 workers, had only 7 non-white apprentices"[11]; and a 1966 Urban League report revealed that "black unemployment stood at ten percent, triple the rate for the entire city . . . even though 148,000 new jobs had been created in the past 18 months. . . . Among those under 24, the jobless rate had reached an all-time high of 25%."[12]

In August 1969, Tyree Scott, a young Black electrician, asked the Central Contractors Association (CCA), an organization of Black contractors, to challenge the exclusion of Black workers from unions and of Black-owned businesses from construction projects. As Scott led protests that closed down federally funded projects worked by white crews, the CCA litigated, arguing that industry practices violated Executive Order 11246. Federal district court judge William Lindberg ordered the parties to work out an agreement, but when the negotiations stalled several hundred Black activists brought business-as-usual to a halt. They protested at University of Washington construction sites "where national television recorded the overturning of bulldozers," marched onto Sea-Tac airport runways to block the planes, and "tied up ticket counters with phony ticket purchases," a strategy pioneered by Saul Alinsky, famously dubbed the dean of community organizing.[13]

Monitoring the turmoil, the Department of Justice filed *United States v. Local 86, Ironworkers* (1970, 1971) against the unions of metal workers, electricians, plumbers, and operating engineers. Judge Lindberg's forty-two-page opinion described flagrantly discriminatory practices: the union withheld job information from Blacks, imposed harder tests and higher standards on Blacks than on whites, required Blacks but not whites to present contractor letters of recommendation before referring them to jobs, referred less-experienced whites over more-experienced Blacks, and excluded Blacks from apprenticeship and membership.[14] The judge ordered several remedial actions, but the unions and construction firms stalled, setting off more protests by the United Construction Workers Association (UCWA), a new organization led by Tyree Scott.[15]

This widely publicized discrimination in Seattle housing, schools, unions, and industries provided the context for *DeFunis*. In 1968 and 1969, when Marco DeFunis was an undergraduate student at the University of Washington, the Black Student Union (BSU) protested the nearly all-white student body, faculty, and curriculum (see below). In 1970, when DeFunis was rejected by the law school, riot police quelled BSU protests on campus.[16] In 1971, when he sued the university, the UCWA shut down seven construction projects on the UW campus and one in the university district.[17] Yet participants in the September 1971 *DeFunis* trial ignored the racial turmoil. DeFunis attorney Josef Diamond, who represented 90 percent of the area's construction firms, claimed that his clients were not concerned with racial minorities (see chapter 4)[18]; and UW attorney James B. Wilson, who had written an article about his own skirmishes with the Mississippi police for providing legal aid to civil rights workers, avoided the subject of racism.[19] Even UW president Charles Odegaard, who testified at trial, never mentioned the campus construction protests or student activism.

THE BLACK STUDENT UNION STORY

In April 1967, before addressing the audience at Garfield High School, Stokely Carmichael spoke to a large crowd of UW students, who enthusiastically received his message that African Americans should take control of their community institutions and use them to better their lives. Afterwards, the UW Afro-American Student Society merged with SNCC's Seattle chapter to form the BSU, which quickly recruited 900 college and high-school students city-wide and orchestrated a fall sit-in at Franklin High School (DeFunis's alma mater).[20] In March 1968, the BSU wrote to President Odegaard, demanding that the university hire Black faculty, counselors, and teaching assistants; offer Black studies courses; eliminate racism in athletics, campus housing, and the Greek system; and improve conditions in the Black community. The assassination of Dr. King on April 4 and the police attack on the Oakland Black Panther Party on April 6 further emboldened BSU members to examine the university admissions process: "Out of a student population of 30,000," they wrote, "there are about 200 Afro-Americans, 20 or so American Indians, and 10 or so Mexican-Americans. The present admissions policies are slanted toward white, middle-class, Western ideals."[21] When meetings with university officials produced little action, the BSU fired off a May 16 letter demanding that the president allocate $50,000 for minority initiatives and then staged a May 20 sit-in at his office. While administrators barricaded themselves in a room and police threatened to remove the students, an ACLU lawyer negotiated with the president.

Afterwards, UW administrators "tried to downplay the sit-in," declaring "that they had not been forced to accept BSU demands but rather had merely restated preexisting policy" and noting that the president had "urged the University community to be more aware of race problems as early as 1965." But *Seattle Times* reporter Marsha King wrote that "the protesting students provided the catalyst. That summer [1968], affirmative action at the University of Washington was born."[22] The university launched the Educational Opportunity Program (EOP), which included vigorous recruitment of minority students, new admissions procedures, financial aid, summer jobs, tutoring, and advising. These measures increased minority enrollments from 150 to 465 for African Americans, 20 to 100 for Native Americans, and 10 to 90 for Chicanos—still, however, anemic numbers in a student body of 30,000.[23]

THE PRESIDENT'S STORY

During his testimony at the *DeFunis* trial in September 1971, President Odegaard presented an affirmative-action history cleansed of the campus and community turmoil. First hearing about complaints of racial discrimination soon after he took office in 1958, he ordered a review of university policies and announced in 1959 that the university would adopt an open-door policy (i.e., requiring few credentials beyond high-school graduation). At the time, he felt that prohibiting discrimination was sufficient to eliminate it, but he had an epiphany at the 1963 commencement ceremony. Reflecting on the hundreds of students who had marched past them, a regent asked, "'Where are the black students?' There were so few that appeared; it just left us with a question, 'Why is it?' With our open-door policy, we had so few that seemed to be coming through." These questions, Odegaard testified, were "in all our minds, because we had been more conscious of racial problems here in Seattle."[24]

That fall he appointed a faculty committee to investigate why the open-door policy had failed to integrate the student body. In court, he described what the committee found:

> Well, more and more as we dug into this, we began to realize that there can be a presumption of legal equality or procedural equality at the University but, in fact, cultural conditions . . . deter certain persons, either by reason of extreme poverty or . . . by reason of separation from the conventional life of the times . . . from acquiring the backgrounds necessary to move into more responsible roles in American life.[25]

His euphemistic language about "cultural conditions" that deterred "certain persons" could not convey to the trial court the education pipeline discrimination, let alone the systemic racism, that prevented students of color from entering or completing undergraduate programs at the University of Washington.

After campus discussion of the 1965 and 1967 committee reports, the administration instituted such proactive measures as outreaching to racial-minority high schools and churches, sponsoring an Upward Bound summer program for disadvantaged high-school students, helping Central District Black students with college applications, giving admissions officials more discretion to consider applicant disadvantages, and providing financial assistance and tutoring for disadvantaged students.[26] In crediting the outreach efforts of minority faculty and students, the president commented paternalistically, "You have to deal with these groups that have been isolated from the mainstream of American life through what amounts to intermediaries who already have come part way . . . into what they would regard as the White System of the University of Washington."[27] At least his archetypal story of UW leaders journeying toward the light had the virtue of commencing at an earlier date than the narrowly framed story that emerged from the trial.

THE TRIAL STORY

The official story of DeFunis's fate begins in 1969–1970.[28] Before graduating Phi Beta Kappa and Magna Cum Laude from the University of Washington in June, he took the Law School Admissions Test (LSAT) twice, scoring 512 (forty-sixth to forty-seventh percentile) and then 566 (sixty-fifth percentile). After applying for admission to the law school's fall 1970 entering class, he was waitlisted and then rejected. During the 1970–1971 academic year he worked nearly fulltime for the Seattle Park Department, completed 21 hours of graduate courses, and took the LSAT for a third time, scoring 668 (ninety-third percentile), clearly an improvement over his previously poor and then mediocre performances.[29] After applying for admission to the law school's fall 1971 entering class, he was once again waitlisted and rejected.

The pretrial materials, witness examinations, and court opinions delineated the 1971 admissions process. The law school required applicants to have an undergraduate degree and submit several documents: transcripts from prior undergraduate and graduate schools, LSAT scores, recommendations from their undergraduate dean and faculty members in their major, and, if they wished, a personal statement. The admissions committee, consisting of five faculty members and two students (a third student was added in the summer of 1971), used several criteria to evaluate the applicants' potential to "make significant contributions to law school classes and to the community at large."[30] The quantitative criteria—the grade point average (GPA) for junior- and senior-year academic courses and the LSAT scores—were combined to make the Predicted First Year Average (PFYA). The admissions committee sorted the 1,601 applicants into three groups: the top group had PFYA scores ranging from 81 to 77, the middle group had scores ranging from 76.99 to 74.5, and the bottom group had scores falling below 74.5. Aware that numerical indicators did not reliably predict whether applicants could make significant contributions to the school and the profession, the committee also considered such qualitative information as the academic status of the undergraduate institution, difficulty of the major, performance in analytic and writing courses, recommendations, extracurricular activities, postgraduate education, work experience, socioeconomic circumstances, and motivation.

The winnowing of applicants proceeded in phases during 1971. At meetings held on February 24, March 29, and April 12, the committee accepted seventy-eight applicants in the top PFYA group, four outstanding minority applicants, and nineteen veterans, while setting aside seven top applicants who seemed less promising on the basis of qualitative information than was indicated by their PFYAs. Meanwhile the chair of the admissions committee rejected most of the applicants in the bottom PFYA range (below 74.5), but set aside fifty applicants who seemed more promising on the basis of qualitative information than was indicted by their PFYAs (none were minority applicants). To prepare for meetings on May 10–14 and 17, the set-aside applications from the top and bottom PFYA groups and all applications from the middle group were randomly assigned to committee members, each receiving about seventy applications and asked to recommend about ten for admission, twenty-five for the waitlist, and thirty-five for rejection. At the May meetings, each reviewer summarized a file and made a recommendation; then the whole committee discussed each applicant and voted. By this process, it determined whom to accept, reject, or place on a waitlist divided into quartiles.[31]

Trial evidence shows that some groups received different treatment from the rest of the applicants. Previously admitted, honorably discharged veterans were automatically accepted irrespective of whether their PFYAs now fell into the low, middle, or high groups. For preliminary review, African Americans were assigned to Vincent Hayes, a second-year Black law student "who had previously served as director of the Governor's Multi-Service Center in Seattle, a job involving considerable personnel evaluation," and to Professor Geoffrey Crooks, who had directed a summer institute held on the UW campus in 1970. The institutes, sponsored by the Council on Legal Education Opportunities (CLEO) at different campuses, provided prelaw education to disadvantaged college students of all races. Also for preliminary review, the files of Chicanos, Filipinos, and Native Americans were assigned to Associate Dean Robert S. Hunt.[32] Although using the same format (file presentation, discussion, and vote), the committee compared minority applicants to one another, but not to nonminority applicants, and "attached less weight to the PFYA in making a total judgmental evaluation as to the[ir] relative ability . . . to succeed in law school."[33]

DeFunis received his rejection notice on August 2, 1971, and on August 19 Josef Diamond filed a complaint in the Superior Court for King County on behalf of DeFunis, his wife, and his parents, claiming that the law school had admitted "candidates whose qualifications and credentials are much below the credentials and qualifications of the plaintiff." The complaint also alleged that the school favored out-of-state applicants:

> That the University of Washington Law School is a state institution supported by the taxpayers and residents of the state of Washington; and taxpayers and residents of the state of Washington are entitled to preference for admission to the state University. At other schools at the University of Washington preference is given to taxpayers

> and residents of the state of Washington. That failure on the part of the defendants to admit said plaintiff to the Law School is unjust discrimination in favor of nonresidents, nontaxpayers, and students who do not have the qualifications possessed by said plaintiff.[34]

After the university unsuccessfully motioned to dismiss the case and the attorneys conducted discovery, the trial began on September 14 and ended on September 16. Judge Lloyd Shorett announced his decision orally and later issued a written Findings of Fact and Conclusions of Law on October 18.[35] He ruled that the university had unconstitutionally discriminated against the plaintiff on the basis of race and ordered the law school to admit him.

In theory, the adversarial testing of witnesses during the discovery and trial should have produced a fuller story than the one that constituted the official record. But in practice the attorneys used narrow time and action frames to craft a narrative about only the two years that DeFunis applied to the law school. This framing excluded inconvenient facts about the DeFunis family's quest for special treatment, the surge in law school applications that disqualified mediocre applicants who previously would have been admitted, and the educational racism that disproportionately eliminated minority students before or during the admissions process. Through clever rhetoric, the attorneys and the judge colored the facts, thereby transmuting the race-neutral claim about a withheld residential preference into the claim of racial discrimination.

THE FAMILY RUMPUS STORY

Among the many omissions from the case record are facts about the DeFunis family's actions. In 1970 and again in 1971, DeFunis applied to law schools at Gonzaga University, Lewis and Clark University, University of California in Berkeley, University of California in San Francisco (Hastings Law School), University of Idaho, University of Oregon, University of Washington, and Willamette University. Although twice rejected by Berkeley and Washington, he received offers from and made deposits to reserve places at Gonzaga, Oregon, and Willamette.[36] When Diamond asked why his client preferred the UW Law School, DeFunis replied that, as a Seattle native who was "acquainted with the setting," he had friends and family there, could get summer jobs, and would be supported by his wife, who worked as a dental assistant.[37] Later in the trial, an admissions committee member read a passage from the letter of recommendation written by his undergraduate advisor: "This guy is a person I would refer to as the planner. He sets his goal and steadily works toward it, come Hell or high water. I admire him in his persistence, but there seems to be the slight tendency of not caring upon whom he might step in the process."[38] Indeed, rather than enrolling in any of the law schools that had accepted him, DeFunis and his family mounted in a pressure campaign to gain admission to his first-choice school.

In a *New York Times* feature article, Nina Totenberg reported that Craig Sternberg, DeFunis's college fraternity brother and a junior attorney in the Seattle firm of Lycette Diamond & Sylvester, put the family in touch with Josef Diamond.[39] When I interviewed Craig Sternberg, he provided more detail:

> I had graduated from the UofW Law School in June of 1970. I knew and had good relationships with most, if not all, of the professors and students on the admissions committee. At the request of one of the professors, I wrote a letter of recommendation for Marco. I thought that his background and grades should have qualified him for the UofW's Law School. I met with Marco on several occasions after he was rejected for the second time, and actually did some research and drafted the complaint. . . . I certainly could not take on a lawsuit of this magnitude without his [Diamond's] permission! His response: if it is good enough for you to pursue, it is good enough for me to take it to court.

That July, Sternberg wrote a complaint at his "kitchen table with Marco providing me facts"; he "completed the draft of the complaint, brought it to Joe and we pursued the case."[40]

As for motive, Totenberg stated that Diamond "was intrigued—partly because the situation offended his sense of rightness, and partly because he had a couple of well-to-do clients who had children not as qualified as DeFunis who were having trouble getting into law school."[41] Sternberg mentioned two motives: "For one thing, he was supporting his young associate. For another, he did not like the idea that our only state supported law school was passing over qualified students in favor of out of state students and students with lesser qualifications."[42] At oral argument before the Supreme Court, Diamond said that, after unsuccessful meetings with university officials, "We had no alternative . . . but to bring a lawsuit." He further volunteered, "As a matter of fact, I have in my office two clients, one girl and one man, waiting for the determination of this [case] to see whether they can get into law school."[43]

But I still wondered why Diamond based his claim of law school discrimination on the allegedly withheld resident preference rather than on alleged minority preferences. Sternberg explained, "The law required the UofW to educate its citizens. This was not a case about race, or affirmative reaction [*sic*]. This was a case about one Washington state resident that was being treated unfairly by admitting out of state students with lesser qualifications—at least in the beginning. The UofW actually raised the issue of affirmative action."[44] Later he repeated the explanation: "This was not a case about affirmative action, race or religion. It was a case about our client. We did not want to make this a race based case."[45] But the facts do not support these explanations because Diamond began making it a race-based case during pretrial discovery and Judge Shorett joined the effort by asking about race in his pretrial guidance (see chapter 4). Clearly, the participants had mixed motives. Sternberg, who had written a letter of recommendation for DeFunis, felt the law school was inventing justifications of its race-conscious admissions program.[46] Diamond, who had a record of winning lawsuits, once told Washington State Supreme Court justice Tom Chambers, who began his career at Lycette Diamond & Sylvester, "'Never allow another lawyer to take control of your case. . . . A lawsuit is like a war."[47]

Determined to make war well before filing the August complaint, Diamond began helping the DeFunis in May or June 1971. Using case documents, docket entries, transcripts, and my interview of Craig Sternberg, I reconstructed the timetable:

- DeFunis took the LSAT exam three times, scoring 512 out of 800 in August 1969, 566 in October 1969, and 668 in December 1970.[48]
- DeFunis had conversations with two different admissions deans before and after learning that he was waitlisted in 1970 and 1971.[49]
- On May 12, 1971, DeFunis was waitlisted for the second time and probably received the notice a week later.
- In a May 24 letter to the UW Law School, Mrs. DeFunis claimed that her son was ill when he took the LSAT in August 1969; Richard O. Kummert, chair of the admissions committee, testified that the letter did not persuade the committee to change its evaluation.[50] According to the university's interrogatory, however, Mrs. DeFunis said her son was ill "on each of the first two takings of the test."[51]
- At trial, DeFunis testified that when he took the August LSAT he did not report any illness to Dr. Kohli, his physician, or to "the proctors at the time of the examination."[52] At trial, Mrs. DeFunis said that she spoke to the doctor three times in May 1971 and wrote to him in June, each time urging him to remember consulting on her son's 1969 illness. Despite the pressure, Dr. Kohli wrote a July 7 letter saying that he had no memory or record of consultations.[53]
- At trial, DeFunis testified that he contacted Diamond in August 1971 but, under cross-examination, he admitted to earlier contact "not for legal assistance, though." When Wilson asked "What sort of assistance did you have in mind if it weren't legal assistance?," he replied "for arrangement of some meetings" so that his parents "would have someone of some importance to go with them who could provide me with legal assistance, perhaps, in the future."[54]
- In late May or early June after DeFunis was waitlisted, Diamond and the parents met with the law school dean and admissions committee chair, who said that "other students [were] better qualified than DeFunis" and declined to provide confidential records "to establish that there were 150 or more better qualified."[55]

- In a June 11 letter to the Board of Regents, Diamond asked to present the DeFunis matter at its June 16 meeting. Former board chair George V. Powell testified that when the letter arrived on June 15 it was too late to add another agenda item. Powell "arranged to have this informal meeting with Mr. Diamond, his clients, and I believe . . . a majority of the Board of Regents." Diamond attended the meeting with the parents and "another person interested at that time."[56] Perhaps this person was, as Totenberg suggested, a client whose child was rejected by the law school.
- After these regents discussed DeFunis's situation with President Odegaard and law school officials, they came away satisfied by the explanation.[57]
- On July 21, the law school admissions committee eliminated DeFunis and others in the two lowest quartiles of its waitlist; by then, Craig Sternberg had drafted the complaint.
- On August 2, DeFunis received a rejection notice, and on August 19, Diamond filed the complaint.[58]

The DeFunis interventions, occurring between the waitlist notice and the rejection notice, reveal a classic escalation strategy—Mrs. DeFunis's May communications with Dr. Kohli and the law school, Diamond's early June meeting with law school officials and his letter to the Regents, the family's June meeting with the regents, and the regents' meeting with the president and dean.

Other accounts reveal why the pressure campaign was unsuccessful. According to a pretrial interrogatory, the admissions committee generally discounted illness claims: "The Committee receives from innumerable applicants statements as to why their LSAT score is not a fair measure of their abilities and many include statements alleging medical infirmities at the time of the test. The Committee has tended to discount most such statements, except for those demonstrating relatively severe symptoms fully verified by a physician. . . ."[59]At trial, Professor Kummert, chair of the committee, also observed that low-scoring applicants frequently claimed that, owing to illness, the test did not measure their true ability.[60]

Moreover, John A. Winterbottom, director of the Educational Testing

Service (ETS) graduate and professional school programs, testified at trial that if a test-taker "became seriously ill to the point where it came to the supervisor's attention," ETS would notate the illness in the score report sent to law schools. "I have seen the [DeFunis] score reports," he added, "and there was no notation."[61] When Diamond prodded Winterbottom to admit that the practice of averaging multiple test scores might disadvantage an ill test-taker,[62] Winterbottom convincingly explained the "practice effect." When a test-taker is ill or anxious while first taking the LSAT, his score "is likely to be somewhat of an under-estimate of his true ability," but when he retakes the test, "the second score, as a result of this practice effect, is likely to be something of an over-estimate of his true ability, and the truth lies somewhere in between," which is why multiple scores were averaged.[63] Indeed DeFunis benefited from the practice effect, his low score of 512 leaping to 566 and then to 668.

The objective of the family's pressure campaign seems to have been gaining not a *reconsideration* of DeFunis's original application but an *enhancement* of it; they were angling to eliminate the two lower scores from the calculation of his PFYA in order to raise his ranking in the applicant pool. Indeed, Diamond endeavored to raise DeFunis's ranking by ignoring testimony that the admissions committee considered only junior-senior grades and insisting that it should have counted DeFunis's A grades for Latin courses taken before his junior year. Would elimination of DeFunis's low LSAT scores have raised his ranking? If my calculations are correct, he would have had a PFYA of 77.73, placing him near the bottom of the top PFYA group.[64] Yet this purely quantitative ranking, as so many trial witnesses pointed out, did not include the qualitative factors considered by the admissions committee.

Failing to achieve their objective with the illness claim, the DeFunis family turned to the regents, first through Diamond's letter asking to discuss the matter at their monthly meeting and then through a private meeting:

> [The family] did not mention the University's policy toward racial minorities. Rather they "explained . . . what good grades [Marco] had and how [he] applied and had been turned down or put on the

> waiting list, and one thing and another, and just asked the Regents to consider the situation and see what, if anything, they could do about it." As a result of this meeting, members of the Board of Regents met with representatives of the Law School to discuss DeFunis's application, but they came away "satisfied" with the Law School's decision not to admit DeFunis.[65]

What can we make of this side-bar activity?

Unquestionably, Diamond, not the senior Mr. DeFunis who was a Seattle furniture salesman, had the background to influence regents.[66] The American-born son of Jewish immigrants who had fled Kiev to escape "the anti-Semitic rule of the Russian czar," Diamond was the first in his working-class family to attend college, earning a UW undergraduate degree in 1928 and a UW law degree in 1931. While practicing law, he presided over a multistate empire of parking lots, auto businesses, hotels, and the Northwest Bank, which he cofounded in 1964.[67] In a 2002 profile, Washington State Supreme Court justice Tom Chambers described Diamond as "one of the state's most dynamic, creative and resourceful lawyers," who not only "represented 90 percent of the construction firms . . . in the city" but held large shares of the legal work in other sectors.[68] In a 2007 obituary, the bank president said Diamond "was probably one of the most powerful people in Seattle, because he had so many contacts."[69] Based on this information, we can surmise that the four regents who were lawyers knew Diamond's reputation and agreed to take the side-bar meeting.[70]

Regent Powell's testimony revealed that at least some of his colleagues had previously acted behind the scenes. Before receiving Diamond's request to meet, he himself was involved in a similar situation: "I had a personal friend . . . who had a daughter who had very good grades and who had been denied [admission]. She was not on the waiting list, and he wanted me to find out what the situation was, so I made inquiry and then for the first time was made aware of the very tight situation in the law school and was informed that this person would probably not be admitted."[71] Yet at trial he stated that state law empowered the seven-member board to delegate administrative responsibilities "to the University administration, the president, and in turn to the faculty and members of the law school."[72] When Wilson asked, "Does the Board of Regents undertake any administrative responsibilities?," Powell replied, "we rely on the president to run the University through his staff and the people he selected to run it."[73] Thus, the regents who communicated with the families of rejected applicants and questioned law school officials transmuted the oversight authority vested in the board as a whole into their own special treatment of the dissatisfied applicants. They surely would not have extended this special treatment to all dissatisfied applicants, if for no other reason than that they would have become full-time grievance officers. This special treatment, enabled by Diamond's personal influence, was discrimination favoring DeFunis.[74]

In his 1970 article for the *University of Toledo Law Review*, Robert M. O'Neil explained that the use of race-conscious admissions to integrate law schools did not prevent white applicants from obtaining a legal education. Rather it modestly redistributed places: "For every [white] student rejected by one law school, opportunities exist at other schools which are objectively as good."[75] But Diamond and his clients had an entitlement perspective: they felt that DeFunis was entitled to attend his first-choice law school and, when rejected, was entitled to exact what he desired.[76] Once caught up in litigation, Diamond desired more—not only his client's admission to the UW Law School but also, as we will see, a holding of racial discrimination. In the chapters that follow, I show how Diamond's race-neutral complaint was racialized during the trial, how systemic racism against minorities was occluded, and how Justice Douglas attempted to reconcile the incommensurable discourses that entered the case.

4

COLORING THE CASE

> This [white] standpoint views white people and their interests as central to, and representative of, humanity. Whites also produce and reinforce the dominant narratives of society—such as individualism and meritocracy—and use these narratives to explain the positions of other racial groups.
>
> —Robin DiAngelo, *White Fragility: Why It's So Hard for White People to Talk about Racism* (2018)

The complaint that Josef Diamond filed in the Superior Court for King County on August 19 claimed that the University of Washington Law School discriminated against Marco DeFunis by failing to give him a state resident preference and admitting students with lower Grade Point Averages (GPAs), Law School Admissions Test (LSAT) scores, and Predicted First Year Averages (PFYAs).[1] The proceedings moved swiftly, taking about fifteen working days for the court to receive the university's response and admissions data, the interrogatories, and a deposition of the law school dean. At the trial, beginning on September 14 and ending on September 16, Diamond called nine witnesses: Marco DeFunis, his wife Lucia, his parents Marco Sr. and Betty Jean, former UW Board of Regents chair George V. Powell, UW president Charles Odegaard, and student members of the admissions committee—Tamara Zorn, Vincent Alan Hayes, and Rochelle Ellen Kleinberg. University counsel James B. Wilson called four witnesses: UW Law School dean Richard L. Roddis; admissions committee chair Richard O. Kummert; Millard Ruud, an American Bar Association consultant on admissions; and John A. Winterbottom, director of the Educational Testing Service (ETS) program that administered the LSAT. In an oral decision of September 22, Judge Lloyd Shorett announced that the law school had discriminated against DeFunis on racial grounds, and in a Findings of Fact and Conclusions of Law issued on October 18 he elaborated on the decision.[2]

Almost every law scholar who wrote about *DeFunis* described it as a dispute over the constitutionality of race-conscious admissions to the law school or more generally the remedial use of racial classifications.[3] These delineations, which manifested the scholarly interest in abstract principles, masked questions about the construction of "discrimination" during the trial phase. Why did Diamond initially allege that the law school discriminated by denying his client a state resident preference? Why did he ignore the actual preference given to underqualified veterans while insinuating that female preferences and anti-Semitism vitiated the admissions process? Who racialized the case so that the judge could "find" (in both senses) racial discrimination against DeFunis?

Racialization, which is the complex discursive process of imprinting racial grammars on social phenomena, operates through myriad vehicles of meaning, most obviously statements, images, and gestures. Its products are not merely racial concepts found in science, law, politics, and religion, images found in the arts and media, or angry fists and fingers thrust in the air. Deeply embedded in society, racial frames like color-blindness and white nationalism pattern the human practices and institutional processes that actualize racial differences, hierarchies, and exclusions. In this chapter, I demonstrate how actors used language in written documents and oral examinations to racialize *DeFunis* during the trial phase. Some of their statements blatantly racialized minority applicants to the law school, while others, when analyzed, revealed implicit racial biases about who could do what within the power-structured relations of race, gender, and status. Although I occasionally speculate on the actors' reasons for choices they made, I am analyzing their white-centric discourse, not their personal psyches. In current research literature, what is called "the new racism" or "aversive racism" manifests itself in (white) professions of color-blindness, defenses of merit, cultural stereotypes, microaggressions, and the absence of people-of-color voices.[4] These and other manifestations of whiteness as the pervasive yet obscured norm constitute the machinery that maintains white privilege in life and, as we will see, in law.

ADMISSIONS PREFERENCES

When I asked Craig Sternberg in a September 2016 interview why Josef Diamond's complaint did not allege racial discrimination against his client, he replied,

> Because I drafted the complaint, and wanted to focus on state preference. . . . I was a young liberal guy, who just graduated from the UofW Law School myself. Politically and probably legally, I was in favor of what became Affirmative Action, but as we got into it, it was clear that the Law School . . . was making up policies and procedures to justify their position. In short, I thought that the Law School went into this period with good intentions, but with no rules, or policies. . . . I think that Joe thought that the Law School was not acting in good faith.[5]

"Good faith," according to *Black's Law Dictionary*, denotes "a state of mind consisting in (1) honesty in belief or purpose" and "(2) faithfulness to one's duty or obligation," while "bad faith" denotes "dishonesty of belief or purpose."[6] Since Sternberg did not conduct trial examinations, the trial transcript does not show whether he acted in good faith, but it does show that Diamond repeatedly crossed the thin line separating candor from canniness during and after the trial.

The Resident Preference

If Diamond had researched California law, he would have discovered that its constitutional provision on educational access applied only to the common schools; yet he insisted that it obliged the university to provide DeFunis with a resident preference. For instance, he asked UW president Odegaard if he was "familiar with a constitutional provision which, I believe, requires the University to prefer resident students." When the president said he was not familiar with it, Diamond read it: "It is the paramount duty of the State to make ample provision for the education of all children residing within its borders, without distinction or preference on account of race, color, caste, or sex." The wording, which obliges the state to provide education for all resident children, makes no mention of universities let alone a preference for in-state applicants. Only when Diamond continued to question Odegaard on this matter did Judge Shorett caution that he should not ask the president to interpret the constitution.[7] Next attempting to establish that the law school violated the (nonexistent) preference for in-state students, Diamond asserted that between 30 percent and 50 percent of the law school students came from outside the state. Before the president could respond, Wilson intervened to note that out-of-state students received 30 percent of the offers but constituted only 20 percent of the enrollment. Thus his intervention missed the point that the state constitution did not require or even address a university resident preference.[8]

Shifting from the resident argument to a merit argument, Diamond enumerated DeFunis's academic achievements, but President Odegaard replied that, with 1,601 applicants competing for 150 places, the law school had to reject many well-qualified students.

> Q [Diamond]: Doctor, are we to understand that your undergraduate students can now look forward to graduating from your university with Magna Cum Laude, Phi Beta Kappa, 3.8 average, and still not be able to get into your law school?
>
> A [Odegaard]: Under the circumstances that have been presented here in terms of competition, unfortunately, this is true.[9]

Given that other witnesses also emphasized the intense competition that resulted in rejecting qualified applicants, Diamond had to nuance his argument. He did so by claiming DeFunis was more qualified than some applicants who received offers and then, with help from the judge (see below), racialized these applicants as less-qualified students of color who benefited from favorable treatment during the vetting process.

The Veteran Preference

During the trial, Diamond learned that the law school gave a particular group of applicants a free pass.[10] Professor Kummert, the admissions committee chair, testified that the school had traditionally readmitted honorably discharged veterans who were inducted into the military before completing the first year and recently extended this privilege to veterans who were inducted before starting their classes. Nineteen of the twenty-three veterans admitted for fall 1971—seventeen white students and two students of color—had lower PFYA scores than DeFunis did. When Diamond asked why the law school admitted them, Kummert replied that it had lower standards in past years when they were originally admitted.[11] So why did Diamond—who complained that the law school admitted "many candidates whose qualifications and credentials are much below the credentials and qualifications of the plaintiff"[12]—avoid targeting these admittees, most of whom were white?

Surely, he wished to sidestep a highly controversial issue at that time—namely that veterans returning from the Vietnam War felt doubly wounded by battlefield injuries and antiwar criticism that indiscriminately lacerated them along with the US government.[13] By targeting veterans, he would have dismayed Americans who believed that those who put their lives on the line for the country were entitled to resume what they left behind, a view he had expressed on returning from his own military service during World War II. In the *Book of Memories* compiled by friends to commemorate Diamond's eighty-fifth birthday, Mel and Johanna Steil, owners of Arctic Furs, recalled that Diamond confronted a colleague who had taken over this business account and "demanded his right, as a returning veteran, to get his job back."[14]

In his Findings of Fact, Judge Shorett bleached the color from the veteran preference, writing that "some students who were admitted in previous years and then went into the Armed Services" were readmitted "without further examination of credentials, although some of these credentials were lower than the plaintiff's."[15] By using "some students," rather than specifically referring to the seventeen white and two Black veterans, he obscured the fact that this preference benefitted mainly white veterans. Similarly, by using the fuzzy "some of these credentials," he avoided naming the multiple criteria used to determine who was qualified.

The Female Preference

After law school officials repeatedly stated that no preference was given to female applicants, Diamond aggressively examined the three student members of the committee. Despite her long examination (filling forty pages of the trial transcript), Tamara Zorn, a second-year law student, was a feisty witness.[16] When he demeaned her for majoring in English at Hunter College, asked for her grade point average, and implied that she could not evaluate applicants with more difficult majors, Zorn replied that she consulted other committee members if she needed information. When he questioned her about a preference for female applications, the dialogue resembled a fencing match. Was a preference given to female applicants, he asked. No, she replied. Could she tell from a file whether the applicant was female? Yes, she could. Did the committee evaluate women differently from men? No, she replied.

But when Diamond asked whether the law students raised questions about the admission of women, Zorn ended the fencing match with an unexpected thrust:

> A [Zorn]: The women students at the law school discussed the admission of women into the law school.
> Q: How?
> A: There was some discussion because of the very small numbers presently at the law school and the very small number of practicing female attorneys, about what could be done to rectify that.
> Q: What was done?
> A: Nothing as far as the University was concerned.[17]

After learning that the university had rebuffed the women students, Diamond dropped the subject and began quizzing her on DeFunis's file, which she had not read until just before testifying in court. After enumerating his achievements, he asked her whether the law school should have admitted him. Zorn replied that his low LSAT scores and his advisor's negative comments made him a less than desirable applicant, a reply that prompted Diamond to abandon this subject as well.

Similarly, Diamond made no headway with Rochelle Ellen Kleinberg, a third-year student who had mastered both assertiveness and taciturnity. When he addressed her as "Mrs. Bancroft," she replied that she used her birth name of Kleinberg. When he quizzed her on her credentials, she informed him she had earned a political science degree from the University of California at Berkeley. When he questioned her ability to evaluate applicant files, she gave terse replies and referred him to the testimony of other witnesses. Thus stymied, he terminated this, the shortest of all the witness examinations he conducted.[18] In contrast, Diamond was able to intimidate Vincent Alan Hayes, a Black student who, while attending law school, also worked as director of the Washington State Multi-Service Center, an agency that served the Black residents of Seattle's Central District. Diamond questioned Hayes on his law school grades, pressured him to admit he had struggled with his classes, noted that he later resigned from the admissions committee, and then grilled him on the twenty or thirty files he had reviewed. Did he read all or only some of the material in each file? He read all the material. Did he receive training in how to read files? No committee members received training. Was he selected for the committee on the basis of a special aptitude? No, but as the Multi-Service Center director he had read many job files.

By all accounts, Diamond was an aggressive lawyer who regarded litigation as an arena for displays of power, but when witnesses violated his assumptions about the status, gender, and race hierarchies he lost his sense of equilibrium. In questioning President Odegaard about the university, he was constrained by the latter's academic status and knowledge. Thus to regain the upper hand, as we saw, he asked the president to step into his area of expertise and interpret a constitutional provision, but the judge terminated the inquiry, stating that legal interpretation fell outside of the president's expertise. But in questioning Zorn and Kleinberg, whom he regarded as lowly female law students, he abruptly ended the examinations when they unexpectedly thwarted his attempts at sexism. His exchanges with Hayes, however, took place within the already racialized trial discourse that depicted minority admittees as inferior to DeFunis (see below). Comfortably situated in the racial hierarchy, Diamond freely derogated Hayes's intellectual abilities and put this Black student in his place.[19]

Insinuations of Anti-Semitism

How Josef Diamond brought anti-Semitism into the case is a more complicated matter. Biographical information shows that he was attuned to it. He told friends the story of his Jewish parents (surnamed Dimerets in Russia) who had fled Kiev to escape persecution. The parents and their three children settled in Los Angeles where Josef was born and soon moved to Seattle where he remained, earning undergraduate and law degrees at the University of Washington, building a law practice, and joining Temple de Hirsch Sinai (which had hosted a freedom school during the Seattle school boycott).[20] When Craig Sternberg, a young Jewish lawyer in his firm, sought permission to pursue the DeFunis case in May or early June, Diamond might have asked how he knew the proposed client, and Sternberg would have replied that they were fraternity brothers in the UW chapter of Sigma Alpha Mu.[21] As UW graduates, both men would have known that Sammy (as it was dubbed) was the most prestigious national Jewish fraternity in an era when Greek organizations were segregated by religion as well as race.

Precisely when Diamond learned his client's religion is blurred by his own coyness. At trial, he asked, "Marco, in addition to your working on the outside [while attending university] . . . did you also do something with reference to your church?" "Yes," Marco replied, "I taught religion school on Sundays."[22] By substituting the word "church" for "synagogue," Diamond implied that he didn't know his client's religion during the trial; yet DeFunis recalled otherwise in his contribution to Diamond's *Book of Memories*:

> Being orthodox, I was required to celebrate two days of the [Rosh Hashana] holiday. It also happened that through Joe's legal tactics, a seat was reserved for me alone at the law school and could not be filled until the trial was concluded. Joe had an afternoon conference with the attorney for the University of Washington and the judge and dis-

> covered . . . that the law school's orientation was going on. The judge . . . told Joe that he recommended I attend one of those days of orientation for which the trial would be recessed. Joe came to me with a smile on his face like the cat that ate the canary and said, "I think it might be a good idea if you went to orientation on the second day of Rosh Hashana. I am not saying that the judge is going to rule in our favor, but he did feel that it would be a good idea if you went."[23]

This description reveals Diamond's tactical agility, previously demonstrated when he orchestrated the end-run to the regents (see chapter 3). Now winning a reserved seat for his client and eliciting the judge's "good idea" to attend orientation, he conveyed this news with a "cat ate the canary" smile.

As the case went forward, Diamond continued to dissemble. In the Washington State Supreme Court, he declared that the admissions committee had arbitrarily and capriciously placed DeFunis "in a classification so far down that he could not enter law school. . . . Thus under the system that was actually followed, the plaintiff could have been rejected because of the color of his hair, *his religion*, his political views or *the fact that he was Jewish*" (my emphases).[24] During oral argument in the US Supreme Court, he feigned ignorance: "We didn't know what his religion was, nor his race, nor whether he belonged to a so-called minority group, nor what constituted a minority group." Later a justice asked:

> QUESTION: What is he? What kind of an American is he?
> MR. DIAMOND: Unh-hunh.
> (Laughter)
> MR. DIAMOND: Well, he comes of Jewish parents. I don't know [*sic*] at the time we brought this action, I think Sephardic Jew, if I'm not mistaken.[25]

Ever tactical, Diamond knew or didn't know his client's religion as the situation required.

In a 1975 article, Erwin N. Griswold, a former US solicitor general and Harvard Law School dean, deplored that *DeFunis* "came to be seen as involving . . . anti-Semitism," adding "it was apparently pure chance that the case became a vehicle for such questions."[26] Anti-Semitism entered the case not by "pure chance" but by Diamond's deliberate tactics: by insinuating anti-Semitism, he could grasp at additional grounds for a weakly grounded complaint and could motivate Jewish organizations to file amicus briefs (see chapter 1). When I asked Craig Sternberg whether Wilson and Diamond encouraged the amici to weigh in, he replied, "I don't know about Wilson, but in our side they contacted us. I do not think that Joe solicited any amici briefs. I do know that many of the amici briefs supported some form of affirmative action, but not the hodge-podge policies that the Law School conjured up to support its position after the fact."[27] Yet most of the Jewish amici in *DeFunis* and later in *Bakke* claimed that affirmative action would roll back the hard-won gains made by Jews who had suffered from historical and contemporaneous anti-Semitism (see chapters 5 and 9).[28]

But why did Diamond only insinuate? If he had lodged a formal complaint, he would not only have to prove that anti-Semitism was a factor in DeFunis's rejection but also would present the courts with the dilemma of balancing the interests of racial minorities who were excluded from top-tier universities against those of Jewish students who were streaming into them. Just a few years after mooting *DeFunis*, the justices would face competing demands for representation in *United Jewish Organizations v. Carey* (1976), a Brooklyn voter redistricting case brought by the Williamsburg Hasidic community. In upholding the splitting of the Hasidim into two districts to cure the dilution of minority voting, the justices in one breath acknowledged the Hasidim's unique religion, culture, and persecution and in the next breath categorized them as generic white voters, thereby erasing the previously racialized identity of this discrete and insular minority group.[29] In this instance, they bleached what had formerly been a racialized religious group.

RACIALIZATION AT TRIAL

In his article, Griswold also observed, "No one thought of the case as involving a major constitutional issue when DeFunis was not admitted to the University of Washington Law School."[30] Craig Sternberg made the same point in his 2016 interview:

> This was not a case about race, or affirmative reaction [*sic*]. This was a case about one Washington state resident that was being treated unfairly by admitting out of state students with lesser qualifications—at least in the beginning. The UofW actually raised the issue of affirmative action.[31]

The trial documents, however, show that participants had racialized the discourse well before UW president Odegaard testified about affirmative action.

The Pretrial Deposition

Diamond began the racialization process while deposing University of Washington Law School dean Richard L. Roddis a week before the trial started:

> Q [Diamond]: Now, what is the policy of the Committee on Admissions with reference to minority groups?
> A: [Roddis]: Well, as to members of certain minority groups, the committee evaluates the qualifications of applicants separately and I think with less emphasis on the undergraduate grades and the L.S.A.T. score than they do with respect to the applicants of the majority groups.
> Q: Would it be fair to say then that the grade qualifications of the plaintiff DeFunis are probably higher than the grade qualifications of some of the minority students who are being admitted to the university?
> A: Yes, sir.[32]

When Diamond made "qualifications" equivalent to GPA and LSAT scores, Roddis hastened to correct him, adding that in a highly competitive applicant pool high scores did not guarantee admission. But as Diamond persisted, Roddis fumbled:

Q: All of the others are more qualified?
A: No, depending again on exactly how one defines "qualification," I suppose. Certainly on the basis of the . . . undergraduate grades and L.S.A.T. score, taking those items alone, there are some other students being admitted who are less qualified.
Q: And if you take into consideration the minority groups that you are allowing in, then on any standard there are some that are less qualified, are there not?
A: Well, part of the reason for separately evaluating the minority students is the feeling that due to educational and cultural disadvantage . . . you simply cannot assess their qualifications on the basis of the grades and the L.S.A.T. score, so it becomes a little difficult for me to say that they are less qualified.[33]

Diamond's statement-like questions declaring that the minority applicants were less qualified than the plaintiff are logically flawed. By equating "qualifications" with GPA and LSAT scores, he conflates the quantified results of white-normed measuring devices with the academic abilities of applicants, thus propagating the stereotype that minority students are intellectually inferior. Although counterfactual, his statements became facts when he instructed Craig Sternberg to read the entire deposition into the trial record.

The Direction on Evidence

At the start of the trial, Judge Shorett gave Wilson a direction on evidence he wanted the university to present:

THE COURT: I want to ask you a question about the minority group. You will have evidence as to how many blacks and how many are Mexicans and so forth?
MR. WILSON: I can provide that . . .
THE COURT: What I want to know, is there more than one minority group, or what numbers are in each one, and is your selection of these particular students for admission based upon some Act of Congress or some type of thought that floats around that there has

> been discrimination by others against them and therefore, they should get favorable treatment?
>
> Are there any figures to show what success they meet with? I am referring to all minority groups in schools of this kind. Have the courts passed upon this question deciding whether or not this constitutes discrimination not permitted by the Constitution? Those are things I will certainly be interested in.
>
> MR. WILSON: Fine. We will certainly prepare those as part of the presentation of our case.
>
> THE COURT: All of us realize that every time you select someone from some other place and put him in the admission group, that means one other must fall out.[34]

In response, Wilson stated that Diamond would have to prove that the school conducted an arbitrary and capricious process that resulted in DeFunis's rejection. Judge Shorett replied, "That's right, I will agree with you. . . . I am not prejudging it now."[35]

But the judge's racialized language indicates that he had already prejudged it. First, his comments display a one-sided interest in obtaining facts about minority applicants—their racial identities and the numbers applying, admitted, and succeeding (or failing) in their studies—rather than obtaining these facts about all applicants irrespective of race. Second, in discussing justifications for race-conscious admissions, the contrast between his disparaging language in "some type of thought that floats around out there" and his unadorned "some Act of Congress" suggests he was predisposed to reject the university's evidence of historical and social discrimination. Third, his use of "favorable treatment" for minority groups indicates his presumption of unfair treatment for nonminority applicants. Finally, the statement that "every time you select someone *from some other place* . . . that means one other must fall out" (my emphasis) reveals his othering of minority applicants; reared in nonmainstream cultures, they are raised up in the rankings to displace mainstream applicants.

Later in the trial, as President Odegaard described the university's turn to affirmative action and Diamond repeatedly objected that his testimony was irrelevant, Judge Shorett commented on fact and law:

> THE COURT: If constitutionally the University can give minority students a preference, then this is relevant to show how this program evolved, and I think, in any event, in a case such as this, which will obviously be reviewed by some appellate court, no matter what I do, this ought to be admitted.[36]

Couched in the conditional "if-then" mode, the statement means that the president's testimony is relevant *only if* a preference for minority applicants is constitutional and *only as* a history of the program's evolution. By relegating the president's facts to background history for a hypothetical legal question, the judge eliminates any probative value they could have in this case.

Witness Examinations

As suggested earlier, Diamond aggressively racialized the trial discourse while questioning witnesses. As a vivid example, we can consider his cross-examination of Millard Ruud, a University of Texas law professor and a prominent leader in several professional associations. As Ruud was describing the Council on Legal Education (CLEO) summer institutes that provided prelaw training for economically and educationally disadvantaged students, this exchange occurred:

> Q [Diamond]: Now, the purpose of the CLEO Institute is to attempt to bring up the low grades of the minority students so they can get into law school?
>
> A [Ruud]: The institute serves several functions. One, to provide . . . to admissions committees, a basis for judging probability of success in addition to the paper criteria. The other is a kind of head start to help the young men and women become more effective students.
>
> Q: Well, you stated that the number of minority group in law school in your Texas college or school is embarrassingly small.

A: Yes.
Q: By that, I take it you mean you feel that there should be more minority groups in law schools?
A: Yes, sir, very strongly.
Q: And part of the purpose, not the main purpose of the CLEO Institute, is to obtain more minority students in law school?
A: The stated purpose is to work with the economically and educationally disadvantaged, and these are predominantly minority group students, predominantly black and Mexican-American students.
Q: So they can and will get into Law school?
A: More importantly, take their places as leaders in their communities as lawyers.
Q: Then I am right, am I not?
A: Yes, sir.
Q: The purpose of CLEO is to get more minority student lawyers.
A: Yes, sir.[37]

Diamond's first question contains two counterfactuals: the case material did not establish that CLEO students had low grades in college, and the institute, which enrolled college graduates, had no impact on their college grades.[38] His subsequent questions insistently rephrase Ruud's statements about the institute purposes until they are distilled to the crassly stated purpose of getting "more minority student lawyers."

Later in the examination, Diamond attempts to discredit Ruud by asking bluntly if CLEO or the university paid him to testify. When Ruud replies he was testifying from his own interest in supporting minority admissions, Diamond plays his trump card:

Q: Now, there is another view with respect to the matter of special admission of culturally deprived people to law schools throughout the country, is there not, than the view you have expressed here?
A: Yes, I am certain there is.
Q: Are you familiar with the articles written by Lino A. Graglia?
A: Lino Graglia is a colleague of mine at the University of Texas.[39]

Whipping out a copy of Lino Graglia's *University of Pennsylvania Law Review* article (see chapter 2), Diamond read several passages accusing law schools of instituting racial quotas and accepting minority students irrespective of whether they were qualified or even culturally deprived.[40] When Ruud mentioned Robert M. O'Neil's article in the *Yale Law Journal,* Diamond expressed his opinion on law school discrimination, Wilson objected, and the judge cautioned Diamond to reserve his personal views for the closing. Inexplicably, Wilson then "waive[d] any redirect examination" of Ruud, thereby forfeiting the opportunity to read passages of the O'Neil's article into the record.[41] Although Judge Shorett received copies of both articles, his written opinion echoed only Graglia's article (see below).[42]

Probably influenced by the Graglia article, Diamond deployed its "reasonable man" rhetoric to interrupt President Odegaard's testimony. As the president explained the administration's growing awareness of racial discrimination, the failure of its "open door" policy, and the implementation of affirmative action, Diamond repeatedly objected, as in this example:

> We are not really attacking a minority program. Our position here is that the law school is admitting students . . . with lower grades and lower qualifications than the plaintiff . . . and also, that they are failing to prefer resident students over non-resident students. . . . Now, I think the University has injected into the trial the matter that some of those that they are admitting . . . with lower grades and qualifications, are minority students. We care not whether they are minority students or whether they are not minority students, and some of them are not. . . . Why are we concerned with the efforts of the University to inaugurate some minority program for minority students, I don't know. I do not believe it is what we are talking about in this trial.[43]

When compared to his aggressively racialized questions for prior witnesses, Diamond's innocent phrasing here—"We care not," "We are not really attacking," and "Why are we concerned . . . I don't know"—must be seen as the now commonplace tactic of white denial. He and his client were not racists; they were defenders of meritocracy. But just as he knew or didn't know his client's religion as the moment required, he did or didn't racialize the applicants as the moment required.

MESSY ADMISSIONS

To be fair, Diamond was able to attack the admissions program because it had irregularities that were not explained in the university's documents and witness testimony. Some witnesses fumbled through vague explanations, others resorted to confusing technical jargon, and inexplicably many of the witnesses were left unguided or unchallenged by Wilson, who was an experienced litigator.

Applicant Information

The admissions committee did not have uniform data across the applicant pool. First, the application form invited, but did not require, students to indicate their racial identities and describe their economic and/or educational circumstances.[44] Some did and others did not provide this information. Second, the committee received letters of reference for CLEO students written by institute faculty but no such additional references for non-CLEO students, and it reviewed these references in late summer but maintained a March 15 deadline for non-CLEO materials.[45] Third, Professor Crooks, who had directed the 1970 institute and attended the 1971 institute, provided his admissions colleagues with oral references for CLEO students.[46] Even if he had the laudable purpose of supporting talented CLEO students, oral references perversely mimicked the well-known "old boy" practice of sidebar communications that allowed gender and racial biases to seep into graduate admissions and faculty hiring.[47]

Applicant Review

Contrary to Diamond's claim, the applicant review process did not include blatantly different treatment of nonminority and minority applicants. For the preliminary review, the committee divided nonminority applicants into three PFYA groups: (1) Individual members reviewed those scoring above 77, accepting some outstanding candidates and setting aside others for future discussion; (2) Individual members reviewed those scoring between 74.5 and 77; and (3) Professor Kummert reviewed those scoring below 74.5, rejecting unqualified candidates and setting aside others for future discussion. An associate dean serving on the committee reviewed applicants identifying as Hispanic, Filipino, and Native American, while Professor Crooks and Vincent Hayes reviewed those identifying as African American.[48] After this preliminary review, the committee members discussed and voted on all set-aside applicants from the top and bottom PFYA groups and all applicants from the middle group. The only applicants who did not receive full committee review were the automatically accepted veterans, immediately accepted applicants in the top PFYA group, and immediately rejected ones in the bottom PFYA group.

Anticipating that Diamond would challenge the preliminary review of African American applicants, Wilson asked Professor Kummert, "Was there any particular reason for giving these two members of the committee that assignment?":

> A [Kummert]: In the sense that Mr. Hayes is the black committee member . . . [and] had, in the nature of his past employment, experience in trying to evaluate credentials of this sort for various positions that he has had responsibility over, and Mr. Crooks . . . as director of the CLEO Program, was actively involved in the examination of applications presented by minority applicants. . . . They were simply assigned in this fashion, largely to get what we thought was the best possible evaluation of the files that are difficult to evaluate.[49]

Later Professor Kummert stated that, in assigning the files of African American applicants to Crooks and Hayes, the committee assumed that a "black person can better interpret the experiences and background and educational opportunities that a black has been exposed to than a white person can."[50] In his comments, we can see the shadow of racism sliding over the preliminary review process. While unfortunately true that few whites of that time understood Black experiences, the file assignment relieved the law school of its responsibility to educate all committee members on the sensitive interpretation of these files.

In questioning Professor Kummert, Diamond repeatedly stated his views and directed the professor to assent to them:

> Q [Diamond]: Now, you separated the minority students from the rest of the students when you considered these applicants, didn't you? . . .
>
> Q: Why did you separate the minority students from the rest of them? . . .
>
> Q: You will agree with me that that is different treatment? . . .
>
> Q: Professor, why would you think that because those files were black [*sic*] and Mr. Hayes was black, that he could better interpret the files and should have the separated files, than anyone else?[51]

His repetition of "separate," which alluded to the *Brown* doctrine that "separate educational facilities are inherently unequal," implied that the file review scheme was unconstitutional. But since the files of all applicant were separated into groups of similarly situated others for preliminary review, one could argue that they received the same fair treatment. The only applicants receiving different treatment were those who did not receive full committee review—the immediately rejected low-scoring applicants, the immediately accepted high-scoring applicants, and the automatically accepted veterans.

Numbers and Weights

To support Dean Roddis's testimony that committee members evaluated "[minority] applicants . . . with less emphasis on the undergraduate grade point average and the L.S.A.T. scores than they do with respect to the applicants of the majority groups," Wilson called two experts on testing.[52] University of Texas law professor Millard Ruud was a consultant on legal education for the American Bar Association, an executive committee member for the Council on Legal Education, and a former board of trustees chair for the Law School Admissions Test Council. Yet when asked to discuss the usefulness of the LSAT in evaluating disadvantaged students, he vacillated:

> One [mistake] is to take it too seriously, and one is not to take it seriously enough. It is not a precise measure . . . but it is exceedingly important. . . . My own personal feeling is that there is no substitute for human judgment and evaluation. . . . Now, you move over to the evaluation of the minority group applicant. There is this common statement that the test is culturally biased. I suppose that is true. The question is whether this bias is any different than the bias in legal education, and there is no really culturally free education.[53]

The gist of this statement was that some experts trusted the LSAT to gauge law school potential and others trusted human judgment, some believed that the LSAT's cultural biases made it a poor predictor of minority performance in law school and others that these biases made it a good predictor of performance in culturally biased legal education. After cautiously straddling all these opinions, Ruud offered a highly technical explanation of LSAT bell curves that confused Judge Shorett, who then asked for clarification.[54]

John A. Winterbottom, director of the Education Testing Service's Graduate and Professional Testing Programs, provided clearer testimony, but Wilson seldom followed up. When he spoke about test validity, already a central issue in employment litigation, Wilson did not ask whether the LSAT's dominant-culture language and contents disadvantaged minority test-takers; and when he stated that test results correlated only with first-year law school grades, Wilson did not ask about the statistical margin of error. By failing to elicit such information, Wilson took the shine off Winterbottom's aura of expertise and undercut the important statement he eventually made. "We are quite aware," said Winterbottom, "that because the test scores are reported numerically . . . there is a kind of seductive appearance of precision about them, and we go to great lengths to urge the law schools using the test scores to remember they are not as precise as they look and that, therefore, they ought to be interpreted with great caution in themselves, and furthermore, they ought always to be used in connection with other information."[55]

Since nothing from Ruud's and Winterbottom's testimony appeared in Judge Shorett's Findings of Fact, it was left to pro-minority amici to explain to the Washington and US Supreme Courts that the LSAT discriminated against minorities by gauging test-takers on language, contents, and skills their prior education had not taught. In the end, no one asked the basic question: If the UW Law School knew that LSAT scores were unreliable predictors of minority potential, then why did it continue to use them?

File Evaluation

University documents and testimony described the admissions committee's formula for calculating PFYAs, its demarcation of three PFYA groups, its assignment of files for review, and its full committee discussions. But describing the procedures is not the same as describing the reasoning that produced admissions decisions, a distinction that Diamond exploited through aggressive witness examination, fact construction, and rhetorical shading.

After reviewing some of the 350 applicant files transported to the courthouse, Diamond questioned Tamara Zorn on notations she had jotted on a file cover. Over Wilson's repeated objections, Judge Shorett let him proceed.

> MR. WILSON: I am going to make the general objection to inquiry which seeks to search the mind of this witness or any of the other witnesses . . . who were members of that committee, as to what was, in their particular mind, that led them to a particular decision in fulfilling their particular duties as a member of their committee. . . . [T]he presumption exists that . . . officials performing their duties are acting . . . legally and acting in compliance with their authority.
>
> THE COURT: Why?
>
> MR. WILSON: . . . the presumption exists that is officials performing their duties are acting properly. They are acting legally and acting

in compliance with their authority. Secondly, I have to cite in our own Washington Court a case that has stated, and . . . the United States Supreme Court has stated that it is not a proper function of the Court to explore . . . the mental processes of these administrative officers who have had the responsibility of making decisions.

THE COURT: Now, it may be well we will get to the point where I will sustain the objection, but I think Mr. Diamond has the right to start this examination, and I will ask you to make your objection to specific questions.

As Diamond resumed, Wilson objected that instead of delving into "the mental processes of this particular member," the court should be concerned with how the admissions process functioned.[56] When Judge Shorett let Diamond proceed, Wilson again objected that a committee member's thoughts while reviewing an application were irrelevant to "whether the process of admissions . . . is in some manner arbitrary or capricious" and to "whether or not Mr. DeFunis should have been admitted."[57] When Diamond moved to enter the files into evidence, Wilson objected that would violate applicant confidentiality.[58]

Continuing to probe Zorn's thoughts, Diamond asked whether her political views influenced her recommendation of an applicant who worked at the ACLU and the Bureau of Indian Affairs. Before she could reply, Judge Shorett interjected a surprisingly prosecutorial question: "Would he have gotten just as favorable a comment if he had been . . . head of the Young Republicans League in some college?" "Yes," Zorn answered, "although that might not be my personal bias. I am interested . . . in the kinds of community center activities that a student shows."[59] Judge Shorett's insinuation that she preferred applicants who worked for progressive organizations resurfaced as a "fact" in the pro-DeFunis dissent written by the chief justice of the Washington State Supreme Court.[60]

FACT AND LAW

On September 22, Judge Shorett delivered an oral decision that contained his legal reasoning but referenced few facts, and on October

18 he issued a written Findings of Fact and Conclusions of Law that contained many facts but almost no legal reasoning. The oral decision began modestly, "Counsel, we all know that this case is of a type that will, and indeed should be, reviewed very quickly by the Supreme Court of the State and so I will just state my views and that Court will get a chance then to review what I have said and eventually decide the matter."[61] Despite promising to "state my views," he ventriloquized Diamond's discourse.

Ignoring evidence that the law school did not consider pre–junior year grades, the judge repeated Diamond's claim that DeFunis's GPA would be "3.8 when you include 9 hours of straight A he received in latin [*sic*] during the first quarter of his junior year," but DeFunis had studied Latin during the summer before his junior year. Ignoring evidence that the law school did not consider postbaccalaureate grades, the judge declared that he "took 24 hours of graduate school courses," receiving A grades for 21 hours and incompletes for three hours.[62] Ignoring testimony that the school averaged multiple LSAT scores in part to neutralize the practice effect, he wrote that DeFunis scored "512 (August, 1969), 566 (November, 1969), and 668 (December, 1970). The score of 668 is within the top 7% of all law school applicants in the nation who have taken the test in the last three years."[63] By locating these misleading statements in the Findings of Fact, he gave them factual status.

The judge also located several imprecise statements in the Findings of Fact. In writing that the law school made offers to seventy-four applicants, including thirty-six minority applicants, who had lower PFYAs than DeFunis did, he failed to mention that thirty-eight of these applicants were nonminorities; this partial recitation of the facts racialized the lower-scoring applicants as students of color.[64] In writing that six of forty-four minorities offered admission, "had qualifications higher than the plaintiff and 38 had qualifications lower than the plaintiff," he provided no defined referent for "qualifications," allowing readers to fall back on Diamond's equation of "qualifications" with only the numerical indicators. Thus eliminating the lower-scoring white applicants who received offers and higher-scoring white ones who, like DeFunis, received rejections, he wrote that "some minority students were admitted . . . prior to and instead of the plaintiff . . . with college grades and aptitude test scores so low that had they been white their applications would have been summarily denied."[65] Through omission and distortion, Judge Shorett collapsed the multiple criteria into only numerical ones and all lower-scoring admittees into only minority admittees. These "facts" allowed him to hold that law school "has discriminated against said plaintiff and has not accorded to him equal protection of the law."[66]

Since the Conclusions of Law section provided virtually no legal reasoning, we must examine the oral decision. Judge Shorett began, "In 1954 the United States Supreme Court in *Brown v. The Board of Education* decided that public education must be equally available to all regardless of race." Then he reasoned, "After that decision the Fourteenth Amendment could no longer be stretched to accommodate the needs of any one race. Policies of discrimination will inevitably lead to reprisals. In my opinion the only safe rule is to treat all races alike and I feel that is what is required under the equal protection clause.[67] Factually, the references to "all regardless of race" bleached the harms of racial segregation experienced by Black children from the *Brown* text, and the reference to treating "all races alike" bleached the stain of racism from his own text. Rhetorically, the statement that the Fourteenth Amendment "could no longer be stretched to accommodate the needs of any one race" trivialized as unnecessary mollification the protection that minorities sought against economic, social, and legal discrimination. Syntactically, the agentless-passive phrasing "policies of discrimination will inevitably lead to reprisals" obscured the massive white violence when courts illegalized segregated schools, union racism, and voter disenfranchisement.[68]

One more passage in the oral decision illustrates Judge Shorett's white-centric reasoning:

> The plaintiff, and others in this group, have not, in my opinion, been accorded the equal protection of the law guaranteed by the Fourteenth Amendment . . . Some difficulty is encountered in determining the proper remedy to correct the discrimination. Only the plaintiff has brought an action. The other eligible applicants have

> not commenced timely suits against the University. I think in law they must be said to have rested on their rights and the principle of laches should prevent suits by them during this ensuing academic year which suits would interfere greatly with the conduct of the law school.[69]

Here he magically brings additional white plaintiffs into existence only to dismiss them by citing the principle of laches, which denies relief to a party that has not made a timely claim. But since nothing in or surrounding the case indicated that other white applicants considered pressing a claim, the commentary on "other eligible applicants" invites future white plaintiffs to challenge race-conscious remedies and thereby turn the judge's white-centric textuality into a white-controlled actuality.

In *Discriminating against Discrimination*, Robert M. O'Neil wrote that "the [*DeFunis*] case was either very simple or very hard—one could say either that the constitution was color blind and forbade all racial classifications, or one could try to differentiate subtly between classifications that hurt and those that helped minorities. Judge Shorett took the easy road."[70] By cherry-picking from a trial discourse short on facts, shorn of minority interests, and speckled with insinuations, he was able to whiten equal protection. Returning to the core issue, I want to ask whether the applicants received different treatment.

The facts show that no single applicant was compared to all other 1,600 applicants. Each previously enrolled veteran was automatically admitted irrespective of his qualifications and without comparison to anyone. Each applicant who received an immediate offer was compared only to others in the top PFYA group, and those set aside for discussion were compared to applicants in the middle PFYA group. Each applicant who received an immediate rejection was compared to others in the bottom PFYA group, and those set aside for discussion were compared to applicants in the middle PFYA group. Each applicant in the middle PFYA group and each minority applicant were compared to others in their groups. Thus all sixteen hundred applicants received the same treatment: the committee divided them into groups in order to compare them to similarly situated others.

Furthermore, all applicants enjoyed special advantages. Veterans benefitted from automatic admission even when possessing qualifications less impressive than those of other applicants. Educationally privileged white applicants who snagged high grades and LSAT scores benefitted from the committee's use of these criteria. DeFunis enjoyed access to the UW Regents, a court order to reserve a place in the entering class, and ultimately an order of admission. Designated minority applicants benefitted from having less emphasis placed on their scores, but they were excluded from the white-against-white trial challenging the very program that provided them with educational opportunity. To echo Garrison Keillor who famously declared that all of Lake Wobegon's children were above average, I would put it this way: In Judge Shorett's court, all applicants, except for the designated minorities, received more than equal treatment.

5

PLYING FACT AND LAW

There are no facts, only interpretations.

—Friedrich Nietzsche, *Notebooks* (1886–1887)

In October 1971, a few days after Judge Lloyd Shorett issued his written Findings of Fact and Conclusions of Law, James Wilson, now joined by Washington attorney general Slade Gorton, gave notice that the University of Washington (UW) would appeal to the state Supreme Court.[1] From February through April 1972, the court received their Brief of Appellants, Josef Diamond's Brief of Respondents (he was joined by two colleagues, Lyle L. Iversen and Craig S. Sternberg), and briefs from fourteen amici curiae.[2] On March 8, 1973, the court issued a 6–2 ruling for the university with a majority opinion authored by Justice Marshall A. Neill, a concurrence by Justice Charles Wright, a dissent by Chief Justice Frank Hale, and another dissent by Justice Robert Hunter.[3]

A month later in what was probably the first law review article on *DeFunis*, Mary K. Hammond stated, "Broadly speaking, the facts are not in dispute as they relate to the basic issues involved."[4] The statement could not have been more wrong because the parties to the appeal had conducted a war of words over the facts recognized by the trial court and the new facts introduced on appeal. Gorton and Wilson detailed the factual errors in Judge Shorett's opinions, the pro-minority amici provided myriad social and legal facts omitted from the trial, Diamond impugned his opponents for introducing facts not in evidence, and the justices themselves tussled over the facts. This chapter interrogates the construction of fact and law, first discussing theories of meaning-making and then examining how the parties used time and action frames to select facts, language to shift their meanings, and logic to link them to the case (or not).

THEORIES OF MEANING-MAKING

Legal-judicial discourse is ordered by a fact/law dualism manifested in its institutional, intellectual, and textual structures. Institutionally, writes Kim Lane Scheppele, the dualism appears as the "division of labor between trial and appellate courts" in which "issues of fact are considered to be virtually fixed at trial, and only issues of law can be raised on appeal." Intellectually, the dualism informs the rule that practitioners should apply a legal principle to the given case facts; and textually it divides opinions into separate sections that recite the facts and argue the legal questions. Scheppele's work challenges two core beliefs—namely, "that deciding the law and deciding the facts . . . [are] different stages of a syllogistic process" and that "law is what needs to be interpreted, but facts are simply true or false."[5] She argues that legal facts are textualized accounts that interpreters delineate and decipher:

> In the courtroom, we don't have the events before us, but instead we have verbal accounts of events. . . . At a trial, actions and harms are converted into accounts and claims. Events are made into texts. And these are texts that . . . are open to interpretation. The "textualization" of social life at trial is magnified on appeal, where judges rarely see the parties to the lawsuit and have only a written record to consult for the evidence. Though they may question counsel at oral argument, judges usually learn the facts of cases in the same way that they learn the law—from reading written documents and working through plausible interpretations of those written texts.[6]

While I agree with this explanation, I note that it glides past the interpretive palimpsest created before and during the courtroom utterances.

When a person states, "At the meeting, committee members assigned applicant ratings," she has already interpreted the activity she observed to make its "who, what, and where" meaningful. The meaning that her auditors make depends upon what they know about the referent's context, because this utterance could refer to Standard & Poor's officials discussing municipal bond applicants, Mayo Clinic doctors discussing drug trial applicants, or UW professors discussing law school applicants. The meaning they make also depends upon the utterance's context because the statement has informational value if she is simply briefing colleagues but evidentiary value if she is testifying in court.[7] When statements delineating a social situation enter litigation, Emmet T. Flood explains, they are reconstructed as facts-for-the-inquiry. From the trial through the final appeal, judges select "from the multiplicity of available characterizations of the facts the interpretation that organizes the relevant facts *in light of the specific inquiry*." In this process, which Flood calls synoptic activity, judges oscillate among the parties' already characterized facts and already interpreted legal principles to select the facts that most closely relate to the legal question(s) they will answer. Thus the meaning of the case is produced by the interplay of linguistically represented fact and law; the facts "assume salience and shape in light of their relevance" to a legal principle, and the principle "becomes meaningful through its application in the particular case."[8]

My analysis in this chapter proceeds on postmodern assumptions about the discursive construction and construal of what we take to be the social and natural world. First, a legal fact, like all facts, is a representation of a social or natural event that someone has already interpreted before couching it in an oral or written statement located in a judicial arena. Second, fact statements do not perfectly correspond to events they purport to represent because the pliability of language enables speakers and writers to produce manifold representations of any particular event. Third, the law's adversarial structure, usually presumed to uncover the "truths" of an event, multiplies representations of facts and laws. Finally, the pliability of language works against the formalist hope that the law can standardize and systematize its discourse.

Formalist Theory and Its Others

Legal formalisms, critical legalisms, and postmodernisms provide different explanations of the law as a power/knowledge formation. In *Postmodern Legal Movements*, Gary Minda traces legal formalism back to Christopher Columbus Langdell, a nineteenth-century Harvard Law School dean and author of the first modern casebook, who sought to make the law a "complete, formal, and conceptually ordered system":

> Completeness meant that the system was capable of providing uniquely correct solutions . . . for every case brought for adjudication. Formality meant that the system was capable of dictating logically correct answers through the application of abstract principles derived from every case. The system was conceptually ordered to the extent that its substantive bottom-level rules were coherently derived from a small number of relatively abstract principles and concepts, creating a holistic system.[9]

Even in this short description, we can see that Langdellian formalism located the law's power in the practitioners' ability to accurately represent facts, consistently apply principles, and systemize the field's concepts and methods.

In adopting the assumption that the law can be a closed, coherent, and correct system of analysis, twentieth-century legal formalism bore a striking family resemblance to New Criticism, the dominant school of literary analysis at mid-century. For example, in their authoritative *Theory of Literature* (1942), Rene Wellek and Austin Warren attempted to create a similarly closed system of literary analysis by differentiating "extrinsic" analysis of a text's historical, social, ethical, or biographical import from their own "intrinsic" analysis of its linguistic and structural features. Both legal and literary formalists sought to insulate themselves from the threats of external reasoning, to derive abstract principles from texts and apply them to other texts, and thereby to gain scientific prestige for their "soft" interpretive disciplines.[10]

Just as Wellek and Warren rejected extrinsic approaches to literature, so Lawrence B. Solum, a contemporary legal formalist, rebuffs critical legal studies, critical race studies, and postmodern theory primarily because they threaten the law's belief in fixed language and rationalist logic.[11] In a 1987 article, he situates himself within humanism's ambit by stating, "We must imagine a progressive and humane social order" and "put away the dogma of indeterminacy." The article criticizes postmodernists for using the twin concepts of language indeterminacy and mystification to argue that legal discourse veils its complicity with systems of domination in order to uphold its own authority.[12] In a 2010 article, he theorizes legal meaning-making as a two-step activity: first the reader performs interpretation to "discover the linguistic meaning . . . of the legal text," and then she performs construction, referencing the linguistic meaning to a legal principle or doctrine to give "a text legal effect."[13] Quoting the First Amendment provision that "Congress shall make no law . . . abridging the freedom of speech," he states that the reader makes its linguistic meaning through familiarity with the English language and ascertains its legal effect through familiarity with judicial doctrine on the time, place, content, and viewpoint of expression.[14] Typically, Solum fails to recognize that linguistic fluidity operates between the two extremes of fixed and indeterminate meaning.

In analyzing language, legal formalism is more restrictive than New Criticism. Where legal formalists recommend making the legal text's linguistic meaning from its lexical, grammatical, and syntactical features, New Critics, who regarded the literary text as a creative amalgamation of literal and figurative language, paid close attention to how figures of speech transmuted meanings. Where legal formalists regard ambiguity as a problem that must be overcome to stabilize the text's meaning, New Critics viewed it as an opportunity to enrich the meaning. In contrast to both formalisms, postmodernists regard ambiguities as the inevitable effects of language when subjected to such writerly or readerly practices as meaning-making, intertextual referencing, textual translation, and temporal or cultural recontextualization. In this chapter, I examine the language practices that made statements about fact and law abundantly meaningful in *DeFunis*.

Fact Taxonomies

Since polysemic language unsettles the law, legal-judicial discourse relies on definitions, taxonomies, and frames to stabilize its facts. The 2001 pocket edition of *Black's Law Dictionary*, for instance, defines "fact" as "an actual or alleged event . . . as distinguished from its legal effect" without remarking on the mediation of language. It goes on to list twenty-four types of facts, including Kenneth Culp Davis's famous distinction between adjudicative and legislative facts.[15] In a 1955 article on judicial notice, Davis defined the former as case-specific facts about "who did what, where, when, how, and with what motive or intent" and the latter as general social facts that "help the tribunal to determine the content of law and policy and to exercise its judgment . . . in determining what course of action to take."[16] His article was a timely intervention into the decades-long attempt to standardize the facts a court could notice, a matter addressed by special committees, the Judicial Conference, the Supreme Court, and the Congress before judicial notice was finally added to the Federal Rules of Evidence.[17] Rule 201(b) Judicial Notice of Adjudicative Facts states, "The court may judicially notice a fact that is not subject to reasonable dispute because it: (1) is generally known within the trial court's territorial jurisdiction; or (2) can be accurately and readily determined from sources whose accuracy cannot reasonably be questioned."[18]

Caitlin E. Borgmann, however, feels that appellate courts need more tools to deal with social facts. She argues that Rule 52(a)(6), which allows trial judges to reject clearly erroneous facts, should be extended to appellate judges so that they can reject clearly erroneous facts in litigant and amicus briefs, such as those taken from junk science or partisan agendas.[19] But other scholars have observed that both trial and appellate courts have refused to notice relevant social facts because of methodological concerns; the social sciences ask different research questions, employ different methods, and thus produce different findings from those of the law.[20] Such concerns ignore a preliminary matter: all narratives use frames that select and slant the facts.

Narrative Frames

Drawing from sociologist Erving Goffman's foundational work, *Frame Analysis: An Essay on the Organization of Experience* (1974), scholars have applied frame analysis to a multitude of genres—novels, news stories, cartoon strips, political speeches, and everyday conversations. William A. Gamson and Andre Modigliani describe the framing of policy debates:

> Every [policy] issue has its own special language and phrases, its characteristic arguments, metaphors, and the like. . . . The ideas in this cultural catalogue are organized and clustered; we encounter them not as individual items but as packages. . . . At the core of a package is its *frame.* A frame is a central organizing idea or story line that provides meaning in an unfolding strip of events, weaving a connection among them. The frame suggests what the controversy is about.

For affirmative-action narratives, the two authors identify prominent thematic frames: the "remedial action" theme of alleviating minority exclusion or underrepresentation; the "delicate balance" theme of designing remedies that do not unfairly burden anyone; and the "reverse discrimination" theme of granting minority preferences that disadvantage whites.[21]

While thematic frames organize and color the story about a social event, time and action frames determine which facts will enter the story. In an article on criminal law, Mark Kelman explains, "Legal argument can be made only *after* a fact pattern is characterized by interpretive constructs. Once these constructs operate, a single legal result seems inevitable, a result seemingly deduced on general principle." Oddly, he uses "interpretive constructs" to denote a narrow time and action frame that limits the facts to the criminal incident itself and a broad one that encompass facts about the perpetrator's history and the circumstances surrounding the incident.[22] Time and action framing, by virtue of regulating which facts flow into the texts that constitute the case, is a form of boundary work, an activity used by all discursive fields to regulate imports from and exports to elsewhere. Fields that maintain permeable boundaries permit in-flows that diversify their contents and methods, while fields (like the law) that maintain relatively impermeable boundaries restrict in-flows that would destandardize their contents and methods.[23]

By applying Gamson and Modigliani's thematic framing to *DeFunis*, we can notice that Gorton and Wilson described it as constitutionally permitted "remedial action" to alleviate minority underrepresentation in law schools; Diamond characterized it as unconstitutional "reverse discrimination" against his well-qualified white client; and DeFunis's amici styled it a quota resembling earlier anti-Jewish quotas in Europe and the United States. But by applying time and action framing, we can see that all three parties, perhaps because their interests converged, narrowed their focus to the 1971 admissions process to exclude inconvenient facts about racism. By contrast, the prominority amici used broad time and action framing to texture their briefs with historical, social, and legal facts about the cumulative racism that excluded minority students from or disadvantaged them in law school admissions.[24]

THE PLAY OF FACT AND LAW

In what follows, I will apply the theorizing above to several of the appellate texts. I begin with Diamond's judicial notice gambit to exclude the facts that contradicted his story about the case. Then I examine how the brief writers and the justices used narrative framing to select the facts, pliable language to characterize them, abstract principles to give them a legal effect, and various modes of reasoning to link them to the admissions dispute.

The Judicial Notice Gambit

In March 1972, as documents flowed to the court, Diamond motioned to strike the pro-minority briefs, objecting that they "would have the court take *judicial notice* of all sorts of things about the relationship of blacks to the community."[25]

> The trouble with judicial notice of this kind is that the court is being asked to judicially know a great many things that may or may not be true. Thus the empirical assumption is made that there is a necessity to have a higher percentage of blacks in the law school. This is not based on anything in the Constitution or statutes and public policy is not drawn out of thin air. Judicial knowledge is supposed to be confined to those things of which well informed people in the community have knowledge. It does not extend to the answer to *controversial* and *arguable questions*.[26]

In this passage, Diamond begins by invoking truth and falsity (noticing "things that may or may not be true") and then performs a series of linguistic transformations.

First, he recharacterizes facts that appeared in the pro-minority texts, most of which were social-science findings, as "the empirical assumption" that more Black students are needed in law schools. Thus Diamond transmutes the factual findings of social-science research in those texts into an "empirical assumption" (or hypothesis) in his text. Next stating that "this is not based in the Constitution or statutes," he adds another layer to the semiotic chain: interpreting rearward, we see that "this" refers to "the empirical assumption," which in turn refers to facts in the pro-minority texts, which in turn refer to social-science findings. Interpreting forward, we can see that "this" (and its semiotic chain) refers to constitutional and statutory texts where Diamond finds only absence. Finally, having implied that the constitutional and statutory texts contain nothing about the need to have more Black students in law schools, Diamond easily slides into the cliché that policy is not drawn from thin air. In short, the passage makes social-science data disappear into "thin air."

But the passage fails to evaporate all facts, because the penultimate sentence references, as the facts a court can notice, those "of which well-informed people in the community have knowledge." Perversely, his invocation of this requirement does not disqualify his opponents' facts about racial discrimination at the university, because this problem had been widely disseminated through Black Student Union activism and media coverage (see chapter 3).[27] Moreover, the final sentence, which claims that courts cannot notice answers "to *controversial* and *arguable questions*," runs afoul of both the Article III requirement that courts can adjudicate only live disputes and the many prior cases that provided answers to highly controversial and arguable racial questions.[28] Despite Diamond's linguistic maneuvers to disqualify the pro-minority briefs, the court permitted the amici to file these briefs and the majority opinion referenced some of their social facts (see below).

Litigant Frames

In their brief, Gorton and Wilson pose two questions of law that situate the case within the narrow time and action frame of the 1971 admissions cycle: "(1) whether, in considering over 1,600 applicants for the approximately 150 positions open for the law class of 1974, the University of Washington could consistently with the Equal Protection Clause, take into consideration the racial background of the applicants and; (2) whether, the denial of respondent's application was the result of the school's minority admission policy."[29] Answering the first question, they state that the admissions committee, in considering racial background, "was guided by a University wide policy which sought to achieve a reasonable representation . . . of persons from certain minority racial and ethnic groups who have been historically suppressed, and excluded from participation in the mainstream of our society."[30] Answering the second question, they state that DeFunis, who ranked below 120 applicants on the waitlist, would not have been admitted even if the 36 minority offers were given to waitlisted applicants.[31]

This rationale contains a semantic shift, here a fallacious slippage from a policy fact to a legal fact: the fact that the admissions program complied with the university policy of providing educational access to historically excluded racial groups does not establish that it was consistent with equal protection jurisprudence.[32] Thus, needing to connect policy to law, Gorton and Wilson broaden their time and action frame. They provide a twenty-two-page review of the law to demonstrate that the law school program has "antecedents . . . in other programs established by legislative and executive actions and given judicial approval." But here they slip from university policy to government policy.[33] Then they state:

> The law as we understand it does treat all races alike insofar as their situations are alike; but chattel slavery, black codes, Jim Crow, restrictive racial covenants, grandfather clauses, and other degradations cannot be quickly erased. The law will treat all races alike only when all races have been treated alike by both law and society so that no one is disadvantaged. The decision now to be made is whether the Constitution . . . forbids the law school . . . to take a small but meaningful step toward correcting the law's past mistakes, by educating minority lawyers to play a significant role in a vital public profession in which they are so critically underrepresented.[34]

After introducing the principle that the law requires the same treatment of similarly situated persons, this rhetorically powerful passage shows that everyone is not similarly situated. It juxtaposes the situation of Blacks under "chattel slavery, black codes, Jim Crow, restrictive racial covenants, grandfather clauses, and other degradations" with the unstated implication that whites have not been subjected to these degradations. It also conveys power relations: the law's "past mistakes" of complicity in societal racism, the law school's "small but meaningful step" of educating minority lawyers, and the possibility that this court might prohibit it from taking this modest step. Yet Gorton and Wilson fail to demonstrate how longstanding societal racism has impacted current minority applicants, thus prompting Diamond to remark disdainfully on the slippage across time and place: "The fact that there has been in some places discrimination against certain minority races in the past does not justify the disregard by the University of the constitutional guarantee of equal protection for persons of another race."[35]

Instead of posing a constitutional question at the beginning of his brief, Diamond declares at the end, "*The real issue in this case*, however, is not the reform of our social or educational system, but is whether one student, Marco DeFunis, Jr., is entitled to have his application . . .

treated on terms as favorable as those accorded to others."[36] Here we see both the personalization of the case and the word substitution in which the principle of treating similarly situated persons the same becomes DeFunis's entitlement to have a consideration "as favorable as" that accorded to "others," namely the minority applicants maligned throughout the brief.

Diamond repeatedly inflates his client's qualifications and describes the committee's criteria as prejudicial:

> Plaintiff was rejected not on the basis of any objective criteria which bear analysis or examination such as grades, test scores or PFYA standing, but on the basis of what were referred to in the testimony as "other things."
>
> . . . The consideration of "other things" included the preferential treatment of certain minorities, and incidentally, may have included adverse treatment of plaintiff because of whatever prejudices may have existed against him.
>
> . . . All of these objective standards were thus shoved aside and on a purely *subjective* basis, and with no justification except unbridled discretion, the Admissions Committee, placed him in a classification so far down that he could not enter law school.[37]

In this syllogistic chain of statements, he dualizes "objective criteria" (equated with scores) and "other things" (equated with prejudices for minorities and against DeFunis) to reach the conclusion that the committee arbitrarily ranked DeFunis too low to enter law school.

Diamond occasionally broadens the time and action frame, as in these statements: "Cases which indicate that race may be regarded for the purpose of *eliminating* discrimination do not say that the black race may be given *special privileges*," and "The mere fact that the 14th Amendment was originally passed to *protect* Negroes does not give Negroes *special* privileges not accorded to persons of other races" (his italics). Repeating the phrase "special privileges" more than thirty times, he argues that equal protection does not permit the rectification of discrimination against minorities "by *creating* discrimination against other races."[38] The fate of his recharacterization, which turns remedial measures into special privileges, would depend on whether the court takes notice of the facts in the pro-minority briefs.

The Pro-Minority Briefs

The authors of the pro-minority briefs faced a predicament. On one hand, the court instructed them to avoid repeating what was said in other briefs. On the other hand, the writers needed to present the facts of societal racism and use them to justify the disputed admissions program.[39] Three briefs tried to demonstrate that the program attempted to provide educational opportunity to racial minority applicants who were dissimilarly situated to white ones.

Writing on behalf of African Americans, Seattle lawyer Philip L. Burton begins his brief with a cascade of dramaturgical statements, such as these two:[40]

> Being Black, and representing a nearly all Black clientele, he knows that his clients are enormously disadvantaged because there is no more than an infinitesimal chance that their case or controversy will be heard by anything but a white, middle-class, or wealthy, judge.
>
> Being Black, and living and working with Blacks, he knows that they believe that Blacks cannot get justice in the white man's courts; and he knows that this is destructive of respect for law and legal institutions, which the legal industry can ill afford.[41]

By using the repetition and cadence of Black preaching, these and the other statements delineate a Black lawyer who, in solidarity with his people, confronts the white justice system. By embedding the views of his Black clients in the drama ("he knows that they believe"), he demonstrates to white readers that how the legal system looks depends on where one stands within its racialized power hierarchy.[42]

Next embedding a prominent Black voice, Burton quotes from a *New York Times* article written by Haywood Burns, director of the National Conference of Black Lawyers:

> Some of the greatest barriers to Blacks receiving fair treatment in the courts today lies not so much from direct racial antipathies as from the structure of the law itself. . . . This historic hostility and neglect have brought about a structural inequality through which the law, by its substantive doctrines and procedural rules, works invidious discrimination against the poor and the nonwhite. Intent is not necessary. Institutionalized bias need never make reference to race or class to remain in its operation and impact highly discriminatory.[43]

Applying Burns's concept of structural inequality to legal education and practice, Burton transitions to a factual voice. "Until the 1950s," he tells readers, "most law schools were completely closed to Blacks by law" and afterwards accepted only token numbers. In 1964–1965, schools certified by the American Bar Association graduated only 200 Black students out of more than 10,000 graduates nationwide. This exclusionary pattern carried into professional practice. In 1971, the nation had one Black lawyer for every 7,736 Blacks compared to one white lawyer for every 631 whites;[44] and Washington state had one Black lawyer for every 3,565 Blacks compared to one white lawyer for every 728 whites.[45] Few or no Black lawyers served as judges, attorneys general, federal and state legislators, or government lawyers.

Next transitioning to a legal voice, Burton declares that the UW Law School, to act in accordance "with its affirmative constitutional duty to disestablish segregation and discrimination in its admissions policy," placed less emphasis on minority GPA and LSAT scores because it "realized that the use of these criteria . . . was in fact discriminatory against prospective minority group students."[46] He links the use of these scores to structural inequality: "Discrimination is committed not only by persons with evil motives, but also by those whose pattern and practice of operation has a discriminatory impact on Black and minority persons. Illegal discrimination has been found in numerous federal court cases where there was no evidence of discriminatory intent."[47] Just so, he reviews court rulings overturning facially neutral policies or practices that disproportionately impacted racial minorities and argues that studies of the LSAT's disproportionate impact on minority test-takers make "a *prima facie* case of racial discrimination."[48]

Finally, Burton cites three precedents in order to invert the meaning of the trial court judgment in *DeFunis*. In *Shelley v. Kraemer* (1948) and *Barrows v. Jackson* (1953), the Supreme Court overturned lower court decisions upholding white housing covenants that barred home sales and rentals to nonwhites; and in *Reitman v. Mulkey* (1967), the Court illegalized a state voter referendum that permitted property owners to sell or rent as they saw fit. In these cases, the Court articulated the principle that state action (the lower court rulings and the voter referendum) illegally enabled private discrimination. Analogizing these cases to *DeFunis*, Burton declares, "the state [i.e., the trial court] has taken action designed to make . . . discriminations legally possible."[49]

Writing for the City of Seattle, Assistant Corporation Counsel Jorgen G. Bader and legal intern Wilbert Maez explain that those who represented this large employer and service provider were well-versed in discrimination law. Indeed, their sixty-seven-page brief brings a wealth of material—federal and state constitutional provisions, civil rights statutes, agency regulations, court rulings, and findings from governmental and scholarly sources—to bear on how testing devices reproduce inequality in employment and education.[50] First they establish that "the principle of Equal Protection authorizes affirmative action programs to effectuate equality of opportunity." To help minorities overcome disadvantages in prior education or training, it permits the use of alternative methods for evaluating abilities that are "not adequately measured by conventional examination procedures."[51]

After providing a lengthy review of testing law and literature, they enter the debate about whether the racially patterned test results reflect the test-takers' nature and/or nurture:

> If minorities did equally well on paper-and-pencil tests, the results would be racially neutral, irrespective of the level of knowledge required, the degree of difficulty of the examination, or the cut-off line that decides the top percentile eligible for filling openings or further interviewing. Racially dissimilar consequences arise only insofar as minorities differ from the remainder of the population.

> . . . The content and level of an examination influence the relative minority representation: the higher the level of knowledge or proficiency probed . . . the greater the opportunity the group with the greater educational achievement or experience has to score high and leave others behind.[52]

Here the authors begin, as do other amici, with the proposition that test-takers are dissimilarly situated individuals whose racially disparate scores reflect their racially disparate prior educations. But they go further than other amici do by providing a sophisticated analysis of test design and norming.

First, Bader and Maez review score distributions that reveal two patterns: minority-group test scores (with the exception of Asian American scores) are underrepresented in the higher-score range and overrepresented in the lower-score range; and the minority test-takers' mean (average) score falls one standard deviation (more or less) below the mean score of a large test-taker pool. Then they explain the patterns. When test language and content reflect the white middle-class education denied to minorities and when white middle-class test-takers vastly outnumber minority test-takers, the mean score for the pool is tilted toward the majority white scores. This tilt in turn produces the standard deviation between minorities and whites, which widens as the test's difficulty increases. Putting the matter another way, the authors state that if all test-takers received the same quality education and if all racial groups had similar numbers of test-takers, scores would reveal individual differences but not racial-group patterns. Their analysis helps readers see that the standard deviation is an artifact of interactive factors—the test language and content, the racial composition of the test-taker pool, and the statistical norming.

The Equal Employment Opportunity Commission, Bader and Maez report, requires employers to analyze such outcomes and, when a test disproportionately disqualifies minorities, to intervene. The employers can limit the test to only majority applicants or can adopt "a higher qualifying score for the majority and a lower qualifying score for disadvantaged minorities" (the latter resembles the UW Law School practice of placing less weight on minority PFYAs than on white ones).[53]

Thus they reach two legal conclusions. First, the fact that a test produces a "disproportionate failure rate among minorities" should "establish a *prima facie* case of violation with the employer obliged to produce a valid explanation" (a point also made by Burton).[54] Second, equal protection requires that similarly situated persons "be treated alike. The facts of American life show that minorities are not similarly situated in opportunities for housing, employment or education due to racial discrimination, and thereby are at an unfair disadvantage on conventional examinations."[55]

Finally, Bader and Maez connect their testing analysis to *DeFunis*. In fourteen pages replete with facts, statistics, and maps taken from authoritative sources (including the state's Kramer Commission[56]), they delineate minority deprivations both nationally and locally. In Washington State, they explain, 70 percent of the Black population resides in Seattle, Tacoma, and Spokane ghettoes where families experience a higher unemployment rate, more segregation into low-pay jobs, and lower wages than their white counterparts. Unsurprisingly, the Black children, who attend substandard schools, have lower scores on tests, higher suspension and drop-out rates, and fewer years of schooling than their white counterparts.[57] While other amici provided broader facts about educational discrimination against minority students, Bader and Maez focus on the dissimilarly situated minority students in Marco DeFunis's age cohort because they would have applied to the UW Law School when he did in 1971.

Writing for the American Indian Law Students Inc., Charles F. Wilkinson and John H. Sennhauser state that they will "advise the Court of relevant considerations relating solely to American Indians," but they organize the brief in a counterintuitive way by placing law in the first sections and facts in the final sections.[58] In the fact sections, they explain why Native American lawyers number little more than two dozen nationwide. Geographically isolated on reservations, socialized into tribal culture, and enrolled in separate schools, Native American students accrue disadvantages all along the education pipeline. Wilkinson and Sennhauser cite several studies showing that these students are insufficiently trained in the normative white language, reasoning, and knowledge needed to win high scores on the tests that screen college and law school applicants. Declaring that "Indians need Indians, not whites" as lawyers, they explain that the former have practical experience with tribal and federal Indian law; know the culture and needs of indigenous communities; are more willing to practice on reservations; and are more personally equipped to develop good attorney-client relationships.[59] These same points appear in an appended letter written by Frederick M. Hart, dean of the University of New Mexico Law School, which had recently launched the country's first Native American prelaw summer program and had placed about fifty students in law schools nationwide.

At the beginning of the brief, Wilkinson and Sennhauser pose two questions of law—namely, whether the Constitution commands colorblindness and which level of review courts should apply to race-conscious admissions. They argue that the trial court's color-blind ruling in *DeFunis* contradicts the massive body of federal Indian law:

> Classification by race . . . is literally nowhere more evident than in regard to American Indians. Congress has enacted a comprehensive statutory scheme which deals with almost every nook and cranny of a reservation Indian's life—matters of education, health, civil liberties, welfare, transfers of land, validity of contracts, testamentary disposition, and expenditures of tribal funds. There are numberless other regulations dealing solely with Indians, including a hiring preference for Indians in the BIA [Bureau of Indian Affairs]. . . . If the trial court's color-blindness is correct, then the above statutory scheme is constitutionally jeopardized.[60]

By juxtaposing the bare-bones reference to "the trial court's colorblindness" with an elaborate description of Congress's color-conscious scheme, they paint the folly of a local judge who ignored or deliberately contravened a massive body of federal law.

On the level of review, Wilkinson and Sennhauser first state that strict scrutiny is appropriate for policies that burden a minority group, while rational basis is appropriate for those that benefit a minority group. Then they cite two cases that reveal how the courts have manipulated the review standard in cases concerning indigenous peoples.

In *Simmons v. Eagle Seelatsee* (1965), the mixed-race descendants of a Yakima Tribe member sued the Yakima Tribal Council over their right to inherit his reservation land. The dispute came to rest on the conflict between a state statute that allowed mixed-race descendants of a tribe member to inherit land and a congressional act that allowed the secretary of the interior to specify the percentage of Native American blood an individual needed to qualify for inheritance. Applying rational basis review, the district court found that Congress had plenary power to make Indian law and added that the quantum blood requirement was a sensible way to preserve Indian land ownership.[61] In *Groundhog v. Keeler* (1971), members of the Cherokee Nation disputed the US president's appointment of W. W. Keeler as the tribe's principal chief, and the district court dismissed the case on grounds that it lacked jurisdiction over internal tribal affairs. On appeal, the Tenth Circuit used racializing language to whiten the Cherokees, describing them as a "civilized" tribe that "ranked high in culture and intellectual receptivity" and had intermarried "with fine members of Scotch families."[62] In dismissing the case, this court stated that the plaintiffs were simply "a group of Cherokees out of power [and] dissatisfied with the officials of a group in power."[63]

Analogizing these two cases to *DeFunis*, Wilkinson and Sennhauser state that for "140 years, American Indians have actually been subjected to a *permissive* standard of interpretation in regard to '*burden*' statutes. . . . For this Court [i.e., the Washington Supreme Court] now to apply a *strict* standard of interpretation to a 'benefit' statute would result in the Indian's being submitted to the worst of both possible worlds."[64] Despite the rhetorical effectiveness of the contradiction they reveal, Wilkinson and Sennhauser skirted the underlying conundrum that the law had defined tribes as the racialized "wards" of the federal government on one hand and as (nearly) sovereign tribal nations on the other hand. Two years later, the US Supreme Court ruled on *Morton v. Mancari* (1974), a case brought by non-Indian employees of the Bureau of Indian Affairs to challenge the secretary of the interior's directive ordering the bureau to give preferences to qualified Native Americans in hiring, training, and promotion. Justice Blackmun, who authored the unanimous opinion, declared that the congressional exemption of Indian preferences "in the narrow context of tribal or reservation-related employment did not constitute racial discrimination of the type otherwise proscribed." He explained that a preference "aimed at furthering Indian self-government" was entirely different from one that discriminated against non-Indians. He added in a footnote, "The preference is not directed towards a 'racial' group consisting of 'Indians'; instead, it applies only to members of 'federally recognized' tribes. . . . In this sense, the preference is political rather than racial in nature."[65] Thus we find another contradiction: in *DeFunis*, Native American law school applicants are a racial group not entitled to special consideration, but in *Mancari* they are a political group entitled to special consideration.

The Pro-DeFunis Briefs

Marco DeFunis's identities as a white, middle-class, Jewish man who was a first-generation college student fit nicely with the identities of the constituencies his amici organizations represented. To support him, these amici personalized their narrative to argue that the race-conscious admissions program discriminated against him. But to represent the interests of their constituencies, they generalized their narratives to argue that the program harmed white-ethnic and Jewish groups. Thus most of the briefs made contradictory statements about the individual versus group scope of facts and laws.

Writing for the National Jewish Community Rights Council, Seattle attorney Jennings P. Felix (who employed DeFunis during and after law school) submitted a skimpy seven-page brief that cited only Lino Graglia's article for the *University of Pennsylvania Law Review* and Raul Hilberg's *The Destruction of the European Jews* (1961). He did, however, attempt to impugn the structural, rather than individual, features of discrimination. When, for instance, he characterized the admissions program as a "dual admissions program" because it allegedly applied lower standards to minority applicants than to white ones, he was appropriating the language of the Supreme Court, which used "dual system" to denote an illegally segregated school district.[66]

Yet, Felix attacks racial classifications as vague and inconsistent structures. As evidence, he states that "the Nazis defined as Jewish any person who had one-quarter Jewish blood," while Southern laws defined as Black any person who had one-eighth or more of African American blood and defined Native Americans as "colored" if they had one-sixteenth or more of Native American blood. From these examples, he concludes that "preferential treatment for 'minority' group members faces an initial hurdle of . . . vagueness, as well as the principle that our constitution requires that state action be 'color blind.'"[67] But this fact-to-conclusion sequence hides inconsistencies: it incorrectly analogizes the Nazi scheme of racializing Jews and the Southern scheme of biologizing African Americans and Native Americans to the admissions procedures that attempt to neutralize the economic and educational effects of racism, and it does not explain how these heinous racial taxonomies of the past justify color-blind procedures in the present.

To tie his claims about "racial preferences" and reverse discrimination together, Felix invokes the "nation of minorities" trope, famously articulated by Justice Felix Frankfurter in *Hughes v. Superior Court of California* (1954) and repeated in Lino Graglia's article (which Felix cites). Here is Felix's version:

> The right to attend law school, just like the right to work, should not depend upon membership in a particular race. Otherwise, other races would have the equal right to be admitted to law school on a racial basis, and the prophetic words of Mr. Justice Frankfurter predict the inevitable outcome that there will be undesirable pressure exerted for admission to law schools "on the ancestral grounds of Hungarians in Cleveland, of Poles in Buffalo, of Germans in Milwaukee, of Portuguese in New Bedford, of Mexicans in San Antonio, of the numerous minority groups in New York, and so on through the whole gamut of racial and religious concentrations in various cities."[68]

The fallacies in this passage are numerous. First, no one has a right, let alone a race-based right, to attend law school, but this false premise grounds the prediction that myriad groups will clamor for their shares of law school places. Second, the passage conflates minoritized racial identity with minoritized (or in some instances majoritized) ethnic identity based on national origin and/or culture. However, it is true that this sort of groupthink motivated white-ethnic hostility toward affirmative action. In 1972, when Felix filed this brief for the National Jewish Community Rights Council, the same organization was attempting to halt the construction of low-cost housing in Forest Hills, Queens. The council feared that racial minorities would move into this predominantly Jewish neighborhood, and its president, Rabbi Seymour Siegel, urged voters to reelect President Nixon in part because he opposed affirmative action.[69]

In a brief written on his own behalf, Seattle attorney George Constable explicitly reminds his readers that Jews suffered from the anti-Jewish "quota system at certain Ivy League colleges during the 1920s," but today "the legal profession is one of the few areas in which Jewish people, who have historically been discriminated against, achieve parity with Christians. . . . Preferential treatment of other minorities will inexorably result in discrimination against Jewish applicants."[70] Half historical fact and half speculative fearmongering, the statement echoes major themes of the anti–affirmative action discourse circulated by Jewish groups during racial conflicts in New York City and other towns (see chapter 1).

Constable, like Felix, invokes the "nation of minorities" trope and uses it here to paint the ripple effect that affirmative-action opponents feared:

> If appellant's program is found to be constitutional, then Jews and other minorities not presently being assisted by the program would be in a position to demand that they either be included, or at least not excluded. . . . The question would then arise as to what is a minority. Even the infamous White-Anglo-Saxon Protestants do not constitute a majority of the population. . . . Eventually, it would appear that virtually everyone could define him- or herself into a minority status and bring him- or herself within the program's ambit. Presumably, this would ultimately necessitate the imposition of a system of quotas whereby each minority group would be admitted

> to the Law School in direct and precise proportion to its percentage in the population as a whole.[71]

What enables Constable's slippery-slope logic—which caroms from the UW admissions program through identity group antagonisms to a system of proportional admissions—is a clever manipulation of what "minority" means, especially when used with such modifiers as "racial," "ethnic," or "religious." The term "racial minority," for instance, denotes not merely the relative size of a group but also its circumstances within a society's power structure—namely, that the group experiences stereotyping, discrimination, and subordination. Constable's minoritization of white-ethnic groups, especially white Anglo-Saxon Protestants, reflects a common anxiety of Jewish and white-ethnic Americans at that time. Knowing that Jews were overrepresented in public university student bodies, social services, and some professions, many Jews feared that discussions of, let alone plans for, proportional representation would diminish their people's hard-won gains.[72] While most white-ethnic groups were not yet overrepresented in universities and professions, they feared that proportional representation would stall their upward mobility.

So far, we have seen that when they opposed race-conscious admissions that benefited grossly underrepresented racial minority groups the amici invoked the groupness of their constituencies. Now we will see how they expunged groupness from equal protection jurisprudence. Writing for the Anti-Defamation League, Robert Baronsky, a prominent Seattle attorney and Jewish community leader, endorsed the trial court judgment that DeFunis was not "accorded the equal protection of the law."[73] Then he launched into an argument that recharacterized equal protection as an individual right. The fallacies in this reconstruction project warrant close inspection.

First, Baronsky racializes DeFunis's rejection, claiming that had he "been a Black or a member of some other minority group, he would have been admitted to the law school, as his objective qualifications were superior to those minority students admitted." Next, he interprets *Brown* as standing for the principles that "public education must be equally available to all regardless of race" and "the state must eradicate state-sponsored segregation which, under no circumstances, could provide equal opportunity for students." Then, he bleaches the racial-group significance of *Brown* from equal protection: "While historically impetus for passage of the Fourteenth Amendment was the movement to bring full citizenship to Blacks, there certainly can be no doubt that it applies to any type of governmentally-sponsored discrimination against individuals based upon arbitrary differences." As support for this proposition, he cites *Yick Wo v. Hopkins* (1896) challenging a building code that penalized Chinese laundries; *Oyama v. California* (1948) challenging the Japanese Alien Land Act; *Douglas v. California* (1963) challenging denial of counsel to an indigent defendant; *Reed v. Reed* challenging a preference for male over female estate administrators; and three school cases. Presumably based on these cases, Baronsky concludes that "race can never be a constitutionally relevant factor in determining admission."[74]

His reasoning is riddled with fallacies. First, the very different facts of these cases, which overturned governmental policies that discriminated against the individual and group plaintiffs, are not analogous to the admissions procedures in *DeFunis*, which sought to remedy the discrimination against minority students. Second, since the cases overturned group-targeted discrimination (against Chinese laundry owners, Japanese landowners, women, etc.), Baronsky has to restyle equal protection as an individual right that protects DeFunis but not the minority applicants. Thus he quotes the famous lines in *Shelley v. Kraemer* (1948), a housing covenant case: "The rights created by the first section of the Fourteenth Amendment, are, by its terms, guaranteed to the individual. The rights established are personal rights." To further support this individualist interpretation, he cites two historic university cases, *Sweatt v. Painter* (1950) and *McLauren v. Oklahoma State Regents* (1950), and states that "both decisions characterized the rights guaranteed by the equal protection clause as personal rights."[75] But since a white homeowner covenant barred the Shelleys, a Black couple, from purchasing a home in a white neighborhood and all-white universities prevented Heman Sweatt and George McLauren, Black applicants, from enrolling, Baronsky has to ignore the racial facts of these cases because they are the inverse of those in *DeFunis*.

In addition to faulty analogical reasoning, Baronsky's individualist rendering of equal protection depends upon misleading syntax:

> If, as argued by appellant, a given racial group has the right to be represented, as a group, in the student body of appellant's law school, then it might be arguable that individuals have to step aside to assure realization of rights belonging to such racial group. But it follows from the decisions cited that there is no such thing as a group right under the Fourteenth Amendment or under this state's Privileges and Immunities claims. They guarantee rights to the individual and to the individual only.[76]

In an "if A, then B" statement, the "A" provides the conditions under which "B" might be true. But Baronsky embeds the "if A, then B" statement in an action frame that is factually false. He is saying if the university argues A (a particular racial groups has a right to be represented), then it could argue B (other individuals will have to step aside). But since the university did not argue that particular racial groups had the right to be represented, the entire "if A, then B" statement is hypothetical. Upon close inspection, we can see that Baronsky's casual attitude toward veracity tarnishes his equal protection claims.

What Justice Neill Wrote

In journeying toward a reversal of the trial court's decision, Justice Neill erodes the boundary between fact and law by interjecting a narrative "voice" that refashions the existing delineations of facts and laws. He begins by posing the legal question: "Broadly phrased, the major question presented herein is whether the law school may, in consonance with the equal protection provisions of the state and federal constitutions, consider the racial or ethnic background of applicants as one factor in the selection of students."[77] Where DeFunis supporters described the admissions program as an unlawful quota scheme and minority supporters described it as a lawful remedy for societal racism, the narrative voice transforms it into a procedure—namely the consideration of racial or ethnic background as "one factor" in applicant review.

The voice also interjects new or marginalized details into the recitation of case facts. It states that the school's applications ballooned from 618 in 1968 to 1,601 in 1971, making applicant selection more complicated, and mentions the "*the continued effects of past segregation and discrimination against Blacks, Chicanos, American Indians* and other disadvantaged racial and ethnic minority groups" (my emphasis).[78] It corrects Diamond's factual errors, observing that the PFYA was only a "preliminary ranking" used to "organize the committee's processing of the applications"; that the "law school had no fixed admissions quota"; that offers "did not follow exactly the relative ranking of PFYAs"; and that the committee exercised "careful and informed discretion based on the evidence appearing in the application files."[79]

On matters of law, Justice Neill was influenced by Robert M. O'Neil, whose articles for the *Toledo* and *Yale* law journals were cited in several amicus briefs, including one that was filed by Joseph H. Gordon and Grant Armstrong but was actually drafted by O'Neil and University of Washington law professor William Anderson.[80] Not only does Neill quote or echo the articles a dozen times, but he fashions his constitutional argument on them, as a few examples will show. In section 2 of his decision, which focuses on "whether racial classifications are per se unconstitutional," he rejects the trial court's color-blind reasoning:

> *Brown* did not hold that all racial classifications are per se unconstitutional; rather, it held that invidious racial classifications—i.e., those that stigmatize a racial group with the stamp of inferiority—are unconstitutional. Even viewed in a light most favorable to the plaintiff, the "preferential" minority admissions policy . . . is clearly not a form of invidious discrimination. The goal of this policy is not to separate the races, but to bring them together.[81]

The last sentence closely paraphrases O'Neil's own statement in the *Yale* article and, explicitly rejecting the arguments of DeFunis's supporters, shifts the discourse from color-blindness to racial integration. Next arguing that racial classification may be used in some circumstances and must be used in other circumstances, Justice Neill reviews recent cases, particularly *Green v. County School Board* (1968) and *Swann v.*

Charlotte-Mecklenburg Board of Education (1971), which upheld race-conscious methods of achieving school integration. Again echoing O'Neil, he states that "consideration of race by school authorities does not violate the Fourteenth Amendment *where the purpose is to bring together, rather than separate, the races*" (my emphasis) and concludes that "the Constitution is color conscious to prevent the perpetuation of discrimination and to undo the effects of past segregation."[82]

As O'Neil had recommended, Justice Neill applies strict scrutiny review to the admissions program and addresses the compelling national interest requirement: "We believe the state has an overriding interest in promoting integration in public education. In light of the serious underrepresentation of minority groups in law schools, and considering that minority groups participate on an equal basis in the tax support of law schools, we find the state interest in eliminating racial imbalance within public legal education to be compelling." In a long footnote, which cites more than a dozen government reports and scholarly articles (including O'Neil's), he rebuffs Diamond's attempt to prevent judicial notice of the amici's extra-record facts. He observes, "In relying on statistical evidence to establish the underrepresentation of minority groups in the legal profession, defendants are supported by ample precedent."[83]

Next considering whether a race-neutral means could be used in place of the law school's race-conscious program, Justice Neill again rebuffs Diamond who, like some of the DeFunis amici, had argued that the proper remedy would be to improve the elementary and secondary education of minority students so that they could compete with non-minority applicants to law school. Justice Neill states, "This would be highly desirable, but 18 years have passed since the decision in *Brown v. Board of Education* . . . and minority groups are still grossly underrepresented in law schools. If the law school is forbidden from taking affirmative action, this underrepresentation may be perpetuated indefinitely." Finally, addressing the narrow-tailoring requirement, he echoes O'Neil's comment that the program assists only "those groups most in need of help."[84]

On the matter of LSAT bias, however, Justice Neill positions the majority justices firmly on the middle ground. On one hand, he rejects the minority amici's claim that the use of test scores effectuates de jure segregation: "We do not, therefore, reach the question of whether there is an inherent cultural bias in the Law School Admissions Test . . . which perpetuates racial imbalance to such an extent as to constitute de jure segregation."[85] On the other hand, he rejects Diamond's claim that only grade and test scores were objective predictors:

> We express no opinion as to whether the LSAT bears a cultural bias which renders the test less reliable as a predictor of law school performance for minority students than for others. But this is certainly a factor which the law school may consider in its discretion [citations omitted]. It would be unnecessary, of course, for the law school to consider race in interpreting the standardized numerical indicators for non-minority students, because the alleged bias operates *in favor* of those applicants (his emphasis).[86]

The meaning of this passage depends on cross-referencing it to the critique of white-normed testing in the City of Seattle brief. While the majority justices decline to comment on the critique, they do understand that the test's racial bias operates in favor of nonminority students. Leaving no doubt, Justice Neill concludes, "The committee may consider the racial or ethnic background of an applicant when interpreting his standardized grades and test scores."[87]

What Chief Justice Hale Wrote

In his dissent, Chief Justice Hale endorses the trial court's judgments that the Constitution is color-blind, racial classifications are per se unconstitutional, and the admissions program deprived DeFunis of equal protection. Summarizing the pro-DeFunis story in language that oscillates between encomium and invective, he twice recounts the plaintiff's lifelong state residency, his graduation from Franklin High School, his GPA, LSAT and PFYA scores, his work for the Seattle Parks Department, and his two rejections. He enlivens the hagiography with satire: "Mr. DeFunis supported his application for admission with every conceivable evidence of competence except possibly an astrological horoscope" and "although a straight A in Latin may speak for little in the current techniques for evaluating law school applicants, one can be sure that John Marshall, Oliver Wendell Holmes, Joseph Story, Benjamin N. Cardozo and John Harlan along with Thomas Jefferson, Abraham Lincoln and Franklin Delano Roosevelt, would have found it impressive."[88]

To discredit the university, Chief Justice Hale declares counterfactually that the case record "reveals, to me at least, another invidious form of discrimination—that against residents of this state"—and adds that the legislature never "conferred such sweeping powers upon the administration or faculty of the university."[89] Impugning the law school's motives, he writes, "In trying to create a national law school by means of procedures now in vogue, the law school must inevitably indulge in what might be deemed an inverse form of discrimination against bona fide residents of the state."[90] More disturbing, he derogates, by name, the three student members of the admissions committee.

To argue that the constitution forbids racial preferences, the chief justice invokes the usually cited precedential cases that overturned antimiscegenation laws and illegalized segregation in public transportation, restaurants, swimming pools, and schools. His discussion of precedents is bookended by citations of *Anderson v. San Francisco Unified School District* (1972), a case successfully litigated by Reynold Colvin, who would be Allan Bakke's attorney. Commenting on the *Anderson* holding that hiring and promotion preferences for minority teachers were unconstitutional, the chief justice wrote, "I think [this holding] expresses the principles which should govern the *DeFunis* case."[91]

In this chapter, I have shown that university and plaintiff briefs used a narrow time and action frame that limited the facts to the 1971 admissions cycle; the pro-minority briefs used a broad frame that encompassed historical, social, and legal facts of racism afflicting minority groups; and the pro-DeFunis briefs vacillated between individual and group pronouncements. Yet all briefs, as well as the court opinions, employed the techniques of language and logic to style the facts for the same purpose—that of resituating a construct, namely "the law school admissions program," within the appellate court's discourse of legal precedents and principles. As the adversarial method demanded, their texts produced the kaleidoscopically shifting meanings of equal protection. When *DeFunis* moved to the US Supreme Court, fundamental contradictions potholed its discourse. Should the justices notice the historical, social, and statistical facts introduced on appeal? Did the abstract principles accurately distill the particulars of different cases? Could the Fourteenth Amendment protect both the group and the individual? In the next chapter, I will argue that only Justice Douglas stepped into the field of contradictions and allowed another discourse to speak.

6

THE MEANINGS OF *DEFUNIS*

> [Contradiction] . . . far from being that from which it must be freed if its truth is at last to be revealed, constitutes the very law of its existence: it is on the basis of such a contradiction that discourse emerges, and it is in order both to translate it and to overcome it that discourse begins to speak.
>
> —Michel Foucault, *The Archaeology of Knowledge* (trans. 1972)

In June 1973, a few months after the Washington State Supreme Court issued its decision, Josef Diamond, with his colleagues Lyle L. Iverson and Craig S. Sternberg, petitioned the US Supreme Court for a writ of certiorari. They sought a reversal of the state court's ruling that the University of Washington Law School admissions program was constitutional and an assurance that Marco DeFunis, who had just completed his second year of law school, could remain enrolled. Washington state attorney general Slade Gorton and university counsel James B. Wilson responded, urging the Court to either affirm the ruling or dismiss the case as already settled, and they assured the Court that DeFunis would remain enrolled. That fall, as DeFunis began his third year, the Court requested memoranda on mootness doctrine; counsel for both parties took the position that the case was not moot.[1] In November 1973, the Court agreed to hear the case and soon received briefs from over four dozen amici, all with longstanding reputations of opposing or supporting affirmative action. DeFunis's amici included the AFL-CIO, Chamber of Commerce, National Association of Manufacturers, B'nai B'rith Anti-Defamation League, American Jewish Congress, and

Jewish Rights Council. The university and minority amici included the American Bar Association, Association of American Law Schools, Council for Legal Educational Opportunity, Mexican American Legal Defense and Education Fund, NAACP Legal Defense and Education Fund, National Council of Jewish Women, and National Organization for Women.

By the time the Court heard oral argument on February 26, 1974, DeFunis was registering for his final quarter of law school, and on April 23, only weeks before his graduation, it issued what scholars would regard as a nondecision. Justice Potter Stewart, writing a per curiam opinion for five justices (himself, Harry Blackmun, Lewis Powell, William Rehnquist, and Chief Justice Warren Burger), declared the case to be moot. Justice William Brennan, in a short dissent for four justices (himself, William Douglas, Thurgood Marshall, and Byron White), reached the opposite conclusion.[2] Only Justice Douglas, in a twenty-eight-page dissent, addressed substantive issues. Most commentators did not hesitate to complain that the Court had dodged vital constitutional and educational questions, leaving academic institutions, applicants, and lawyers to grope through the fog of affirmative-action discourse.[3]

The confusions and contradictions are what interest me once again. In previous chapters, we saw that the parties to *DeFunis* divergently constru(ct)ed the case facts, social facts, and legal questions from the seemingly incompatible discourses of history, social science, statistics, and everyday experience. In this chapter, I highlight some problems in the oral argument and the mootness opinions before moving to a close reading of Justice Douglas's dissent, which commentators have described as inconsistent. Where they attributed the inconsistencies to the justice's personal ambivalence about affirmative action, I argue instead that they are the effects of the incommensurable discourses he sought to reconcile. Where they claim the dissent does not cohere, I argue that his critique of the Law School Admissions Test (LSAT) is the linchpin that holds it together.

MOOTING THE CASE

Conventional wisdom advises court watchers not to speculate on the basis of exchanges at oral argument what the justices will say in their opinions. Nonetheless, we should read some of these exchanges indexically because, as it turned out, they pointed to aspects of the *DeFunis* opinions. In this instance, the two main opinions reached opposite conclusions about whether the case was moot, but they used the same narrative frame, reasoning, and language. By contrast, Justice Douglas's dissent violated several conventions of format, language, fact, and law, thus confusing readers who in turn attributed these textual features to Justice Douglas's state of mind. In short, I will argue that textual analysis should not rest on speculations about the author's psyche.

Oral Argument

Even a cursory reading of the oral argument transcript reveals that Josef Diamond, Slade Gorton, and most of the justices adopted the lower courts' discourse characterized by a narrow time and action frame to bracket the 1971 admissions cycle, binary logic to pit DeFunis against minority applicants, and the use of "qualifications" to denote only grades, test scores, and predicted first-year averages. Perhaps in keeping with the adversarial ethos, Justice Stewart, who was sympathetic to the plaintiff, took the lead in questioning Diamond while Justice Brennan, who was sympathetic to the defendant, took the lead in questioning Gorton.

In his opening statement, Diamond tediously recited DeFunis's achievements during and after his college years, the family meetings with university officials and regents, the argument that his client had been displaced by less-qualified minority admittees, and the decision to file suit. During this soliloquy, he mentioned that he had obtained a court order "requiring the university to produce the files and the records of some of those who were being admitted," and, after examining 300 or 400 of the 1,600 files, concluded that applicants with PFYAs below 74.5 "were automatically eliminated, with the exception of the minorities." When Justice Stewart interrupted to ask about low-scoring veterans, Diamond replied, "Yes, there were some returning servicemen . . . we're raising no question about the returning servicemen." Next the justice wanted to know whether Diamond had "randomly chosen [the 300 or 400 files], or . . . did that represent a particular category." He replied, "We requested all of the minority groups . . . and some of the additional others"[4] Although Diamond consistently embroidered his uninvited statements about the allegedly less-qualified minority applicants, he was unable give precise answers to questions about them. When Justice Brennan asked him to identify the groups that benefited from race-conscious admissions, he struggled to name African Americans, Chicanos, and American Indians, leaving Justice Stewart to remind him of Filipino Americans. To cover for this floundering, he claimed that the admissions committee had no way to determine the applicants' racial identities.

The exchanges revealed Diamond's manipulations of the facts. First, by examining all of the minority files but only a few of the others, he drew a sharp boundary around the evidence he could present at trial. Second, by ignoring the lower-scoring veterans and higher-scoring minority applicants, he could focus even more narrowly on those minority applicants who had lower numerical scores than his client. Only later as Justice Douglas questioned Slade Gorton about the law school criteria did the latter state that "the law school was not simply looking for 150 persons with the highest predicted first-year averages" but instead used several other criteria to determine who was qualified for admission.[5]

Most of the justices used language that overpersonalized the plaintiff and impersonalized the applicants of color. They asked the attorneys whether DeFunis had registered for his final quarter, whether the school might turn him away, whether he had passing grades, whether he served on law review, whether the state would permit him to take the bar examination, and whether his court-ordered enrollment would delegitimate his law degree. Consistently referring to the applicants of color as "minorities," "blacks," and twice as "Negroes," they asked which groups were the designated beneficiaries, how the law school identified them, whether it had a pro-rata (i.e., group-based) acceptance scheme, and whether their success rate in completing their studies and passing the bar examination was lower than that of white students.

Justice Blackmun, for instance, asked Diamond, "If he does graduate and if this decision of the Washington Court is affirmed, will he, nevertheless, be eligible to take the Washington bar examination? Even though your Supreme Court has said he was been illegally in law school?" As Diamond wandered through a reply, finally declaring that his client was "entitled to know" that his degree was "legally his" and not conferred "by default," Justice Rehnquist interrupted:

> Question [Rehnquist]: I don't see how you could call his degree won by default, then, if we held the case were moot.
>
> Mr. Diamond: No, I am not saying that his degree would be won by default. I am saying that he is in law school illegally. The fact that he is making his grades, and he is going to get his degree because he has passing grades, and I think he is near the top of his class. So . . . on that score we have no problem.[6]

During his presentation, Gorton addressed Diamond's misrepresentations. "It is not correct," he said, "to characterize the State Supreme Court's decision as saying he was illegally in law school. The State Supreme Court decision said that the program of admissions adopted by the law school was valid, and that he was not deprived of equal protection." DeFunis, he stated, "was only marginally qualified when he was compared with all of the people who were admitted into the school. There were 1601 applications. Most of them were qualified people. Three hundred and thirty were eventually given letters . . . of admission. On the basis of his predicted first-year average (PFYA), Mr. DeFunis ranked about 290th in that group of 330."[7] Curious about this ranking, I contacted the Law School Admissions Council, which provided data indicating that his LSAT scores placed him at about the seventy-fourth percentile of all scores reported nationwide for 1969–1970.[8] But DeFunis's ranking did not influence Chief Justice Burger, who asked Gorton, "Does it really make any difference to the basic issues in this case whether he [DeFunis] was No. 1 or No. 290?"[9]

By contrast, Justice Douglas quizzed Gorton on the possibility of LSAT bias against racial minority test-takers:

Question [Douglas]: Mr. Attorney General, when I was teaching law many years ago, I discovered to my consternation that these tests, these so-called tests had built-in racial bias. Is there any finding in this record as to your test?

Mr. Gorton: There is no finding in the record, Mr. Justice Douglas, because neither party wished to bring that subject up. Obviously Mr. DeFunis would not make that claim, and the University of Washington did not attempt in court to prove that it engaged in previous racial discrimination. . . .

Question: No, even when I was teaching, I couldn't find out how they did it; but it was very subtle, built-in system to see that certain minorities didn't get into school.

Mr. Gorton: Mr. Justice Douglas, I don't think that there has ever been, at least in this school, any kind of such deliberate attempt. I think that because of the difference, because of the effects of racial discrimination, that happens in fact, even with what you called, in the *Griggs* case, for example, a test which is neutral on its surface. And you might very well, in a proper case, find that the predicted first-year average had a built-in racial bias.[10]

Here we see Justice Douglas expressing his own experience-based hunch and wanting evidence of test bias. But Gorton equivocates, first admitting that the litigants had a converging interest in omitting evidence of LSAT bias, next denying that the law school had deliberately discriminated, and then acknowledging that in a "proper case," such as *Griggs*, the Court might overturn a facially neutral test that produced racially disparate results, if used deliberately. Douglas would develop his hunch about test bias into the central critique of his dissent.

The Mootness Opinions

The justiciability doctrine, based on the Article III provision that limits federal court review to cases or controversies, imposes several requirements: to have standing to pursue a lawsuit, the would-be plaintiff must be injured or be in imminent danger of injury; the parties must have a true adversarial relationship; and the decision, if favorable, must give relief to the injured party. If conditions change at any point in the process from trial through appeal so that one or more of the requirements are no longer met, the court can declare the case to be moot. Nevertheless, mootness doctrine provides for certain exemptions. The "voluntary cessation" exemption allows a case to proceed when the accused party halts the challenged action (often to avoid liability) but is likely to repeat it when the hubbub dies down. The "short-term conduct" exemption similarly allows a case to proceed when it involves a short-term event, such as an election or a pregnancy, that would let the accused party evade review merely because the clock has run out on the particular event. The "class-action" exemption allows a case to proceed when the named plaintiff no longer meets one or more of the requirements, but the members of the certified class continue to meet them.[11] In what follows, I show that by reading the justices' opinions through the lens of mootness doctrine versus the lens of discourse analysis we see different aspects of their strategy.

Justice Stewart's per curiam opinion concluded that the case was moot. Writing that "DeFunis brought the suit on behalf of himself alone, and not as the representative of any class," he approached mootness by way of Article III jurisprudence, which dictated that a case must present a live dispute and affect the plaintiff's rights. Thus after confirming that the plaintiff did not represent members of class who might have kept the dispute alive, he stated that DeFunis had already received the relief he sought—admission to the law school and assurance that he could complete his final quarter.[12] Then he writes,

> DeFunis will never again be required to run the gantlet of the Law School's admissions process, and so the question is certainly not "capable of repetition" so far as he is concerned. Moreover, just because this particular case did not reach the Court until the eve of the petitioner's graduation from law school, it hardly follows that the issue he raises will in the future evade review.

Analyzing the passage doctrinally, we can see two maneuvers. By overpersonalizing the case to the plaintiff, Justice Stewart can justify his camp's position that "the Court cannot, consistently with the limitations of Art. III of the Constitution, consider the substantive constitutional issue tendered by the parties," and by warning that the issue he raised would not evade review in the future, he indicates that some justices would welcome future cases that provide them with the opportunity to pronounce on race-conscious admissions.[13]

Analyzing the passage discursively, we can see the contradictions. The tone of certainty varnishing it does not hide the aporia, the impasse when facing a difficult contradiction. The Stewart camp refuses to enter the space of national conflict over race-conscious remedies to render a decision on the constitutionality of this program; yet the camp creates a new contradiction when stating "the judgment of the Supreme Court of Washington is vacated, and the case is remanded for such further proceedings as by that court may be deemed appropriate."[14] Since the Stewart camp felt its own court lacked jurisdiction because the case was moot, why did it exercise its power by nullifying the state court's judgment and remanding for further proceedings? Some scholars argued that the Stewart opinion left only the trial court judgment standing; others argued that its remand would allow the state justices to opine (or not) on the legality of race-conscious admissions; and still others wondered why the Supreme Court didn't dismiss the case and avoid the complications.[15]

Accusing the Stewart camp of "straining to rid itself of this dispute," Justice Brennan also strained when, to keep the dispute alive, he similarly overpersonalized the plaintiff. If "unexpected events—illness, economic necessity, even academic failure"—were to prevent DeFunis from graduating, he would have to reenroll and "might once again have to run the gantlet of the University's allegedly unlawful admissions policy." A decision would "insure [*sic*] that, if for some reason petitioner did not graduate this spring, he would be entitled to re-enrollment at a later time on the same basis as others."[16] But if these unlikely events occurred during DeFunis's last term, the law school could provide him with sick leave, financial aid, or permission to retake a course in the fall term.[17] Justice Brennan's other reason for deciding the case—namely, that it was "ripe for decision on a fully developed factual record with sharply defined and fully canvassed legal issues"[18]—simply doesn't square with the deficient trial record and the parties' kaleidoscopic interpretations of fact and law. Thus where the Stewart rationale created procedural contradictions, the Brennan rationale created empirical contradictions.

In short, I have argued that the two camps used the same reasoning to reach opposite conclusions about justiciability: by applying mootness doctrine to a case so particularized to DeFunis's fate in the 1971 admissions cycle, they avoided any discussion of the consequences for minority applicants who were seeking access to legal education and minority communities that were seeking access to legal services. But the two camps expressed different views on the amici prognostications about a ruling that the admissions program was unconstitutional. University supporters warned that a ruling of unconstitutionality would roll back the post-*Brown* progress toward equal educational opportunity; minority supporters feared that it would solidify structural racism in education and elsewhere; and DeFunis supporters welcomed it as preventing the spread of anti-white quotas throughout society. The Stewart camp rebuffed the amici, insisting that the case's mootness "depends . . . upon the simple fact that DeFunis is now in the final quarter" of law school, while the Brennan camp admonished its colleagues for avoiding an issue that "concern[s] vast numbers of people, organizations, and colleges and universities, as evidenced by the filing of twenty-six *amicus curiae* briefs."[19]

The camps did agree on one consequential point. Justice Stewart stated, "there is no reason to suppose that a subsequent case attacking these [race-conscious] procedures will not come with relative speed to this Court"; and Justice Brennan wrote, "Few constitutional questions in recent history have stirred as much debate, and they will not disappear. They must inevitably return to the federal courts and ultimately again to this Court."[20] They were correct: two months later, *Bakke* began its long journey to the high court.

THE DOUGLAS DISSENT

Although law scholars saluted Justice Douglas for addressing substantive issues, they felt his dissent was riddled with inconsistencies. In a 1975 article, Larry M. Lavinsky, who had served of counsel for the Anti-Defamation League's amicus brief to the US Supreme Court, described it as "an opinion in which eloquence and insight are mingled with ambivalence and ambiguity."[21] Daniel Steiner, who moderated a 1975 *DeFunis* panel, remarked that Douglas expressed "his views in a rather lengthy discussion of what the case was all about and which way it should be decided," but "some of us feel there was not great clarity in that opinion." Panelist Robert M. O'Neil was uncharacteristically blunt: "If one needs confirmation of the whole Court's dilemma, one need only look at the paradoxes and inconsistency of Mr. Justice Douglas' separate tortured opinion."[22] Confronted by the textual contradictions, some scholars simply ignored them, others cherry-picked the statements that supported their views, and still others interpreted them psycho-biographically.[23]

Twenty-four years later, psycho-biographical interpretation retained its strong grip on textual ambiguities. Elaborating on "the depth of Justice Douglas's ambivalence," Jim Chen noted that in *Wright v. Rockefeller* (1964) the justice argued that the government should not demarcate voting districts along racial lines, and in *DeFunis* he "decided to try mending affirmative action without ending it," but only after vacillating. In conference, he criticized "both race-conscious admissions and the use of standardized tests," and then he circulated drafts of the dissent alternately rejecting or accepting the constitutionality of race-conscious admissions before settling on the final version.[24] Initially I too interpreted the dissent this way, wondering whether its awkward phrasing and contradictory statements reflected Douglas's declining health, which eventuated in a major stroke later that year, but then I reminded myself that psycho-biographical interpretation is the default method for readers steeped in liberal-individualist ideology.

Interpretive Schemes

To interpret new texts, ordinary and expert readers alike deploy previously learned reading strategies. As Annette Kolodny explained in a landmark 1980 essay,

> what we are taught to read well and with pleasure, when we are young, predisposes to certain specific kinds of adult reading tastes. For the professional literary critic, the process may be no different, but it is at least more conscious. Graduate schools, at their best, are training grounds for competing interpretive paradigms or reading techniques: affective stylistics, structuralism, and semiotic analysis, to name only a few of the more recent entries. The delight we learn to take in the mastery of these interpretive strategies is then often mistakenly construed as our delight in reading specific texts.[25]

From this abbreviated statement, we can infer that interpretation is customary because we redeploy on current texts the strategies we learned while reading previous ones, and it is constitutive because each strategy makes visible and meaningful a particular set of textual features. As the predominant reading strategy in the United States' liberal-individualist society, psycho-biographical interpretation is used by ordinary people when they make sense of a "befuddled" grandmother's wandering tale; by financial analysts when they explain the "nervous" stock market's free-fall; by scholars when they declare that daffodil imagery expresses the poet's joy or chiaroscuro conveys the painter's angst; and by law practitioners when they identify textual traces of the framers' intent or the criminal's motive. The assumption behind these interpretations is that the person (or personified entity) is an intentional being that expresses its subjectivity in language and other mediums.

Rather than using this reading strategy to explain the dissent's inconsistencies as expressions of Justice Douglas's personal ambivalence about race-conscious admissions, we can ask why they appear in this text and how they function there. I will argue that Justice Douglas enters the space of aporia—the places where contradictions, paradoxes, and dilemmas bubble to the surface of the textualized case—and attempts to reconcile the seemingly incommensurable discourses wielded by the parties. As we have seen, these discourses—of admissions qualifications and procedures, racially patterned test-score statistics, DeFunis's personal story, minority group histories, and abstract legal principles—produced divergently characterized facts and divergently reasoned law.

As noted earlier, the Stewart and Brennan opinions used the familiar method of reasoning, namely applying principles (mootness doctrine) to particulars (case facts), but Douglas used dialectical reasoning. His narrative thus proceeds through a series of thesis/antithesis commentaries to reach a synthesis or, to put it in the familiar language, to reach the conclusion that the factual record was too deficient to support a pronouncement on law.

The Dissent

The dissent consists of three sections—the first summarizing the UW Law School admissions process, the second providing a critique of the LSAT and GPA, and the third attempting to weave the discourses of admissions, testing, experience, and law into a coherent narrative about equalizing educational opportunity. As readers, we will find ourselves journeying through a deteriorating prose style as the smooth writing of the summary gives way to the awkward syntax, obscure statements, and oscillating positions of subsequent sections. The meanings we make as we read the passages sequentially will depend on whether we also read cross-referentially to notice the relationships among elements situated in different textual locations.

Section 1 summarizes the facts on record—the number of applicants, the criteria, the file assignments, the evaluation procedures, and the offers of admission. It notes that the committee accepted thirty-seven minority applicants: "Of these, 36 had Averages below DeFunis' 76.23, and 30 had Averages below 74.5 and thus would ordinarily have been summarily rejected. . . . There were also 48 nonminority applicants admitted who had Averages below DeFunis. Twenty-three of these were returning veterans . . . and 26 were others" deemed to deserve admission on grounds of other factors.[26] The paragraph that follows the summary appears to validate Diamond's claim that the minority admittees displaced his client:

> It is reasonable to conclude from the above facts that while other factors were considered by the Committee, and were on occasion crucial, the Average [i.e., PFYA] was for most applicants a heavily

> weighted factor, and was at the extremes virtually dispositive. A different balance was apparently struck, however, with regard to the minority applicants. Indeed, at oral argument, the respondents' counsel advised us that were the minority applicants considered under the same procedure as was generally used, none of those who eventually enrolled at the Law School would have been admitted.[27]

This passage introduces a chain of propositions: the PFYA was a heavily weighted factor in evaluating most applicants; it was less heavily weighted in evaluating minority applicants; thus Diamond claimed that if it had been applied consistently none of the minority applicants would have been admitted. But the opening clause, "It is reasonable to conclude from the above facts," introduces complexity. By using agentless-passive phrasing ("It is reasonable to conclude") and hedging the reasonableness with a qualifier ("from the above facts"), Justice Douglas shifts the entire passage into the epistemic modality, which always functions to convey the speaker's certainty or doubt about propositions that follows. In other words, the paragraph is subtly stating that the propositions seem reasonable if based only on the summarized case facts.

The next passage addresses the law school's authority to determine its admissions goals and criteria:

> Clearly it is not for us but for the law school to decide which tests to employ, how heavily to weigh recommendations from professors or undergraduate grades, and what level[s] of achievement on the chosen criteria are sufficient to demonstrate that the candidate is qualified for admission. What places this case in a special category is the fact that the school did not choose one set of criteria but two, and then determined which to apply to a given applicant on the basis of his race. The Committee adopted this policy in order to achieve "a reasonable representation of minority groups." . . . Although it may be speculated that the Committee sought to rectify what it perceived to be cultural or racial biases in the LSAT or in the candidates' undergraduate records, the record in this case is devoid of any evidence of such bias, and the school has not sought to justify its procedures on this basis.[28]

Embedded in this passage but without attribution are allusions to the parties' characterizations of the admissions scheme: DeFunis supporters delineated it as a dual system with different criteria for white and minority applicants; university supporters stated that the criteria advanced the university goal of achieving reasonable minority representation; and minority supporters contended that LSAT bias disproportionately eliminated minority applicants. The somewhat petulant wording of last sentence, which notes that the record contains no evidence that the law school sought to rectify the LSAT's alleged racial bias, implies that Douglas finds something to be objectionable, but what? Is it the deficient case record itself, or the law school's failure to introduce such evidence, or factually unsupported speculations about such bias? Readers are left to feel uncertain.

The final passage in section 1 begins with a syntactically complex statement that increases this uncertainty: "It thus appears that, by the Committee's own assessment, it admitted minority students who, by the tests given, seemed less qualified than some white students who were not accepted, in order to achieve a 'reasonable representation.'"[29] Readers should not take this sentence as a wordy version of the typical subject-verb-object (SVO) format, because the embedded phrases change its meaning. If it used SVO syntax, it would say, "The committee acknowledged that it accepted less-qualified minority students in order to achieve reasonable representation." But the phrases "by the tests given" and "seemed less qualified" change the meaning to "by using these tests, the committee made the minority students seem less qualified than white ones." Similarly, the phrase "by the Committee's own assessment" suggests that the committee, although knowing the tests had this effect, nevertheless persisted in using them. Finally, the opening clause "It thus appears," which casts this statement in the epistemic modality, suggests that Justice Douglas again has doubts about something. It is the tests themselves, the committee's disregard for their effects, or the rendering of minority students as "less-qualified"? The readers' fog of uncertainty created by the lexicon of appearing, seeming, and speculating is dispelled by the LSAT critique in section 2.

Justice Douglas weaves this narrative from many extrarecord

scholarly and scientific sources as well as his own observations. He begins with a salute to John Henry Wigmore, the legendary teacher and scholar of legal evidence who, at a time when law schools accepted almost all applicants, advised them to weed out the laggards in rigorous first-year law courses. As law schools came under pressure from rising applications, they turned to testing, at first the Ferson-Stoddard Law Aptitude Test and later the LSAT, which Justice Douglas dissects.

> The test purports to predict how successful the applicant will be in his first year of law school, and consists of a few hours' worth of multiple-choice questions. But the answers the student can give to a multiple-choice question are limited by the creativity and intelligence of the test-maker; the student with a better or more original understanding of the problem than the test-maker may realize that none of the alternative answers are any good, but there is no way for him to demonstrate his understanding. . . . "If he is subtle in his choice of answers it will go against him. . . . If he is strong-minded, nonconformist, unusual, original, or creative . . . he must stifle his impulses and conform as best he can to the norms that the multiple-choice testers set up in their unimaginative, scientific way. The more profoundly gifted the candidate is, the more his resentment will rise against the mental strait jacket into which testers would force his mind."[30]

Justice Douglas blends into this critique of the test's format and content a quotation from *The Tyranny of Testing* (1962), a book that rocked the testing establishment because the author, Banesh Hoffmann, a distinguished professor of physics and collaborator of Albert Einstein, used empirical methods to reveal the flaws of multiple-choice testing.[31] Yet the passage does more than inform the dissent's readers about the flaws of testing in experiential language they, as former test-takers, will understand; it cultivates their self-esteem by inviting them to identify with gifted students. High-scoring readers can flatter themselves on acing the test, lower-scoring readers can take comfort in resisting its pedestrian thinking, and all readers can resent the straitjacket format.

In the next passage, based on research by Thomas M. Goolsby Jr.,

Justice Douglas argues that test scores do not gauge all of the factors that contribute to performance in law school.

> Most of those scoring in the bottom 20% . . . do better than that in law school—indeed six of every 100 of them will be in the *top* 20% of their law school class [Goolsby citation omitted]. And no one knows how many of those who were not admitted because of their test scores would in fact have done well were they given the chance. There are many relevant factors, such as motivation, cultural backgrounds of specific minorities that the test cannot measure, and they inevitably impair its value as a predictor. Of course, the law school that admits only those with the highest test scores finds that on the average they do much better, and thus the test is a convenient tool for the admissions committee. The price is paid by the able student who for unknown reasons did not achieve that high score—perhaps even the minority with a different cultural background. Some tests, at least in the past, have been aimed at eliminating Jews.[32]

This passage introduces three more groups of students that have reasons to resent testing—lower-scoring students who can be high performers in law school, lower-scoring minorities with backgrounds the test cannot measure, and Jews who were historically targeted by exclusionary tests. By exemplifying how the test works against virtually all students—gifted and average, higher and lower scoring, white and minority, Jewish and non-Jewish—the critique reaches out to diversely positioned readers.

Next Justice Douglas addresses the unreliability of LSAT scores, this time echoing statements made during the trial and once again quoting Banesh Hoffman:

> The school can safely conclude that the applicant with a score of 750 [out of a maximum 800] should be admitted before one with a score of 500. The problem is that in many cases the choice will be between 643 and 602 or 575 and 528. The numbers create an illusion of difference tending to overwhelm other factors. "The wiser testers are well aware of the defects of the multiple-choice format

> and the danger of placing reliance on any one method of assessment to the exclusion of all others. What is distressing is how little their caveats have impressed the people who succumb to the propaganda of the test-makers and use those tests as though they were valid substitutes for judgment."[33]

The statement that "numbers create an illusion of difference" echoes John A. Winterbottom's trial testimony that numbers have a "seductive appearance of precision about them, and we go to great lengths to urge the law schools using the test scores to remember that they are not as precise as they look." It also references the dissent's own testing lexicon of "appearing" and "seeming."[34] The bluntly worded quotation from Hoffman's book revives the dissent's innuendos that law schools, though aware that the LSAT makes minority applicants appear less qualified, nevertheless continue to use it.[35]

By now, Douglas's contemporaneous readers should realize that section 2 admonishes the UW Law School for using the LSAT as a convenience, Diamond for insisting it is an objective tool, and the amici for objecting to only its anti-minority or anti-Semitic effects. Today's cross-referencing readers might also recall Michel Foucault's analysis of tests and grades in *Discipline and Punish* (1975). The book demonstrates how disciplinary institutions, such as the school, the military, and the prison, used these devices to quantify individuals' personal and social qualities, to rank them relative to others, to construct the mean and the norm, to mark the deviations, and thus to create the objective "truth" of the human sciences.[36] In *DeFunis*, we can see these dynamics at work. When Mrs. DeFunis claimed that her son was ill while taking the LSAT and Diamond claimed that the law school should have incorporated his pre–junior year Latin grades, they were attempting to raise his PFYA score and thus his ranking in the applicant pool. When his supporters described the PFYA as an objective indicator, they were attempting to endow their claims with the "truth" of quantification. Paradoxically, these parties wanted the law school to clamp down on the lower-scoring minority applicants the disciplinary apparatus that had rejected the mediocre plaintiff.

Justice Douglas concludes the LSAT critique with this statement:

since the UW Law School "presented no evidence to show that adjustments [to minority scores] . . . were used in order validly to compare applicants of different races," the Court has "no choice but to evaluate the Law School's case as it has been made."[37] This statement refers to the record principle, which obliges the Court to consider only the facts included in the trial record. Coming at the end of section 2, it encapsulates the dissent's thesis-antithesis structure, already exhibited in section 1's summary of the case facts and section 2's presentation of the missing social facts.

Section 3 is punctuated by pronouncements of law, such as these, that some scholars interpreted as affirming Justice Douglas's tilt toward color-blindness:[38]

- "Once race is a starting point educators and courts are immediately embroiled in competing claims of different racial and ethnic groups that would make difficult, manageable standards consistent with the Equal Protection Clause."
- "There is no constitutional right for any race to be preferred."
- "The Equal Protection Clause commands the elimination of racial barriers, not their creation in order to satisfy our theory as to how society ought to be organized."
- "So far as race is concerned, any state-sponsored preference to one race over another in that competition is in my view 'invidious' and violative of the Equal Protection Clause."[39]

Instead of fishing these statements from different pages of section 3 and stringing them together to argue that Justice Douglas would have illegalized the law school's admissions program, we must read the section straight through to see that it oscillates among delineations of case facts and social facts, statements about racially discriminatory and racially neutral practices, and metacommentaries on the discourses of law and life. This reading strategy reveals how Justice Douglas's dialectic finally synthesizes a resolution.

Section 2, as we have seen, concludes with the thesis that "we have no choice but to evaluate the Law School's case as it has been made." Section 3 begins with an antithesis:

> The Equal Protection Clause did not enact a requirement that law schools employ as the sole criterion for admission a formula based on the LSAT and undergraduate grades, nor does it prohibit law schools from evaluating an applicant's prior achievements in light of the barriers that he had to overcome. A black applicant who pulled himself out of the ghetto into a junior college may thereby demonstrate a level of motivation, perseverance, and ability that would lead a fairminded [*sic*] admissions committee to conclude that he showed more promise than the son of a rich alumnus who achieved better grades at Harvard. That applicant would be offered admission not because he is black, but because as an individual he has shown he has the potential, while the Harvard man may have taken less advantage of the vastly superior opportunities offered him.[40]

This paragraph, which references earlier discussions of tests and grades, states that the equal protection clause does not require law schools to consider only these criteria and does not prohibit them from considering applicants' backgrounds. Thus it seems to substitute for the race of the Black applicant his "background" of overcoming economic and educational disadvantages.

While both the pro-minority and pro-DeFunis amici used racializing language to describe applicant qualifications, Justice Douglas explains why background consideration is racially neutral:

> Such a policy would not be limited to blacks, or Chicanos, or Filipinos, or American Indians, although undoubtedly groups such as these may in practice be the principal beneficiaries of it. But a poor Appalachian white, or a second generation Chinese in San Francisco, or some other American whose lineage is so diverse as to defy ethnic labels, may demonstrate similar potential and thus be accorded favorable consideration by the Committee. The difference between such a policy and the one presented by this case is that the Committee would be making decisions on the basis of individual attributes, rather than according a preference solely on the basis of race.[41]

Together the two passages acknowledge that the racist and classist structuring of American society produces diverse applicants, whose capabilities cannot be measured by tests and grades predicated on a normative type. Inverting the commonplace trope, Justice Douglas observes, "The melting pot is not designed to homogenize people, making them uniform in consistency. The melting pot . . . is a figure of speech that depicts the wide diversities tolerated by the First Amendment under one flag."[42] Despite some mixing of metaphors, the passages above explain why standardization fails to comprehend dissimilar people shaped by dissimilar backgrounds.

To set up another thesis/antithesis pair, he turns to claims made by DeFunis supporters. The admissions committee, they argued, used different standards, "with the result that the Committee admitted minority applicants who, in the school's own judgment, were less promising than other applicants who were rejected," and, in seeking reasonable representation of minority students, must have had some number in mind. Douglas responds, "Without becoming embroiled in a semantic debate over whether this practice constitutes a 'quota,' it is clear that, given the limitation on the total number of applicants who could be accepted, this policy did reduce the total number of places for which DeFunis could compete—solely on account of his race."[43] Although rebuffing the DeFunis supporters' "quota" language and the university supporters' "reasonable representation" language, Douglas seems to agree with the former that the admissions policy reduced the number of places for which DeFunis could compete "solely on account of . . . race." He concludes this passage with a quote from *Loving v. Virginia*: "The clear and central purpose of the Fourteenth Amendment was to eliminate all official state sources of invidious racial discrimination in the States."

But then comes the antithesis: "The Law School's admissions policy cannot be reconciled with that purpose, unless cultural standards of a diverse rather than a homogeneous society are taken into account."[44] The qualifier—"unless cultural standards of a diverse rather than homogeneous society are taken into account"—is the pivot to elaborating the antithesis.

> The key to the problem is the consideration of each application *in a racially neutral way*. Since the LSAT reflects questions touching on cultural backgrounds, the Admissions Committee acted properly in my view in setting minority applications apart for separate processing. These minorities have cultural backgrounds that are vastly different from the dominant Caucasians. Many Eskimos, American Indians, Filipinos, Chicanos, Asian Indians, Burmese, and Africans come from such disparate backgrounds that a test sensitively tuned for most applicants would be wide of the mark for many minorities.[45]

In what I consider to be rank dishonesty, opponents of race-conscious admissions repeatedly decontextualized the phrase "*in a racially neutral way*" to argue that only the use of numerical scores complies with the Fourteenth Amendment's purpose of eliminating state-sponsored discrimination. But this passage makes the inverse argument that the use of the LSAT, which is not a racially neutral test of applicants who have diverse backgrounds, cannot be reconciled with the Fourteenth Amendment's purpose. Thus Justice Douglas states unambiguously that to neutralize test bias the committee acted appropriately "in setting minority applications apart for separate processing."

Continuing to elaborate on background differences, he again resorts to the epistemic modality:

> I do know, coming as I do from Indian country in Washington, that many of the young Indians know little about Adam Smith or Karl Marx but are deeply involved with the spirit and philosophy of Chief Robert B. Jim of the Yakimas, Chief Seattle of the Muckleshoots, and Chief Joseph of the Nez Perce which offer competitive attitudes toward life, fellow man, and nature.
>
> I do not know the extent to which blacks in this country are imbued with ideas of African Socialism. Leopold Senghor and Sékou Touré, the most articulate of African leaders, have held that modern African political philosophy is not oriented either to Marxism or to capitalism. . . . But at least as respects Indians, blacks, and Chicanos—as well as those from Asian cultures—I think a separate

> classification of these applicants is warranted, lest race be a subtle force in eliminating minority members because of cultural differences.[46]

The first-person pronoun in the phrases "I do know" and "I do not know" undoubtedly encouraged some readers to conflate the narrative voice with Justice Douglas's personal knowledge of Native Americans in his home state of Washington. Indeed in "William O. Douglas, the Supreme Court, and American Indians," Robert H. Keller Jr. argues that the justice's comments on Native Americans in this case and previous ones derived from his extensive personal knowledge of Native American peoples.[47] While the biographical information is interesting, it detracts from the language features I have been foregrounding—in this instance, the epistemic certainty that normative criteria cannot capture the distinctiveness of Native American culture.

Earlier Justice Douglas concluded that the admissions committee acted appropriately in giving minority applications separate consideration. After the paragraphs quoted above, he restates this conclusion twice: "But at least as respects Indians, blacks, and Chicanos—as well as those from Asian cultures—I think a separate classification of these applicants is warranted lest race be a subtle force in eliminating minority members because of cultural differences"; and again, "My reaction is that the presence of an LSAT is sufficient warrant for a school to put racial minorities into a separate class in order to better probe their capacities and potentials."[48] The passage that follows leaves no doubt that Justice Douglas's extra-record LSAT critique functions as the linchpin of the dissent:

> The merits of the present controversy cannot in my view be resolved on this record. A trial would involve the disclosure of hidden prejudices, if any, against certain minorities and the manner in which substitute measurements of one's talents and character were employed in the conventional tests. . . . The case, in my view, should be remanded for a new trial to consider, *inter alia*, whether the established LSAT's [*sic*] should be eliminated so far as racial minorities are concerned.[49]

Perhaps because the passages I have quoted are followed by a five-page discussion of precedential cases overturning racial discrimination, practical suggestions for how to conduct a racially neutral admissions process, and further pronouncements on equal protection, readers may miss their significance. Those passages delineate the aporia, the central contradiction of not only the "reverse discrimination" logic of the plaintiff's supporters but also the liberal-individualist logic of the courts that heard *DeFunis* and would hear *Bakke*.[50] The white middle-class normed LSAT and the diverse cultures of racial minority groups were incompatible. Rather than minority applicants failing the test, the test failed them.

At the end of the dissent, where a conventional opinion would locate a holding or command, this statement appears:

> My view is only that I cannot say by the tests used and applied that he [DeFunis] was invidiously discriminated against because of his race. I cannot conclude that the admissions procedure of the Law School of the University of Washington that excluded DeFunis is violative of the Equal Protection Clause of the Fourteenth Amendment. The judgment of the Washington Supreme Court should be vacated and the case remanded for a new trial.[51]

In isolation, this passage epitomizes what psycho-biographical interpreters take to be Justice Douglas's ambiguity about race-conscious remedies. They could read "I cannot say" as expressing either his indecision about whether the admissions program discriminated against DeFunis or his unwillingness to declare that it did so discriminate. They could read "I cannot conclude" as expressing either his indecision about whether the program violated the equal protection clause or his conviction that it did not. But here, as elsewhere, the qualifying phrase, "by the tests used and applied," refers readers to his critique of instruments that cannot gauge the past or future performance of those who diverge from white-normed expectations. Operating within legal-judicial discourse, Justice Douglas reaches the correct conclusion in calling for a new trial to fill the gaping hole in the factual record; operating outside of legal-judicial discourse, he steps into the space of aporia and dialectically resolves the contradictions that psychobiographical readers have attributed to him.

My four chapters on *DeFunis* have focused on the discourses surrounding the case and swirling within it—the racial conflicts that roiled the Seattle community and rocked the University of Washington campus, the behind-the-scenes actions that precipitated the litigation, the trial that colored the case, and the brief and opinion writers who made it a discourse wracked by contradictions. They demonstrate that the rules constraining what could be said were overcome by the rhetoric proliferating what was said; the trust that the adversarial method would uncover the truth was tarnished by the deficient record; and the idealized concept of academic merit was frustrated by the barriers to educational opportunity.[52] The conflicts surrounding *DeFunis* and the contradictions manifested in it would burst forth in the *Bakke* story. This version of reverse discrimination, which gained potency from media coverage, political pressure, and numerous amicus briefs, threw the parties' interpretive ingenuity into overdrive and once again marginalized minority interests.

PART III

THE *BAKKE* CASE

7

SLANTING THE STORY

The Truth must dazzle gradually
Or every man be blind—

—Emily Dickinson, "Tell all the truth but tell it slant—" (#1263, 1890)

Regents of the University of California v. Bakke presented the US Supreme Court with constitutional questions it had dodged in 1974 by declaring that *DeFunis v. Odegaard* was moot. The two cases bore more than a superficial resemblance. Both featured rejected white male applicants who claimed, initially or later, that race-conscious admissions programs deprived them of enrollment in professional schools and thereby violated their right to equal protection. Both went forward with inadequate factual records that did not prevent the parties from making bold assertions about the admissions programs, the applicants, and the meaning of equal protection. Both sparked frenzied interest from numerous advocacy groups, educators, law scholars, public intellectuals, journalists, and ordinary Americans. In the chapters that follow, I will show how *Bakke*, like *DeFunis*, was shaped by discursive strategies that filtered the facts, slanted the legal arguments, and dug the divide between judicially textualized "racial discrimination" and socially constructed "systemic racism."

THE OFFICIAL STORY

Court documents, journalism, and scholarship told an almost identical story about the admissions program at the medical school on the University of California's Davis campus (UCD) and the fate of Allan Bakke therein. When the school opened its doors in fall 1968, the entering class of fifty students included three Asian Americans but no African Americans, Mexican Americans, and Native Americans. Slightly more diverse in 1969, the entering class of fifty students included eleven Asian Americans, two African Americans, one Mexican American, and no Native Americans.[1] In 1970, the school implemented a special admissions program for economically and educationally disadvantaged applicants, and in 1971 it increased the entering class size to one hundred places, designating sixteen for special admissions and eighty-four for regular admissions. Out of approximately 450 entering places from 1970 through 1974, the special program admitted 71 minority applicants—26 African Americans, 33 Mexican Americans, and 12 Asian Americans—but no economically and/or educationally disadvantaged Native Americans or whites.[2]

Two committees that used somewhat different review processes evaluated the applicants. In the regular admissions program, a large committee eliminated applicants with Grade Point Averages (GPAs) under 2.5 on a 4.0 scale and, for those remaining in the pool, invited approximately one out of six to interviews. Next, five-member subcommittees rated interviewees on their Medical College Admissions Test (MCAT) scores, general and science GPAs, quality of the undergraduate curriculum, letters of recommendation, extracurricular activities, character, motivation, contemplated type and location of practice, and interview performance. Added together, the individual ratings, which could range from zero to 100, produced a total benchmark score at or below a perfect 500; a year later when the rating subcommittees were increased to six members the perfect score rose to 600. Since the applications arrived over a period of six months, the regular admissions committee reviewed them in batches and made "rolling offers," periodically compiling a waitlist to be sure the entering class would fill.

The task force (occasionally called the "special committee"), which evaluated applicants to the special admissions program, consisted of medical faculty and students, some white and some minority. During the 1972–1973 admissions cycle, its members did not serve on the regular admissions committee, but during the 1973–1974 admissions cycle some individuals served on both committees. Although this committee followed the same review process, it did not adopt a 2.5 GPA cutoff and invited approximately one out of five applicants to interview. After assigning benchmark scores, it made recommendations to the regular admissions committee, which could accept a special applicant, reject him/her, or request more information. The task force committee could fill, but was not required to fill, sixteen places; in 1973 and 1974, it filled fifteen places and transferred the sixteenth place to the regular program.[3]

For the fall 1973 entering class, the 2,664 applications began to arrive in July 1972, some months before rolling admissions decisions were made. Entering the process very late, Allan Bakke submitted an application in January 1973 and attended a March interview conducted by Dr. Theodore West, who wrote a positive evaluation. Although he received a benchmark score of 468 out of 500, the committee rejected him because by that time it had already mailed 123 of the total 160 offers and considered no one with a benchmark score below 470.[4] Two weeks after receiving the rejection letter in May, Bakke wrote to Dr. George H. Lowrey, chairman of the admissions committee and associate dean of student affairs, asking for reconsideration; receiving no reply, he wrote again, complaining that the admissions program was biased in favor of racial minorities. Dr. Lowrey turned the matter over to his staff assistant, Peter C. Storandt, who encouraged Bakke to reapply for admission to the fall 1974 entering class.

Reapplying early in the 1973–1974 cycle, Bakke was one of 3,737 applicants competing for 100 places. In August 1973, he attended two interviews, a new procedure for all applicants. Medical student Frank Gioia communicated a favorable impression, but Dr. Lowrey reported that Bakke "was very unsympathetic to the concept of recruiting minority students. . . . One of his main reasons . . . was that this decreased his own chances of getting into medical school. . . . [He is] a rigidly oriented young man who has a tendency to arrive at conclusions based more upon his personal impressions than upon thoughtful processes using available sources of information."[5] Case evidence revealed that four committee members gave Bakke high ratings, one gave a slightly lower rating, and Dr. Lowrey gave him such a low rating that his benchmark score of 549 out of 600 actually fell below that of the previous year.[6] Rejected again, Allan Bakke began his long trek to the Supreme Court.

In April 1974, immediately after receiving notification of this second rejection, Bakke filed a racial-discrimination complaint with the Department of Health, Education, and Welfare and engaged Reynold H. Colvin, a San Francisco attorney who had litigated against an affirmative-action program for minority administrators in the public school system. In June, after the Supreme Court issued its mootness ruling in *DeFunis*, Colvin filed suit in the Yolo County Superior Court of California. Alleging that the special admissions program had violated his client's nondiscrimination right under the California Constitution, Title VI of the Civil Rights Act of 1964, and the Fourteenth Amendment, he asked the court to find the program unlawful, enjoin the medical school from considering race in admissions, and order Bakke's admission. Heard by retired Judge F. Leslie Manker, the case moved swiftly from a September 1974 trial to a March 1975 decision that the admissions program was unlawful under all three provisions. Judge Manker declined to order admission because Bakke had not proved that he would have been admitted but for the special program and instead ordered the medical school to reconsider his application without taking race into account.

When both parties appealed—Bakke claiming that the trial court should have ordered his admission and the university contesting its judgment against the program and its injunction on considering race—the California Supreme Court agreed to hear the case and soon received briefs from counsel and amici. At the March 1976 oral argument, Chief Justice Donald R. Wright and six associate justices questioned the two attorneys, Reynold Colvin for Bakke and Donald L. Reidhaar for the university, about racial discrimination, the special program, and possible alternatives. Issuing an Opinion of the Court in September 1976, Justice Stanley Mosk and five colleagues held that the program had unconstitutionally discriminated against Bakke and remanded to the trial court, noting that the burden of proof fell to the university to show that Bakke would not have received an offer in the absence of the program. When the university stipulated that it could not do so, the justices instructed the trial court to order Bakke's admission to medical school.[7] Only Justice Matthew O. Tobriner dissented in a blistering opinion.

As the UC Regents considered whether to appeal to the US Supreme Court, "more than a dozen minority groups urged the[m] . . . not to do so" because the evidence was too weak to uphold the special program. Some groups opposed an appeal, insinuating that the regents wanted a negative ruling that would undermine the program, but others supported an appeal lest the state court ruling encourage the illegalization of similar programs across the country.[8] In December 1976, the university petitioned the Supreme Court, which, as Justice Powell later stated, "granted certiorari to consider the important constitutional issue."[9]

MISSING IN ACTION

Owing to their single-minded focus on whether Bakke experienced racial discrimination, scholars who wrote about the case generally failed to consider the other types of discrimination that in fact did vitiate the medical school's admission process. Some of these discriminations were revealed in pretrial documents and trial testimony but were not addressed by the trial court; others, exposed by journalists and amici after the trial concluded, were not addressed by the California Supreme Court. As a result, the official record that went forward to the US Supreme Court omitted or oversimplified what should have been delineated as the biased treatment of applicants along the lines of age, time of application, inconsistent standards, spousal status, and family wealth or prominence.

Age Discrimination

Bakke was born in 1940 to middle-class Minnesotans, his father working as a mailman and his mother as a teacher in Minneapolis, which they soon left to move the family to South Florida. After graduating from Coral Gables High School, a de jure white-only school, Bakke enrolled at the University of Minnesota with the assistance of an ROTC scholarship, earning a BS in engineering in 1962 and taking a year's worth of graduate courses. In 1967, after serving in the Marine Corp for four years, including a seven-month tour in Vietnam, he accepted the position of research engineer at the Ames Research Center, a NASA laboratory near Palo Alto, California. While at Ames, he earned an MS in mechanical engineering at Stanford University in 1970, took premed courses at Stanford and San Jose State University, and spent countless hours as a hospital volunteer.

In 1971 at the age of thirty-one, Bakke began investigating the possibility of obtaining a medical degree. Concerned about his age, he queried several medical schools on their policies, applied to two for the fall 1972 entering class, and did not receive invitations to interview. When asked in a pretrial interrogatory about the reasons they gave, he said, "The University of Southern California stated that my application was not sufficiently strong. Northwestern stated that my age was above their stated limit."[10] For the fall 1973 class, Bakke applied to eleven medical schools and addressed the age issue in his UCD application, which Bernard Schwartz quoted in his book:

> "Although I am 32 years old, the usual factors which detract from an older applicant do not apply in my case." He stressed the medical prerequisite courses he had taken, which "removes the question of current academic inclinations and aptitudes." Above all the statement stressed, "I am in excellent health. Actuarially it may be predicted that I might not serve as a physician as long as a younger applicant. But I believe my high general level of health, good health maintenance habits, and balanced outlook offset these cold statistics."[11]

Although interviewing at four medical schools (Mayo Clinic, Minnesota, Stanford, and UCD), he was rejected by all eleven schools to which he had applied.

For the fall 1974 class, he again applied to eleven schools and again received rejections. According to his pretrial interrogatory, the medical schools at Georgetown, Cincinnati, and Wake Forest gave no reasons; the Mayo Clinic stated his record was weaker than those of applicants who were accepted and waitlisted; and Stanford, UC Davis, UCLA, Minnesota, South Dakota, and Wayne State mentioned the heightened competition. Only the University of California at San Francisco stated that his "age was a negative factor," but it likely was a negative factor elsewhere.[12] Indeed, when Bakke queried schools about their age limits, the UCD Medical School had replied, "when an applicant is over thirty, his age is a serious factor which must be considered. . . . The [admissions] committee believes that an older applicant must be *unusually highly qualified* to be seriously considered" (my emphasis).[13] After interviewing Bakke for the 1973 entering class, Dr. Theodore West wrote in his committee report that he was "'a well-qualified candidate for admission . . . whose main handicap is the unavoidable fact that he is now 33 years of age,'" the "well-qualified" suggesting he was not regarded as "unusually highly qualified." Dr. West added, "'I sensed an air of frustration and emotion which I attribute to his concern about the impact of age and the fact that this probably is about the last chance for him to apply.'"[14]

While deposing Dr. George Lowrey during the summer of 1974, Colvin asked about age limits:

Q [Reynold Colvin]: Does the medical school have a policy with respect to the age of applicants?

A [Lowrey]: There is no defined age or cut off age.

Q: Do you remember a discussion of age with respects [*sic*] to Mr. Bakke's application?

A: No.

Toward the end of the deposition, UCD attorney Donald Reidhaar followed up:

Q: Doctor Lowery [*sic*], I believe you also testified that you did not recall a discussion of age regarding Mr. Bakke's application, is that correct?

A: Yes, that is correct.
Q: Do you know whether age was considered as a factor in passing on his application in either 1973 or 1974?
A: As with all other information that is on the application, I am sure it was taken into consideration, yes.[15]

Despite Dr. Lowrey's wavering memory, the evidence suggests that Bakke's age was a negative factor at UCD as well as a disqualification at Northwestern and UC San Francisco.

Although the literature on medical schools of that era does not identify which ones had age-limit policies, some of the *Bakke* briefs argued that age limits worked against lower-income applicants who needed to work during and after college. One brief noted that in 1972 16.2 million white Americans and 10.2 million minority Americans had incomes falling below the federal poverty threshold, thus implying that a larger number of white students than minority students needed to earn income from work that in turn delayed college graduation and medical school application.[16] Another brief noted that in 1973 8.4 percent of white Americans and 29.6 percent of minority Americans fell below the poverty threshold, thus implying that a greater proportion of minority students than white ones needed income from work that delayed their progress.[17] The two data sets exemplified the malleability of facts. Although numbers indicated that more whites were poor and percentages indicated that poverty was more prevalent among minorities, both data sets failed to focus on the subsets of poor individuals who actually applied to medical schools.

Those of us who participated in 1970s campus activism remember that many professional and graduate programs used age limits to disqualify female applicants who took time off during and after college to carry out family duties.[18] Indeed, just one year after the *Bakke* decision, the Supreme Court ruled on *Cannon v. University of Chicago* (1979), a case brought by thirty-nine-year-old Geraldine Cannon, who challenged the thirty-year age limit at the University of Chicago Medical School and the thirty-five-year age limit at the Northwestern University Medical School (which had rejected Bakke). She claimed that the age limits, which disproportionally disqualified women, were "not valid predictors of success in medical schools or in medical practice."[19] After the trial court ruled against her, the case circled from the appeals court to the Supreme Court and back to the appeals court. The US justices were concerned with the technical question of whether, under Title IX, Cannon had a private right to sue or only the right to file a complaint with the Office of Civil Rights (OCR). Inexplicably, they ignored the problem of administrative paralysis. By 1972, the OCR was so inundated by discrimination complaints that it transferred thousands to the Equal Employment Opportunity Commission (EEOC); by 1974, the EEOC itself had backlogged 85,000 complaints (1,500 in higher education alone) and took an average of thirty-two months to resolve each one. Thus it is no surprise that Cannon, who filed an EEOC complaint in April 1975, still had received no response by May 1979 when the Supreme Court ruled against her or that Bakke, who received no EEOC response at all, decided to pursue litigation.[20]

We might be tempted to conclude that medical schools illegally discriminated when they imposed age limits or higher standards on older applicants, but at that time no statute illegalized age discrimination in higher education. The Age Discrimination in Employment Act of 1967 (ADEA) prohibited discrimination in employment but not in education and protected only those who were forty or older.[21] The Age Discrimination Act of 1975 (ADA), which mirrored the sweeping language of Title VI of the Civil Rights Act, stated that "no person in the United States shall, on the basis of age, be excluded from participation in, be denied the benefits of, or be subjected to discrimination under, any program or activity receiving Federal financial assistance."[22] Although the ADA applied to all federally funded programs and protected all ages, its implementation was delayed until 1979 because Congress required a preliminary study of its impact on federal laws.[23] Thus if Bakke had alleged what looks like age discrimination to us today, the complaint would have fallen outside the ambit of the law.

Procedural Irregularities

Several irregularities in the admissions process opened a space for other types of discrimination. According to Dr. Lowrey's written declaration, the school did not set a firm application deadline, instead reviewing applications as they arrived over the course of six months and mailing acceptance letters in batches:

> For the 1973 class acceptances were mailed monthly from December through May. For the 1974 class acceptances were sent in January, February, and March. Thus, many applicants are accepted before other applicants have applied and a late application which might have been accepted earlier may be rejected.[24]

As the rolling admissions proceeded, the committee raised its standards, thus discriminating in favor of early applicants who had less impressive qualifications than later ones and discriminating against later applicants who were expected to have more impressive qualifications than those receiving early offers.

As a second procedural irregularity, the committee reevaluated some applicants who belatedly submitted positive material such as a glowing letter from the college dean; in giving these applicants a new "rating somewhat higher than" the original one, it provided special treatment that was not enjoyed by applicants who did not know they could belatedly submit material.[25] To provide a nondiscriminatory review, the committee should have set a firm application deadline, used consistent standards to evaluate all applicants who met that deadline, and disregarded late additions to already evaluated files.

A third procedural irregularity allowed bias to creep into applicant evaluation. When Colvin deposed Dr. Lowrey, he asked, "How are the oral interviews organized?" The doctor replied, "There is no specific instruction given. Each individual [interviewer] has had some experience sitting in with a member of the faculty who has had many past interviews and . . . our students will do this four or five times before they begin the interviews themselves."[26] But interviewing entails a finely tuned skill-set; social-science students, for instance, are taught how to design structured and unstructured interviews, devise preliminary questions, respond with follow-up questions, and simultaneously juggle the tasks of managing the conversation, observing the body language, and recording the interview. Even highly trained interviewers never achieve complete uniformity because interviewee answers vary in length, content, language, and supra-linguistic features. Moreover, as we will see in *Bakke*, interviewer stereotypes and biases can contaminate the interviews.

Interview Contamination

Dr. West, who conducted Bakke's March 1973 interview, gave an enthusiastic report to the admissions committee:

> He is a pleasant, mature person, tall and strong and Teutonic in appearance (not surprising from his Minnesota background). A believer in personal health and fitness, he is careful about his diet and vices, runs every day and genuinely intends to improve on the actuarial statistics. . . . He seems completely unprepossessing; he was not dynamic or aggressive and articulated well in all areas except his response to my request that he express for me some of his reasons for changing from engineering to medicine. During that phase his conversation was more halting, more introspective. . . . On the grounds of motivation, academic record, potential promise, endorsement by persons capable of reasonable judgments, personal appearance and demeanor, maturity and probably contribution to balance in the class I believe that Mr. Bakke must be considered as a very desirable applicant to this medical school and I shall so recommend him.[27]

During the 1960s and 1970s, stereotyping was a common practice in the education and employment sectors. Not surprisingly, Dr. West paints Bakke as a strong, clean-living, nonaggressive, verbally fluent Teutonic man and interprets these traits indexically as signs that he is a "very desirable applicant." Gripped by the same stereotype, journalists and scholars who later commented on the case also described him as a well-built, fair-skinned, blond, blue-eyed man of Norwegian descent.[28] Although working for Bakke, stereotyping worked against female and African American candidates; white male decision-makers routinely interpreted their appearance, demeanor, and speech as signs that they were too deviant from gender and racial norms to succeed.[29]

Also troubling was Dr. Lowrey's aversion to Bakke's views on minority admissions program. After receiving his first rejection notice, Bakke wrote to the doctor on May 30, 1973, asking to be placed on the waitlist and to audit courses as a special student.[30] Receiving no reply, he wrote again on July 1:

> I am convinced that a significant fraction [of applicants] . . . is judged by a separate criterion. I am referring to quotas, open or covert, for racial minorities. . . . I realize that the rationale for these quotas is that they attempt to atone for past racial discrimination. But instituting a new racial bias, in favor of minorities is not a just solution. In fact, I believe that admissions quotas based on race are illegal. For this reason I am inquiring of friends . . . about the possibility of formally challenging these quotas through the courts. My main reason . . . would be to secure admission for myself—I consider the goal worth fighting for in every legal or ethical way.[31]

Bakke's fluent quota language indicates he had already learned about discrimination lawsuits and was using the threat of litigation to pressure the medical school into admitting him. Underestimating the danger, Dr. Lowrey asked Peter C. Storandt to respond to Bakke, a decision that set the stage for collusion between Storandt and Bakke (see below).

When Dr. Lowrey interviewed Bakke in the next application cycle, they inevitably clashed over minority admissions. No matter who initiated the discussion, Dr. Lowrey was at fault for not informing Bakke that the topic was irrelevant to the interview's purpose of ascertaining his potential for medical training and practice. Worse, he allowed his hostility to corrupt his report to admissions committee:

> I found Mr. Bakke to be rather limited in his approach to the solution of the difficulties in improving the delivery of medical care. Part of this was undoubtedly due to lack of information but the disturbing features of this was that he had very definite opinions which were based more on his personal viewpoints than upon a study of the whole problem. His opinion of the special selection of minority students is stated in one of his letters. He was very unsympathetic to the concept of recruiting minority

> students so that they hopefully would go back to practice in . . . presently neglected areas. . . . One of his main reasons . . . was that this decreased his own chances of getting into medical school. . . . It may well have been the interviewer's fault, but my own impression of Mr. Bakke is that he is a rather rigidly oriented young man who has the tendency to arrive at conclusions based more upon his personal impression than upon thoughtful processes using available sources of information. This may be a rather severe criticism but I certainly felt this way about him. . . . I would rate him acceptable but certainly not an outstanding candidate for our school.[32]

The report reveals that both men had tunnel vision in pursuing their objectives: Bakke, criticizing the minority program for decreasing his chance of acceptance, used the language of law to lever himself into medical school, while Lowrey, defending it for recruiting minorities who would practice in neglected communities, used the language of character to block Bakke's move. Both men formed hasty impressions based, respectively, on resentment of the school's minority program and resentment of Bakke's criticism of it.

In a reply memorandum submitted to the trial court, Colvin didn't mince his words:

> It becomes evident not only that Dr. Lowrey disagreed with plaintiff's position regarding special admissions, but also that the dispute over the program caused Dr. Lowrey to downgrade plaintiff during the interview. Dr. Lowrey in effect penalized plaintiff for challenging the University's Special Admissions Program. . . . The university, acting through Dr. Lowrey, cannot reasonably be allowed to downgrade plaintiff for opposing a discriminatory university policy, and yet, at the same time claim that because he was thus downgraded he could not have been accepted even if there were no Special Admissions Program.[33]

At that time, downgrading was commonly used to disqualify women in student admissions and faculty hiring; decades later, it was used by ideologically motivated peer reviewers to disqualify applicants for National Endowment for the Humanities research awards.[34] Dr. Lowrey's report, clearly skewed by his hostility toward a "troublemaker," lowered Bakke's benchmark score. Four committee members gave him 96, 94, 94, and 92 while Dr. Lowrey and the sixth member gave him 86 and 87 for a total of 549 out of 600 that would have been about 565 without the downgrading.[35] At oral argument, California Supreme Court Justice Stanley Mosk snapped, "In reviewing Dr. Lowrey's evaluation of Bakke, more than half . . . is about Bakke's views on minority admissions. What does that have to do with Mr. Bakke's potential ability to someday remove my appendix?"[36]

The Dean's Admissions

From the start, Colvin argued that the UCD admissions program functioned as a two-track, racial quota with sixteen of the one hundred places reserved for minority applicants and the other eighty-four places left over for non-minority applicants.[37] Reidhaar responded that the special program sought to diversify the medical school and profession by admitting economically and educationally disadvantaged applicants, that courts traditionally deferred to academic institutions on educational matters, and that Bakke would not have been admitted in the absence of the program.[38] Neither attorney accurately described the admissions scheme, which actually had multiple tracks. I have already identified four tracks: typical applicants had to be highly qualified but older ones had to be even more highly qualified, and early admittees had to rise above a benchmark cut-off score but later admittees had to rise above a higher cut-off score. Two more tracks came to light as Colvin deposed Dr. Lowrey:

> Q: I am curious. I really do not understand how the hundred were chosen. I understand, I think, how the 16 were chosen, but how were the other 83 or 84 chosen?
>
> A: For the most part, they were chosen on the basis of the [benchmark] rating.
>
> Q: Yes?

A: But there were exceptions to that.
Q: Those exceptions were made by the committee as a whole?
A: Some, yes, because of further information, a letter from a dean of the Applicant's undergraduate school would come through and be very strong and this would make that original rating somewhat higher than it had been. Other considerations were taken into account. If an individual was married to a member who had already been accepted and whose rating was quite high, but perhaps not quite high enough to be accepted on the basis of the rating alone, that individual would be accepted, providing they did not have the opportunity to go to another medical school.[39]

These "exceptions" were actually two more admissions tracks. On a fifth track, the committee reevaluated and reranked applicants who belatedly added positive material to their files, a process differentiating them from applicants who received only one review. On a sixth track, the committee made offers to somewhat less-qualified spouses of already accepted medical students that, on merit, would have gone to better qualified applicants. Breezing right by these "exceptions," Colvin avoided learning about yet another track

In July 1976, three months before the California Supreme Court ruled, *Los Angeles Times* reporter William Trombley revealed that UCD Medical School dean John C. Tupper had been accepting underqualified applicants who had wealthy or influential parents.

> In at least eight instances and possibly more the dean of the UC Davis medical school intervened to assure the admission of students who ordinarily would not be admitted or whose chances for admission were questionable. . . . "Frequently these cases involved the children of prominent Sacramento-area physicians and politicians," said Peter L. Storandt, a former assistant dean at the UC Davis school of medicine. . . . In one case Tupper admitted the son of a wealthy businessman who ranked below at least 90 other applicants and who did not meet the UC Davis minimum grade-point requirements in undergraduate science courses. On another occasion, Tupper changed a student evaluator's rating of an applicant

> from 90 to 97, to make sure the applicant was accepted. In a third instance the dean admitted the son of a VIP without requiring him to go through the normal admissions process. In most of the other cases Tupper disregarded recommendations of the school's student-faculty admissions committee and accepted students whose ranking ordinarily would not have earned them places in the school.[40]

Before Trombley exposed Dean Tupper's favors, which began as early as 1972 when Bakke first applied to UCD, George Sutherland, a UCD medical student, had written about them in articles for the fall 1974 and spring 1975 issues of the school newspaper. Moreover, the dean's favors were known at the school: Dr. Lowrey told Trombley that he had "complained to Tupper, without result," and Storandt acknowledged that he knew but "there was no way I could object and continue my employment." When confronted, Tupper told Trombley, "in the University of California, deans of professional schools have final authority over admissions,"[41] thus avoiding the question of whether deans should discriminate in favor of underqualified applicants from prominent families.

In a follow-up story published a week later in the *Los Angeles Times*, Trombley quoted high-ranking officials. William K. Coblentz, a San Francisco lawyer who served as chairman of the UC Board of Regents, said he would ask UC president David S. Saxon to conduct an investigation of all UC medical schools. President Saxon, who admitted reading about the dean's practice "with great interest and damned little pleasure," said, "For many, many reasons I really would be loath to interfere with that . . . but on the other hand we should not have procedures in which the same kind of general standards are not applied to everyone." A university spokesman said that UCD Chancellor James H. Meyer "plans no investigation of Tupper's actions because 'he still feels he doesn't have any evidence' that the dean violated guidelines set for deans of UC professional schools."[42]

When the US Supreme Court agreed to hear *Bakke* in October 1977, *Washington Post* reporter Lou Cannon revived the scandal. He wrote that Dean Tupper, who felt he had "the right to admit five of the 100 incoming students [each year] on his own authority," had admitted "the son and daughter-in-law of the chancellor at the Davis campus, Emil Mrak." Cannon requoted Mrak's earlier statement in the *Los Angeles Times* article: "The dean should have five or six students a year for the good of the university and the good of the community. If he can't do that, why the hell have a dean? You might as well put a secretary in there." Speaking to Cannon, the *Bakke* attorneys were dodgy. Reidhaar said he knew about the "preferential admissions policy favoring well-connected applicants," but these "practices have now been 'relegated to history' and were never raised in the legal history of the Bakke case." Colvin said, "One of the reasons they were not raised is that [I] didn't know of the existence of such policies until long after [my] involvement in the case," But Sutherland and Trombley broke the story while Colvin was defending his client in the California Supreme Court. Only George Sutherland, then a pediatric intern, candidly stated, "'It was the dean's program that kept Bakke out every bit as much as the minority program.'"[43]

THE ASSISTANT'S ASSIST

In 1973 when Dr. Lowrey assigned Bakke's complaint to Peter C. Storandt, a staff assistant in the medical school's Office of Student Affairs and Admissions, the two men developed a relationship that veered from cordiality into collusion. Three letters documenting the relationship were appended to a US Supreme Court brief submitted by the Urban League and sixteen other organizations, including the UCD Law School.[44] Storandt's July 18 letter, which begins with "Dear Allan" rather than the more appropriate "Dear Mr. Bakke," responds to his May 30 letter to Dr. Lowrey proposing that the medical school wait-list him and/or permit him to audit classes. As was proper for a staff member trying smooth ruffled feathers, Storandt commends Bakke on his qualifications (though going too far in revealing that he rated in "the top ten percent of our 2,500 applicants in the 1972–73 season") and states that the medical school had to reject "some remarkably able and well-qualified individuals, including, this year, yourself." Addressing Bakke's request to audit classes, he writes, "The regulations of the

University of California do not permit us to enroll students in the medical school on any other basis than full-time, however, so that even your suggestions for adjacent enrollment cannot be enacted." Then he turns to the age issue: "Your dilemma—our dilemma, really—seems in your mind to center on your present age and the possible detrimental influence this factor may have in our consideration of your application. I can only say that older applicants have successfully entered and worked in our curriculum and that your very considerable talents can and will override any questions of age in our final determinations."[45] He recommends that Bakke apply for early admission to UCD's medical school, thereby learning by October 1 whether the school will offer him a place or move his application to the regular pool to be vetted later.

But then Storandt inappropriately offers a research plan that would support Bakke's threatened litigation:

> you might consider taking my other suggestion which is then to pursue your research into admissions policies based on quota-oriented minority recruiting. The reason that I suggest this coordination of activities is that if our decision is to defer your application for admission, you may then ask AMCAS [American Medical College Application Service] to send it elsewhere as well. Your interest in admission thus would become more generalized and your investigation more pointed.[46]

In other words, by applying to other medical schools Bakke would maximize his chances of acceptance and by identifying schools with race-conscious admissions programs he would maximize his opportunities for litigation. The rest of the July 18 letter leaves no doubt that Storandt is pushing Bakke toward litigation. Urging him to research *DeFunis v. Odegaard*, which was brought by a law student "on the very grounds you outlined in your letter," he helpfully supplies a case summary, information on the medical school's evaluation of minority students, and the names of experts who could assist Bakke his research—Professor Robert Joling, an attorney specializing in medical law at the University of Arizona College of Medicine, and Martin S. Begun, associate dean at the New York University School of Medicine.[47]

In his August 7 reply, Bakke thanks Storandt "for taking time to meet with me last Friday afternoon. Our discussion was very helpful to me in considering possible courses of action. I appreciate your professional interest in the question of the moral and legal propriety of quotas and preferential admissions policies." On Friday, August 3, according to Joel Dreyfuss and Charles Lawrence, Bakke left Palo Alto around 4 p.m. and drove 100 miles to the Davis campus to meet with Storandt.

> They shook hands. Storandt offered Bakke a cup of coffee and tried to make small talk. Bakke brushed the chitchat aside and pressed Storandt for information about admissions procedures and the performance of minority students at the Davis Medical School. Storandt was reminded of a character out of a Bergman film, "somewhat humorless, perfectly straightforward, zealous in his approach; it was really striking; he was an extremely impressive man and I felt he deserved a straight answer."[48]

According to Dreyfuss and Lawrence, Storandt told Bakke that the special program had not accepted any disadvantaged whites and had filled its sixteen set-aside places with minority admittees who had lower grades and test scores than those of whites.

By the end of the meeting, "Bakke knew nearly as much as Storandt about the admissions procedures at Davis," but he did not know that the dean had admitted underqualified white applicants. Although "Storandt had learned about [the dean's admittees] soon after he came to Davis in 1972," he was more critical of the special program. According to Dreyfuss and Lawrence:

> Storandt had always been ambiguous about the Task Force that selected minority students for the medical school. He was bothered by the fact that no whites had been selected by the Task Force, although it professed to consider all disadvantaged applicants. He felt compromised because he had to answer questions from white applicants in ways he felt were not totally honest in order to cover up the faculty's failure to develop a well-thought-out and carefully articulated rationale for the program.[49]

As suggested by his concern for rejected white applicants and his litigation advice to Bakke, Storandt's moral compass pointed to the zone of whiteness.

Bakke's August 7 letter displays how much he had learned. Reminding Storandt that his "first concern is to be allowed to study medicine, and that challenging the concept of racial quotas is secondary," he adds, "the quota issue is unquestionably a more significant goal because of its direct impact on all applicants."[50] Then he outlines two litigation plans. According to Plan A, he would apply to UCD for early admission and, if accepted, would somehow "retain standing to sue Stanford and UCSF [University of California at San Francisco] in order to officially pose the legal questions involved." According to Plan B, he would apply to UCD for early admission and, before receiving an early decision in October, would confront Stanford in August or September, demanding "immediate admission as an alternative to a legal challenge of their admitted racial quota." If Stanford capitulated, then he would sue UCD and UCSF or, if also admitted to UCD, he would still sue UCSF.[51] After complimenting Storandt for being "so responsive, concerned, and helpful to me," he asks whether UCD would welcome litigation "as a means of clarifying the legal questions involved," whether minority students performed adequately, and whether any statistics were available. Tellingly, he provides his phone number should Storandt wish to talk and adds, "If you are in the Sunnyvale area and would like to visit us, Judy and I would be happy to have you."[52] This offer of a sociable visit suggests a budding friendship.

Storandt's August 15 reply is more professional in tone if not in substance. After complimenting Bakke for having "carefully arranged your thinking about this matter," Storandt provides more guidance. On Plan A, which calls for applying to UCD but not Stanford and UCSF, he notes that Bakke would not have standing to sue the latter universities. For that reason, he prefers Plan B "with the proviso that you press the suit—even if admitted—at the institution of your choice." To answer Bakke's questions about minority student performance, he suggests "researching these issues in the *Journal of Medical Education*, where an extensive bibliography has accumulated in the last few years," and adds this comment:

> At Davis, such students have not required "official" tutoring, although they and many of their classmates have organized an impressive series of study sessions during the year. A few of them—perhaps ten percent—have taken longer than four years to complete the M.D. degree (but not more than one year longer). Their performance on the first part of the National Board of Medical Examiners' test series has been mixed—half of the current third year class "minority" students failed to qualify as passing the first time they took the examination; all of our "minority" students have passed the appropriate levels of the test by the time of their graduation. Part two, based on the clinical years of a medical education, seems to pose no such problems for these students.

If nothing else, this passage demonstrates Storandt's ambivalence: he attempts to paint the minority students in a negative light but refrains from falsifying the facts. In closing, Storandt cautions Bakke, with unintended irony, about "the need for careful evaluation of these facts and opinions."[53] A few days later, on August 19, Bakke writes to Storandt, confirming that he will proceed with the modified Plan B. The two men continued to exchange letters in November and December 1973 although by then Bakke had reached out to others. In a December letter to Storandt, read by Allan P. Sindler but not appended to his book, Bakke writes, "'I have heard from Mr. DeFunis, and expect to receive some helpful information from him." Also, according to Sindler, Bakke had been referred to Reynold H. Colvin.[54]

In its January 1977 brief, the Urban League brief argued that Storandt's assistance to Bakke indicated that "the University's primary aim was to 'set the stage' for a judicial determination of the validity of its Task Force program."[55] In February, the *Los Angeles Times* featured Don Speich's carefully researched story about Storandt's collusion with Bakke. In June, the National Conference of Black Lawyers brief argued that the case did not meet Article III requirements: "This requirement of adversariness of necessity precludes the Court from entertaining a suit where there has been collusion between the parties."[56] As evidence, it summarized the Bakke-Storandt correspondence and Storandt's comment to Speich: "He candidly admitted that he had encouraged Bakke to begin the lawsuit and had acted out of concern that the program in question and others like it were not fair or constitutional."[57] But the brief inaccurately claimed that Storandt's actions constituted institutional collusion because Speich's article shows he acted on his own and only afterwards did UCD officials participate in a cover-up of the collusion. Storandt said he informed "[Dean] Tupper that this correspondence had occurred, and it looked like Bakke was going to bring a suit against the university. I wanted him to be aware of my role."[58] Dean Tupper replied that Storandt "'shouldn't worry' because he had acted in 'good faith,'" and Dr. Lowrey confided, "it was made clear to Storandt that nobody at the school would object if he chose to look for a job elsewhere."

Storandt told Speich, "If I had it to do all over again . . . there wouldn't be any letters from me. I might have talked to him on the phone (but would) have insisted that our conversations be off the record." Thus in retrospect Storandt regretted his actions not for being collusive but for being insufficiently clever. He also explained what prompted his actions:

> "I was quite struck with him. He was a very, very vigorous moralist. He was like a character out of a Bergman film . . . a Calvinist. He was very, very straight (and) he showed an unusual willingness to fight for a principle and to ferret out compromise and avoid it." If Bakke had been "somebody who was a wishy-washy twerp and had said 'I am going to sue you,' I would not have given him the time of day," Storandt said. But, he added Bakke wasn't like that, "he was so vigorous."[59]

The evidence suggests that Storandt had acted from mixed motives: his dislike of the special admissions program, his solicitude for rejected white applicants, and his attraction to Allan Bakke's Teutonic magnetism.

In this chapter, I have shown that many factors—the higher standards for older applicants, the higher bar for later applicants, the offers to less qualified spouses of already admitted students, the dean's offers to underqualified applicants with prominent parents, Dr. Lowrey's hostility to Bakke, and Storandt's collusion—vitiated the admissions process. In the next chapter, I will argue that the expedited trial distilled the facts of this complicated social situation into the relatively simple facts-for-adjudication that allowed Judge Manker to find an equal protection violation.

8

TEXTUALIZING *BAKKE*

In theory there is no difference between theory and practice. In practice there is.

—Attributed to Yogi Berra

In theory, legal-judicial discourse is ordered by a fact/law dualism propped up, like twin towers undergoing renovation, by a scaffolding of institutional structures, legal doctrines, precedents, rules of evidence and procedure, and textual conventions. Kim Lane Scheppele describes the institutionalized dualism:

> The division of labor between trial and appeals courts is also premised on a sharp distinction between law and fact. Answers to questions of fact are considered to be virtually fixed at trial, and only issues of law can be raised on appeal. Appeals courts, because they do not have the parties present and do not have an opportunity to hear all the evidence presented orally, are thought to be poorly situated to work out what happened and are supposed to limit their review to questions of law in which they have special expertise.[1]

In *Scientific Evidence and Equal Protection of the Law*, Angelo N. Ancheta explains that trial courts are "the first line of the judiciary in almost all constitutional cases; even if precedent-bound in addressing the legal issues, they must first engage in adjudicative fact-finding to establish the context and record for constitutional claims." This fact-finding

> is predicated on the assumption that the clash of interests and evidence that each party produces out of self-interest will result in an eventual "truth" and thus a correct and just resolution of the dispute. . . . The elaborate rules of procedure and evidence, including cross-examination, provide rigor to the adversarial process so that evidence presented by one side is not assumed to be right or true. But with this system of adversarial justice comes the potential for evidence and arguments to be prejudiced . . . [because] winning the case is the primary interest of parties and their advocates, not necessarily ensuring that the judge or the jury arrives at the correct "truth."[2]

In theory the adversarial principle—manifested while taking depositions, examining witnesses, and contesting written or physical evidence—will ensure the production of factual "truths" to which judges apply the law.

But what happens if the litigants have converging interests in obscuring some of the facts? What happens if parties with different interests are excluded from the discovery and trial? What happens if the litigants' attorneys and the judge use language that similarly constructs the facts and laws of the disputed social situation? These conditions, I will argue, enabled the plotting of *Bakke* as a narrow story about reverse discrimination against a white plaintiff.

PLOTTING THE CASE

Recall that Allan Bakke was rejected by the UCD Medical School in May 1973, collaborated with Peter Storandt on a litigation plan, and contacted Marco DeFunis, who provided copies of his case documents. One document, the Anti-Defamation League's amicus brief, cited *Anderson v. San Francisco Unified School District* (1972), a class action brought by white teachers to challenge the school district's use of race-conscious measures to retain minority administrators during a time of layoffs, a practice that the US District Court for Northern California found unconstitutional.[3] Counsel for the white teachers was Reynold

H. Colvin, a senior partner in a small San Francisco law firm, a former member of the city's board of education, and a former president of the local chapter of the American Jewish Committee. Apparently, he opposed affirmative action because he felt it discriminated against whites and "substitut[ed] group rights for individual rights."[4]

When they met in January or February 1974, Colvin advised Bakke to wait for the Supreme Court ruling on *DeFunis*; then on June 20, about two months after the nondecision, Colvin filed a complaint at the California Superior Court in Woodland, a small town in rural Yolo County north of Sacramento. According to Joel Dreyfuss and Charles Lawrence III, who interviewed several people associated with the case, he had two goals: "While the thrust of legal action would aim at getting the special admissions program declared illegal, the real objective was to get Bakke admitted in time to join the fall class."[5] Thus motivated to streamline the proceedings, he chose to represent Bakke alone rather than a class of white applicants and to select the rural court whose docket he thought would be less crowded than those of the San Francisco and Sacramento courts.[6] As it turned out, the Woodland court had a case backlog and asked retired Judge F. Leslie Manker to hear *Bakke*.[7]

UCD was represented by Donald L. Reidhaar, a graduate of the UC Berkeley Law School who had joined the UC Office of Counsel in 1962 and was promoted to general counsel in 1973. Described as a meticulous and self-effacing lawyer, he too had "expressed doubts about the constitutionality of racial preferences," warning the UC president in a May 1974 memorandum that the Fourteenth Amendment, Civil Rights Act, and executive agency regulations prohibited race-based preferences.[8] Receiving Colvin's complaint on the day it was filed, Reidhaar sent three of his staff lawyers to Davis, where they interviewed Dr. C. John Tupper (the medical school dean), Dr. George H. Lowrey (the admissions committee chair), Peter Storandt (a staff assistant), Drs. Lindy Kumagai and Sarah Gray (the former task force chairs), and a few others.[9] Some of the interviewees felt the lawyers were hostile to affirmative action or anticipated winning the case without much effort and noted they didn't follow up on references to Dean Tupper's admission of underqualified students.[10]

During the summer, the lawyers conducted a limited discovery: on

July 23, Colvin deposed Dr. Lowrey; on August 7, Bakke completed UCD's short written interrogatory; and on August 29, Reidhaar submitted Dr. Lowrey's written declaration, which clarified some of the information given at the deposition. Meanwhile the two lawyers submitted their own briefs to the trial court. Seeking an order to admit Bakke to the medical school, Colvin declared that his client was more qualified than the minority admittees and described the admissions program as a racial quota system. For his part, seeking a ruling that the medical school could consider race as one factor in admissions, Reidhaar emphasized that the training of minority doctors served important needs of the medical school and profession.

Feeling pressured by the impending fall term, Colvin initiated a private conversation with Reidhaar that was described by Dreyfuss and Lawrence:

> He met with Reidhaar to discuss the possibility of a faster and less costly resolution. "Look," he said to Reidhaar, "Allan Bakke belongs in medical school. He should have been admitted in the first place. There's a law of the universe that there is always room for one more, so why don't you find another cadaver for Mr. Bakke up there at Davis? He will go to medical school. There will be no more lawsuit, and since there are no other plaintiffs in this case, it will be over."[11]

Reidhaar rejected the offer in order to seek a ruling on the program's constitutionality, but who had directed him to do so? Later interviewing the regents, Dreyfuss and Lawrence learned that Reidhaar had briefed them on "the case at their July [1974] meeting, but several who attended the closed-door meeting do not recall any specific instructions to the general counsel."[12] Their memory loss probably resulted from a need to distance themselves from the exposés circulated by journalists and amici while the case was appealed (see chapter 7).

At a September 27 hearing on the motion to admit Bakke to the medical school, Colvin "told Reidhaar that he was willing to let the hearing serve as the trial in the case. This meant there would be no more discussion, no further testimony, and no further discovery or gathering of evidence." Although "surprised when Colvin made that offer," Reidhaar agreed.[13] Thus except for the lawyers' arguments at this short hearing, the trial was entirely textualized; the facts were provided only by their briefs, Dr. Lowrey's deposition and declaration, Bakke's cursory interrogatory, and admissions information supplied by the medical school. Excluded were facts that could have been provided by Tupper, Storandt, Kumagai, Gray, and expert witnesses; they could have testified to California's history of minorities in medical education and practice, the effects of the medical school's admissions criteria on minority applicants, and the status of healthcare in underserved minority communities.[14]

Since so much of the case focused on racial minorities—Colvin arguing that the special admissions program discriminated in their favor and Reidhaar that it remedied discrimination against them—the exclusion of their voices is particularly troubling. In a 1979 article aptly titled "The Case for Minority Participation in Reverse Discrimination Litigation," Edward Chen blasted Justice Powell for concluding that the record, which was clearly deficient, failed to prove that the medical school was remedying its own past discrimination. Although others lamented the deficient record, Chen was one of the few to analyze how reverse discrimination litigation suppressed minority interests:

> The cases demonstrate that the assumptions underlying the traditional adversary model of litigation are inapposite in the reverse discrimination context. The adversary system presupposes that two parties representing dramatically opposite interests will litigate all relevant facts and legal issues. But in reverse discrimination suits, there are three distinct sets of interests and viewpoints—those of (1) the plaintiff challenging the legality of the affirmative action program, (2) the defendant administering or enforcing the program, and (3) the program's beneficiaries.[15]

Chen further explains why two-party litigation would exclude evidence of prior discrimination against minorities. To avoid future litigation and protect their institutional authority from judicial intervention, universities would not invoke prior discrimination as a justification for their affirmative action programs; and to avoid weakening their claims, white plaintiffs would discount any evidence of discrimination introduced by other parties, such as amici. Chen contends that robust interest representation, which gives people a say in judicial decision making that affects them, protects not only the interests of minorities but also the integrity of the adjudicatory process.[16]

Not surprisingly, the universities in *DeFunis* and *Bakke* failed to introduce the gritty facts of education pipeline discrimination that disqualified many minority students for professional school application, of admissions criteria that disproportionately eliminated many who did apply, and of white privileges—such as superior education, economic resources, and parental influence—that warped the competition for places in an entering class. In both cases, the imposition of narrow time and action frames limited the facts to the fate of a single white man during two admissions cycles, thus displaying only the harms he allegedly experienced while obscuring the harms minorities experienced before the special admissions programs were implemented and would experience if they were discontinued.[17] *Bakke* raises an additional question: when Colvin and Reidhaar agreed to textualize the trial, they would have needed Judge Manker's consent because, according to several provisions in the 1965 California Evidence Code, courts decided questions about the admissibility of evidence.[18] By consenting to forego the trial, the judge enabled the attorneys to exclude not only minority interests but also what could have been operative facts in the case.

LOCATING THE FACTS

After filing his June 20 complaint, Colvin deposed Dr. George H. Lowrey on July 23; Reidhaar filed his response on July 31; Colvin submitted Bakke's interrogatory and his own memorandum on fact and law in August; and, at the end of August, Reidhaar provided Dr. Lowrey's written declaration and his own memorandum on fact and law. Rather than interpreting the documents as simple interest-inflected renderings of social events, I will analyze how the authors racialized their facts and claims, thereby locating them within or outside *Bakke*'s zone of "truth."[19]

Initial Filings

At barely three pages, Colvin's complaint asserted a cause of action—that is, a set of facts that depicted harm, relief, and standing to sue. In general, he narrowly framed his story: in 1973 and 1974, Bakke, who was fully qualified to attend medical school and made timely applications, was rejected solely on account of his race because the admissions committee, composed of minority members, conducted two separate review processes and filled a quota of sixteen special places with less-qualified minority students. Some of these facts were incorrect: Bakke's first application arrived belatedly, the committee had white as well as minority members, and it filled fifteen special places in both years. Another claim—that Bakke was more qualified than minority admittees—depended on the flawed presentation of admissions data originally furnished by the university (see below). Other claims misrepresented cause and effect. Colvin claimed, for instance, that the special program "invidiously discriminated against [the plaintiff] on account of his race" in violation of the equal protection clause, the state constitution, and the Civil Rights Act, but Bakke, who was not economically or educationally disadvantaged, was ineligible to apply for special admissions. He claimed that Bakke would "suffer substantial and irreparable harm" from UCD's rejections, but Bakke's plan to trade his successful career as a NASA scientist for medical training was thwarted by ten other schools, not only UCD, a fact entered into evidence. Finally, he claimed that "a bonafide and genuine dispute exists" between the parties "as to plaintiff's right to be admitted to said Medical School"[20]; however, no law or policy provided any applicant with a right to be admitted to a medical school.

In less than three pages, Reidhaar's First Amended Answer declared that Colvin's facts did not support a cause of action or justify relief. Varnishing his reply with elevated rhetoric, he claimed that the medical school "considered the minority group status of qualified applicants as a factor in filling a limited number of spaces in each year's first year class for the purpose of promoting diversity in the student body and the medical profession and expanding medical education opportunities for persons from economically or educationally disadvantaged backgrounds." He asserted that the "petitioner would not have been admitted . . . even if there had been no such special admissions program" and countered that using "minority group status as one factor in determining whether such applicants have disadvantaged backgrounds is consistent with the Equal Protection Clause," the California Constitution, and the Civil Rights Act.[21] But in his First Amended Cross-Complaint for Declaratory Relief, also filed on July 31, Reidhaar contradicted his anti-standing argument, writing that "an actual controversy . . . now exists between the University and Cross-Defendant relating to whether the special admissions program" violates these constitutional and statutory laws.[22]

Although skimpy, these documents showed that Colvin was better than Reidhaar at plotting the case. By dualizing the issues—the more qualified Bakke versus the less qualified minority admittees, the higher standards for regular applicants versus the lower ones for special applicants, and nondiscrimination laws versus discriminatory admissions practices—Colvin made them congruent with the two-party dispute format and the fact/law division that structured legal-judicial discourse. But by claiming that Bakke had a "right to be admitted to said Medical School," he ventured into uncertain territory. In *Brown v. Board of Education* (1954), Chief Justice Earl Warren, author of the unanimous opinion, clarified who had a right to what: "Today, education is perhaps the most important function of state and local governments. Compulsory school attendance laws and the great expenditures for education both demonstrate our recognition of the importance of education to our democratic society. . . . Such an opportunity, where the state has undertaken to provide it, is a right which must be made available to all on equal terms."[23] The right to education existed under specific conditions: if state law promised a free and equal public school education to all resident children and decreed compulsory school attendance, then this education was a right that had to be available on equal terms. As Jack Balkin explained in an article on *Brown*, "States can forego public education completely, but once they provide public education they have constitutional duties of fairness and equality under the Equal Protection Clause."[24]

What the *Brown* Court meant by education available "on equal terms" would be muddied in later cases. Some school cases suggest that the Court understood the phrase to denote integrated schools but not equal-quality schools. In *Green v. County School Board of New Kent County* (1968) and *Swann v. Charlotte-Mecklenburg Board of Education* (1971), the Court made it clear that a school district's choice plan, which allowed students to opt for different schools, did not excuse it from its constitutional obligation to integrate schools. But in *San Antonio Independent School District v. Rodriguez* (1973), which alleged that the Texas funding scheme had created educational inequalities among public schools located in property-poor and property-rich districts, Justice Lewis Powell (who would write the compromise opinion in *Bakke*) firmly rejected the plaintiffs' claim that the state was obliged to equalize school funding and quality. "It is not the province of this Court," he wrote, "to create substantive constitutional rights in the name of guaranteeing equal protection of the laws," adding that no right to education was "explicitly or implicitly guaranteed by the Constitution."[25] But since the Constitution could not have provided a right to public school education because public schools did not exist when the framers wrote it, how could Colvin claim that Bakke had a right to be admitted to the UCD Medical School? Obviously, he had to racialize the alleged wrongs and rights.

Racialized Language

In *Bakke*, the medical school had inadvertently adopted a racialized discourse. Dr. George Lowrey explained that the "1973 application forms were prepared by the Davis Campus and referred to 'disadvantaged' backgrounds; [the] 1974 forms were prepared by American Medical Colleges Admissions Service (AMCAS), a nationwide application processing service, and the form referred to 'minority group' applicants."[26] When engaging AMCAS, no doubt because it could more efficiently process the massive applicant pool, which grew from 2,500 in 1973 to 4,000 in 1974, perhaps school officials failed to scrutinize the application form or perhaps they asked to modify its racialized language but were told they could not.[27]

Whatever the reason, the result was that the school added the language of race to that of economic and educational disadvantage, a point Colvin exploited when deposing Dr. Lowrey:

> Q [Colvin]: Did all of those who indicated a minority ethnic identification under Question 13 or who answered Question 15 in the affirmative become applications which were referred to the Task Force? . . .
>
> A [Lowrey]: If we had a black student whose father was a physician and who had gone through four years of pre-med school with little difficulty and by this I mean consecutive years, he would not be considered a minority student as designated on the question here. He would not be considered a Task Force applicant.
>
> Q: He would have two qualifications, a minority student and educationally or economically disadvantaged?
>
> A: That is right.[28]

Although Lowrey's first answer indicated that the eligibility criterion was economic and/or educational disadvantage, Colvin asserted that it was based on both disadvantage and minority identity. This racialization enabled him to interrogate Lowrey on the mean scores of regular and special applicants in 1972–1973 and 1973–1974.[29] On discovering mean score disparities, he then parroted the *DeFunis* claim that the special admittees, who were minorities, were less qualified than the regular admittees, all of whom he incorrectly assumed to be non-minorities.

Colvin's claims became case facts because Reidhaar did not depose former task force chairs, Drs. Lindy Kumagai and Sarah Gray, who could have corrected the errors.[30] In a letter to the *Sacramento Bee* dated January 4, 1977, Dr. Gray wrote that the task force committee sought "highly motivated and promising students with backgrounds of educational deprivation" and, during the initial screening, transferred nondisadvantaged applicants to the regular admissions pool. It also found that minority applicants were more likely than white ones to meet the additional criterion of intending to practice medicine in poor minority communities. She explained,

> Although grades, test scores, and disadvantage factors are used in the initial screening of these applicants, the students who are finally selected for admission are chosen because they present the strongest evidence of a serious desire to eventually return to a disadvantaged area similar to that from which they came (mainly inner city ghetto, rural area, or Indian reservation) to provide health care. . . . With those criteria, it is not surprising that most of the students who have entered the program have come from racial minorities.[31]

By failing to examine the task force chairs, Colvin and Reidhaar obscured these facts, most crucially the requirements that special applicants of any race had to be economically and/or educationally disadvantaged and had to present strong evidence of intending to practice in underserved minority communities. Consequently, the higher courts were able to discount the amici facts showing that few white physicians actually served minority communities, instead of understanding that these facts supported the requirement on intended location of practice.

Separate and Segregated Admissions

Initially claiming that "racial minority and majority applicants went through separate segregated admission procedures,"[32] Colvin ramped up the rhetoric in his August 7 Memorandum of Points and Authorities:

> There is no question here but that Bakke's exclusion from the University of California Medical School at Davis was a result of a racial classification. Bakke was not permitted to compete for all the places in the entering class of the Medical School. He was excluded solely because of his race from a significant number of places which were set aside and reserved for other races. Had Bakke been a member of racial minority such exclusion would have been unconstitutional. For as the U.S. Supreme Court held in *Sweatt v. Painter*, the exclusion of a black applicant from a state university law school solely because of his race is a violation of the Equal Protection Clause. If the Constitution prohibits exclusion of balks [sic] and other minorities on racial grounds it cannot permit the exclusion of whites on racial grounds.

> For it must be the exclusion on racial grounds which offends the Constitution and not the particular skin color of the person excluded.[33]

Logic seems to carry the passage, but language does the heavy lifting. Using the epistemic modality in "There is no question here," the narrator directs readers to accept the veracity of his following statements, which take the declarative mood commonly used for expressions of fact. By placing Bakke in front of passive verbs—he "was not permitted" and "was excluded"—the statements foreground his alleged victimization; moreover, the repetition of "exclusion," "excluded," "racial," and "race" produce strong rhythmic and semantic effects that emphasize the race-based injury inflicted on him. All of the claims are counterfactual because, regardless of whether Bakke was a minority or white applicant, he could have applied for special admission only if he were economically and/or educationally disadvantaged, which he was not.

Furthermore, in citing *Sweatt v. Painter* (1950) as a precedent for *Bakke*, Colvin makes its factual contents disappear. Heman Sweatt, a Black applicant to the University of Texas (UT) Law School, was automatically rejected in a state that had de jure segregation. The state court delayed the lawsuit so that Texas could hastily establish a separate Black law school, which consisted of a tiny faculty and substandard facilities, a tactic scorned by the US Supreme Court when it held that the situation violated the equal protection clause and ordered Sweatt's admission to the UT Law School.[34] Colvin's analogy between *Sweatt* and *Bakke* attempts to make the two plaintiffs fungible by extracting them from the contexts in which de jure racism caused Sweatt's automatic rejection and the disadvantage criterion caused Bakke's ineligibility to compete for special admission. Only by hiding these social contexts can Colvin extract the *Sweatt* principle and apply it to *Bakke*.

Moreover, even the skimpy facts in evidence contradict Colvin's claim that the UCD Medical School maintained two separate admissions processes. The admissions committee, according to Dr. Lowrey's declaration, consisted of approximately fourteen to fifteen faculty members and the same number of student members, all chosen by the dean of the medical school. For the initial evaluation, subcommittees of the whole committee screened regular applicants and the task force subcommittee screened special applications to determine whether each applicant "showed sufficient promise to be invited for an interview."[35] Regular applicants were interviewed by one faculty member in 1972–1973 and separately by one faculty member and one student member in 1973–1974, while special applicants were interviewed jointly by a faculty member and two student members in both years. After reading files and interview reports, each subcommittee member rated each interviewee on a scale of 0–100; the regular subcommittees had five screeners in 1972–1973 and six in 1973–1974, while the task force subcommittee had six in both years. Then each subcommittee reported to the whole admissions committee, which in turn could accept its recommendations, reject them, or request further information. Although regular and special admissions differed in minor details concerning the number of subcommittee members and interviewers, Colvin's claim that the two processes "paralleled but never intersected" was factually incorrect because the power to admit, reject, and waitlist applicants was vested in the committee as a whole.[36]

Reidhaar must have realized that Colvin's reiteration of the phrase "separate, segregated admissions" put the university in a difficult position, because his August 30 Memorandum of Points and Authorities attempted to revise the story. First, he declared that the medical school goal was not to segregate the races but "to *encourage* integration of the races in the school and in the professions." Then he argued, "Where segregation results directly or indirectly from past or present racially motivated public policies the Constitution has been held to *require*" affirmative action to integrate the races; but "where there is racial imbalance not resulting from racially motivated public policies the courts have *permitted* the public agency to remedy that imbalance by giving preference to minorities."[37] Ironically, Reidhaar's memorandum, together with admittee data, revealed the school's de facto segregation before instituting the special program and used the unfortunate language of preferences that would be echoed by the courts.

Quota and Competition

Colvin argued that Bakke was the victim of a racial quota because he was excluded from applying for the sixteen special admissions places and thus could compete for only the remaining eighty-four places. This argument is counterfactual in several respects. As previously noted, Bakke did not meet the requirements of disadvantage or intended location of practice to apply to the special admissions program, which in turn filled only fifteen places in 1973 and 1974.[38] More significantly, none of the applicants was able to compete for all one hundred places. From this total, fifteen places were filled by special admittees, another five or six were filled by the dean's less-qualified admittees, and perhaps two more were filled by less-qualified spousal admittees, thus reducing the number of competitive places to seventy-seven or fewer. Recall also that the school expected higher qualifications from older than younger applicants and from later than earlier applicants, so older and later applicants would have had much slimmer chances at admission. In short, the number of places for which Bakke could compete was probably less than twenty because he failed to meet several criteria: younger age, prominent parents, previously admitted spouses, economic or educational disadvantage, and an expressed interest in practicing in underserved communities.

It is particularly disappointing that the trial record contained no information on the social construction of applicant merit. No one explained that privileged white students benefitted from high-quality K–12 schools, AP courses, expensive extracurricular activities, college test tutoring, admission to elite colleges, and the educational advantages they furnished. No one explained that upper- and middle-class white students benefitted from the MCAT's white-normed language and contents. No one explained that low-income students, disproportionately those of color, lacked the privileges that constructed individual merit.[39]

Data on Who Was Qualified

To argue that his client was more qualified than special admittees and some regular admittees, Colvin used the university's statistical table:

Table 8.1: Bakke Compared to Classes Entering in 1973 and 1974

	Science GPA	*Total GPA*	*MCAT Verbal*	*MCAT Quantitative*	*MCAT Science*	*MCAT General*
		Class Entering in Fall 1973				
Bakke	3.44	3.46	96	94	97	72
Regular admittees	3.51	3.49	81	76	83	69
Special admittees	2.62	2.88	46	24	35	33
		Class Entering in Fall 1974				
Bakke	3.44	3.46	96	94	97	72
Regular admittees	3.36	3.29	69	67	82	72
Special admittees	2.42	2.62	34	30	37	18

Note: The table initially appeared in Reynold H. Colvin and Robert D. Links, Brief for Respondent in Opposition (filed 6 January 1977), in Slocum, vol. 1, 11; it reappeared in Justice Powell's opinion, *Regents of the University of California v. Bakke* 438 U.U. 265 (1978): 277–278, footnote 7. The note indicates that the data come from case records 210, 223, 231, and 234, presumably furnished by the UC Davis medical school. Yet the data in the Colvin and Powell tables are not entirely identical: for Bakke's Science GPA, Colvin listed 3.45 and Powell listed 3.44; for the overall GPA, Colvin listed 3.51 and Powell listed 3.46. I have duplicated Justice Powell's data and have replaced table abbreviations with words.

The table shows that Bakke's individual numbers were higher than the regular admittee mean numbers with three exceptions: his 1973 total GPA was lower than the mean (3.46 to 3.49), his 1973 science GPA was lower than the mean (3.43 to 3.51), and his 1974 MCAT general score was the same as the mean (72 to 72). For all categories, his individual scores were higher than the special admittee mean scores.

As evidence, this table comparing Bakke's individual scores to group mean scores is deeply flawed. Since it does not show within-group distributions, we do not know how many individuals in each group scored above or below Bakke and by how much. To use the 1973 total GPA as an example, Bakke's individual GPA was 3.46, the regular admittee mean was 3.49, and the special admittee mean was 2.88. We know from other evidence that the dean's admittees and spousal admittees had lower GPAs and that special admittees had individual GPAs ranging from 2.11 to 3.76.[40] Thus lacking within-group distributions, we do not know how many regular and special admittees had GPAs above, approximating, or below Bakke's GPA and whether those with lower GPAs had comparable MCAT scores and more impressive qualitative criteria. We do not know why most of the regular admittee mean scores and some of the special admittee scores were lower in 1974 than in 1973. Nor do we know how the MCAT, which was normed to dominant-culture education, impacted disadvantaged applicants of any race. In short, the table does not show that Bakke was more qualified than others, but Judge Manker and later Justice Powell accepted it at face value.[41]

Standing

Colvin argued that but for the sixteen special admissions places (actually fifteen places) Bakke would have been admitted to the medical school and thus had standing to bring this lawsuit. Predictably countering that he would not have been admitted even if the special places did not exist, Reidhaar provided several facts. When Bakke applied belatedly for 1973 entering class with a benchmark score of 468, fifteen applicants with a 469 score were ahead of him, but no one below 470 received offers; when he applied for the 1974 class with a benchmark score of 549, twenty applicants with higher scores and twelve with the same score did not receive offers.[42] Since the numbers suggest that Bakke would not have been among the fifteen regular applicants receiving offers in the absence of the special places, Reidhaar declared that he did not have standing to challenge the program. Both standing arguments are questionable.

Recall that Colvin had asked the court to order Bakke's admission (mandatory relief), enjoin the medical school from continuing special admissions (injunctive relief), and declare the admissions scheme to be unlawful (declaratory relief). Reidhaar countered that the court could grant relief only if a "trial on the merits" proved the plaintiff's standing and harm; the only harm, he added, was that Bakke would have to wait for one year to reapply to medical school: "The University urges, in view of the lack of irreparable injury to Plaintiff and the complex, sensitive and important nature of the matters at issue that this discretion [the court's discretion to enjoin] not be exercised here so that those issues will receive a full airing at the trial on whether a permanent injunction should be granted."[43] Yet within days of arguing for "a full airing at the trial," Reidhaar agreed to forego the trial. His position was blatantly contradictory: no harm because the thirty-four-year-old plaintiff (already disadvantaged by his age) could reapply and no relief unless warranted by a full trial, which he then agreed to forego.

THE JUDGE'S STORY

Judge Manker was not deterred by the underdeveloped factual record. On November 11, 1974, he circulated a twenty-six-page Notice of Intended Decision, and on March 6, 1975, he issued a three-page Addendum to Notice of Intended Decision, a six-page Findings of Fact and Conclusions of Law, and two-page Judgment. He concluded that the task force program, by setting a quota that favored minority applicants, violated constitutional and statutory laws; that the "unfair and arbitrary admissions procedure" warranted judicial intervention; and that Bakke was "entitled to have his application considered without regard to his race or the race of any other applicants." But he withheld the requested order of admission, concluding that the evidence did not show Bakke would have been admitted in the absence of special admissions.[44] Through a linguistic analysis of the Notice of Intended Decision, we will see how he constructed the facts to support this ruling.

Speech act theory differentiates between constative utterances, which describe something in the natural or social world, and performative utterances, which create something in the social world.[45] A speaker's statement, "Yesterday John wed Jean," is a constative utterance that could be factually true if the wedding occurred or untrue if it was cancelled. A priest's statement to John and Jean, "I pronounce you man and wife," is a performative utterance that creates their marriage. In "How Performatives Work," John R. Searle identifies further distinctions among performatives. The utterance "I promise to visit you on Wednesday" is a performative that creates a linguistic fact (a promise), but whether it creates a social fact (a visit) depends upon whether the speaker actually does visit on Wednesday. Similarly, the committee chair's utterance "I adjourn the meeting" is a performative that creates a social fact if the members obediently disperse, but creates only a linguistic fact if the members buck the chair to vote on agenda items.[46] The marriage and meeting examples suggest that the ability to create certain social facts rests on the speaker's institutional authority and the nature of the social context. Although judges have broader authority than priests and stronger authority than committee chairs, their pronouncements do not always transform linguistic facts into social facts, as was illustrated by the massive resistance to *Brown*'s school desegregation mandate.

Legal-judicial discourse is full of performatives that create social facts: the utterances "I order the defendant into custody" and "We remand to the court below for a new trial" result in the social activities of detaining a person and retrying a case. What gives these performatives a social effect, as Searle explains for similar commands, is they are uttered by a speaker who occupies the requisite position of authority over other actors within the judicial apparatus and according to the discursive rules.[47] Pintip Hompluem Dunn notes that some judicial performatives use actor-action syntax, as in "I order" or "We remand," while others use agentless-passive syntax, as in "It is ordered" and "It is remanded." Both syntactical forms create the social acts to which the words refer because the utterances meet the conditions just explained, but the agentless-passive syntax performs another function. By using the grammatical structure of constatives—namely, the existential verb "is" to present a factual proposition ("The grass is green")—the agentless-passive utterance "suggests that the judges are mere observers of the law, just as a person can be a mere observer of the characteristics of grass."[48]

The judge-as-observer syntax reveals that the authority to create facts lies not with the judge as a person but with the rule-bound discourse that his professional persona inhabits. Just so, the linguistic and genre conventions of legal texts can also create social facts. The phrase "Findings of Fact," when used as a section title in a court opinion, is performative in two senses: it bestows factuality on the section's depictions of social circumstances, and it gives these facts an operational value because they (are supposed to) ground the opinion's conclusions of law. Applying this analysis to Judge Manker's Notice of Intended Decision, I will show that he seems to follow the conventional method of selecting from among all the facts alleged in case documents those he regards as the operative facts grounding his legal conclusions.

After a short introduction, Judge Manker devotes five pages to nearly verbatim summaries of the lawyers' claims. He repeats Colvin's claims that the medical school used "separate, segregated admission procedures with separate standards for admission," accepted "less qualified" minority applicants, maintained a minority "quota of 16%," and denied Bakke admission solely "on account of his race," thus causing him irreparable harm. Then he repeats Reidhaar's claims that the admissions committee considered race as one of several factors; that its purpose was to promote diversity in the medical school and profession; and that it would not have accepted Bakke in the absence of the special places. Although Bakke was not entitled to court-ordered admission, Reidhaar claimed, the parties had a genuine dispute over the constitutionality of the admissions scheme.[49] Judge Manker's close summary gives the impression that he performed a meticulous review, but his conclusions suggests otherwise.

He begins, "First, the Court is of the view that plaintiff's complaint states a cause of action."[50] If taken as a constative, the sentence is a literally correct description of Colvin's text, which does make statements about the cause of action. But the introductory phrase, "the Court is of the view," casts the statement in the epistemic modality and signals its performative effect. The statement tells us that the judge, denoted by the ritual metonym of "the Court," views the complaint as providing facts that give the plaintiff the right to pursue litigation against the defendant. In particular, the judge implies that the complaint's facts delineate a social situation in which the defendant caused material, social, and/or symbolic harm to the plaintiff who thus qualifies for relief. But so far, Judge Manker has only summarized the claims made by the two lawyers. How does he select and slant just those facts that fit his legal analysis?

First, he rejects the university's counterclaim: "the Court will consider defendants' contention that plaintiff has no standing to bring this action, in which the Court finds no merit."

> The allegations of the complaint herein show a clear and important interest in the plaintiff in the subject matter and outcome of the litigation. He even alleged that but for the complained of special admissions program he would have been admitted to the medical school as a student. Whether this allegation has been sustained by the evidence will be discussed later. But clearly plaintiff has alleged his right to bring this action.[51]

Here Judge Manker identifies two bases for Bakke's standing—his interest in the lawsuit's subject matter and outcome, and his allegation that but for the special program he would have been admitted to medical school in the absence of the special program. Whether the evidence supports this allegation the judge defers to a later discussion.

Later in the Notice, after he has adopted Colvin's characterization of the special admissions program, Judge Manker returns to standing:

> Having found . . . that this special program is racially discriminatory the question might be asked whether the plaintiff is in a position to object thereto in view of the fact that he did not apply to this special program as a disadvantaged student. The Court feels that a white student who had applied for the special program and been refused purely on the basis of his race would have been in a much stronger position to question this practice than the plaintiff.[52]

This passage makes three points: it encapsulates Colvin's claim that the special program is racially discriminatory, implicitly recognizes that disadvantage is an eligibility requirement, and hypothesizes that a disadvantaged white student who was refused admission on the basis of his race would be in a stronger position to challenge it than Bakke was. The circular reasoning begins and ends with the not fully articulated assumption that the program discriminated by refusing to admit white students on the basis of their race. Recall, however, that applicants of any race had to meet the program's eligibility criteria of economic and/or educational disadvantage and intended practice in low-income minority communities.

Since Bakke did not meet these criteria, Judge Manker has to construct what he regards as the factual basis of his standing to sue:

> Nevertheless, the use of this special admissions program did substantially reduce plaintiff's chances of successful admission to the medical school for the reason that 16 places in the class of 100 were set aside for this special program; the plaintiff was in fact competing for one place not in a class of 100 but in a class of 84 which reduced his chances of admission by 16 percent. Whether the plaintiff would have actually been admitted in either of the two years absent this program will be discussed later in this memo.[53]

As previously indicated the facts are incorrect, because each year the total number of competitive places was reduced not only by fifteen places for special admittees but by places given to less-qualified spousal and dean admittees. Moreover, simply stating the number of noncompetitive places is not the same as proving they caused or contributed to Bakke's rejection. In a multivariable situation that also included age bias, interviewer's animus, his MCAT scores, his engineering background, and his belated premed courses, who is to say which ones weighed heavily in the rejection? Perhaps to avoid complexity, Judge Manker again postpones a discussion of whether he would have been admitted in the absence of the special program.

Some fifteen pages later, he finally addresses the matter: "With reference to plaintiff's contention that he would have been admitted to the medical School had it not been for the special admissions program, the Court finds that this contention has not been supported by the evidence."[54] First he quotes Dr. Lowrey, who claimed that Bakke's application was strong enough to warrant an interview but not strong enough to earn an offer even without the special program. Then he undercuts the claim: "Dr. Lowrey seems to indicate that the plaintiff would not have been admitted yet there appears to the Court to be at least a possibility that he might have been admitted absent the 16 favored positions on behalf of minorities."[55] By using the phrase "seems to indicate" and ignoring university data on the number of rejected applicants who ranked ahead of Bakke in both years, Judge Manker creates the "possibility that he might have been admitted." This "possibility" is a linguistic fact masquerading as a social fact.[56] Since his *belief* that a "possibility" might have existed is not evidence that the possibility actually did exist, let alone concrete evidence that Bakke would have been admitted but for special admissions, Judge Manker has to create more facts.

After quoting from case documents that described the program's use of multiple admissions criteria, he observes:

> It is interesting to note that in the years . . . in which plaintiff applied for admission, no white person applying for consideration as a disadvantaged applicant was accepted. Furthermore, it is interesting . . . that since the program was instituted in the year 1969 not a single white person has been admitted under this so-called disadvantaged program. It seems to the Court that this program must be judged upon the basis of how it is carried out not by what defendants may claim it to be. The University announcement of the program does not indicate that it is limited to minority groups and in fact counsel for the defendant in his oral argument and in his brief has insisted that it is not exclusively a minority program but that it is one in which minority status is simply considered as one factor in determining a disadvantaged status.[57]

Here again the judge uses the epistemic modality ("it is interesting," "it appears") and the metonymic "the Court" to lend veracity to his precipitous slide from the program's nonracial criteria as stated in case documents to the racialized outcome of admitting no white applicants. Although the record lacked information on why the program did not admit white applicants (see below), Judge Manker states his legal conclusion:

> Based on the evidence in this case the Court finds that this special program of admissions . . . is in fact a program open to and available only to members of racial minority groups and that it excludes

> consideration of applicants who are members of the white race. It appears to this Court that it logically follows that such program discriminates in favor of minority racial groups and against the white race.[58] It would appear to the Court that the evidence in this case does establish that the medical school had in fact established quotas for this so-called special program and carried that out in their admissions practices.[59]

Here the text uses the epistemic "it appears" and metonymic "the Court" to slide from racialized admittees to the characterization of the program as a discriminatory quota scheme.

Despite the tactics for communicating veracity, the five passages quoted above contain distortions of facts about the social situation they purport to represent. Factually, the record shows the number of whites who applied for special admissions—six for the fall 1971 class, twenty-one for the fall 1972 class, and seventy-three for the fall 1973 class.[60] It also shows that the task force chair reviewed all special applicants, both white and minority, to determine if they were truly disadvantaged and transferred nondisadvantaged ones to the regular admissions pool. But the record does not indicate how many of the one hundred white applicants failed to meet the eligibility requirements (disadvantage and intended location of practice) and were transferred to the regular pool or how many remained in the special pool but failed to meet other criteria. Without these facts, one cannot conclude that the special program discriminated against white applicants.

Although the fourth passage asserts "Based on the evidence in this case the Court finds," the judge creates linguistic facts that do not refer to evidence or the lack thereof. In the first and second passages, "it is interesting" introduces his statements that the special program admitted no whites. In the third one, "it seems" introduces his inference that the program must be judged on its effect. In the fourth and fifth passages, "it appears" and "it would appear" introduce his conclusions that the special program discriminated for minority applicants and against white applicants through a quota favoring the former. Each of these prefatory clauses conveys the writer's attitude toward the veracity of the information that follows. That something seems to have occurred to the writer is not evidence that it actually occurred. In other words, he has created linguistic facts that reside in his text but do not refer to facts residing in other texts that represent the disputed social actions. Of course those texts, as I have shown, selected and slanted their facts.

The previous chapter and this one examined the construction of the *Bakke* story that went forward on appeal. By truncating the discovery, the lawyers barred information that should have entered the proceedings. By relinquishing the adversarial method of witness examination, which at least promised to test the alleged facts, they textualized the case. By freeing language to do its work, they made ungrounded claims about social activities. By selecting the claims that fit his legal conclusions and embedding them in an epistemic discourse of "seeming" and "appearing," the judge constructed the illusion of judicial "truth." In theory, as Yogi Berra said, there should have been no difference between theory and practice; in practice, there was.

9

THE DISAPPEARANCE OF RACISM

> Simply because you do not have evidence that something exists does not mean that you have evidence that it doesn't exist.
>
> —Donald Rumsfeld, NATO Press Conference, 6 June 2002

Soon after the Yolo County trial court issued its ruling in *Bakke*, counsel for both parties decided to appeal—Donald Reidhaar hoping to gain a reversal of the holding that the medical school admissions program was unconstitutional and Reynold Colvin seeking an order to admit Bakke to the school. In May 1975, Reidhaar petitioned for a transfer from the state appeals court to the California Supreme Court on grounds that a case of such importance should not get bogged down in multiple litigations.[1] Agreeing to hear it, the high court received briefs from nine amici curiae along with briefs from Reidhaar, John F. Lindberg, and Gary Morrison (hereafter Reidhaar) representing the university and Colvin and Robert D. Links (hereafter Colvin) representing Bakke.[2] The court held oral argument on March 18, 1976, and released two opinions on September 16: Stanley Mosk's six-justice opinion found against UCD on virtually all matters, and Matthew O. Tobriner vigorously dissented.

For emphasis, Justice Mosk placed the holding at the beginning of the opinion: "We conclude that the program, as administered by the University, violates the constitutional rights of nonminority applicants because it affords preference on the basis of race to persons who, by the University's own standards, are not as qualified for the study of medicine as nonminority applicants denied admission."[3] Applying strict scrutiny, he noted that it required the university to prove that "the special admissions program is necessary to serve a compelling governmental interest and that the objective of the program cannot reasonably be achieved by some means which would impose a lesser burden on the rights of the majority."[4] He acknowledged that the medical school's objectives of integrating the student body and improving minority healthcare "meet the exacting standards required to uphold the validity of a racial classification. Nevertheless, we are not convinced that the University has met its burden of demonstrating that the basic goals of the program cannot be substantially achieved by means less detrimental to the rights of the majority."[5]

In a full-throated dissent, Justice Tobriner chastised his colleagues for misconstruing facts, precedents, and doctrines.[6] By attributing to the Grade Point Average (GPA) and the Medical College Admissions Test (MCAT) a predictive accuracy they did not have, they assumed that the special admittees were less qualified than the regular ones. By misinterpreting precedents, they failed to differentiate invidious racial classifications that excluded minorities from benign ones that aimed to integrate them. The majority, he wrote, had inverted equal protection doctrine: "It is anomalous that the Fourteenth Amendment that served as the basis for the requirement that elementary and secondary schools could be *compelled* to integrate, should now be turned around to *forbid* graduate schools from voluntarily seeking that very objective."[7]

In chapter 7, I recounted many social circumstances that were omitted from or misrepresented in the official story. In chapter 8, I examined how the truncated discovery, waived trial, and language techniques excluded not only the nonracial types of discrimination against Bakke but also the interests of current and future minority applicants. Here, I continue my investigation of reverse-discrimination discourse to show how it modulated during the appellate phase. But this investigation does not follow the well-worn path traveled by mainstream scholars who have made high-level arguments about equal protection as a concept enshrined in the Constitution, canonized by opinions in landmark cases, and debated by dueling factions.[8]

Instead, I am interested in how the participants in the appeal dematerialized equal protection so that it could not produce justice in the social world. By "dematerialized," I refer to the techniques of language and logic that enabled them to evacuate facts, misconstrue precedents, and extract principles. The process of draining representations of social circumstances from their narratives shifted the juridical ontology from an inquiry into what allegedly did happen in the social realm to what should happen in the conceptual realm.[9]

FACTS

In a 2012 article, Jeffrey C. Dobbins explores what happens to new evidence "that was not presented to the trial court but is presented to the appellate court." The willingness of appellate courts to entertain new evidence, particularly when offered by amici, is constrained by the record principle. This principle obliges the parties "to submit their cases in full in the trial court," the trial court to make a "determination of facts," and the appellate court to confine itself to adjudicating "contentions that were initially made in the trial court."[10] Quoting from *Black's Law Dictionary*, Dobbins defines new evidence as "something (including testimony, documents and tangible objects) that tends to prove or disprove the existence of an alleged fact" and defines facts as "something that actually exists, an aspect of reality." Although the dictionary's definition reiterates the formalist assumption that facts are real-world events that exist independently of the language that constructs them as such, Dobbins acknowledges that appellate courts encounter not "raw facts" but textually delineated facts. He notes that amicus briefs, which typically delineate historical, social, and statistical facts, are "a particularly significant source of new evidence on appeal."[11]

Scholars view such fact-laden briefs as a genre originating from Louis Brandeis's appellate brief in *Muller v. Oregon* (1908), which challenged a policy requiring shorter working hours for female employees than male ones. Brandeis famously devoted nearly one hundred pages of his brief to a review of studies purportedly showing that long working hours harmed women; even though the parties did not cite these studies at trial and social scientists disputed some of their findings, the Court felt that the information helped it understand the case. Thus, Dobbins writes, "Brandeis's success in *Muller* guaranteed that his extra-record, science-laden brief . . . would be modeled in a number of subsequent cases."[12] Yet the pro-minority fact-laden briefs gained no traction in Justice Mosk's *Bakke* opinion. In what follows, I summarize the new evidence provided by several amicus briefs and then show how Justice Mosk dismissed most of it.

New Evidence on Medical School Admissions

In documenting the history of minority exclusion from medical education, the pro-minority amici began with Howard University and Meharry Medical College, founded after the Civil War to provide postsecondary education to African Americans and for nearly a century the only institutions training Black physicians. Not until 1943 did a white institution, Rush Medical College in Chicago, graduate a Black physician, and as late as 1964 eighteen of the nation's eighty-five medical schools enrolled no Black students. In 1969–1970, when Black students were 2.39 percent of medical students nationwide, Howard and Meharry enrolled 1.46 percent, while all mainstream schools enrolled only 0.93 percent.[13] That same year, medical schools nationwide enrolled only ninety-two Mexican Americans (0.0025 percent of all thirty-seven thousand students), and in 1974–1975 they enrolled 638 Mexican Americans (1.2 percent of all students).[14] Also in 1974–1975, they enrolled perhaps eighteen Native Americans, a guesstimate because no one was tracking their numbers in medical education and practice.[15] The UCD medical school manifested this exclusionary pattern. From 1968 to 1970, it enrolled two Blacks, one Chicano, and no Native Americans out of 200 students. From 1971 to 1974, the special program accepted twenty-six of the total twenty-seven Blacks who were enrolled, thirty-three of the thirty-nine Chicanos, and the sole Native American student.[16]

While the amici attributed the exclusionary patterns to the

well-documented racial discrimination that occurred in the education pipeline leading to medical school application, the Association of American Medical Colleges (AAMC) also described the continuation of white dominance during the era of medical school expansion. Between 1959 and 1974, when applications rose from 14,952 to 42,340, first-year places increased modestly from 8,173 to 14,763, yielding a drop in the admissions rate from 55 percent to 35 percent.[17] Under pressure to diversify the student body, medical schools tempered their reliance on GPA and MCAT scores by adding qualitative criteria, but studies showed that it primarily benefitted white male applicants. In 1974, 28,179 white men applied to medical schools nationwide. While 6,732 of these white men had GPAs above 3.30 and MCAT science scores above 600, 1,784 were rejected and 4,313 lower-scoring white men were admitted.[18] In 1975, when 108 of the nation's 121 medical schools had implemented race-conscious admissions programs, white (predominantly male) applicants received 84.2 percent of the offers and filled 82.3 percent of places.[19]

New Evidence on the GPA and MCAT

At trial and on appeal, Colvin insisted that Bakke's GPA and MCAT scores objectively proved that he was more qualified for medical school than minority students admitted by the task force program.[20] Instead of discussing these devices, Reidhaar attributed the "gross under-representation of minorities" at medical schools to "the effects of past societal discrimination," demurring that "although the University of California has never had a policy of racial discrimination, it is well recognized that such discrimination is . . . 'an evil . . . which in varying degrees manifests itself in every part of the country.'"[21]

The pro-minority amici, following the path laid out by those in *DeFunis*, provided a robust critique of the GPA and MCAT as racially discriminatory devices. The National Lawyers Guild (NLG) contended that they reflected racial inequalities in lower-level education: for example, the lack of science and math courses at minority schools and the steering of minority students away from these courses at integrated schools disqualified some for college and prevented others from succeeding in premedical college studies.[22] The Mexican American Legal Defense and Education Fund (MALDEF) cited more than a half-dozen law cases and three state-level reports finding that Hispanic students in California, Texas, and Colorado attended segregated schools that failed to provide adequate instruction; for example, only 12,000 of the nearly 800,000 Chicano students in California received bilingual instruction in 1972–1972. The courts in California and elsewhere must have known about language barriers to public school education because the US Supreme Court, in ruling on *Lau v. Nichols* (1974), found that the San Francisco school district, by providing only English instruction to eighteen-hundred Chinese-speaking students, denied them meaningful access to education.[23]

Summarizing the findings of a University of California report, MALDEF clearly delineated the carry-forward effects of discrimination in the education pipeline:

> Discrimination against minority students at the primary and secondary levels continues and is perpetuated by discrimination at the college and post-graduate levels. . . . The cumulative educational deficit created by the state's failure to afford Chicano students with equal educational opportunity bars these students from successful entry into the University system. Rather, traditional examinations and other entry criteria—criteria which themselves have never been validated by reliable predictive indices for minorities—effectively complete the discrimination circuit of minority students' education by shutting them out of higher education entirely.[24]

The NLG similarly observed that the carry-forward effects worked with entrance tests to cause "the 'exit from flow' of potential minority physicians from high school through medical school."[25] The amici's "circuit" and "flow" metaphors illustrate the filtering dynamic: the state's failure to provide minority students with adequate schooling created cumulative disadvantages along the way to high-school graduation, and the use of entrance tests reflecting the education they were denied barred them from college and medical school.

The pro-minority amici cited numerous studies showing that the

GPA and the MCAT (which had barely changed since its adoption in the 1940s) were invalid devices for measuring test-takers' current abilities and future performance. The AAMC summarized the findings: "(1) studies show no correlation between grades and test scores and subsequent academic performance for blacks, (2) if traditional 'predictors' are used, optimum validity is achieved by separate equations or 'cut-off' scores for each race/sex subgroup and (3) certain background, interests, attitudes, and motivations are useful in predicting the success of minority students but not of white students."[26] The American Medical Students Association (AMSA) also noted, "A compilation of the social science literature . . . indicates that [the] MCAT (1) is culturally biased against rural and minority Americans; (2) has content unrelated to the specific study of medicine; (3) is unrelated to success in either medical school or medical practice; and (4) is an unjustified expense to the poor applicant."[27]

AMSA bluntly denounced the trial lawyers and judge for omitting evidence on the GPA and LSAT as devices that produced discriminatory effects:

> Underpinning the logic of the court's opinion below is the assumption that prior to the institution of its special admissions program, Davis Medical School was operating a "neutral" admissions system which depended wholly on the individual applicant's "merit." Understandably, Mr. Bakke sincerely shares this assumption and, of course, counsel for the Medical School had little incentive to challenge it since to do so would be to admit the existence of the prior discrimination. Therefore, the record below is rather scanty on what Amicus believes to be the crucial issue in this case: whether or not Davis had been operating a discriminatory admissions program which it was required to correct.[28]

AMSA claimed that UCD's own admission data revealed the GPA and MCAT's discriminatory effect: in 1968, the medical school admitted no Blacks or Chicanos; in 1969, the new special admissions program admitted two Blacks and one Chicano; and from 1970 to 1974, the program admitted a total of thirty-three Chicanos, twenty-six Blacks, and one Native American. Concluding that the school had no choice but "to take affirmative action to remedy the de facto segregation," AMSA cited prior cases upholding race-conscious remedies.[29]

New Evidence on Minority Healthcare

To document another effect of minority exclusion from medical training, the amici provided shocking data on minority physicians and minority healthcare. The NLG reported that, out of 320,903 active physicians in 1972, the nation had 5,478 Black physicians and a Black population 23.5 million, yielding a ratio of one Black physician for every 4,298 Black persons; and California had 769 Black physicians and a Black population of 1,400,143, yielding a ratio of one Black physician for more than 1,800 Black people.[30] MALDEF reported that Mexican Americans, at 4 million persons, were California's largest minority group; yet if all 250 Chicano physicians nationwide were practicing in California, the ratio would be one Chicano physician for every 16,000 persons. Moreover, since most California Chicanos and Latinos spoke no or little English, they encountered language barriers to healthcare; most facilities serving these populations lacked bilingual medical professionals, translators, and Spanish-language materials.[31] The NLG argued that the lack of healthcare, particularly for those ravaged by poverty, caused catastrophic outcomes comparable only to those in developing countries of Africa and South America. Compared to whites, minority infant and maternal mortality rates were double or triple, life expectancy was ten years shorter, doctor visits were 25 percent fewer, and disability and work loss rates were much higher.[32]

Pieced together, the amici information traced the effects of discrimination in two dimensions. One was the life-course impact: separate and unequal schooling saddled individual minority students with deficits that halted their progress through the education pipeline leading to medical school. The other was the community impact: the shortage of minority (and non-minority) doctors in minority communities resulted in unacceptably poor outcomes for those with both treatable and terminal conditions. Admittedly, the lack of regression analysis showing the relative strength of factors that contributed to the status of minorities in medical training, practice, and care encouraged Bakke supporters to attribute the racial disparities to individual choices, but they invoked the record principle as their first line of defense.

The Record Principle

Repeatedly adverting to this principle, Colvin stated that "the record in this case contains no evidence to support the special admissions program"; the university failed "to cite any intrinsic evidence to justify the asserted goals of the special admissions program" or introduce any "evidence whatever to prove that the instant quota is the only method capable of achieving their objectives."[33] While these claims were literally false, the university's facts were insufficiently trenchant and thus led to its fatal stipulation. On September 30, 1976, two weeks after the California Supreme Court announced its opinion, Reidhaar conceded that the university "cannot meet the burden of proving that the special admissions program did not result in Mr. Bakke's failure to be admitted."[34] To prove that the program was not a factor in Bakke's rejection, Reidhaar would have had to offer not only carefully disaggregated information on virtually all applicants but also the damning facts about preferences for younger applicants, spouses of enrolled students, offspring of prominent parents, and underqualified students admitted by the dean. So how did Justice Mosk make the inconvenient university and amici facts disappear?

Time and again, he adopted Colvin's "no evidence" tactic. Rejecting the university's evidence that disadvantaged white applicants could apply for special admission, he wrote in a footnote, "*The record is not clear* as to how and to whom the material regarding the special admissions program was distributed." Rejecting the university's evidence that a preference was given to applicants intending to practice in underserved communities of northern California, he wrote in a footnote, "Bakke does not challenge the preference accorded to applicants from the northern part of the state. . . . Indeed, *the record does not indicate* that any applicant in 1973 or 1974 was granted a preference because he planned to practice in Northern California" (my emphases).[35]

Rejecting the amici's evidence that the medical school excluded minority students before it instituted special admissions, he wrote, "there is *no evidence* as to the nature of the admission standards prior to 1969, when the special admissions program began. . . . Thus the fact that few minorities were accepted before 1969 was not necessarily the result of the absence of a preference for minorities strictly on racial grounds." Rejecting the amici's information on GPA and MCAT bias, he wrote, "There is *no evidence in the record* to indicate that the University has discriminated against minority applicants in the past. Nevertheless amici curiae ask that we find, by analogy to the employment discrimination cases, that the University's reliance on grade point averages and the Medical College Admission Test in evaluating applicants amounted to discrimination in fact against minorities." Rejecting the amici's claim of past discrimination, he wrote, "Neither party contended in the trial court that the University had practiced discrimination, and *no evidence* with regard to that question was admitted below. Thus on the basis of the record before us, we must presume that the University has not engaged in pat discriminatory conduct." He then added in a footnote, "Admittedly, neither the University nor Bakke would have an interest in raising such a claim. But this fact alone would not justify us in making a finding on *a factual matter not presented below*" (my emphasis).[36]

Under cover of the record principle, the majority justices dismissed virtually all university and amici information on the cynical rationale that it did not appear in the clearly deficient record produced by the deliberately truncated discovery and waived trial. Yet they undoubtedly understood that educational discrimination had disadvantaged California applicants to the UCD Medical School. Just a few years earlier in *Serrano v. Priest* (1971), Justice Mosk and five of his colleagues found that California's school financing scheme, which consigned low-income, predominantly racial-minority students to underfunded and educationally inferior schools, violated their right to equal protection.[37]

PRECEDENTS

In legal-judicial discourse, facts are supposed to ground arguments by precedent, which in turn utilize analogical reasoning.[38] According to cognitive scientists, analogical reasoning is three-step process: in retrieval, a person seeks possible source analogs for the situation presented by the target analog; in mapping, she identifies similar features of the source and target analogs; and in transfer, she uses the source features to illuminate the target. Although generally consisting of this process, analogical reasoning serves different purposes. In literary works, analogy functions expressively to transfer meanings from the source analog to the target analog in more detail than a metaphor or simile could do. In instructional settings, it functions heuristically, using the source analog that represents a known situation to illuminate the target analog's situation. In legal settings, precedents entail obligation: after a lawyer performs the retrieval, mapping, and transfer processes, he is obliged to answer a legal question in the target case the same way it was answered in the source case, not because he thinks it is the best practical, moral, or political answer but because it is the previously sanctioned answer. Just so, writes Frederick Schauer, "when presented with a situation in which the very same issue was decided previously by the same (even if differently staffed) Supreme Court, the current Court is obliged to reach the same conclusion about the same issue."[39] Likewise, Dan Hunter states, "Prior analogs, called precedents, are used to predict, explain, or justify the outcome of the currently undecided case."[40]

By linking cases to other cases, precedents bring consistency to legal-judicial discourse, but this effect can be attenuated. First, brief writers with diverging interests can provide different selections from and characterizations of the facts in the case at hand; then the writers can select either different precedents or the same one with its own selectable facts, dicta, and principles.[41] In an article on legal analogy, Jacob M. Carpenter advises novices to "carefully explain the details about the precedent case and then explicitly explain . . . which fact from the precedent case is like which fact from the present case, how or why those facts are similar, why those facts are important for similar reasons, [and] what benefit those facts both further."[42] In short, I am pointing out that since every case consists of constellated details that are not identical to those of possible precedents, brief writers have the flexibility to select what best serves their particular client's interests and their own argument.

Second, some law scholars distinguish between surface features, which are said to be the case facts, and structural features, which are said to be "the effect that the facts have on the parties or on the law," such as causing a harm or embodying a principle.[43] In an article on analogical reasoning, Cass Sunstein explains that lawyers must "decide when [fact] differences are relevant. To make this decision, they must investigate cases with care in order to develop governing principles." As an example, he notes that the facts of a case challenging a neo-Nazi march in Skokie, Illinois, differed from those of a case challenging a Klan rally in Hamilton County, Ohio, partly because the large Jewish community of Skokie, many of whom were Holocaust survivors, argued that marchers wearing full Nazi regalia including swastikas would be a life-threatening event. "This is indeed a difference," he remarks, "but American law currently decrees it irrelevant. It appears unprincipled . . . for the states to ban prohibitions on political speech except when the speaker is associated with the Holocaust." But the facts, which Sunstein doesn't describe, do bear a resemblance. The large African American and Jewish populations of Hamilton County might also have viewed the Klan rally, in which members wore robes and hoods, carried firearms, burned a cross, and spoke about getting rid of African Americans (always denoted by the "n" word) and Jews, as a provocation for life-threatening vigilantism.[44]

I mentioned the two cases not to argue that the Supreme Court was wrong to illegalize an Illinois statute and three Hamilton County ordinances as overly broad restrictions of speech or to argue that certain types of hate speech should be restricted, even if they don't incite lawless action. Rather, I will argue that the distinction between surface facts and structural principles is underanalyzed in racial discrimination cases. There the so-called surface facts manifest patterned social relations that in turn determine the meaning of the principle that presumably binds the source and target cases. With these cautions in mind, I examine some of the analogizing in *Bakke*.

The University Precedents

In 1930, with a grant from the Garland Fund in Boston, the NAACP hired attorney Nathan Margold, a recent Harvard Law School graduate, to study segregation and devise a legal strategy. His report recommended mounting a series of lawsuits to challenge *Plessy v. Ferguson*'s

(1896) "separate but equal" doctrine and win judgments that segregated schools were unconstitutional. When Charles Hamilton Houston, dean of the Howard University Law School, became special counsel to the NAACP, he began with equalization lawsuits that would compel states to provide comparable postgraduate programs for Black students; he reasoned that when the duplicate programs proved too costly to establish, the courts would compel them to integrate their white-only programs. The legal team, which included Thurgood Marshall who succeeded Houston as the NAACP's legal director in 1938, won five landmark cases: *Murray v. Pearson* (1936), *Missouri Ex Rel. Gaines v. Canada* (1938), *Sipuel v. Board of Regents* (1948), *Sweatt v. Painter* (1950), and *McLaurin v. Oklahoma State Regents* (1950).[45]

In his Reply Brief, Colvin located his citations of these cases in an argument about judicial intervention: "In the face of a clear factual record, defendant asserts that the courts are powerless to interfere with the administration of the quota policy."[46] Although the statement is counterfactual because the record was grossly deficient and the university did not assert the courts were powerless to intervene, Colvin cited the historic cases as authoritative:

> Even before it decided the *Brown* case, the Supreme Court declared void various graduate and professional school programs because the academic institutions involved had discriminated on the basis of race. In *Sweatt v. Painter* . . . for example, the court ordered the University of Texas to admit an applicant who had been excluded from the university's law school because of his race. (See also, *McLauren v. Okla. . . . Sipuel v. Board of Regents . . . Missouri ex. Rel. Gaines v. Canada . . .*). The instant case, similarly, is an appropriate one for judicial relief. The record herein clearly demonstrates that defendant's special admissions program discriminates on the basis of race and thereby lessens the chances that non-minority persons will be admitted to the medical school.[47]

Here Colvin links four of the five historic cases to *Bakke* by extracting the principle that courts do intervene and order relief in cases of unlawful racial discrimination.

The facts of the source and target cases are not analogous. In each historic case, a Black person (four men and one woman), who applied to an all-white postgraduate program (four law schools and one graduate education program), was summarily excluded because the state maintained a de jure system of segregation. In *Bakke*, a white person, who applied to a nearly all-white medical school, was rejected after being reviewed in a multicriteria evaluation process. His rejection, as I have suggested, resulted from a number of factors including preferences for younger applicants, spouses of enrolled students, and offspring of prominent parents; interviewer bias; and Bakke's own ineligibility for special admission. Thus in applying the abstract principle enunciated in the source cases to the target case, Colvin made a false analogy. It was fallacious because the social relations in which the university actions occurred in each case were what gave the facts and principle their meaning.

The Brown Precedent

One would expect *Brown v. Board of Education* to figure as an important precedent because the Court's relatively short opinion, which implicitly repudiated *Plessy*'s "separate but equal" rationale, asserted the harms, stigmatic and otherwise, that segregation inflicted on Black children. Colvin does not reference *Brown*, but Reidhaar attempts to analogize it to *Bakke* in an imprudently worded passage:

> In extending the special "suspect classification" protection to minority groups, the United States Supreme Court carefully avoided a finding that advantaged Caucasians, like Mr. Bakke, are entitled to this same special protection. The Court has acted to strike down invidious discrimination, but its decisions . . . indicate that a racial classification is invidious only to the extent it excludes, disadvantages, isolates, or stigmatizes minorities or is designed to segregate the races. See *Brown v. Board of Education*. . . . It is fanciful to argue that Mr. Bakke or other non-minorities are stigmatized by feelings of inferiority because of the special admissions program. And the purpose of the special admissions program is to *encourage* integration of the races in the medical school and in the profession.[48]

Reidhaar's imprudent language about "advantaged Caucasians, like Mr. Bakke" overwhelms his central point that the special admissions program actualizes *Brown*'s integration mandate. Moreover, he wobbles between talking about minority students and talking about the abstract concept of "racial classification"; hypothesizes about the *Brown* Court's speech acts; and hinges special protection on the symbolic harm of stigmatization, as well as the social harms of exclusion and isolation.

The passage provoked Justice Mosk to hyperbole: "That whites suffer a grievous disadvantage by reason of their exclusion from the University on racial grounds is abundantly clear. The fact that they are not also invidiously discriminated against in the sense that a stigma is cast upon them because of their race . . . does not justify the conclusion that race is a suspect classification only if the consequences of the classification are detrimental to minorities."[49] The tiff between the two men highlights their different renderings of "suspect classification": for Reidhaar, it is a concept that should protect social groups subjected to chronic exclusion, disadvantage, and stigmatization; for Mosk, it is it a concept that should prohibit any policy that classifies by racial traits, irrespective of whether they stigmatize. Mosk's taxonomic abstraction allows him to foreground the "grievous disadvantage" experienced by white applicants to the medical school while backgrounding those inflicted upon minority applicants.

Entering the fray, Justice Tobriner foregrounds the harms inflicted on minorities:

> Beginning with *Brown v. Board of Education* . . . [courts] struck down racial classifications embodied in segregation laws, laws that, by officially excluding minorities from the principal governmental and social institutions utilized by the majority of Americans, stigmatized members of minority groups and consigned them to inherently inferior treatment. . . . More recently, courts have perceived the invidiousness of a somewhat more subtle use of racial classifications, and have invalidated laws embodying such classifications which coerced, facilitated or encouraged private discrimination against minorities or the preservation of a segregated society. . . .

> In all of these cases the racial classifications at issue were utilized, explicitly or covertly, to stigmatize, exclude or accord inferior treatment to minorities.

On his rendering, racial classification is more than a taxonomic abstraction because, when an invidious one is inscribed in laws, it actuates or at least validates the social practices of segregating, excluding, and stigmatizing minorities. UCD's racial classifications, he states, "are worlds apart from the invidious racial classifications deemed constitutionally suspect in prior cases"; rather than excluding "any particular racial group from participation in the medical school," they are "aimed at ensuring that qualified applicants of all racial groups are actually represented in the institution."[50]

Interpreting the meaning of *Brown* for *Bakke*, the two justices dramatized the anticlassification and antisubordination perspectives described in John Hart Ely's "The Constitutionality of Reverse Racial Discrimination" (1974). Peering at *Brown* through the lens of colorblindness, Justice Mosk bleached segregation's harms to minority students and extracted the anticlassification principle that all racial classification is unconstitutional; gazing through the lens of color-consciousness, Justice Tobriner recognized segregation's harms to Black students and extracted the antisubordination principle that distinguished remedial uses of classification from oppressive ones.[51]

The Antimiscegenation Precedents

Insisting that the UCD admissions process was unconstitutional, Colvin again cited *Sweatt* along with two more cases—*McLaughlin v. Florida* (1964), overturning a Florida law prohibiting interracial cohabitation, and *Loving v. Virginia* (1967), overturning a Virginia law prohibiting interracial marriage.

> Nearly a generation ago, the United States Supreme Court ruled that the exclusion of a black applicant from a state university law school solely because of his race was a violation of the equal protection clause [citing *Sweatt*]. Ever since, the unvaried holding of

> the United States Supreme Court decisions and the teaching of contemporary history have been the same: discrimination on the basis of race is illegal, immoral, unconstitutional, inherently wrong and destructive of a democratic society. "Over the years, this court has consistently repudiated '[d]istinctions between citizens solely because of their ancestry' as being 'odious to a free people whose institutions are founded upon the doctrine of equality'" [quoting *Loving* and citing *McLaughlin*].[52]

Here Colvin links these antimiscegenation cases to *Bakke* by expunging the case facts and contexts in order to extract only the principle that racial distinctions among people are illegal, immoral, and undemocratic.

But the purpose of antimiscegenation laws challenged in *Loving* and *McLaughlin* was to prevent the mixing of a Black person and a white person in a domicile or a marriage, while that of the UCD program was to facilitate the mixing of diverse races in the medical school's student body and facilities. Seen in context, they were also different in effect: the antimiscegenation laws, for instance, denied Black partners of white persons the parental authority and spousal inheritance that white couples possessed, while the medical school (presumably) provided medical students of all races with the same learning opportunities. Without facts, Colvin's readers do not have to think about the differences between a Black-white couple in a private domicile and a multiracial student body in a public medical school, policies that prevent or promote racial mixing, and the availability of ancillary rights and resources.

The "Effect" Precedents

In arguing that the admissions program was unconstitutional, Colvin divided the purpose of the UCD admissions policy from its effect. He begins with this statement: "The fact that defendant intended its quota to favor minority groups does not justify the quota. It is not the purpose, but, rather, the *effect* of a racial classification that commands its invalidation."[53] Factually speaking the school did not have a quota, but Colvin's phrase "that defendant intended its quota to favor minority groups" appears as a dependent clause in an SVO sentence: "The fact [that X] . . . does not justify the quota." This syntax turns his own embedded quota allegation into a textualized fact. Next Colvin declares that the effect, not the purpose, of "a racial classification" is what makes it invidious. The proposition concerns an abstraction (racial classification) devoid of any factual content, such as data showing that the special admissions program harmed white applicants and, for obvious reasons, data showing the harm to minorities excluded from medical training before the program was implemented.[54] Then as legal support for his contention that courts should look to a policy's effect, Colvin cites three precedents.

In *Burton v. Wilmington Parking Authority* (1961), a Black man sued a restaurant, located in a public parking facility, for refusing to serve him. The central issue was whether the Wilmington Parking Authority, which owned, leased, and managed the facility, was implicated in the restaurant's racial discrimination. After determining that the authority was a state agency funded by tax revenues and subject to state law, the Supreme Court found—without any discussion of effect—that by failing to include the required nondiscrimination provision in the leasing contract it facilitated the restaurant's private discrimination.[55] The fact patterns of the source and target cases diverged: *Burton* concerned the state agency's failure to prevent the restaurant's exclusion of a Black customer on the basis of race, while *Bakke* concerned the state medical school's rejection of a white applicant on the basis of a multifactor evaluation process.

In *Palmer v. Thompson* (1971), a court ordered the city of Jackson, Mississippi, to desegregate five public parks. To avoid integrating the park swimming pools, the city closed four pools and transferred the fifth one to the YMCA, which operated it as a white-only facility. The Supreme Court acknowledged that some evidence supported the plaintiff's claim that the city was hostile to integrated swimming pools; other evidence supported the city's claim that it could not operate integrated pools safely; and no evidence supported the claim that the city facilitated the YMCA's white-only pool. Demurring that it was "difficult or impossible for any court to determine the 'sole' or 'dominant' motivation behind the choices of a group of legislators," the Court stated that the closure of "the public pools to black and white alike" had a racially neutral effect.[56] Colvin's analogy is inapt factually and contextually. Factually, both entities took action, the city closing park pools to prevent their integration and the medical school implementing special admissions to promote its integration. Contextually, the actions had different effects: white people, but not Black ones, could continue swimming at the many privately owned white pools in Jackson, but white applicants could not continue to fill all or nearly all of the places at the medical school. Thus the Jackson effect, which maintained the white monopoly of resources, was the obverse of the UCD effect, which interrupted it.

In *Wright v. Council of the City of Emporia* (1972), initially filed in 1965, Black students challenged the historically segregated school system in Greensville County, Virginia. When the district court accepted the plaintiffs' integration plan, public officials resisted by splitting the county into two political jurisdictions and two school districts in order to maintain white schools in the city of Emporia and Black ones in county outskirts. The Supreme Court wrote that, although the officials professed a benign purpose, "we have focused upon the effect—not the purpose or motivation—of a school board's actions"; based on enrollment data, it concluded that the effect of the new districting was state-facilitated school segregation.[57] Here again the segregative effect of the districting scheme in *Wright* was the obverse of the integrative effect of the admissions scheme in *Bakke*. In sum, the principle that should have linked all four cases is that the Constitution requires the racial integration of public facilities. That principle was upheld in *Burton* and *Wright*, skirted in *Palmer*, and sidelined during the *Bakke* appeal.

The Swann *Precedent*

Repeatedly cited in *Bakke* briefs and opinions, *Swann v. Charlotte-Mecklenburg Board of Education* (1971) was a notorious desegregation case that spent nearly six years bouncing between the district and appeals courts before finally arriving at the Supreme Court. Admonishing the school board, Chief Justice Warren Burger stated testily that for seventeen years the Court had never hesitated to intervene when school authorities defaulted on their affirmative duty to integrate the schools. Among the many vexing issues in *Swann* was the extent to which "racial balance or racial quotas may be used as an implement in a remedial order to correct a previously segregated system."[58] The school board objected to the district court's order that it make efforts to reach a 71–29 percent ratio in individual schools, which matched the ratio of white to Black students in the district. Supporting the district court, the chief justice declared,

> We see therefore that the use made of mathematical ratios was no more than a starting point in the process of shaping a remedy, rather than an inflexible requirement. From that starting point the District Court proceeded to frame a decree that was within its discretionary powers, as an equitable remedy for the particular circumstances. . . . In sum, the very limited use made of mathematical ratios was within the equitable remedial discretion of the District Court.[59]

Predictably citing *Swann*, both Reidhaar and Colvin distorted its facts to fit their arguments.

Reidhaar analogized *Swann* to *Bakke* in an attempt to defend the admissions program's allocation of eighty-four regular places and sixteen special places. After noting that the *Swann* court "held that school authorities may assign minority students to a particular school so that the minority percentage of the student body is the same as the minority percentage of the whole population of the district," he observed that the "16 seats under the special admissions program . . . is far below the percentage of disadvantaged minorities in the California population."[60] While the *Swann* court precisely referenced the white/Black student percentages at each school to the white/Black student percentages in the school district, Reidhaar references the sixteen special places to the percent of disadvantaged minorities in the whole California population. His ratio is both overinclusive because most of California's disadvantaged minorities were not college graduates seeking admission to the UCD Medical School and underinclusive because some minorities who sought admission lived outside of the state.[61]

By contrast, Colvin endeavored to differentiate *Swann* from *Bakke* by using word substitution and quotation cherry-picking:

> In *Swann*, the issue was how best to integrate an elementary and secondary school system so as to guarantee that there would not be a separate (and hence, unequal) elementary school system. The court clearly did not require the use of a quota; indeed it may not even have *permitted* one. "If we were to read the holding of the district court to require . . . any particular degree of racial balance or mixing, that approach would be disapproved and we would be obliged to reverse" (quoting Chief Justice Burger).[62]

In the chief justice's text, the comment quoted above functioned as a foil does in a fictional text, namely as the folly that contrasts with the wise or good. Here the hypothetically disapproved "particular degree of racial balancing" sets up the opinion's approval of the district court's method—namely its use of a flexible ratio that served as a starting point in fashioning an equitable remedy. Thus decontextualized, the quotation that appears in Colvin's text distorts the factual and legal import of the *Swann* opinion.

Next, Colvin differentiates the court's remedy in *Swann* from the medical school remedy in *Bakke*, writing that "in *Swann* no one was deprived of an education."

> As Mr. Justice Douglas has noted, "the *Swann* policy would not impinge constitutional rights, because no one would be excluded from a public school, and no one has a right to attend a segregated public school." [cites *DeFunis v. Odegaard*]. In the instant case, defendant sought to impose a "particular degree of racial balance" [again quoting Chief Justice Burger] and thereby has denied access to the medical school to certain non-minority persons because of their race. Due to these factors, the legal conclusions reached by the United States Supreme Court in *Swann* do not control the instant case.[63]

Colvin is right that *Swann* is an inapt analogy for *Bakke*, but for the wrong reason. The analogy is legally inapt because the Virginia and

California constitutions promised all resident children an education at the public schools, but did not similarly promise an education at state universities.[64] The analogy is also practically inapt: since the medical school could not enroll all who applied, the standard is not whether it rejected Bakke or anyone else, but whether it provided applicants, all of whom were dissimilarly situated by not only academic criteria but also gender, race, class, age, family status, and geography, with an equitable vetting process.

Responding to Colvin, Reidhaar argued that the law permits race-conscious remedies for racial discrimination, that the university's purpose is to integrate the medical school and profession, and that race is only one factor (not a determinative factor) in special admissions. But in so arguing, he stated, "the efforts to integrate primary and secondary schools, like the efforts to integrate the medical school and the medical profession here, both entail some harm to some non-minorities."[65] Piqued by his casual attitude toward white harm, Justice Mosk rejected the analogy:

> Whatever the inconveniences . . . to achieve integration, no child is totally deprived of an education because he cannot attend a neighborhood school, and all students, whether or not they are members of a minority race, are subject to equivalent burdens. . . . The disadvantages suffered by a child who must attend school some distance from his home or is transferred to a school not of his qualitative choice, cannot be equated with the absolute denial of a professional education, as occurred in the present case.[66]

Here again, Justice Mosk adopts Colvin's white-centered perspective and ignores the statutory context that differentiates public schools from medical schools, an approach that provoked his only dissenting colleague.

With simmering anger, Justice Tobriner entered the debate about legal rights and harms:

> No one can realistically assert that white-Anglo students who have been transferred from schools with better facilities and more experi-

> enced teachers to presently "unequal" schools as part of the desegregation process have not suffered at least some detriment that would not have suffered "but for" their race. The fact that such children have "no right to a segregated education" . . . does not distinguish past desegregation decisions from the instant case since it is equally true that medical school applicants have no right to a segregated medical education.[67]

But then he observes, "Whenever there is a limited pool of resources from which minorities have been disproportionately excluded, equalization of opportunity can only be accomplished by a reallocation of such resources; those who have previously enjoyed a disproportionate advantage must give up some of that advantage if those who have historically had less are to be afforded an equitable share."[68] Although the language may seem coldly economistic, it translates the dispute over the admissions program into the discourse of distributive justice.

The DeFunis *Precedent*

Factually, *DeFunis* would seem to be an apt analogy for *Bakke*, but legally, as Justice Mosk explained, it offered no guidance. After the Supreme Court vacated the Washington Supreme Court judgment for the defendant and remanded to that court, the state justices reached no further conclusions.[69] The lack of definitive conclusions did not deter *Bakke* participants from snipping morsels to feed their arguments. In arguing that racial classifications have harmful effects, Colvin lifts a long paragraph from the Douglas dissent that caroms from the "nation of minorities" trope through the problems of segregation and stigmatization. Then he states, "Mr. Justice Douglas noted that race could be used only in a 'neutral manner,'" a two-word phrase he snips from the Douglas's long explanation of why LSAT bias warranted eliminating the test or reviewing minority students separately.[70]

Using a more sophisticated cut-and-paste method, Reidhaar snips *DeFunis* quotations from their diverse contexts and rearranges them as steps in his argument. For example, he declares that the Washington Supreme Court "found that a minority admissions program at the

University of Washington Law School, very similar to the special admissions program at issue here, served a compelling interest." Next he quotes from the Washington opinion: "We believe the state has an overriding interest in promoting integration in public education. In light of the serious under-representation of minority groups in the law schools, and considering that minority groups participate on an equal basis in the tax support of the law schools, we find the state interest in eliminating racial imbalance within public legal education to be compelling."[71] But then he quotes Justice Douglas's "I cannot conclude that the admissions procedure of the Law School of Washington that excluded DeFunis is in violation of the Equal Protection Clause of the Fourteenth Amendment." Of course, the quote was preceded by Douglas's extensive critique of the LSAT biases that disadvantaged racial-minority test-takers, a topic Reidhaar assiduously skirted lest he imply that MCAT discriminated against its racial-minority test-takers.[72] In short, by sequencing his own statement, the Washington Supreme Court passage, and the Douglas sentence, Reidhaar creates a paper chain of logical reasoning.

Justice Mosk locates two short *DeFunis* quotations in footnotes, one stating that the UW Law School admissions policy was not benign with respect to whites and the other that no race had a constitutional right to be preferred.[73] A third quotation, located in his text, repeats a Douglas passage that Colvin had quoted at greater length: "The Equal Protection Clause commands the elimination of racial barriers, not their creation in order to satisfy our theory as to how society ought to be organized. The purpose of the University of Washington cannot be to produce black lawyers for blacks, Polish lawyers for Poles, Jewish lawyers for Jews, Irish lawyers for Irish. It should be to produce good lawyers for Americans."[74] Justice Mosk uses this passage to call out what he regards as the university's parochialism in assuming that minority doctors would be more likely than white ones to serve minority communities and to reject the amici's evidence showing that white doctors seldom practiced in these communities.

The Griggs *Precedent*

For all the talk about evaluating a policy on its social effect rather than its stated purpose, one might expect the brief and opinion writers to pay close attention to the gatekeeping devices that sat at the center of *Griggs v. Duke Power Co.* (1971). Brought on behalf of Black plaintiffs, the NAACP claimed that a Duke Power plant had engaged in discriminatory practices first by refusing to hire Black workers in any job category but menial labor and later by requiring prospective workers to hold a high school diploma and pass two intelligence tests, criteria that effectively barred Blacks from nonmenial job categories. After reviewing Title VII provisions, testing studies, and job performance data, the Supreme Court found that these criteria were unrelated to job duties, did not predict for Black workers' on-the-job performance, and, regardless of the employer's intent, discriminated against Black workers who were disadvantaged by inferior education.[75] In what follows, I summarize two of the several pro-minority amici arguments that analogized *Griggs* to *Bakke*.

In an exhaustive eighteen-page survey of testing law and literature, the National Lawyers Guild restated the *Griggs* principle that when a test results in a disproportionate failure rate among minorities compared to whites, the burden of proof shifts to the employer to show that it is a valid means of selecting employees. After establishing that the courts had applied this principle to cases of alleged discrimination in employment, jury service, and education, the NLG quoted Justice Douglas's comment that the deficient factual record in *DeFunis* justified a retrial that examined the LSAT for any biases against minority test-takers. Applying this advice to *Bakke*, the NLG reviewed two dozen studies showing that the GPA and MCAT scores, which reflected prior educational disadvantages, had little or no predictive value for minority performance in medical school courses, clinical instruction, and professional practice.[76] The NLG concluded, "Given the fact that the[se] two main traditional criteria for medical school admissions have been shown by numerous researchers to have little or no relationship to medical school and professional performance, it would be unjust, and violative of the Equal Protection Clause, for those criteria to be utilized against minority applicants."[77]

Also applying *Griggs* to *Bakke*, the American Medical Student Association declared that "A testing device which excludes non-whites from job opportunities is *prima facie* discriminatory." Then it addressed key differences between the two cases:

> While *Griggs* concerned a claim under Title VII of the 1964 Civil Rights Act, courts have applied its reasoning to cases involving equal protection. . . . Although *Griggs* concerned job hiring policies instead of admissions to professional schools, both involved artificial barriers to career opportunities. It follows, therefore, that a testing device such as MCAT which Davis admits operates to exclude minorities is suspect under *Griggs*. The burden then passes to the medical school to show that there is a demonstrable relationship between the test and performance on the job.[78]

The *Bakke* trial court, AMSA wrote, ignored the issue of MCAT validity and simply assumed that "Anglos who had through 'merit' earned the 'right' to attend Davis Medical School were deprived of that right due to the special admissions program." Thus, it urged the California Supreme Court to either reverse the trial court or remand "with directions to permit interested parties to intervene to present evidence of the discriminatory nature of the admissions program" before special admissions was implemented.[79]

Justice Mosk's disposal of the amici's testing facts and *Griggs* precedent is laced with irony. First he states that the medical school is not required to adhere to strict ranking based on GPA and MCAT scores; instead it may "consider . . . that low grades and test scores may not accurately reflect the abilities of some disadvantaged students," may determine the weight to give to scores, and may "consider other factors."[80] Case records showed that this is precisely what the admissions committee did. Next, he declares that courts do not approve race-conscious remedy without findings of past discrimination:

> Amici curiae ask that we find, by analogy to the employment discrimination cases, that the University's reliance on grade point averages and the Medical College Admissions Test in evaluating

> applicants amounted to discrimination in fact against minorities. Amici claim that the application of these quantitative measures by the University had resulted in the exclusion of a disproportionate number of minority applicants, that grades and test scores are not significantly related to a student's performance in medical school or in the profession, and that the test is culturally biased.[81]

But since the amici had cited many studies showing that the GPA and MCAT had a racially discriminatory effect, Justice Mosk once again invokes the record principle to dismiss their evidence: "Neither party contended in the trial court that the University had practiced discrimination, and no evidence with regard to that question was admitted below. Thus on the basis of the record before us, we must presume that the University has not engaged in past discriminatory conduct." Appended to this statement is a footnote: "Admittedly, neither the University nor Bakke would have an interest in raising such a claim. But this fact alone would not justify us in making a finding on a factual matter not presented below."[82]

In the previous chapter and this one, I have demonstrated that social and textual practices made the pro-minority facts in *Bakke* disappear. The truncated discovery, the waived trial, and the appellate court's failure to remand were social practices that prevented minority witnesses and intervenors from entering the judicial arenas. The invocation of the record principle to reject the pro-minority amici facts, the faulty analogizing of factually dissimilar cases, and the ascent to abstract principles that, like one-size-fits-all garments, cloaked the white plaintiff in equal protection were textual practices that left current and future minority applicants out in the cold.

These outcomes were discussed in somewhat different language by *Bakke* brief writers and later commentators. The AMSA brief argued for a retrial or an appellate rehearing:

> Minority applicants have just as much at stake in the outcome of this litigation as Mr. Bakke and probably much more than the Re-

gents. . . . The outcome of this litigation will have a direct effect on the careers of thousands of young Black, Chicano, Asian, and Native American men and women who now have a realizable aspiration to become doctors. It would be shameful if a decision adverse to their interests were made without permitting them an opportunity to present evidence.[83]

Similarly, the NAACP brief stated, "Amicus are especially distressed that the California Supreme Court . . . should take a step backwards from the decision of the Washington Supreme Court in *DeFunis v. Odegaard*." Urging the court to order a retrial, it declared that the "wholly inadequate and almost non-existent" trial record could "be traced directly to the fact that the real parties in interest were not represented"—those parties being "Blacks, Mexican-Americans, Asians, Native Americans, and other minority persons who will as a result of this decision be denied the opportunity to become doctors."[84]

In advocating for an intervenor to represent people of color groups that had a stake in the outcome of the case, the two briefs were raising the issue of interest impairment addressed at length in subsequent scholarship on reverse-discrimination litigation. Edward Chen's "The Case for Minority Participation in Reverse Discrimination Litigation" (1979) and Emma Coleman Jones's "Litigation without Representation: The Need for Intervention to Affirm Affirmative Action" (1979) discussed several factors that vitiated *Bakke*, among them adherence to the two-party dispute format, appellate deference to the deficient record, prioritization of litigant information over amici information, the inchoate notion of due process for nonlitigant parties, and constraints on intervention imposed by Rule 24 of the Federal Rules of Civil Procedure. Jones, seeking a way around the Rule 24 constraints, enumerated several interests that could have been articulated. Minorities, she wrote, had the same interests as the white plaintiff in competing for medical school places and obtaining a medical education, but they had additional interests in revealing UCD's prior de facto discrimination, protecting the remedial program, and providing minority access to healthcare. Chen and Jones concluded that absence of minority intervention in reverse-discrimination cases diminished the integrity of the adjudicatory process by contravening the democratic principles of interest representation, equity, and procedural due process.[85]

Paraphrasing Donald Rumsfeld, I would add that the deliberate exclusion of facts about systemic racism from *DeFunis* and *Bakke* did not prove the absence of systemic racism from the social and educational circumstances that precipitated the cases. Despite the tactics used by the plaintiffs' supporters to whiten discrimination in these cases and subsequently by conservative organizations to smother race consciousness, which I discuss in the final chapter, systemic racism would continue to gash the social fabric for decades to come.

10

PLACES

Whenever there is a limited pool of resources from which minorities have been disproportionately excluded, equalization of opportunity can only be accomplished by a reallocation of such resources.

—Justice Matthew Tobriner, Dissent, *Regents of the University of California v. Bakke*, California Supreme Court

On December 14, 1976, the University of California (UC) petitioned the US Supreme Court for a writ of certiorari. In addition to Donald Reidhaar and Gary Morrison, its distinguished legal team consisted of Archibald Cox, a Harvard law professor who had served as US solicitor general during the Kennedy era and special prosecutor in the Watergate investigation before his firing during the infamous Saturday Night Massacre; Paul J. Mishkin, a prominent constitutional law scholar at the UC Berkeley Law School; and Jack B. Owens, who had clerked for Justice Lewis Powell in 1973–1974 before joining a prestigious San Francisco law firm.[1] On January 6, Reynold H. Colvin and Robert D. Links (hereafter Colvin), again representing Allan Bakke, asked the Court to deny the writ. Known as an astute attorney Colvin had previously won a ruling in *Anderson v. San Francisco Unified School District* (1972) for the white plaintiffs who challenged the school board's race-conscious policy of protecting minority administrators during a lay-off process.[2] Unsurprisingly, the two teams polarized the dispute, respectively arguing that the Constitution protected UCD's plenary power to determine its admissions program or Bakke's right to attend the medical school.

On February 22, after three rounds of voting accompanied by the strenuous objections of Justice William Brennan who felt that *Bakke* was a weak vehicle for deciding constitutional questions, the Court decided to hear the case and scheduled oral argument for October 12.[3] Over the next seven months, it received 57 amici briefs totaling 1,400 pages and representing 240 organizations and individuals.[4] Among the distinguished brief writers were future Supreme Court justice Ruth Bader Ginsburg, Children's Defense Fund founder Marian Wright Edelman, former assistant attorney general Burke Marshall, and civil-rights lawyers Jack Greenberg and Joseph Rauh Jr. *DeFunis* participants reappeared. Brief writers included Slade Gorton and James Wilson for Washington State, Jennings P. Felix and Marco DeFunis for Young Americans for Freedom, Larry Lavinsky for the Anti-Defamation League, and Harry B. Reese for the Law School Admissions Council. Frequently cited authorities included Robert M. O'Neil's law review articles, Justice Douglas's dissent, and former University of Washington president Charles Odegaard's new book, *Minorities in Medicine* (1977).[5]

External pressure was mounted soon after the California Supreme Court ruled on September 16, 1976. In November, the Conference of Black Lawyers urged the UC Regents not to appeal the case but instead to reaffirm the institutional commitment to affirmative action, establish a "broadly representative" commission to review all admissions programs for compliance with the Fourteenth Amendment, and appoint a special counsel to issue opinion letters and conduct any necessary litigation. "The University," said attorney Ralph Smith, was "disinclined to adopt this point of view" and pursued the appeal.[6] On January 14, several weeks before the Court decided to hear the case, Emma Coleman Jones and Peter D. Roos, who represented seventeen organizations, urged the Court to "vacate the decision below and remand for the taking of further evidence." Describing *Bakke* as raising "perhaps the most important equal protection issue of the decade," they declared that minorities, who "have not participated in the litigation," now "risk jeopardy of their rights on an inadequate record." They stated that the record lacked evidence on whether California's segregated schools disadvantaged minority applicants, whether the medical school had discriminated in the past, whether the MCAT was biased against minority test-takers, and whether Bakke's rejection was owing to special admissions.[7] In a reply brief, the university team stated there was no need to document "societal discrimination and instances of *de jure* segregation in state public schools" because this history "is formally recognized in numerous opinions and holdings of state and federal courts" and no need to seek evidence that the medical school intentionally discriminated because it never did. "The full record leads to one conclusion only—Bakke came so close to admission that it cannot be demonstrated one way or another whether he would have been admitted absent the special program."[8]

When the Court granted the writ, many parties escalated the pressure. The media stoked the controversy, particularly in New York, where the *New York Times* featured Jewish and white-ethnic criticisms of government agencies charged with overseeing affirmative action.[9] Black leaders—notably, Vernon Jordan of the National Urban League, Jesse Jackson of Operation PUSH, Bayard Rustin of the A. Philip Randolph Institute, Benjamin Hooks of the NAACP, and Coretta Scott King—activated their constituents, who harried the administration with phone calls, telegrams, and demonstrations. The Black Congressional Caucus announced that the Department of Justice's (DOJ) Motion to Participate in Oral Argument was "not fully representative of all of the constituent branches of government and in particular not fully representative of our views as Members of Congress." After accusing the DOJ of attempting to qualify "the decisions of this Court" that race-conscious measures could "remedy the effects of societal discrimination," the caucus bluntly asserted minority interests: "The constitutional mandate to overcome the status of inferiority and exclusion imposed upon minority peoples cannot be balanced against the possible impact of these reasonable measures on random individuals who are not members of excluded groups. . . . There is no balancing to be done."[10] The National Conference of Black Lawyers warned that "to decide the 'merits' [of the case] . . . would be to say that the most significant civil rights ruling of this decade should henceforth be associated with a case as defective and as tainted as this is." It accused the litigants of collusion, citing Peter Storandt's assistance to Bakke in developing a litigation plan and the university's failure to request a full trial. Outraged by the university's statement that obtaining a ruling on race-conscious admission was more important than arguing about whether Bakke should be admitted, the Conference stated, "The notion that a decision on this issue . . . will be sufficiently 'definitive' so as to put this entire issue to rest reflects a perception that is not in accord with reality."[11]

Meanwhile, Black leaders were dismayed by the Carter administration's tepid response. When first approached by the university, Solicitor General Wade McCree (the second African American to hold this post) and Assistant Attorney General Drew Days III (the first African American to head the civil rights division) were reluctant to become involved in what they regarded as a weak case. But President Jimmy Carter directed Attorney General Griffin Bell to prepare a brief; drafted by Days and revised by McCree's assistant, it was delivered to the president, who asked his adviser Stuart Eizenstat to review it.

> [Eizenstat] criticized its style, organization, and tone. But the content was even more important, and Eizenstat considered that a political disaster. The brief supported the admission of Bakke, declared the admissions program at Davis unconstitutional, and gave tentative support to the use of race in admissions. . . . He said the language of the brief would harm the government's affirmative action programs and added that the trial record was too thin to warrant support for Bakke's admission.[12]

In September, an anonymous source leaked the brief to Black leaders, who personally contacted McCree, while their Black colleagues in the cabinet and Congress pressed for a stronger position on affirmative action. The media hyped the entire drama, to the displeasure of the Court: "The Chief Justice and Justice Blackmun told McCree that the entire Court was offended," and McCree told "Attorney General Bell that the Justices felt the newspaper accounts subjected them to improper public pressure when they were about to hear oral argument."[13]

When the Maginot Line that legal-judicial discourse had drawn around the Court to shield it from external influences failed, the conflict surged into *Bakke*, generating tensions that left their traces in the justices' conference memoranda and Justice William J. Brennan's private account. These documents, published years later, reveal that the Court's deliberations were prolonged by not only Justice Blackmun's two-month absence while recovering from surgery at the Mayo Clinic but also the justices' inability to agree on legal standards. They debated whether to apply Title VI analysis and if so whether an individual had a right to sue under this provision, or whether to apply constitutional analysis and if so whether a race-conscious program could meet the strict scrutiny requirements. The Brennan account notes that Justice Thurgood Marshall was so "livid over LFP's [Justice Powell's] opinion which he regarded as racist" that he "shot back tartly, 'I will not join *any* part of the opinion.'"[14]

On June 24, 1978, the Court released six opinions. Justice John Paul Stevens (joined by Chief Justice Warren Burger, Justice Potter Stewart, and Justice William Rehnquist) stated that they would affirm the California Supreme Court's ruling that the special admissions program "violated Title VI of the Civil Rights Act of 1964 by excluding Bakke from the Medical School because of his race" and also its order directing the UCD Medical School to admit him.[15] Justice William Brennan (joined by Justices Byron White, Thurgood Marshall, and Harry Blackmun) stated that they would reverse the lower court's holding that the special admissions program was unconstitutional, its order directing Bakke's admission, and its injunction prohibiting the medical school from considering race in the admissions process.[16] Authoring separate opinions, Justice White maintained that Congress did not intend for private lawsuits to enforce Title VI; Justice Marshall recounted the sordid history of American racism to argue that the law did not prohibit race-conscious remedies; and Justice Blackmun emphasized that judges were ill-equipped to address matters concerning medical education and practice. Justice Powell attempted to straddle the polarized camps. Siding with the Stevens camp, he found the special admissions program to be unlawful but on constitutional rather than statutory grounds and affirmed the order of admission. Siding with the Brennan camp, he reversed the lower court injunction prohibiting any consideration of race in admissions and famously declared that it could be one of many factors considered in the individualized reviews of applicants.[17]

The opinions stimulated everyone's interpretive ingenuity. Newspaper articles topped by blaring headlines described the outcome as a win for racial quotas or for race-conscious remedies, and scholars published over 500 articles in the first two years.[18] Rather than adding yet another interpretation to this bulging archive, I will examine the language and logic that constructed four models of discrimination—"societal discrimination," "education pipeline discrimination," "racial quota," and "proportional representation"—in select briefs, oral argument exchanges, and conference memoranda. Strumming beneath this work of linguistic construction was a fierce battle over the distribution of societal resources. The concept of "places" in the UCD Medical School, which erupted onto the textual surfaces, was its synecdoche.

"SOCIETAL DISCRIMINATION"

In the Brief for Petitioner, Paul Mishkin, Jack Owens, and Donald Reidhaar pose this legal question: "When only a small fraction of thousands of applicants can be admitted, does the Equal Protection Clause forbid a state university professional school from voluntarily seeking to counteract effects of generations of pervasive discrimination against discrete and insular minorities by establishing a limited special admissions program that increases opportunities for well-qualified members of such racial and ethnic minorities?"[19] In describing the admissions program, they foreground chronic racial discrimination against minorities and the university's modest attempt to counteract its effects, but their extravagant rhetoric does the heavy lifting. It understates the number of possible admittees while overstating the size of the applicant pool ("small fraction of thousands of applicants"), and it understates the scope of special admissions while overstating its salutary effects (a "limited special admissions program" that counteracts "generations of pervasive discrimination"). Indexically, this last phrase points to their construction of "societal discrimination" in the argument that follows.

The brief devotes twenty-seven pages to historical, social, and statistical facts that delineate "societal discrimination" and another fifty pages to legal argument that periodically references the construct. The authors note that most minority students applying to the UCD Medical School in 1970 attended segregated "elementary school in 1954, the year this Court decided *Brown v. Board of Education*," and, owing to the backlash against integration, completed their education at segregated schools in California and southern states.[20] Rather than following this cohort through the education pipeline, the authors leap forward to the "ramifications of societal discrimination for minority doctors [that] extend to every aspect of their professional lives."[21] Black physicians, they state, are denied clinical appointments, specialty certification, hospital affiliation, medical school appointments, and professional association membership. Contending that these barriers restrict the number of Black doctors, they compare white ratios to Black ones: one white physician for 640 white patients but one Black physician for 4,348 Black patients nationwide and for 15,000 to 20,000 Black patients in the Deep South.[22] Next they claim that the shortage of minority doctors affects minority communities which, compared to white ones, suffer much higher rates of stillbirths, infant and maternal deaths, preventable childhood diseases, untreated acute and chronic illnesses, and death from illness in all age groups. Refuting the claim that white doctors treat minority patients, they cite studies showing that the preponderance of those who practice in minority communities are doctors of color. Training more such doctors, they declare, "is not a philosophical position, it is a statistical position. It is justified not on the basis of the theory of differences of color, but on the practical necessities of the deprivation of peculiar enclaves within our society that we need to be concerned with a new racially selective education."[23]

Circling back to medical school admissions, Mishkin, Owens, and Reidhaar narrate the advent of race-conscious admissions. In 1948, twenty-six of the nation's seventy-seven medical schools overtly prohibited Blacks from applying; in 1964, most schools at public and private universities had all-white student bodies; and as late as 1971 all schools still had predominantly white student bodies. As applicant pools ballooned, medical schools that had relied on GPA and MCAT scores to vet applicants slowly realized that these devices "continued to limit admission almost exclusively to whites." To remedy this situation, they first put more emphasis on applicants' written statements, letters of recommendation, and personal interviews; later, they adopted race-conscious admissions to bring their mission "more closely into line with a broad range of educational imperatives and pressing needs in the profession and the larger society." Although deftly using statistical and experiential facts to animate "societal discrimination," the authors did not demonstrate its effects in *Bakke*, as the justices would later note.[24]

Writing for the American Civil Liberties Union (ACLU), three distinguished law school professors—Norman Dorsen (New York University Law School), Ruth Bader Ginsburg (Columbia University Law School), and Frank Askin (Rutgers University Law School)—reference "societal discrimination" only once. At the end of the brief, they state, "Centuries of *societal discrimination* and oppression were not and could not have been reversed that one day in 1954. To this day the Fourteenth Amendment's promise remains unfulfilled" (my emphasis).[25] Instead, they repeatedly use the phrase "systemic discrimination" and close synonyms, whose workings they depict in theoretical terms. They note that ACLU members had conducted a vigorous debate on the "need to eradicate the *cumulative effects* of *systemic discrimination* against minorities." They describe the special admissions program as "a plan plainly designed to ameliorate *systemic discrimination* against minorities." They state that California, having "*long discriminated* against minorities," now attempts "to redress the *harsh and cumulative disadvantages* imposed on minorities." They warn the Court that a decision for Bakke would strip government agencies of the "authority to prevent *projection of past and continuing systemic discrimination* long into the future" (my emphases).[26] They borrowed the phrase "systemic discrimination" and the concept of "cumulative disadvantages" from the theory of distributive justice advanced by Scottish philosopher Alexander Dunlop Lindsay and American philosopher John Rawls. After citing both men, the authors quote from Rawls's *A Theory of Justice* (1971): "inequalities of wealth and authority, are just only if they result in compensating benefits for everyone and, in particular, for the least advantaged members of society."[27]

The Justices

Unfortunately, neither the university's facts nor the ACLU's theory persuaded three justices that the construct of "societal discrimination" accurately represented social reality. In his conference memorandum, Chief Justice Burger stated that the university's argument "proceeds on the dubious assumption that minorities are readily identifiable 'blocs' which in some way *function as units* and are generally harmed or benefited in roughly the same degree by the same external forces. . . . The university desires to remedy the general effects of broad historic social discrimination, not discrimination by the university or the state but by society at large, in and outside California" (my emphasis).[28] Here he objects that the concept of "societal discrimination" presumes too much uniformity in group identity and behavior, too much consistency of harms or benefits, and too much time and action in framing the discrimination story.

In a conference memorandum that some scholars consider an early draft of his opinion, Justice Powell wrote:

> The state certainly has a legitimate and substantial interest in addressing or eliminating, where feasible, the disabling effects of discrimination. . . . In the school cases, the States were required by court order to redress the wrongs worked by specific and identifiable racial discrimination. That goal was far more focused than the remedying of the effects of "societal discrimination," a concept of injury that may be ageless in its reach into the past. We have never approved a classification that aids persons perceived as members of victimized groups at the expense of other innocent individuals in the absence of adjudicated, legislative, or administrative findings of constitutional or statutory violations.[29]

At first Justice Powell reiterates the chief justice's objection to "societal discrimination" as an overly broad concept that presumes too much group uniformity, time, and action. But then he introduces a new concern, which he seems to project onto his colleagues ("We have never approved"): they are troubled by the material effects of redress on white people. The phrase "at the expense of other innocent individuals" indicates that he (and perhaps his like-minded colleagues) understood the implications of the ACLU's references to distributive justice—namely that justly compensating Native Americans, African Americans, and Hispanic Americans for centuries of subjugation and exploitation would tax the resources traditionally monopolized by relatively privileged whites.

In his memorandum, Justice Rehnquist also notes that prior decisions upheld remedies for only "identifiable victims of particular discriminatory practices" and then rejects the idea that minority applicants to the medical school are "victims of generalized past discrimination."[30] The university, he continues,

> is assuming that every minority applicant who worked his way through school has been discriminated against. While it is clear that every person who has suffered racial discrimination on account of being a member of a minority is, by definition, a member of a minority, I am unwilling to agree that every member of a minority has been discriminated against. . . . The fit between the two groups (members of minority groups and persons who have been discriminated against on account of membership in a minority group) is far from exact and thus an insufficient basis for use of racial classifications.[31]

This passage invokes the fallacies of overinclusive and underinclusive classification explained in Joseph Tussman and Jacobus tenBroek's widely read article, "The Equal Protection of the Laws" (1949).

In analyzing classification, Tussman and tenBroek deployed Aristotelian logic, which is essentialist in assuming that intrinsic traits can differentiate groups and rationalist in assuming that syllogistic reasoning can produce knowledge. "To define a class," they state, "is simply to designate a quality or characteristic or trait or relation, or any combination of these" that differentiates classes from one another and determines an individual's membership in a class. Consequently, "Individual *X* is a member of class *A* if, and only if, *X* possess the traits which define class *A*."[32] Their statement reverses the usual syllogistic order which proceeds from a universal proposition to a conclusion: All members of group A possess trait #3 (universal affirmative statement); If individual X possesses trait #3 (conditional statement); Then individual X is a member of group A (conclusion). To exemplify classificatory fallacies, Tussman and tenBroek note that the wartime policy of interning Japanese Americans was overinclusive because it assumed that all Japanese Americans were a threat to national security and underinclusive because members of other groups were a threat to national security.

Justice Rehnquist draws on overinclusivity to reason that two groups—members of a given minority group and persons experiencing discrimination as members of this group—are not coextensive because not all members of the given minority group have experienced discrimination. The problem with this abstractly reasoned claim is its empirical and theoretical naivety. To support the claim empirically, one would have to survey either all members of the given minority group or a carefully designed representative sample of members. The results would tell us what we already know: generalizations cannot accurately cover a multiplicity of particulars, and outliers do not disprove the generalization. To explain individual and group racial identities, one would have to describe how identity ascription occurs. People ascribe racial identity to themselves and others based on signifiers denoting ancestral, bodily, linguistic, or cultural traits that differentiate the classes in an already existing racial taxonomy. The traits and taxonomy are preconditions for the recognition of racial identities, racial group memberships, and racial discrimination. Even when people know their society's racial taxonomy, they make mistakes such as concluding that a brown-skinned, Spanish-speaking, self-ascribed Anglo is a Latinx person.

Perhaps the most troubling aspect of the justices' rejection of "societal discrimination" is their intolerance of anomalies (or outliers), which are inevitable in all knowledge fields, as suggested by studies of paradigms and anomalies.[33] In *The Structure of Scientific Revolutions* (1962), T. S. Kuhn explained that as scientists pursue their work according to the reigning paradigm anomalies inevitably appear, prompting them to tinker with the paradigm and eventually to embrace a previously marginalized alternative that explains what seemed aberrant under the old paradigm.[34] In an article on retro-recognition, Alan Lightman and Owen Gingerich also note that sometimes current "anomalies are recognized only after they are given compelling explanations" by a new paradigm. Thus scientists may perceive the anomalous phenomenon but "leave it unquestioned and ignored"; only when a new paradigm explains it do they retroactively recognize it was anomalous under the old one.[35]

In general, the recognition of anomalies advances knowledge. Just so, the Court in its education cases, had expanded its paradigmatic interpretation of the Fourteenth Amendment as crafted to protect African Americans so that it protected others grouped by race, sex, national origin, and native language. But confronted by an anomalous white man who demanded protection from a race-conscious program designed to provide relief to minorities, they reasserted rather than replaced the individualist discrimination paradigm. Deploying the comfortably familiar Enlightenment rationality, they segmented societal discrimination's time and space, broke its process into discrete acts, dissolved the "groupness" of minorities, and whitened the color of the allegedly victimized individual.[36] Such are the dangers of abstract reasoning when untethered from the empirical ground.

"EDUCATION PIPELINE DISCRIMINATION"

Behind the justices' radical disaggregation of "societal discrimination" was a profound unease, shared by Bakke supporters, with the social and statistical facts that the pro-minority amici used to delineate "education pipeline discrimination." Writing for a dozen Mexican American organizations, Vilma S. Martinez and her colleagues had recounted "the abysmal history of racial discrimination against Mexican Americans in California and the Southwest." They used data on Mexican American income, employment, housing, and imprisonment to describe the cycle of multigenerational poverty enabled by discrimination in the education pipeline where most students attended substandard schools, acquired below-grade skills, and dropped out.[37]

"The foregoing statistics," they write, "clearly show that the severe racial/ethnic disparities which prompted responsible public officials to institute affirmative action programs still exist."[38] Next they provide a data-rich review of medical training and practice across the nation and in California that revealed the barriers to minority physicians and the consequences for minority healthcare. Like the California Supreme Court briefs, this one demonstrated that the "critical [healthcare] needs of these communities have not been addressed by an all-white medical profession" that lacked the language skills, cultural understanding, and motivation to treat people of color living in ghettoes, barrios, and reservations.[39]

Pipeline Filters

Other briefs narrowed their time and action frames to focus on the current cohort of medical school applicants. Writing for the Law School Admissions Council (LSAC), Northwestern University law professor Harry B. Reese used data from the Department of Health, Education, and Welfare (HEW) and professional associations to argue that the exclusion of minority students from "graduate and professional schools in the 1970's must be seen . . . as the culmination of an educational process that began in the elementary schools in the 1950's."[40] Among students born in 1954 who might have applied to medical schools in 1976, 85 percent of whites and 68 percent of Blacks graduated from high school in 1972; 47 percent of white graduates and 38 percent of Black graduates entered college in fall 1972; and 29 percent of white students and 11 percent of Black students graduated from college. Of the last group, 45 percent received their diplomas from historically Black colleges.[41]

Next Reese superimposes this student cohort on the timeline of nondiscrimination laws. The typical twenty-two-year-old applying to professional schools in 1976 was born when the Court ruled on *Brown* (1954), reached fourth grade before the Civil Rights Act (1964) was enacted, and entered high school when, in *Green v. County School Board* (1968), the Court expressed its frustration with the tenacity of school segregation. Indeed in 1970, over half of the nation's "black population

. . . (11,640,000 of 21,970,000) lived in the South where racial segregation in education was required by explicit state statutes," and the rest lived in the North and West "where racial segregation had been accomplished, also *de jure,* through official establishment of discriminatory school district boundaries and attendance zones."[42] Data from court cases and HEW studies showed that 88.4 percent of Black students and 72.1 percent of all minority students attended unlawfully segregated schools. "These figures," Reese declares, "provide a ready answer to the question of why the pool of potential minority applicants to graduate and professional schools is severely limited. . . . More than three of every four have been unlawfully shunted into racially segregated public schools, where they have received an inferior education."[43]

Turning to the impact of admissions criteria, Reese explains that studies of the 1976 applicant pools for law and medical schools consistently find that "applicants from minority groups subjected to unlawful educational segregation rank significantly lower than white applicants on the conventional measures of academic achievement." The disparities, he argues, reflect prior educational inequalities, because grades and tests "measure abilities which are taught, acquired, and developed in formal education. A different, inferior education naturally tends to produce different, inferior scores."[44] As a foil to his analysis, he calls out theories of genetic inferiority and cites a 1970 article by Arthur Jensen (see below).

Writing for the Black Law Students Association (BLSA) at the University of California, Berkeley, Ephraim Margolin deepens the analysis. The lower courts in *Bakke,* he states, erroneously assumed "that minority candidates were 'less qualified' and therefore in need of a preference" because the record contained no evidence on biases in the admissions process: "The first biasing factor is the personal interview of candidates. These interpersonal sessions were unstructured and the interview summaries were unstandardized. . . . There is a substantial potential for both the debilitating influence of racial prejudice on the rapport between candidate and interviewer and the injection of personal biases by interviewers into the summaries."[45] The record contained evidence of Dr. Lowrey's bias against Bakke and the admissions committee's bias for spouses of enrolled students, while news stories disclosed the dean's bias for underqualified applicants from prominent families.

Since the record contained no evidence of MCAT validity, Margolin fills the gap, stating that "a critical review of published research indicates that the MCAT is not a valid indicator of performance as a medical student, an intern or resident, or a practicing physician. . . . Thus, heavy reliance on MCAT scores made candidates from different racial backgrounds seem unequally qualified." As support, he cites twelve studies of student cohorts at several dozen of medical schools that found little or no correlation of test scores with grades in medical school classes, performance in clinical settings, graduation rates (92 percent for lower-scoring students and 93 percent for higher-scoring students), or professional practice. Although the studies show that "the MCAT is, at least, a very poor indicator of a candidate's qualifications to study or practice medicine," the court "did not consider these findings and had no other evidence before it to justify its conclusion that minority candidates were less qualified."[46]

Where other amici discussed the dominant-culture language, logic, and contents of standardized tests, Margolin analyzes test norming:

> Bias is introduced into a test whenever a test is normed on one group and used to evaluate members of another group. . . . The MCAT was normed to students taking the test in 1951 . . . at a time when there were virtually no minority candidates for medical school. This bias is likely to be even larger than for a test normed on a representative sample of the population, where minority representation would still be proportionately small.

When test-takers are compared interracially, the MCAT's norming to white middle-class scoring results in an average minority-to-white score gap of 105 to 155 points that makes minority test-takers appear less likely to succeed in medical school. However, statistical studies comparing minority and white students nationwide show that the score gap "is not reflected by a similar performance gap in medical school."[47]

Similarly asserting that the undergraduate GPA was an unreliable indicator of future performance, Margolin cites studies showing that it was slightly more predictive of medical school performance than the MCAT but varied more within each racial group than between racial groups. In short, Margolin demonstrates that interview bias, MCAT norming, and GPA unreliability allowed the California Supreme Court to conclude that minority admittees were less qualified than Bakke. "The reluctance of the University to present evidence," he asserts, "should not excuse the lower court's ignoring such evidence presented by *amici* [citation omitted] and conjuring reverse discrimination instead."[48]

The Justices

Reese and Margolin dramatically narrowed the timespan of "societal discrimination" to the 1954–1976 period, the action to the education pipeline, and the victims to the current applicant cohort. One might think this specificity would satisfy justices who were all too familiar with discrimination in the K–12 pipeline, but instead at oral argument they questioned the attorneys on other topics. Did they think the case fell under the Fourteenth Amendment, Title VI, or both? Would they have made the same arguments if the number special admissions places had been lower or higher than sixteen? Should Asian Americans have been eligible for special admission? In preconference memoranda, the justices ruminated on principles that could be extracted from prior cases: Did the cases require deference to school and university authorities or the use of strict scrutiny review? Did they provide guidance on discrimination in the absence of intentionality, on the differentiation of invidious racial classifications from benign ones, and on special protection of racial minorities? Only Justice Brennan mentioned the MCAT and GPA studies. Thus the shadow of consensus slid away from the facts and toward the utilization of abstract principles to illegalize the UCD admissions program.

"RACIAL QUOTA"

In his Brief for Respondent, Colvin ostentatiously reprised the quota language he had used in the lower courts:

> Is Allan Bakke denied the equal protection of the laws in contravention of the Fourteenth Amendment to the United States Constitution when he is excluded from a state operated medical school solely because of his race as a result of a racial quota admission policy which guarantees the admission of a fixed number of "minority" persons who are judged apart from and permitted to meet lower standards of admission than Bakke?[49]

This powerful statement, located at the beginning of the brief, delineates the admissions policy as a "racial quota" guaranteeing "a fixed number" of places to minority applicants reviewed separately from and meeting lower standards than Bakke. Note that the terms "policy" (rather than "program"), "guarantees," and "fixed number" all imply intention to discriminate.[50]

Rather than providing facts to support this claim, Colvin creates the appearance of factuality by inserting, into the sixty-one-page brief, fifty-seven mentions of "quota" and such synonyms as "racial percentages" and "racial ratio." This passage is typical:

> Petitioner has formally adopted a *preferential racial quota* and has *set aside 16 of the places* for members of designated racial and ethnic minority groups. In doing so, petitioner has prevented Bakke, solely because of his race, from competing for the *16 quota places.* Petitioner does not dispute *this fact* and . . . concedes that it cannot refute Bakke's claim that he would have been admitted to the medical school had there been *no quota.* Because *the quota* reveals *the true nature* of the special admissions program, petitioner seeks to evade this aspect of the case. . . . *The record* herein, however, *establishes beyond doubt* that the special admissions program is *in fact* a *racial quota* (my emphases).[51]

Here Colvin uses metonymy, a linking device, to create a chain of signifiers—special admissions→sixteen set-aside places→a racial quota→the program's "true nature"—and places the chain within assertions about its factuality ("does not dispute this fact," "established beyond a doubt," and "in fact"). These techniques give "racial quota" a factual status in his text, but the facts included in and deliberately omitted from the record do not support the claim that Bakke could not compete for all one hundred places "solely because of his race." He did not meet the eligibility criteria to compete for places given to economically or educationally disadvantaged applicants or to compete for places given to applicants with medical school spouses, prominent parents, or the dean's acceptances. If he had been able to compete for all one hundred places, his benchmark score of 549 out of 600 put him at the ninety-second percentile, which was not the top tier of the huge applicant pool.[52]

The Bakke Amici

Unsurprisingly the Bakke amici embed heavy-handed quota language in statements about the academic inferiority of minority applicants. Writing for the Queens Jewish Community Center and Jewish Rights Council, Benjamin Vinar claims that "numerous applicants including the respondent Mr. Bakke . . . were *excluded* by reason of this *dual program*; while students with *far lower objective indicia* of excellence were admitted on the basis of their membership in certain *racial or national groups*" (my emphases).[53] Writing for Young Americans for Freedom, Jennings P. Felix and Marco DeFunis state that the school "gave *preferences* to certain 'minorities' by admitting them with *lower qualifications* than certain whites and, further, *reserved sixteen places* for the minorities" (my emphases).[54] Writing for the Order of the Sons of Italy in America, Judith R. Cohn and Robert L. Blacksberg contend that "*white applicants* whose qualifications are such that they would have been admitted if a *quota* of spaces were not *reserved for members of the preferred race* are *denied* the opportunity to attend medical school" (my emphases).[55]

To examine the quota narrative more closely, I turn to a brief written by Philip B. Kurland and seven more attorneys (hereafter Kurland) for the Anti-Defamation League, New York City Council of Supervisors and Administrators, National Jewish Commission on Law and Public Affairs, Jewish Labor Committee, and UNICO National. These five organizations played leading roles in the racial conflict over New York schools, the complaints against fifty-two universities, and the anti–affirmative action litigation against the State University of New York Downstate Medical Center and the City College of New York Biomedical Program (see chapter 1).[56] After describing each of the amici organizations in glowing terms, Kurland explains why they oppose UCD's alleged racial quota:

> The "*numerus clausus*," the *racial quota* that is involved in this case, is of particular concern to the amici because of the long history of *discrimination against Jews and others* by the use of *quotas*, both in Europe and in the United States. This brief is not an argument on behalf of any single minority, but on behalf of the free and open society mandated by the Constitution. It may be noted, however, that after only three or four decades of non-discriminatory admissions, in which creed, color, and ethnic origin have been rejected as appropriate criteria for university admissions, the universities, which for centuries set the style in *excluding or restricting Jewish students and those of various other religious, racial, and ethnic minorities*, may again be able to do so, again in the name of enlightenment and diversity, if the decision below is not affirmed (my emphases).[57]

Kurland uses "numerus clausus" (Latin for "closed number"), which denotes the quotas historically imposed on Jews and "others" at European and American universities, to imply that UCD's program is the latest episode of virulent anti-Semitism that spanned centuries and countries.

In the twenty-four pages that follow, "quota" metastasizes in his text and such section headers as: "The racial admissions quota utilized by the Petitioner deprived Respondent of his constitutional rights to equal protection of the laws," "Racial quotas are intrinsically malign," and "There is no state interest that can justify the use of a racial admissions quota."[58] Midway through the brief, Kurland finally defines the term:

> By definition a *quota* is a means of allocating scarce rights, goods, or services. If there were enough places at California's medical schools for all who wished to take advantage of them there would be no

> need for a *quota*. A *quota* arbitrarily . . . grants benefits to some by denying them to others. A *racial quota* is a measurement of an individual by a standard that must be wholly irrelevant in fact as well as law to the function for which the individual is being measured, the benefit he is to receive, or the hardship that is to be imposed (my emphases).[59]

Read literally, the passage turns medical school places into one of the valuable goods distributed on the basis of applicant identity rather than merit. Read symptomatically, however, it points to a contradiction.

In objecting that the quota allocates valuable goods to identity groups, the Jewish and white-ethnic amici exhibit their own "groupness." The ADL brief explicitly states that race-conscious admissions restricts the numbers of "Jewish students and . . . other religious, racial, and ethnic minorities." The Order of the Sons of Italy brief declares that it harms "persons of Italian origin, as well as . . . other members of the 'majority' white population." The Queens Jewish Community Council and Jewish Rights Council brief complains that it "is precisely the kind of system which for so many centuries was used to disadvantage members of the group we represent—the Jewish people." Meaning to criticize this Jewish sense of "groupness," Justice Blackmun lapses into genetic determinacy: "It is to be noted that nearly all the responsible Jewish organizations who have filed amicus briefs here are [on] one side of the case. They understandably want 'pure' equality and are willing to take their chances with it, knowing that they have *the inherent ability to excel* and to live with it successfully" (my emphasis).[60]

The Justices

During oral argument, comments about quotas reveal that the lawyers and justices believed that language was separable from facts about social events which, I have argued, are linguistic constructs. When Archibald Cox stated that the sixteen special admissions places did not constitute a quota that limited the number of minority admittees, Justice Powell responded, "Now the question is not whether the 16 is a quota. The question is whether the 84 is a quota." As Cox continued to talk about the sixteen places, Justice Stevens interrupted, "Mr. Cox, the facts are not in dispute . . . does it really matter what we call [the] program?" Cox replied, "if we call it a quota, knowing the facts and deciding according to the operative fact," then the semantics "couldn't matter less."[61] Stevens and Cox were not the only ones who believed that language did not construct facts. When Justice Powell asked whether the litigants had a factual controversy, Colvin replied that they were disputing the admissions quota, which "had a lot of factual elements to it," and added that the university's word "goal" was "a real misuse of language." Clearly exasperated, Justice Rehnquist interposed, "That really is a matter of characterization rather than strictly a fact. As I understand it, there were 16 places set aside for minority applicants and . . . you're certainly free to argue from that what you want about quotas and goals but that really goes beyond the strict factual matter."[62]

In his conference memorandum, Justice Powell similarly wrote that "the parties fight a sharp preliminary action over the proper characterization of the special admissions program. Petitioner prefers to see it as establishing a 'goal' of minority representation in the medical school. Respondent echoing the courts below labels it a racial quota. This semantic distinction is beside the point." But the justices' dismissal of the two terms as mere semantics masks their operations within legal-judicial discourse: "quota" invites a judgment of unconstitutionality that would halt the disputed social action, while "goal," the term used in federal agency regulations concerning affirmative action, invites a judgment that would permit or prescribe that social action. For Bakke supporters, wording mattered: they weaponized "quota" because it denoted an illegal practice. For Justice Powell, terminology didn't matter: "Whether this limitation is described as a quota or a goal, it is a line drawn on the basis of race."[63] According to this statement, "quota" and "goal" are merely linguistic varnish dabbed onto the factual "line drawn on the basis of race," itself, ironically, a metaphorical clause.

Irritated by Colvin's quota language, Justice Marshall used legal-judicial language to attack what others insisted were the unvarnished facts. At oral argument, he stated that the information on special admissions, which appeared in Dr. Lowrey's deposition, was hearsay because the doctor was employed at another university when the program was designed and adopted. During their long exchange, Colvin insisted the information was fact, Marshall insisted it was hearsay, and Colvin pushed back, stating that "it would only be hearsay in the sense that it related to the historical origin of the rule but it is not hearsay as it related to the way the rule was imposed in the two years [that Bakke applied]."[64]

Hearsay, according to *Black's Law Dictionary*, denotes "testimony that is given by a witness who relates not what he or she knows personally, but what others have said. . . . Such testimony is generally inadmissible under the rules of evidence."[65] Generally hearsay statements are not considered evidence because the person originally making the statements, if absent from the court, cannot be put under oath and cross-examined. This delineation of hearsay surfaces three issues. First, in bifurcating statements into those made by a witness who observed an event and those made by a witness who restates what someone else said about the event, it does not recognize, as I have argued throughout this book, that people do not directly apprehend events. Only through language do they make perceptual impressions meaningful. Second, the information presented in Dr. Lowrey's deposition and declaration, Bakke's interrogatory, and university documents more closely resembled hearsay than fact because it was not tested by witness examination at (the waived) trial. Third, university documents showed that the medical school admitted fifteen special applicants each year Bakke was rejected, but whether this number signified a quota benefitting less qualified admittees, a step to reach the goal of integrating the student body, or a cohort of admittees who met the admissions criteria was the work of linguistic characterization. Thus contrary to the justices' claim that facts and words were separable, what passed for facts about the social world always consisted of words.

"PROPORTIONAL REPRESENTATION"

Alarmed by the abundant information on systemic discrimination and the demands for minority inclusion, Bakke supporters feared that a ruling for the university would validate the idea of proportional representation that in turn would ripple across societal sectors to erode the near-monopolies of white groups over the nation's material and symbolic resources. Colvin thus links racial quotas in education to group proportionality in the professions:

> It ["quota"] implies that rights to education, training and consequent career opportunities, ideally open to all on an equal opportunity basis, will now be officially categorized by group membership. One would not become a doctor, lawyer, engineer or account, but a Black doctor, a Chicano lawyer, an Asian engineer, or an American Indian accountant. Admission to each profession or trade would be limited according to the relative size of each ethnic group.[66]

Here echoing Justice Felix Frankfurter's commentary on proportional representation in *Hughes v. Superior Court* (see below), Colvin proceeds to deconstruct "groupness." Who, he asks, decides which groups are entitled to career training? Will they receive benefits in proportion to their national, state, or local population? Which criteria determine racial group membership? "Need one be a 'full-blooded' American Indian to qualify? Or is one grandparent sufficient? Or one great-grandparent? Are we to become involved in the testing of legal rights according to blood lines?"[67] Although objecting to this biologizing of race, Colvin had biologized it all along when asserting that tests objectively gauged the academic inferiority of minority applicants.

To demonstrate more vividly the proportionality panic that gripped Bakke supporters, I turn to a brief written by eleven attorneys for eight Jewish, Polish, Italian, and Hellenic organizations. Citing the lead author, Howard L. Greenberger, who represented the American Jewish Committee, I argue that the brief relies on lexical substitutions, commonsensical statements, and slippery-slope logic to construct a narrative that transforms the places allocated by the UCD admissions program into a nationwide proportionality disaster.[68] Greenberger begins by noting that the trial court "found that the Medical School's admissions policy . . . utilized a racial quota and had discriminated against Bakke because of his race." After summarizing the case and the interests of the amici, he proceeds to the argument section, there connecting the alleged racial quota to group proportionality. First, he claims that "petitioner's argument necessarily means that there is a 'proper proportion' of representation of each group in each profession or calling." Then he observes, "Not surprisingly, the University insists that its special admissions program should not be viewed as a 'quota.' Since 'quota' is a painful word to many people because it is reminiscent of past injustices, it is often replaced by a euphemism such as 'ratio' or 'reasonable representation.'"[69] Next he discredits the university's defense of special admissions by citing *Hughes v. Superior Court of California* (1950). This case was precipitated when picketers in the Black town of Richmond, California, demanded that local Lucky grocery stores hire Black workers in proportion to Black customers. After a state court enjoined the picketers and held them in contempt for continuing to picket, they challenged the injunction which, they claimed, stifled their speech as protected by the due process clause of the Fourteenth Amendment. Justice Felix Frankfurter famously wrote,

> To deny to California the right to ban picketing in the circumstances of this case would mean that there could be no prohibition of the pressure of picketing to secure proportional employment on ancestral grounds of Hungarians in Cleveland, of Poles in Buffalo, of Germans in Milwaukee, of Portuguese in New Bedford, of Mexicans in San Antonio, of the numerous minority groups in New York, and so on through the whole gamut of racial and religious concentrations in various cities. States may well believe that such constitutional sheltering would inevitably encourage use of picketing to compel employment on the basis of racial discrimination.[70]

This passage, which I described in previous chapters as giving rise to the "nation of minorities" trope, caroms from the Richmond picketing to the total restructuring of society along the lines of ethno-proportionality (notably all the groups he names, except "Mexicans," are white ones).

Drawing on this passage, Greenberger repeatedly glissades down the slippery slope from medical school places to universal proportionality:

> In effect, therefore, petitioner [in *Bakke*] is arguing that there is a "proper" proportion of representation for each group and that certain minorities have a right, entitled to recognition as a "compelling state interest," to have available a substantially proportionate number of doctors for their use. If this is so, minority groups have an equal right to a proportionate number of hospital personnel, prosecutors and judges, and so forth.[71]
>
> Petitioner's theory, of course, would apply with equal validity to psychologists, social workers, bankers, businessmen, political officeholders, and a broad spectrum of economic, professional and governmental occupations with equally profound and divisive implications. The result would be a race-conscious society in which a proportionate number of places in colleges, professional schools and occupational categories would be set aside for members of particular racial and ethnic groups.[72]
>
> Far from being regarded as abhorrent, invidious and irrelevant, racial and ethnic classifications would be officially sanctioned and recognized in all walks of life; each professional or officeholder would be regarded, and would regard himself, as a representative of the group from whose quota he comes; and individual aspirations would be limited by the proportionate size of the group to which the individual belongs.[73]

From these three hyperbolic passages, which refer to the competition for places in higher education and dozens of occupations, we can gauge the panic felt by the amici constituents who, as white elites and white ethnics, enjoyed out-sized shares of the nation's resources.

Construing Statistics

To discredit arguments for minority representation, some of the Bakke supporters simply repudiated data on racial discrimination, but others attacked statistical research itself. Writing for the Pacific Legal Foundation, Ronald A. Zumbrun, John H. Findley, and William F. Harvey took their readers through a labyrinthine narrative with many factual gaps and distortions. They begin by declaring that the university asks the

Supreme Court to "engage in the kind of legislative assumption which once was made by the Congress in Section 402 of the Civil Rights Act of 1964."[74] Providing no further information, they simply named a provision that had directed the US commissioner of education to conduct a survey of public-school equality and, within two years, to deliver a report to the president and Congress. Commissioner Francis Keppel recruited Johns Hopkins University sociologist James S. Coleman, who led a team of social scientists that surveyed 600,000 students, 60,000 teachers, and 3,100 schools nationwide. The Coleman report, titled *Equality of Educational Opportunity* (1966), fueled heated debates among educators, statisticians, and policymakers. After organizing a Harvard seminar on the Coleman report, statistician Frederick Mosteller and sociologist Daniel P. Moynihan published some of the papers in their coedited volume, *On Equality of Educational Opportunity* (1972).[75]

Relying mainly on the Harvard book, Zumbrun and his colleagues argued that the Coleman findings undercut Congress's assumption that "schools which Negro children attended would prove to have inferior facilities."

> Coleman found that was not the case [citing Mosteller and Moynihan]. Furthermore, it was found that the range of performance within each school was greater than school-to-school variations, at all grade levels, for all racial and ethnic groups [citing the Coleman report]. From Coleman's findings, one could reasonably conclude that no one was being shortchanged by the nation's public school system, at least within large geographic regions, and that everyone was being afforded an opportunity to maximize whatever academic potential he brought to school with him [citing Mosteller and Moynihan].

Thus they assert that the Coleman report's "actual findings," which contradict the university's "broad social allegations" and "historical revanchism," should caution the *Bakke* justices against using "simplistic assertions . . . as a basis for constitutional decision making."[76] Again drawing on the Mosteller and Moynihan book, Zumbrun and his colleagues state that the Coleman finding of "a statistical disparity . . . between the median test scores of Negro pupils and the median test scores of white pupils" should not "be used to establish 'group inequalities.'" In *Bakke*, they complain, the university "suggest[s] that a statistical disparity between the numbers of whites and blacks in the Davis Medical School establishes a history of past discrimination which justified the use of 'reverse discrimination' in admissions to create a racial balance."[77] Their arguments, however, ignore the flaws in both books that scholars had previously identified.

In a 1972 review of Mosteller and Moynihan's book, education scholar Diane Ravitch, who was then writing *The Great School Wars: New York City, 1805–1973* (1974), observed that the Coleman report had "unleashed a wide variety of interpretations."[78] Affirmative-action supporters read it as proof that race-conscious remedies were needed to equalize education, while opponents read it as proof that individual ability determined educational performance. Soon after the report appeared, Arthur R. Jensen, a Berkeley professor of education psychology and psychometrics, published two highly controversial articles. In "Social Class, Race, and Genetics: Implications for Education" (1968), he reviewed research on the environment vs. heredity question, and in "Selections of Minority Students in Higher Education" (1970) he argued that the white-Black disparity in educational attainment was largely owing to racial differences in intelligence as reflected by scoring on IQ tests.[79] Citing the latter article in his Law School Admissions Council brief, Harry Reese remarked that using "educational attainment as the measure of ability, while refusing to come to grips with . . . past [educational] discrimination as the obvious cause, would involve the tacit . . . adoption of a premise of genetic inferiority."[80]

Most scholars praised the Coleman survey as "the second largest social-science research project ever conducted in the United States" but noted that it was hampered by the short timeline, nonparticipation of large school districts, and simplistic "inputs" and "outputs." The inputs consisted of basic data on school facilities, per pupil expenditures in districts rather than schools, and family background from "highly fallible student reports"; and the outputs consisted of scores on standardized tests administered to students at mostly segregated schools.[81]

Statisticians criticized the design, data, and interpretations. In a 1973 article for the *Journal of the American Statistical Association*,

Anthony E. Boardman faulted the Coleman study for being empirically unsound, limited in scope, and overgeneralized, and faulted the Mosteller and Moynihan reanalysis for using untested models of educational attainment, too few variables, and insufficiently disaggregated data. Both the study and the reanalysis, he wrote, did not look "specifically at Puerto Ricans, Mexican Americans, American Indians or Orientals," a mistake that *DeFunis* and *Bakke* brief writers repeated by equating "minorities" with "Blacks," as if other groups of color did not exist.[82] Statistically, they barely existed because education researchers were not closely tracking other groups than African Americans and Chicanos.

In a 1975 article for the *American Educational Research Journal*, Ronald P. Carver criticized the Coleman study's output design. It used standardized test scores to compare individual student performance to averaged student performance, organized the scores to reveal disparities by race and class, and analyzed the data along only two axes. One axis showed how much racial group variance was attributed to differences in student ability and motivation versus how much was attributed differences in school facilities, curriculum, and teachers; the other axis showed how much racial group variance occurred within individual schools versus how much occurred across schools. In other words, each axis had a two-factor proportion: out of 100 percent variance, the study attributed X percent to student ability and Y percent to school conditions. Thus the findings concerning racialized student and school differences were artifacts of a psychometric test designed to reveal averaged student performance, a classificatory scheme designed to reveal group disparities, and a statistical model designed to reveal a two-factor proportion, all at a single moment in time. Carver concluded that a study which tested student performance against learning standards, incorporated more factors, and tracked student performance longitudinally would have produced very different findings.[83]

"Statistical Discrimination"

Rather than disputing or misrepresenting statistical findings, Benjamin Vinar's brief for the Queens Jewish Community Council and the

Jewish Rights Council created the new concept of "statistical discrimination." He begins by criticizing the evidence in *Brown*:

> Current affirmative action programs are essentially an outgrowth of some of the curious reasoning indulged by this Court in its rationale in *Brown v. Board of Education* [citation omitted]. In *Brown*, where the Court finally faced head-on the law which it had promulgated some 60 years earlier in *Plessy v. Ferguson* [citation omitted], it rightly held that *Plessy* . . . was wrong, but it did so on an inappropriate rationale.

The Court, he continues, was persuaded by "*sociological and psychological statistical evidence* . . . that such governmental discrimination had deleterious side effects upon the psyches and learning incentives and abilities of the children of minority groups . . . and that *for that reason* such [segregation] laws were necessarily unconstitutional" (his italics).[84]

Next Vinar conflates the use of psychological and sociological statistics with de facto segregation, turning both into artifacts with no social referents: "Plainly, if psychological and sociological statistics rather than straightforward legal criteria were to become our guidepost, then it was apparent that the psychological and sociological fact of statistical 'de facto segregation,' with or without government order, was disadvantageous to minority groups. *Ergo*, governments were now to be deemed to have the obligation to correct such 'de facto segregation' wherever it existed." Then, like other Bakke supporters, he slides down the slope to proportional representation: "Step by step we have witnessed the incursion by the courts and administrative agencies into virtually every walk of the citizenry's life":

> Jobs for minority groups have been ordered to be created by "uncreating" them for their existing white occupants. Minority quotas for schools have been ordered to be met by compulsory busing . . . More and more it has become statistical integration for the sake of statistical integration which is the desired goal. No matter what the effect on the individual child . . . the ultimate goal is that it be good for the group affected.[85]

And then, as with other Bakke supporters, groupthink bubbles to the surface of the text.

"This concept of group statistical rights," Vinar asserts, "is precisely the kind of system which for so many centuries was used to disadvantage members of the groups we represent—the Jewish people. It is the *numerous clausus* by which numbers of Jews in universities were controlled in Germany, Austria, and Russia."[86] Quite obviously, Vinar's reasoning proceeds through a substantively misleading chain of equivalences: statistical evidence→statistical discrimination→statistical rights for minorities→anti-Jewish quotas. At the end of the brief, he returns to statistics, writing, "Ethnic, religious, and racial surveys and censuses by government agencies, followed by decrees to 'integrate' statistically on an ever more compounding basis (a populations shift year by year and day by day), are things without end."[87] When Vinar wrote this brief, the two organizations he represented were fighting to block school and housing integration in the New York metro area (see chapter 1).

The meanings of *DeFunis* and *Bakke*, I have argued throughout this book, were constructed by mechanisms of language and law. Some participants depicted these cases as win-lose disputes between an indignant white plaintiff and an intransigent university; others cast them as metaphysical duels between the abstract principles of color-blindness and color-consciousness; and still others delineated them as litigation designed to maintain systemic racism. Through their own words, the lawyers and judges demonstrated that the dispute over professional school places was a synecdoche for the wider societal combat over which races could possess how much of the nation's material and symbolic goods. In spinning arguments, the defenders of white privilege freed the principle of color-blindness to bleach the real-world consequences of systemic racism.

The last word goes to Theodore M. Shaw, associate director and counsel of the NAACP Legal Defense and Education Fund, whom I interviewed in 2002. "Now," he said, "color-blindness is being used as a tool to get people to say that you can't do anything affirmatively about racial inequality because in order to do that you have to take race into account. What they've done is made mere race-consciousness into the evil. It's never been the evil; white supremacy and racial oppression have been the evil."[88]

PART IV

THE REPRISE

CONCLUSION: INSTALLING THE NEW RACISM

> When a racial group's collective prejudice is backed by legal authority and institutional control, it is transformed into racism, a far-reaching system that functions independently from the intentions or self-images of individual actors.
>
> —Robin DiAngelo, *White Fragility* (2018)

The participants in *DeFunis v Odegaard* and *Regents of the University of California v. Bakke*, as I have shown throughout this book, used the infinitesimal mechanisms of language and law to select the facts and principles that constituted "reverse discrimination" as a new object of litigation and "systemic racism" as its rejected "other." Although the cases generated an abundance of statements in briefs, court opinions, and media coverage purporting to show that race-conscious admissions procedures discriminated against white applicants to university programs, something more powerful was needed to dismantle affirmative action in higher education. This final chapter demonstrates that the conservative movement, by expanding, reorienting, and operationalizing its organizations during the post-*Bakke* era, sought to install what critics now call "the new color-blind racism."

For those interested in theory, I will argue that discourses need generously resourced organizations in order to make structural change. For those interested in action, I will describe the rise of cultural conservatism, the founding of new organizations that managed dozens of anti–affirmative action initiatives, and the impact of these initiatives on college applicants. Then I will describe conservative proposals for making structural change and analyze the organizational forms that enabled the coordination of activity. The short finale revisits the disconnect between "racial discrimination" in legal discourse and "systemic racism" in lived experience.

THEORIES

In the introduction to this book, I described discourse as an ensemble of actors and actions, organizations and processes, material objects and symbolic elements, bound together by particular relations. To illustrate this concept, I borrowed a simple example from Ernesto Laclau and Chantal Mouffe's "Post-Marxism without Apologies": as two workers build a brick wall, one asks the other to hand him a brick, which he then cements into the unfinished wall. Laclau and Mouffe explain that the workers, their actions (handing and cementing), the material objects (bricks, cement, and trowel), and statements ("hand me a brick") are parts of the total operation of building a brick wall. "This totality[,] which includes within itself the linguistic and the non-linguistic, is what we call *discourse*."[1] But notice that this example omits certain features of discourse—not only the bricklayers' socialization into the trade practices required to build the wall but also the whole dimension of organizational dynamics. What Laclau and Mouffe describe is the routinized practices of individual actors, not the spatially and temporally distanciated processes of organizations that Anthony Giddens analyzes in *The Constitution of Society*. These organizations, as I will explain shortly, have the power to produce and circulate "truths" (or, if one prefers, ideology) that in turn empower them to act in other ways.

While it may seem obvious that legal-judicial discourse participates in the power/knowledge regime of the United States, we owe to Michel Foucault the analysis of how power depends upon discourses that produce "truth." In "Two Lectures" (1976), he describes two models of power that emerged from the field of political economy over the course of the eighteenth and nineteenth centuries. The juridical model conceives of power in terms of individual rights: one has "a right, which one is able to possess like a commodity, and which one can in consequence, transfer or alienate, either wholly or partially, through a legal act or through some act that establishes a right, such as takes place through cession or contract." Juridical power is also exercised by institutions that can order action (e.g., the order to admit Bakke to medical school), prohibit action (e.g., rulings that found race-conscious admissions to be unconstitutional), and permit action under certain restrictions. By contrast, the economic model conceives of power as systemic functionality; it resides in modes of production and reproduction that depend upon class domination and subjection.[2] In the United States, this power was exercised through racial bondage in the plantation regime, labor exploitation in the era of industrialization, and now the financialized class relations of neoliberal capitalism.

In his work, Foucault traces the shift from the top-down exercise of power in old sovereign regimes to the circulation of discursive power throughout the capillaries of modern society:

> In any society, there are manifold relations of power which permeate, characterize, and constitute the social body, and these relations of power cannot themselves be established, consolidated nor implemented without the production, accumulation, circulation and functioning of a discourse. There can be no possible exercise of power without a certain economy of discourses of truth which operate through and on the basis of this association. We are subjected to the production of truth through power and we cannot exercise power except through the production of truth.

By the production of truth, Foucault means knowledges that are produced by authoritative institutions, at one time institutions of religion and since the late nineteenth century those of medicine, crime, sexuality, and other human sciences. To understand how a power/knowledge regime operates, Foucault advises us to "conduct an ascending analysis," which begins by examining "its infinitesimal mechanisms" and then tracks how they are "invested, colonized, utilized, involuted, transformed, displaced, [and] extended" as they circulate through society.[3] Throughout this book, I have examined these small mechanisms; now I will ascend to the larger ones, the organizations and the flows of human, informational, and financial resources.

CULTURAL CONSERVATISM

As noted in the introduction, the conservative movement exercised its power through an organizational infrastructure of think tanks, advocacy organizations, legal defense funds, training programs, media outlets, and legislative networks. The construction of this infrastructure responded to the recent intensification of partisan politics within the much longer trajectory of professionalizing the production of knowledge. In the United States, this professionalization began with the nineteenth-century institutionalization of the modern disciplines at research and land grant universities and accelerated through twentieth-century boundary-crossing developments. These developments included the flow of foundation and government funding to academic institutions, the resulting proliferation of specialisms, the World War II hybridization of academe to the military-industrial complex in science and technology projects of national importance, the postwar growth of universities that increased their capacity to train professionals, and the involvement of experts in governance.[4]

In *The Idea Brokers: Think Tanks and the Rise of the New Policy Elite*, James Allen Smith describes the incorporation of academic liberals into the Kennedy and Johnson administrations where, as advisors and other officials, they helped the presidents navigate complex social issues like racism, poverty, and crime. The use of knowledge expertise in governance captured the attention of those working in the nonacademic policy sector who saw it as an opportunity to gain influence. This sector, according to John L. Campbell and Ove K. Pedersen, was traditionally "dominated by a number of prominent state policy research organizations and several rather scholarly private ones." But as partisan rancor intensified during the 1980s and 1990s, conservative entrepreneurs founded "more aggressive and competitive private policy research organizations" to break the liberal monopoly on expert knowledge. They used these organizations not merely to oppose New Deal programs, civil rights reforms, and Keynesian economics but to create a "marketplace" of policy ideas.[5]

Before the Reagan revolution, conservative organizations tended to function within particular spheres. The American Enterprise Institute (1938), Heritage Foundation (1973), Cato Institute (1974), and other think tanks were "idea brokers" that produced policy papers and press releases. The Intercollegiate Studies Institute (1953), Young Americans for Freedom (1960), National Journalism Center (1976), and Leadership Institute (1979) trained conservative students for positions in mainstream and movement organizations. The Moral Majority, founded by Jerry Falwell Sr. and Paul Weyrich in 1979, quickly became the largest organization to mobilize the Christian Right in advocacy and lobbying activities.[6]

During the 1980s, Christian Right leaders and neoconservative intellectuals, who had been peripheral to the movement's free-market economic agenda, gained more visibility for cultural issues. While religious leaders emphasized family values and intellectuals sounded warnings about academic leftism, the Free Congress Foundation (founded by William F. Buckley Jr., Frank Chodorow, and Paul Weyrich in 1953) merged these concerns in two influential publications. The anonymously authored *Cultural Conservatism: Toward a New Agenda* (1987) argued that, as the movement pursued its economic agenda, "America has been suffering from cultural drift" that gradually emptied "the nation's values of their content"—namely, Western Judeo-Christian culture. Borrowing the sociological concept of mediating institutions that stand between individuals and the larger economic, political, social, and cultural systems, the book maps out policies for families, schools, jobs, religious institutions, and safety net programs.[7] *Cultural Conservatism: Theory and Practice* (1991), edited by William S. Lind (a paleoconservative critical of cultural Marxism) and William H. Marshner (a theology professor intent on reviving religious values), combined papers by such intellectuals as Russell Kirk, William Bennett, and Michael Levin with those by movement and governmental officials. Explicitly criticizing the conservative preoccupation with economic issues, the book recast in conservative terms the traditionally progressive critiques of sexism, racism, Eurocentrism, public schools, and higher education.[8]

Although troubled by the Free Congress Foundation's emphasis on culture, economic conservatives were familiar with the cultural issues addressed by neoconservative intellectuals whose work was published in highly regarded and widely read magazines like the *National Review* and *Commentary*. These authors, cued by New Left critiques of the university, had mounted an attack on academic institutions, which they regarded as incubators of radical left ideology and activism. Through books, journals, public lectures, and press conferences, these and other conservative intellectuals circulated a political correctness discourse that censured research on gender, race, and class, multicultural teaching, poststructuralist theory, speech codes, affirmative-action programs, and progressive student groups.[9]

To understand how this massive discourse was produced and circulated, I visited conservative organizations in 1991–1992 and again in 2001–2002. During the first round of visits, I discovered that new organizations had burrowed inside academe. The National Association of Scholars (1987), headquartered in Princeton, New Jersey, had spawned dozens of chapters and was using its journal, conferences, and publicity machine to denounce tenured radicals (i.e., leftists, feminists, multiculturalists, and poststructuralists) and progressive trends in academe. Creating a powerful echo chamber, the Madison Center for Educational Affairs (MCEA), founded by William J. Bennett in 1990 after his stint as Reagan's secretary of education, had launched the Collegiate Network. Consisting of seventy conservative student newspapers located on sixty-six campuses across the country, it circulated inflammatory articles on race, gender, sexuality, and leftism to more than 600,000 readers. As sidelines, the MCEA awarded grants to conservative authors, published a guide to activism on campus, and made referrals for summer internships at the Washington Legal Foundation and the Center for Individual Rights (see below). In these few examples, we can see how cultural conservatism brought the subject of universities into the field of conflict and how organizations, through the channeling of financial, human, and informational resources, mounted an attack on them.

ANTI–AFFIRMATIVE ACTION INITIATIVES

Meanwhile, outside of academe, I discovered that second-generation conservative organizations were wielding the power of the law against affirmative action. From the 1990s onward, three of these combative organizations took the lead: the Center for Individual Rights (CIR) (1989) litigated academic reverse-discrimination and speech cases; the American Civil Rights Institute (ACRI) (1996) orchestrated state-level voter referenda banning affirmative action; and the Center for Equal Opportunity (CEO) (1995) provided research and advocacy.[10]

In 2001, when I interviewed the CIR director of legal and public affairs Curt A. Levey at the organization's Washington, DC, headquarters, I learned that this public interest law firm (PILF), which was funded by foundations, legal fees, and direct-mail gifts, had less than a dozen lawyers and support staffers. Though small, it maximized its clout by carefully selecting cases from a large number of potential "walk-in" and "over the transom" plaintiffs and by reaching out for assistance to the American Civil Rights Institute, Center for Equal Opportunity, National Association of Scholars, and the Federalist Society. The CIR, Levey said, viewed discrimination and affirmative action in higher education as synonymous: "I know some people like to say that preferences—racial preferences, gender preferences—are a way of implementing opportunity," but "opportunity cannot be accomplished by discriminating."[11]

His support for this position rested heavily on his interpretation of the *Bakke* opinions:

> The universities . . . try to rely legally on Justice Powell's opinion in . . . *Bakke*. Although none of the other justices joined him in this point, people at least have argued that this was the holding of the Court. . . . Again, our position would be that if you're using race you're violating the equal protection clause of the Constitution and Title VI of the 1964 Civil Rights Act. But . . . even if we concede for argument's sake that Powell's opinion is a law, are you complying with Powell's opinion? Our position is that most of the selective universities in this nation are not even coming close to complying with Powell's opinion.[12]

Later in the interview, when I asked how we might explain the underrepresentation of minorities and women in particular institutions and fields, he replied,

> Part of the reason we're called the Center for Individual Rights is because . . . you have to look at people as individuals. There is no concept in the Constitution about group rights: women as a group, minorities as a group, aren't entitled to some percentage of the jobs. . . . So the fact that there's not the right proportion of women or minorities is not in and of itself a problem that needs to be remedied.[13]

In 2001 and again in 2002, I interviewed Roger Clegg, vice president and general counsel of the Center for Equal Opportunity.[14] He described the CEO as an educational organization focused on civil rights, bilingual education, and immigration, adding, "it's also fair to call us an advocacy organization because we do have a point of view." When I asked how the staff made this point of view known, he said they write for print and digital media, appear on radio and television programs, meet with government officials, and testify before Congress. They also filed amicus briefs in CIR cases and assisted the ACRI with California Proposition 209 and Washington Initiative 200. These activities were directed by Edward Blum, who would later orchestrate the voting rights case of *Shelby County v. Holder* (2013); the reverse-discrimination case of *Fisher v. University of Texas* (2013, 2016); and the Students for Fair Admissions lawsuits against admissions programs at Harvard, North Carolina, and Texas.[15]

Clegg explained that the CEO opposed "the use of preferences on the basis of race, ethnicity, or sex" in admissions and employment. "We can have a debate about whether that discrimination is justified or not," he stated, "but it is discrimination" that violates the Constitution and the Civil Rights Act of 1964.[16] Clegg, like Levey, rejected the concept of underrepresentation. "It's wrong," he said, "to assume that any time you have a numerical imbalance something sinister is going on, that it must be because of discrimination of the effects of discrimination." Women often make the "personal choice" to enter "some fields rather than others" or "interrupt their careers to a greater degree than men." Similarly with race, he added, "you have to be careful because if there's such a thing as 'underrepresentation' then necessarily there's such a thing as 'overrepresentation.' If you believe there are not enough blacks and Hispanics at the law school . . . then you are saying there are too many Jews or Asians."[17]

In 2002 when I interviewed Kevin Nguyen, executive director of the American Civil Rights Institute, the ACRI had gathered nearly 980,000 signatures to place the Racial Privacy Initiative (RPI) on the California ballot.[18] Designated as Proposition 54, it prohibited state and local governments from collecting data on race, ethnicity, and national origin, but made exceptions for data needed to comply with federal law, conduct medical research, and carry out law enforcement activities.[19] When I asked Nguyen about the thinking behind the RPI, he explained that data collection forced individuals

> to pick between the racial heritage of one parent over another or one grandparent over another when they're confronted with these questions and boxes. . . . All we're doing is giving ourselves the warm, comforting blanket of racial data when, in fact, the data are inherently corrupt and unfortunately corrupt public policy. What I mean by that is that racial data have no scientific value because if they did they would have standards and consistency. . . . None of the scientists and none of the lay people can agree on what "race" is, what constitutes a racial group, and beyond that what the labels mean.[20]

Nguyen's comment echoed two tropes used in *Bakke*, the percentage-of-blood policies and the nation-of-minorities trope, to repudiate data that made racial groups visible. He contended that racial "data feed into the theory of disparate impact," which in turn requires "that we must achieve some sort of proportional representation in our workforce, our colleges, and our contracting."[21] Ending with an emotional appeal, he said, "We don't want to leave them [our children and grandchildren] a society where, in the case of Jewish Americans or Asian Americans, their entry into a prestigious public college depends upon how well their group is doing at the time."[22]

His mention of these groups reminded me of the frequent invocation of anti-Jewish quotas in *Bakke* and of California Proposition 187 (1994), which restricted the access of undocumented immigrants to many government services and benefits. The proposition, Nguyen explained, "was passed by an overwhelming margin with strong support from minority voters as well as legal immigrants . . . [because] the California economy was in the tank and people were very much concerned about the lack of government resources to serve all of California's residents and citizens." When I asked whether low-income people were voting from their own economic interests, he adverted to the law: "People who were law-abiding citizens and residents felt that their taxes should go into services for citizens and legal residents and that it wasn't fair to subsidize or completely support those who were in this country illegally."[23] When I asked whether the ACRI saw any relationship between immigration and affirmative action, his long answer again adverted to the law: We should apply the same principles to everyone, but instead we apply the principles inconsistently to groups that, as groups, do not have constitutionally guaranteed rights.[24] Yet, as we will see next, the anti–affirmative action initiatives mounted by these organizations had racially disparate group impacts.

California

In 1995, Governor Pete Wilson issued an executive order banning affirmative action at state universities, and a month later Ward Connerly persuaded the University of California Regents to approve Resolution SP-1 banning affirmative action in the UC system.[25] In 1996, Connerly and Dusty Rhodes, president of the *National Review*, founded the ACRI, which went on to orchestrate bans in eight states. That same year California voters approved the ACRI's Proposition 209, which provided that "the state shall not discriminate against, or grant preferential treatment to, any individual or group on the basis of race, sex, color, ethnicity, or national origin in the operation of public employment public education, or public contracting."[26] The impact of Resolution SP-1 and Proposition 209 was dramatic. At UC Berkeley, the number of Black freshmen plunged from 258 in 1997 (pre-ban) to 95 in 1998, a 63 percent decline[27]; system-wide Black and Hispanic enrollments declined by 131 percent and 148 percent, while white and Asian American enrollments increased by 115 percent and 451 percent respectively.[28]

Subsequently California legislators enacted the Four Percent Plan, which guaranteed the top 4 percent of each high-school graduating class admission to a state university, though not necessarily their first choice. They assumed that, "given *de facto* racial segregation in the state's high schools," the plan would be a race-blind way to increase minority enrollments at state universities.[29] But studies tracking applicants, admittees, and enrollees showed sharp declines for Blacks, Hispanics, and Native Americans, steady or fractionally lower outcomes for Whites, and large increases for Asians across the UC system.[30] The declines were troubling because, as the Black and Hispanic populations burgeoned, their share of high-school diplomas and UC applications increased, but so too did their rejections.

Affirmative-action opponents knew that "deep inequalities plagued California's public education system" and "suggested that the only fair way to redress the under-representation of certain minority groups in higher education was to address the unequal opportunities in K–12 education," but they did not bring "the same zeal to the fight for K–12 educational equality that they brought to ending affirmative action."[31] Indeed, *Williams v. California*, a case filed in 2000 by the American Civil Liberties Union for thousands of Black and Hispanic students, exposed the appalling conditions at destitute schools—overcrowded and cancelled classes, noncredentialed teachers, textbook and supply shortages, leaking roofs, shuttered bathrooms, and rat and mold infestations.[32] Magnifying the school inequalities, UC required applicants to "complete fifteen or more courses in seven different subject areas" and awarded extra points for advanced placement and honors courses, but the destitute schools offered students of color few such courses.[33]

In 2002, as noted earlier, the ACRI successfully campaigned to place the Racial Privacy Initiative on the November ballot, but it was defeated. When I mentioned to Theodore M. (Ted) Shaw, then associate director and counsel of the NAACP Legal Defense and Education Fund, that it was marketed as protecting individual privacy from the uses of racial data, he reframed it as speech suppression: the RPI, he said, "is not a matter of racial privacy; it is a matter of censoring race, of making race something we can't talk about."[34]

Texas

In 1992, the CIR's Michael F. Rosman and Vincent A. Molloy filed *Hopwood v. Texas*, on behalf of Cheryl Hopwood and three white men who were rejected by the University of Texas Law School. The district court, which denied intervention on behalf of minority students, ruled for the university; the Sixth Circuit Court of Appeals, which also denied intervention, ruled against the university. Sending shock waves through the affirmative-action community, the circuit court declared that Justice Powell's opinion was not binding, student diversity was not a compelling governmental interest, and race could not be a factor in admissions.[35] Broadly interpreting the ruling, Texas attorney general Daniel C. Morales declared that it banned race-conscious measures in admissions, financial aid, hiring, and retention at all public universities and federally funded private ones.[36] At UT Austin, Hispanic applicants to the law school dropped by 15 percent and Black ones plunged by 42 percent. System-wide, Hispanic applicants dropped by 17 percent and Black ones dropped by 21 percent; at UT Austin Black admittees slid from 501 in 1996 to 419 admittees and only 163 enrollees in 1997.[37]

When the US Departments of Justice and Education took the position that the *Hopwood* decision was incorrect, Texas legislators enacted the Ten Percent Plan (TPP), which guaranteed high-school students in the top 10 percent of their graduating class admission to a state university of their choice.[38] Supporters thought the TPP, by drawing from segregated schools, would increase Black and Hispanic enrollments at flagship campuses. At UT Austin, Black enrollees fell from 4.9 percent of the student body in 1995 (pre-*Hopwood*) to 2.7 percent in 1997 and then rose to 3.4 percent in 2002; Hispanic enrollees fell from 14.7 percent to 12.6 percent and then crept up a fraction of a percent.[39] The situation was worse than the numbers indicated, because by 2010 Texas was a majority minority state, with the third largest number of Black people (behind New York and Florida) and the second largest number of Hispanic people (behind California) as shares of the total state population.[40] Studies showed that the Hispanic share of all high-school diplomas had increased dramatically, the Black share had increased modestly, and the White and Asian shares had decreased; yet both *Hopwood* and the TPP resulted in lower ratios of Hispanic and Black applicants, admittees, and enrollees but higher ratios of White and Asian ones.[41]

While discussing the situation. Ted Shaw observed, "You have case after case in Texas [names several]. You have a lot of history in Texas; none of that was context in *Hopwood*. In fact, the court acted as if nothing that had happened in the past had any relevance for the present conditions."[42] By ignoring history, the Sixth Circuit court and the TPP framers repeated it.

Florida

In 1999 the ACRI decided to launch an affirmative-action referendum in Florida. Fearing it would hurt his brother's chances in the 2000 presidential election, Governor Jeb Bush preempted the threat by issuing the One Florida Initiative, which banned affirmative action in education, employment, and government contracting. To soften the blow, he also announced the Talented Twenty Program, which guaranteed the top 20 percent of each high-school graduating class admission to the state university system.

When state senator Kendrick Meek and representative Anthony Hill arrived at the governor's office to demand public forums on One Florida, a staffer turned them away with racially insulting language. Meek and Hill alerted the media and staged a twenty-five-hour sit-in that ended when the governor agreed to hold three forums. As protestors inside and outside the auditoriums disrupted the forums, national civil rights organizations worked with dozens of local groups to mount a get-out-the-vote campaign that, according to Julian Bond, NAACP board chair, increased the African American vote in the presidential election by 60 percent. But the election was vitiated by state lists that made registered voters ineligible to vote, police intimidation of Black voters, poll closings, misaligned ballots, hidden ballot boxes, and the aborted recount of ballots with hanging and dimpled chads. Bond remarked, "The margin of victory in Florida was the margin of disenfranchisement in Florida, and that, of course elected George Bush as president."[43]

At the University of Florida, from 2000 (before One Florida) to 2001, Black admittees dropped from 1,671 to 1,046 and enrollees dropped from 829 to 461. Subsequently the numbers rose to 659 in 2002, 676 in 2003, and 726 in 2004. Moreover, the Talented Twenty program failed to mitigate university segregation: from 2002 to 2004, Florida A&M University was 96.2 to 98 percent Black; the University of Florida and Florida State University were 10 to 11 percent Black; and most other universities ranged from 1.6 to 8.5 percent Black.[44] Reporting on the outcomes of the One Florida and Talented Twenty Initiative ten years later, an *Orlando Sentinel* article cited data showing that as the proportions of Black and Hispanic high school graduates increased their proportions among freshmen at state universities decreased or stagnated. Former Governor Bush told reporters, "'I would say the results are pretty good,'" and system chancellor Frank Brogan, who had served as Bush's lieutenant governor, said that One Florida had "abolished 'quotas.'" Other One Florida supporters blamed the declines on the weak economy, rising tuition, limited university growth, and the enrollment of Talented Twenty students in out-of-state universities (a flow the state did not track).[45]

Washington

In July 1997, the CIR's Michael Rosman filed *Smith v. University of Washington Law School* on behalf of three white plaintiffs—Katuria Smith rejected in 1994, Angela Rock rejected in 1995, and Michael Pyle rejected in 1996. Reprising *DeFunis*, the law school admissions committee, again chaired by Richard Kummert, weighted the GPA and LSAT heavily and used race as a factor to diversify the entering class. Gaining class certification to represent all white students applying for admission from 1994 onward, Rosman sought a summary judgment that the admissions program violated constitutional and statutory law.[46]

Meanwhile, the ACRI, which had unsuccessfully pressured the state legislature to enact an affirmative-action ban, collected enough signatures to place Initiative 200 (I-200) on the 1998 ballot. The wording, which prohibited state-sponsored preferences based on race, ethnicity, sex, or national origin, was a cover for illegalizing affirmative action.[47] Although opposed by major corporations and by Governor Gary Locke, who told the *Seattle Times* that people were misled by the preference language, it passed with 58 percent of the votes.[48] When the Ninth Circuit Court of Appeals finally heard *Smith*, it stated that the admissions program did not violate the Constitution, but it had to comply with I-200.[49] At the University of Washington, the 945 Black undergraduates in 1998 (before I-200) dropped to 744 in 1999, a 21 percent decline. Black freshmen plunged from 124 in 1998 to 74 in 1999, a 40 percent decline, but then crept up to 115 in 2001. The law school enrolled one Black student among 158 first-year students in 1998 and again in 2000, and the medical school enrolled one Black student among 175 first-year students in 1998 and again in 2000.[50]

Michigan

In 1997, the CIR's Michael Rosman worked with Kirk O. Kolbo, Larry Purdy, and other lawyers at the Minneapolis-based Maslon Law Firm to sue the University of Michigan (UM). In *Gratz v. Bollinger*, the lawyers represented two white plaintiffs, Jennifer Gratz rejected by the university's College of Literature, Science, and the Arts (LSA) in 1995 and Patrick Hammacher, rejected in 1997. They asked the district court for class certification to represent all rejected applicants who were not African American, Hispanic, or Native American. The court, which denied intervention on behalf of minority students, found that the 1995–1998 admissions procedures functioned as an unconstitutional racial quota.[51] In *Grutter v. Bollinger*, the lawyers represented Barbara Grutter, a white applicant to the law school rejected in 1996, and also sought class certification.[52] The district court denied intervention on behalf of minority students and declared the admissions program to be unconstitutional. The Sixth Circuit Court of Appeals permitted intervention and ruled for the law school, but before it could rule on *Gratz* the parties appealed to the Supreme Court.

When minorities were finally allowed to intervene, the NAACP Legal

Defense and Education Fund, American Civil Liberties Union, Mexican-American Legal Defense and Education Fund, and Citizens for Affirmative Action's Preservation represented African American and Latino students in *Gratz*, while Miranda Massie, a Detroit lawyer, represented Black, Latino, Asian Pacific, and Middle Eastern students in *Grutter*. The intervenors, Massie emphasized, presented robust evidence "about educational conditions for Black, Latina/o, and Native American students," "bias in the LSAT and college GPA," "the benefits of affirmative action," "the history of the struggle for integration in schooling," and "the professional achievements and social contributions of minority alumni at the UM Law School."[53] The effect of the Supreme Court's ruling for the university in *Grutter* was short-lived because, in January 2004, the ACRI launched the Michigan Civil Rights Initiative (MCRI) to nullify it.[54] The MCRI, led by Jennifer Gratz, collected 317,575 signatures to place Proposal 2 on the November 2006 ballot.[55] After voters approved it, the Coalition to Defend Affirmative Action. . . . By Any Means Necessary (BAMN), sued, claiming that Proposal 2 used misleading language that defrauded voters and violated the Voting Rights Act. The Supreme Court declined to interfere.[56]

Looking back at reverse-discrimination lawsuits, we can see strategic shifts in the choice of plaintiffs: individual white male plaintiffs in *DeFunis* and *Bakke*→individual white women in *Hopwood, Grutter,* and *Fisher*→white female and male plaintiffs in *Smith*→white female and male plaintiffs representing a class in *Gratz*→Asian Americans as a racial group in *Students for Fair Admissions v. Harvard University* and *Students for Fair Admissions v. University of North Carolina*. Although the trajectory that eventuated in class or group plaintiffs contradicted the conservative positions that equal protection was an individual right, the lawyers were obviously attempting to maximize the effect a favorable ruling would have. And although conservatives had long objected to the use of statistics to reveal racism, the SFFA lawyers used them to argue that Harvard's admissions program exacted a racial penalty on Asian American applicants to achieve racial group balancing.[57] Moreover, the choice of white female plaintiffs was an obvious wedge strategy designed to fracture traditional female support for affirmative action. Similarly, by mounting referenda and lawsuits in states experiencing minority population growth, immigrant flows, and economic downturns, the initiatives deepened the anxieties of low- and middle-income white families over their access to material and social resources. Just so, in my interviews with officials of conservative organizations, two pushed back against the idea of equitably distributing resources to people of color: Curt Levey demonized people (implicitly those of color) for believing "'we're entitled to our share; we will not stop demanding until the percentages match exactly the percentages in the general population'"; and Kevin Nguyen invoked (implicitly white) self-interest by stating, "the less we rely upon contextual or historical rights, privileges, and entitlements, then the better off we will be as individuals."[58]

SYSTEMATICITY

It may seem paradoxical that the conservative movement, which was so intent on masking systemic racism, had systematically deployed its organizational infrastructure. Systemic thinking was present in conservatism since at least the post–World War I emergence of neoliberalism in Europe and reappeared at the start of the reverse-discrimination era in a memorandum written by an unlikely source. In August 1971 just a few months before his nomination to the US Supreme Court, Lewis F. Powell Jr., then a partner in the largest law firm in Virginia, met with officials of the US Chamber of Commerce, who invited him to write a memo. Titled "Attack on American Free Enterprise System," the thirty-four-page memo lays out an action plan.[59] In it, Powell lambasted communists and other revolutionaries "who would destroy the entire system, both political and economic" and named the following individuals: ACLU director William Kuntsler, who had defended Civil Rights, Black Power, and New Left activists; consumer-protection activist Ralph Nader, who had founded Public Citizen (1971) earlier that year; Yale law professor Charles Reich, who had published *The Greening of America* (1970) about the revolution in consciousness and culture; and Frankfurt School theorist Herbert Marcuse, described only as a "Marxist faculty member at the University of California at San

Diego." Powell was also distressed by social science professors who, as "stimulating teachers," "prolific writers," and textbook authors, exerted undue influence on students and colleagues.[60]

After chastising business leaders for their reluctance to confront their critics, Powell detailed several offensive strategies. In the business sector, executives should appoint corporate vice presidents whose primary responsibility is "to counter—on the broadest front—the attack on the enterprise system," and the Chamber should finance "careful long-range planning and implementation." In the knowledge sector, the Chamber should build its own "staff of highly qualified scholars in the social sciences," maintain a speaker's bureau, and conduct evaluations of social-science textbooks; pressuring colleges, it should demand balance in the social-science faculty, insist on equal time for speakers, and request specific courses to be taught in graduate schools of business.[61] In the media sector, he also proposed an outside-inside strategy that combined external pressures, such as monitoring the media, demanding equal time, and filing complaints with the Federal Communications Commission, with infiltration by publishing pro-enterprise articles, books, and advertisements in the mainstream media.

To influence government, he urged businesses to lobby Congress and state legislatures, mobilize stockholders, and educate voters on the benefits of free enterprise. As for the courts, he stated, "Under our constitutional system, especially with an activist-minded Supreme Court, the judiciary may be the most important instrument for social, economic, and political change. Other organizations and groups, recognizing this, have been far more astute in exploiting judicial action than American business." Noting that the ACLU had generated scores of cases and amicus briefs, he urged the Chamber to build its own "highly competent staff of lawyers" authorized to select cases, engage in litigation, and appear before the Supreme Court.[62]

Powell did not discuss conservative public interest law firms, but others would. In *The Rise of the Conservative Legal Movement: The Battle for Control of the Law* (2010), Steven M. Teles provides a richly detailed history of conservative PILFs, law programs, professorships, and the powerfully networked Federalist Society. The first-generation PILFs—state and regional firms that focused on local free-enterprise issues—included the Pacific Legal Foundation (Sacramento, 1973), Landmark Legal Foundation (Kansas City, 1973), Southeastern Legal Foundation (Marietta, Georgia, 1967), Atlantic Legal Foundation (Larchmont, New York, 1977), Mountain States Legal Foundation (Denver, 1977), New England Legal Foundation (Boston, 1977), and Washington Legal Foundation (Washington, DC, 1977). At first, these firms, which sought to advance the pro-business agenda and maximize the return on donor investment by writing amicus briefs for many cases—coordinated only loosely with other organizations.[63]

Yet the firms were structurally meshed with business organizations. In "With Charity for All," a 1984 article for the *Yale Law Journal*, Oliver A. Houck provides a chilling account of the first-generation PILFs as wholly owned subsidiaries of American business officials who funded them, served on their boards, and shaped their dockets. He credits Michael J. Horowitz's report to the Scaife Foundation, titled "The Public Interest Law Movement: An Analysis with Special Reference to the Role and Practice of Conservative Public Interest Law Firms" (1980), with seeking "to divorce these PILFs from the business community."[64] Teles notes that the Horowitz report, which was widely distributed to conservative donors and activists, precipitated a rethinking of conservative movement organizations. Horowitz, a liberal in his previous career as a law school student and civil rights instructor in the segregated south, admired liberal PILFs for their high moral tone, legal specialization, and academic outreach. He advised conservative PILFs to follow their example and litigate problems that disempowered people, such as small business and consumer regulations, gerrymandering, racial quotas, and ghetto housing, schools, and crime.[65] Learning from the Horowitz report as well as their own work in first-generation PILFs and Reagan-era government agencies, the second-generation entrepreneurs founded smaller PILFs located in or oriented to the nation's capital that would specialize in certain issues, pursue original litigation, and coordinate with advocacy organizations.

First- and second-generation conservatives exercised power through articulatory mechanisms—that is, structures that linked their organizations to one another or meshed them to the machinery of government. One such mechanism, the interlocking directorate, had been analyzed by sociologist G. William Domhoff in his widely read book, *Who Rules America?* (1967). Domhoff demonstrated that individual powerbrokers who served on multiple corporate boards functioned as "interlocks" that allowed these companies to coordinate their financial and political interests. Applying this concept to conservative organizations, we would notice that board members of the Madison Center for Educational Affairs, which sponsored the network of conservative student newspapers, were affiliated with the Free Congress Foundation, Hoover Institution, Intercollegiate Studies Institute, and National Association of Scholars. As a powerful "interlock," Paul Weyrich was a cofounder, executive director, and/or board member of the Heritage Foundation (1973), the America Legislative Exchange Council (1975), the Free Congress Research and Education Foundation (1977), the Christian Voice advocacy group (1977), the Moral Majority (1979), and National Empowerment Television (1993), an interactive recruitment medium used to broadcast conservative ideology, organizational activities, and activist training programs to local sites.

Conservatives also deployed another articulatory mechanism, the umbrella councils, that was pioneered by the civil rights movement. One type, which linked leaders within a specific sector, was prefigured by the Southern Christian Leadership Conference (SCLC), a group of Black clergy who coordinated Black church activism after the 1956 Montgomery Bus Boycott. Among the conservative umbrella councils, the Philanthropy Roundtable, originally an informal network in the 1970s, was institutionalized in 1987 under the auspices of the Institute for Educational Affairs (itself founded by Olin Foundation president William E. Simon and neoconservative intellectual Irving Kristol). Another type, which linked organization across sectors, was prefigured by the Leadership Conference on Civil Rights (LCCR). From 40 organizations in 1950, the LCCR grew to over 200 civic groups, academic and professional associations, research institutes, public interest law firms, and a wide spectrum of identity-based organizations.[66] In the mid-1970s, the Heritage Foundation launched a similar version, the annual Resource Bank meetings attended by conservative organization leaders, policymakers, and intellectuals. In a 1991 interview for the foundation's *Policy Review*, President Edwin Feulner signaled a turn to cultural conservatism—"Heritage is going to become more active and involved in cultural and family issues, which are more and more going to be at the cutting edge of conservatism"[67]—and then used the 1992 Resource Bank meeting, titled "Ideas Have Consequences: A Conservative Battleplan for the 1990s," to sell it. At the meeting, which I attended, speakers explained how the blending of cultural and economic rhetoric could function, like a multipurpose tool, to rivet conservative factions, clasp unaligned citizens, and split the liberal coalition.[68]

A third articulatory mechanism is best exemplified by the expansive operations of the Federalist Society. According to Steven Teles, the society emerged from a "symposium on federalism at the Yale Law School held in April 1982." The organizers, a small group of law students at Yale University and the University of Chicago, had the modest aim of providing an opportunity for the exchange of conservative and libertarian ideas, but the symposium "attracted enormous attention in the national press, in the conservative movement, and among conservative law students." With guidance from prominent conservatives, the students gained financial support from conservative foundations and built the organization. It consisted of student, faculty, and lawyer divisions, which spawned campus and local chapters, and practice groups that addressed particular areas of law. Many of the society's activities focused on building human capital—for instance, recommending law students for academic fellowships funded by conservative foundations; placing young lawyers in positions with government, PILFs, and private firms; maintaining a clearing house that connected conservative PILFs with pro bono lawyers; and assembling a pool of candidates for judicial appointments.[69] By 2015, the Federalist Society had approximately 40,000 members, 200 student chapters on campuses, and 75 lawyer chapters in major cities.[70]

In *Ideas with Consequences: The Federalist Society and the Conservative Counterrevolution* (2015), Amanda Hollis-Brusky describes the society as a political epistemic network (PEN) operating in the field of the law where struggles occur over problems and solutions. Both Hollis-Brusky and John L. Campbell and Ove K. Pederson, in their 2014 book on the production of policy ideas, note that PENs, unlike traditional epistemic networks of scientists and scholars, blur the boundaries between knowledge and power. Just so, the Federalist Society produces actionable intellectual capital: the contents of its lectures, conferences, and publications explain and justify legal frames, concepts, and narratives that conservative judges can incorporate into opinions and conservative experts can recirculate in other venues.

To circulate its knowledges, Hollis-Brusky notes, the Federalist Society developed a large roster of experts to speak to the media, Congress, and state legislatures, and began reaching out to Tea Party leaders.[71] This process of using experts to channel ideas to various sectors was not new. During 1992 visits to the Heritage Foundation, I learned that it distributed the *Annual Guide to Public Policy Experts*, which listed 2,000 scholars with expertise in 77 fields, to an array of media, nongovernmental, and governmental entities. It also marketed its ideas, sending policy reports to thousands of syndicated columnists, news reporters, and opinion-page editors whose endorsements the Heritage staff clipped, assembled, and sent to Congress members and staffers to convey the actuality or appearance of public pressure.[72]

Hollis-Brusky describes Federalist Society members as conduits for the organization's actionable knowledge and names several prominent members—law school professors, lawyers (among them, the CIR's Michael Greve and the CEO's Roger Clegg), government official, and sitting judges—who have deployed the ideas in their work sites. Geographer Walter Nicholls further illuminates the territorial and relational dynamics of PENs. Located in particular places, the PEN meetings, conferences, facilities, and other venues function as contact points for mobile actors, who in turn function as vehicles that transmit its ideology and action agenda into the spaces where power/knowledge contests occur. This ideology, an ensemble of ideas, values, and commitments transmitted through events and communication technologies, sustains cohesion among distant place-based actors.[73]

The academic literature that focuses on how conservative lobbyists, leaders, and funders influence members of Congress does not sufficiently depict the hybridization of the movement's dynamic organizational network to the machinery of government. To understand hybridization, which occurs on a larger scale than lines of influence, we need to follow the flows of movement policy ideas into government entities and the return flows of government resources and regulations to society. In "Why Democracy Will Be Hard to Do" (2008), I tracked the flow of several initiatives targeting higher education from conservative organizations into Congress, which transformed them into policies, regulations, and funding decisions that in turn affected higher-education institutions along with those seeking to enter or already residing in them. The examples included educational restrictions on beneficiaries of Personal Responsibility and Work Opportunity Reconciliation Act of 1996 (the welfare reform act); funding decisions concerning the Pell Grant, Perkins Loan, and Upward Bound programs; earmarked grants for academic research on security issues; regulations imposed on area studies and identity studies program; and actions protecting religious institutions from the separation-of-church-and-state doctrine.[74] Subsequent publications like Jane Mayer's *Dark Money: The Hidden History of the Billionaires Behind the Rise of the Racial Right* (2017) and Nancy MacLean's *Democracy in Chains: The Deep History of the Radical Right's Stealth Plan for America* (2017) have analyzed in frightening detail the episodes of movement-government hybridization, such as those engineered by the Koch empire.

All of these activities, as Lewis Powell anticipated in his 1971 memorandum, required enormous sums of money. By the early 1990s, major conservative donors such as the Bradley, Coors, JM, Koch, Olin, Scaife, and Smith Richardson Foundations were practicing strategic philanthropy. Still the best record of that period, Sally Covington's *Moving a Public Policy Agenda: The Strategic Philanthropy of Conservative Foundations* (1993), written for the progressive National Committee for Responsive Philanthropy, provides hard data on grants awarded by twelve leading foundations for the years 1992 through 1994. These twelve foundations provided a total of $210 million in grants: $79.2 million to national think tanks and advocacy groups, $9.1 million to regional and state think tanks, $10.5 million to public interest law firms and legal projects, $23 million to conservative programs in academe; $16.8 million for scholarships and fellowships to train students in economics, political science, law, and public policy; $7.6 million for chairs and professorships; and many millions more for media watchdog groups, conservative media, book authorship, conferences, and lectures.

Among the organizations mentioned above the Heritage Foundation received $8,979, 852, the Free Congress Foundation received $5,097,200, the Intercollegiate Studies Institute received $2,639,100, the Madison Center for Educational Affairs received $1,995,580, the National Association of Scholars received $2,170,000, the Federalist Society received $1,514,500, and the Center for Individual Rights received $1,251,100.[75]

The Supreme Court ruling in *Citizens United v. Federal Elections Committee* (2010), which prohibited government from limiting expenditures on campaign communications, strengthened the financial power of organizations, particularly conservative ones. It enabled dark money to pour into electoral politics and, with the aid of gerrymandering and disenfranchisement tactics, elect members of Congress who enacted conservative policies and confirmed conservative judges.[76] As the conservative movement's organizations grew richer, the material resources and rights available to racial minorities, immigrants, and low-income whites grew poorer.

In this book, I have argued that *DeFunis* and *Bakke* were badly crafted and decided. To support this argument, I restored to each case what legal-judicial discourse had banished—the racial turmoil in local communities, the maneuvers by rejected white plaintiffs and their attorneys to gain their objectives, the amici accounts of systemic racism, and the sidelined interests of minority applicants and communities. I also analyzed how brief and opinion writers used the mechanisms of language—narrative framing, grammatical and syntactic structures, figurative devices, and lexical choices—to racialize facts, empty precedents of their social content, enunciate abstract principles, and bleach racism from equal protection. By restoring these dimensions to the two cases, we can see that these tools helped the plaintiffs, attorneys, and judges install a new form of color-blind racism that diminished the opportunities available to already disadvantaged people of color.

But let's step back from the details of these cases and take a moment to consider the larger landscape that emerges from the mists of the 1970s. Race-conscious admissions programs were a minuscule intervention into the massive racism that structured K–12 schools, trades and professions, housing, community facilities, social programs, financial services, retail venues, policing, voting, and all the other sectors of activity. The fierce battle over race-conscious admissions programs reveals, to me at least, that the white opponents—whether plaintiffs and their attorneys, organizations and their funders, or judges who wrote learned rationalizations of the programs' unconstitutionality—were determined not to cede an ounce of the nation's material and symbolic resources to communities of color.

When I complained to Ted Shaw that the courts seemed unable to comprehend the materiality of systemic racism as manifested in housing, schools, jobs, nutrition, and healthcare, he said that brief writers had to operate within the constraints imposed on them:

> Our milieu . . . [is] we're lawyers, we're in the courts. I think we can and should say to the Court, "You're wrong about this so-called societal discrimination stuff." But we could spend 30 or 40 pages on that issue alone, just laying it out and making those arguments, and we'll miss the arguments on the facts of this case and the arguments we can make within the case law that's governing the disposition of these cases now. So that's the triage decision that we have to make.[77]

His comment raises what I regard as an urgent question about a legal-judicial discourse that prioritizes page limits over thorough problem analysis, clings to the notion of linguistically unrefracted facts, and sidelines the interests of communities of color—all in an effort to stamp abstract principles onto the welter of lived experiences. Today, in spring 2020, we once again witness the yawning gulf between the law's abstract "racial discrimination" and the multiracial crowds pouring into the streets to demand justice for people of color. What, if anything, will the scholars, the lawyers, and the judges do to save the law from itself?

NOTES

INTRODUCTION

1. Ellen Messer-Davidow, "Manufacturing the Attack on Liberalized Higher Education," *Social Text* 36 (Fall 1993): 40–80; "Dollars for Scholars: The Real Politics of Humanities Scholarship and Programs," in *The Politics of Research*, ed. E. Ann Kaplan and George Levine (New Brunswick, NJ: Rutgers University Press, 1997), 193–233; "The Struggle for the Academy," in *Encyclopedia of American Cultural and Intellectual History*, ed. Mary Kupiec Cayton and Peter W. Williams, 3 vols. (New York: Scribner's, 1999), vol. 2, 237–251; "*Rosenberger v. Rectors and Visitors of the University of Virginia:* From Discourse and Dollars to Domination," *South Atlantic Quarterly* 98, no. 1 (Fall 2001): 868–893; "Why Democracy Will Be Hard To Do," *Social Text* 86 (Spring 2006): 1–35; and "Caught in the Crunch," in "Academic Freedom and Intellectual Activism in the Post-9/11 University," ed. Edward J. Carvalho, special issue, *Works and Days* 26, nos. 1–2 (2008–2009): 399–419. For books reviewing the war against higher education, see John K. Wilson, *The Myth of Political Correctness: The Conservative Attack on Higher Education* (Durham, NC: Duke University Press, 1995); Jeffrey Williams, ed., *PC Wars: Politics and Theory in the Academy* (New York: Routledge, 1995); and Michael Berube and Cary Nelson, eds., *Higher Education Under Fire: Politics, Economics, and the Crisis of the Humanities* (New York: Routledge, 1995).

2. See Bernard Schwartz, *Behind Bakke: Affirmative Action and the Supreme Court* (New York: NYU Press, 1988), 45–47 (quotation 46); Joel Dreyfuss and Charles Lawrence III, *The Bakke Case: The Politics of Inequality* (New York: Harcourt Brace Jovanovich, 1979), 162–171; Howard Ball, *The Bakke Case: Race, Education, and Affirmative Action* (Lawrence: University Press of Kansas, 2000), 70–77; Lee Lescaze, "Blacks Decry 'Neglect' by White House," *Washington Post*, 29 August 1977; Bill Peterson, "Proposed Justice Dept. Brief Draws Fire of Rights Groups," *Washington Post*, 9 September 1977; Bill Peterson, "Justice Dep. Brief Irks Black Caucus, Civil Rights Groups," *Washington Post*, 9 September 1977; "Blacks Urge Carter to Back 'Affirmative Action,'" *New York Times*, 10 September 1977; William Claiborne, "Hill Black Caucus

Warns Carter on Stand on Quotas," *Washington Post*, 13 September 1977; Simon Anekwe, "NAACP Seeks Meeting with Carter on Administration Stand on Bakke," *New York Amsterdam News*, 24 September 1977; and Bill Neikirk, "Blacks Score Points with Carter," *Chicago Tribune*, 25 September 1977.

3. A search of HeinOnline Core US Journals reveals that 514 articles, comments, and notes on *Regents of the University of California v. Bakke* were published in 1978–1979 alone. The majority focused on US Supreme Court opinions—explicating them, debating the issues, and speculating on the implications for affirmative-action programs. See, for example, Kent D. Lollis, "Right to Education: *University of California v. Bakke*," *Black Law Journal* 6, no. 2 (1979), 265–275 (20 citations); Earl M. Matz, "A Bakke Primer," *Oklahoma Law Review* 32, no. 1 (1979): 119–137 (603 citations); Robert M. O'Neil, "Bakke in the Balance: Some Preliminary Thoughts," *California Law Review* 67, no. 1 (January 1979): 143–170 (946 citations); and David F. Schwartz, "Discriminatory Intent and Disproportionate Impact: A Postmortem of Regents of the University of California v. Bakke," *California Western Law Review* 15, no. 2 (1979): 179–218 (26 citations). Among the few articles that provided a critical perspective on the entire case from its precipitating circumstances through its final phase, one of the best is Ralph R. Smith, "Reflections on a Landmark: Some Preliminary Observations on the Development and Significance of Regents of the University of California v. Bakke," *Howard Law Journal* 21, no. 1 (1978): 72–127 (50 citations). Even fewer articles discussed the US racial formation and its ideological underpinnings. As contrasting examples, Guido Calabrisi's "Bakke as Pseudo-Tragedy" (*Catholic University Law Journal* 28, no. 3 [1979]: 427–444 [6,165 citations]) is a relatively traditional discussion of the clash between the meritocratic concept of equal opportunity and the idea of reparations for historically subjugated groups, while Alan David Freeman's "Legitimizing Racial Discrimination through Anti-Discrimination Law: A Critical Review of Supreme Court Doctrine" (*Minnesota Law Review* 62, no. 6 [July 1978]: 1049–1120 [802 citations]) offers a sweeping critique of legal individualism's erasure of minority group subjugation. I have included citation counts to show that articles written by prominent law scholars or published in mainstream law reviews received more attention than those written by pro-minority scholars or published in minority law reviews. Reputation and race intersected to marginalize the work of minority scholars and to carry the official *Bakke* story, reiterated in Justice Lewis Powell's opinion, into the case's robust afterlife. As one exception to this trend, I would note that Derrick Bell's articles from 1970 through 1980 routinely received over 2,000 citations, whether published in mainstream or Black law journals.

4. At bottom, I argue, legal language constructs and interpretation construes both fact and law. For traditional approaches to legal interpretation, see William N. Eskridge Jr., Philip P. Frickey, and Elizabeth Garret, *Legislation and Statutory Interpretation* (St. Paul, MN: Foundation Press, 2000); Antonin Scalia, *A Matter of Interpretation: Federal Courts and the Law* (Princeton, NJ: Princeton University Press, 1997); Stephen Breyer, *Active Liberty: Interpreting Our Democratic Constitution* (New York: Vintage, 2003); Aharon Barak,

Purposive Interpretation in Law (Princeton, NJ: Princeton University Press, 2005); and the overview in Sotirios A. Barber and James E. Fleming, *Constitutional Interpretation: The Basic Questions* (New York: Oxford University Press, 2007). The formalist distinction between linguistic and legal interpretation in Lawrence B. Solum's "The Interpretive-Construction Distinction," *Constitutional Commentary* 27, no. 1 (Fall 2010): 95–118 contrasts with critical analyses of the fact/law dualism and the linguistic construction of facts. For critical analysis, see Kim Lane Scheppele, "Facing Facts in Legal Interpretation: Questions of Law and Questions of Fact," *Representations* 30, no. 1 (Spring 1990): 42–77; David L. Faigman, "Normative Constitutional Fact-Finding: Exploring the Empirical Component of Constitutional Interpretation," *University of Pennsylvania Law Review* 139, no. 3 (January 1991): 541–613; Emmet T. Flood, "Fact Construction and Judgment in Constitutional Adjudication," *Yale Law Journal* 100, no. 6 (April 1991): 1795–1814; Scheppele, "Cultures of Facts," *Perspectives on Politics* 1, no. 2 (June 2003): 363–368; Angelo N. Ancheta, *Scientific Evidence and Equal Protection of the Law* (New Brunswick, NJ: Rutgers University Press, 2006); Caitlin E. Borgmann, "Appellate Review of Social Facts in Constitutional Rights Cases," *California Law Review* 101, no. 5 (October 2013): 1185–1248; and Faigman, "Evidentiary Incommensurability: A Preliminary Exploration of Reasoning from General Scientific Data to Individualized Legal Decision-Making," *Court Review* 50, no. 2 (2014): 52–60.

5. The history and work of the SCE is recounted by the essays in a special edition of *Works and Days*. See "The Society for Critical Exchange, Phase I: 1975–1988," ed. Patricia Harkin, *Works and Days* 25, nos. 1–2 (2007). The history of the GRIP remains unwritten. Replacing "Literary Studies" with "Knowledge" in the group title, David Shumway and I led the attempt to create a hybrid field we dubbed "the new knowledge studies" from the late 1980s through the 1990s. We organized two conferences held at the University of Minnesota (1989 and 1992) and another, with sociologist Richard Harvey Brown, at the University of Maryland (1991). We coedited special issues of *Poetics Today* and *Social Epistemology*, and, with David Sylvan, a book series at the University Press of Virginia. The inaugural volume was *Knowledges: Historical and Critical Studies in Disciplinarity*, ed. Ellen Messer-Davidow, David R. Shumway, and David J. Sylvan (Charlottesville: University Press of Virginia, 1993).

6. In a 2002 article on *Board of Trustees of the University of Alabama v. Garrett* (2001), a disabilities case, sociologist Pamela Brandwein observes, "Inquiries into the nature and conditions of permeability between academic disciplines, the legal academy, and constitutional law are much needed. We need to understand how established constitutional contexts have been changed via interchange with the academic disciplines and the legal academy." See Pamela Brandwein, "Constitutional Doctrine as Paring Tool: The Struggle for Relevant Evidence in University of Alabmaa v. Garrett," *University of Michigan Journal of Law Reform* 35, nos. 1–2 (Fall 2001/Winter 2002): 37–80 (quotation 55).

7. Thomas F. Gieryn, "Boundary-Work and the Demarcation of Science from Non-Science: Strains and Interests in Professional Ideologies of Scientists,"

American Sociological Review 48, no. 6 (December 1983): 783. For a fuller account of boundary-work, see Julie Thompson Klein, *Crossing Boundaries: Knowledge, Disciplinarities, and Interdisciplinarities* (Charlottesville: University Press of Virginia, 1996).

8. Tony Becher, *Academic Tribes and Territories: Intellectual Inquiry and the Culture of Disciplines* (Milton Keynes, UK: Society for Research into Higher Education and Open University Press, 1989), 37.

9. For important work on institutional and disciplinary diversification, see Burton R. Clark, *The Higher Education System: Academic Organization in Cross-National Perspective* (Berkeley: University of California Press, 1983); Andrew Abbott, *The System of Professions: An Essay on the Division of Expert Labor* (Chicago: University of Chicago Press, 1989); and Mattei Dogan and Robert Pahre, *Creative Marginality: Innovation at the Intersections of Social Science* (Boulder, CO: Westview Press, 1990). These and other authors, including Becher and Klein, agree that following their formation in the late nineteenth to early twentieth century academic disciplines have proliferated specialisms (or subfields) within their precincts. The diversity that results fosters knowledge change at two levels—alternatives to the discipline's core concepts and methods, and hybridization with other specialisms in the interstices among disciplines. Of course, knowledge change can be limited by the discipline's mechanisms for controlling its practitioners, policing its boundaries, and maintaining objects of analysis that do not overlap those in other disciplines (as, for instance, "race" and "racism" do).

10. Corinne Blalock, "Neoliberalism and the Crisis of Legal Theory," *Law and Contemporary Problems* 77, no. 4 (2014): 71–104.

11. See John Locke, *Two Treatises of Government: A Critical Edition*, ed. Peter Laslett (Cambridge, UK: Cambridge University Press, 1966). For an early article explaining the intellectual crosscurrents around patriarchal and liberal-individualist theory during the seventeenth century, see Melissa A. Butler, "Early Liberal Roots of Feminism: John Locke and the Attack on Patriarchy," *American Political Science Review* 72, no. 1 (March 1978): 135–150. The landmark work on possessive individualism was C. B. Macpherson's *The Political Theory of Possessive Individualism: Hobbes to Locke* (New York: Oxford University Press, 1962). In "Possessive Individualism at 50: Retrieving Macpherson's Lost Legacy" (*Good Society* 21, no. 1 [2012]: 132–150), Peter Lindsay acknowledges Macpherson's debt to Marxian thought but also foregrounds differences arising from their respective individualist and structuralist orientations. Yet I would argue that the problem of progressive appropriation in Locke, Marx, and Macpherson should be re-read through the lens of Rosa Luxemburg's explanation of capitalist accumulation and imperialism in "The Accumulation of Capital—An Anti-Critique" (1913) (*Rosa Luxemburg: Reflections and Writings*, ed. Paul LeBlanc [Amherst, NY: Humanities Books, 1999], 175–197).

12. For a short account of the emergence of neoliberalism, see John F. Henry, "The Historic Roots of the Neoliberal Program," *Journal of Economic Issues* 44, no. 3 (June 2010): 543–550. For background on neoliberalism, see David Harvey, *A Brief History of Neoliberalism* (Oxford, UK: Oxford University Press,

2005); and the much fuller account by Pierre Dardot and Christian Laval, *The New Way of the World: On Neoliberal Society,* trans. Gregory Elliott (London: Verso, 2013). For a critical account of Chicago School projects, see Naomi Klein, *The Shock Doctrine: The Rise of Disaster Capitalism* (New York: Metropolitan Books/Henry Holt, 2007). Scholarly interest in neoliberalism was heightened by the 2007–2008 subprime mortgage crisis and the ensuing economic meltdown, which demonstrated that the carnage, in the US and globally, traveled along the intersecting lines of gender, race, socioeconomic class, and nationality. See Maurizio Lazzarato, *The Making of the Indebted Man: An Essay on the Neoliberal Condition,* trans. Joshua David Jordan (Amsterdam: Semiotext[e], 2011); "Race, Empire, and the Crisis of the Subprime," special issue, ed. Paula Chakaravartty and Diane Ferreira da Silva, *American Quarterly* 64, no. 3 (September 2012); and Ellen Messer-Davidow, "Investing in Higher Education: Debtors, Bettors, Lenders, Brokers," in special issue, "Saving the Humanities from the Neoliberal University," ed. Ronald Strickland, *Humanities* 6, no. 2 (March 2017). For an overview of structural adjustment programs, see Sarah Babb, "The Social Consequences of Structural Adjustment: Recent Evidence and Current Debates," *Annual Review of Sociology* 31 (2005): 199–222. Most studies of development loans focus on countries or regions in Africa and Latin America; almost uniformly they note the devastation of poor and low-income populations in such areas as agricultural work, education, and healthcare.

13. *Citizens United v. Federal Elections Committee* 558 U.S. 310–485 (2010). For two linguistic genealogies of "person" and "corporation" see Sanford A. Schane, "Corporation Is a Person: The Language of a Legal Fiction," *Tulane Law Review* 61, no. 3 (1986–1987): 563–610; and Jonathan A. Marcantel, "The Corporation as a Real Constitutional Person," *University of California Davis Business Law Review* 11, no. 2 (Spring 2011): 221–266. The articles examine the historical and constitutionally contemporaneous meanings of these two terms as well as theories that construct the corporation as a collective of persons, an independent real-world entity, or a legal fiction. The crux of the matter is (1) whether the law should provide the corporation with the same natural attributes and rights it attributes to the human person; (2) whether it should recognize that this collective has different attributes and rights; and (3) whether it is obliged for the sake of consistency to provide other human collectives, such as racial groups, with comparable attributes and rights.

14. Anthony Giddens, *The Constitution of Society: Outline of a Theory of Structuration* (Berkeley: University of California Press, 1984), xxiii.

15. Giddens, 22. Giddens uses the term "discursive" with respect to formal rules; I have substituted "textual" (meaning the modes of oral and written language) because the theory of discourse that informs my work regards discourses as encompassing subjects, objects, concepts, actions, and processes in particular types of relations.

16. Giddens, 171.

17. Stephen Resnick and Richard Wolff, "Althusser's Liberation of Marxian Theory," in the *Althusserian Legacy*, ed. E. Ann Kaplan and Michael Sprinker (London: Verso, 1993), 63.

18. Michel Foucault, *The Archaeology of Knowledge and the Discourse on Language,* trans. A. M. Sheridan Smith (New York: Pantheon, 1971), 151.

19. Ernesto Laclau and Chatal Mouffe, "Post-Marxism without Apologies," *New Left Review* 166 (November–December 1982): 82 (short quotation and long quotation).

20. Foucault, *Archaeology of Knowledge*, 40–55.

21. Michel Foucault, *The Order of Things: An Archaeology of the Human Sciences* (New York: Random/Vintage, 1971). In the famous preface, Foucault begins with a passage from Borges quoting a Chinese encyclopedia's taxonomy of animals that demonstrates "the limitation of our own [thinking], the stark impossibility of thinking *that*" taxonomy (xv) and then proceeds to explain the epistemic ground, table, or field that orders knowledge constructs (see xv–xxv). For those needing help with this book, I recommend Gary Gutting, *Michel Foucault's Archaeology of Scientific Reason* (Cambridge, UK: Cambridge University Press, 1989).

CHAPTER 1. FRENEMIES

1. Slade Gorton and James B. Wilson, "Brief of Respondents in Opposition to Amicus Curiae Briefs of the Anti-Defamation League of B'nai B'rith and the American Federation of Labor and Congress of Industrial Organizations" (filed 21 February 1974), in Ann Fagan Ginger, ed., *DeFunis versus Odegaard and the University of Washington: The University Admissions Case, The Record* (Dobbs Ferry, NY: Oceana, 1974), vol. 2, 604–606. Two scholars who wrote books about the case also commented on the alignments: Robert M. O'Neil, *Discriminating Against Discrimination: Preferential Admissions and the DeFunis Case* (Bloomington: Indiana University Press, 1975), 135–136; and Allan P. Sindler, *Bakke, DeFunis, and Minority Admissions: The Quest for Equal Opportunity* (New York: Longman, 1978), 203–204.

2. Gorton and Wilson, "Brief of Respondents in Opposition to Amicus Curiae Briefs of the Anti-Defamation League of B'nai B'rith and the American Federation of Labor and Congress of Industrial Organizations," 609–610.

3. See Howard Ball, *The Bakke Case: Race, Education, and Affirmative Action* (Lawrence: University Press of Kansas, 2000), 77–85 (on amici), 70–77 (on government); and Sindler, *Bakke, DeFunis, and Minority Admissions*, 241–253 (on amici and government).

4. Information in John David Skrentny, *The Ironies of Affirmative Action: Politics, Culture, and Justice in America* (Chicago: University of Chicago Press, 1996), 73.

5. *Report of the National Advisory Commission on Civil Disorders* (Washington, DC: US Government Printing Office, 1 March 1968). On 3 March, Bantam Books issued the first edition; 30,000 copies were sold in the first three days and over 1.6 million were sold by July (Sales information from Jerome Karabel, "How Affirmative Action Took Hold at Harvard, Yale, and Princeton," *Journal of Blacks in Higher Education* 48 [Summer 2005]: 63). Despite wide media coverage, the report, along with its documentation of systemic racism, faded

from public memory—only to be "discovered" all over again through media coverage of today's Black Lives Matter movement.

6. Nicholas Pedriana and Robin Stryker, "Political Culture Wars 1960s Style: Equal Employment Opportunity-Affirmative Action Law and the Philadelphia Plan," *American Journal of Sociology* 103, no. 3 (November 1997): 656 (quotation). For accounts of Nixon's campaign strategy and the revived Philadelphia Plan, also see Hugh Davis Graham, *The Civil Rights Era: Origins and Development of National Policy, 1960–1972* (New York: Oxford University Press, 1990), 325–35; and Skrentny, *Ironies of Affirmative Action*, 177–209.

7. For Nixon, Agnew, and Janus strategy, see Thomas Byrne Edsall and Mary D. Edsall, *Chain Reaction: The Impact of Race, Rights, and Taxes on American Politics* (New York: W. W. Norton, 1991), 74–98 (Agnew quotation, 85). When Blacks rioted in Baltimore after the assassination of Dr. King, then-governor Agnew excoriated Black leaders for "'refusing to renounce such radicals as Stokely Carmichael and H. Rap Brown" (Edsall and Edsall, 85) and described Black Power leaders as "Hanoi-visiting . . . caterwauling, riot-inciting, burn-america-down type of leaders" (William T. Martin Riches, *The Civil Rights Movement: Struggle and Resistance* [New York: St. Martin's Press, 1997], 100). In fall 1969, he called antiwar protesters "an effete corps of impudent snobs" (Maurice Isserman and Michael Kazin, *America Divided: The Civil War of the 1960s* [New York: Oxford University Press, 2000], 268). Later that year at a Republican dinner, he railed against student protesters on campuses as glib, impudent, pseudo-intellectual anarchists (Alexander Bloom and Wini Breines, eds.,*"Takin' It to the Streets": A Sixties Reader* [New York: Oxford University Press, 1995], 355–358).

8. "Kerner, Cook Will Be Cited by B'nai B'rith," *Chicago Tribune*, 21 April 1968.

9. Irving Spiegel, "Jews Troubled Over Negro Ties: Long Civil Rights Support Strained by Antagonisms," *New York Times*, 8 July 1968.

10. Bill Kovach, "Racist and Anti-Semite Charges Strain Old Negro-Jewish Ties," *New York Times*, 23 October 1968.

11. Spiegel, "Jews Troubled Over Negro Ties."

12. Kovach, "Racist and Anti-Semite Charges."

13. On this same point, see John Kifner, "Blacks vs. Jews," *New York Times*, 26 January 1969; and for a somewhat later article, see Peter I. Rose, "Blacks and Jews: The Strained Alliance," *Annals of the American Academy of Political and Social Science* 454 (March 1981): 55–69.

14. Jerald E. Podair, *The Strike That Changed New York: Blacks, Whites, and the Ocean Hill-Brownsville Crisis* (New Haven, CT: Yale University Press, 2002), 10–13 (quotation 11).

15. Podair, *Strike That Changed New York*, 13–15.

16. See Herbert Hill, "Racism within Organized Labor: A Report of Five Years of the AFL-CIO, 1955–1960," *Journal of Negro Education* 30, no. 2 (Spring 1961): 109–118; Ray Marshall, "Unions and the Negro Community," *ILR Review* 17, no. 2 (January 1964): 179–202; and Paul Frymer, *Black and Blue: African Americans, The Labor Movement, and the Decline of the*

Democratic Party (Princeton, NJ: Princeton University Press, 2011), chapter 3, "The NAACP Confronts Racism in the Labor Movement," 44–69.

17. Jane Anna Gordon, *Why They Couldn't Wait: A Critique of the Black-Jewish Conflict over Community Control in Ocean Hill-Brownsville (1967–1971)* (New York: Routledge, 2001), 32 (school numbers); Podair, *Strike That Changed New York*, 16 (dual system quotation).

18. Podair, 17.

19. Podair, 23, 41.

20. Podair, 22–36 (school desegregation, PAT, and EQUAL), 27 (quotations of PAT members).

21. See Clarence Taylor, *Knocking at Our Own Door: Milton A. Galamison and the Struggle to Integrate New York City Schools* (New York: Columbia University Press, 1997), 23–32 (Galamison's background), 91–175 (boycott); and Richard D. Kahlenberg, *Tough Liberal: Albert Shanker and the Battles Over Schools, Unions, Race, and Democracy* (New York: Columbia University Press, 2007), 57–58 (Galamison and Shanker).

22. Maurice R. Berube and Marilyn Gittell, "The Lines Are Drawn," in *Confrontation at Ocean Hill-Brownsville: The New York School Strikes of 1968*, ed. Maurice R. Berube and Marilyn Gittell (New York: Praeger, 1969), 13.

23. M. A. Farber, "Brooklyn Sit-In Bars 2nd Hearing by School Board," *New York Times*, 21 December 1966; and Podair, *Strike That Changed New York*, 71–73. These sources report that Galamison confronted the board's vice president, whereas Clarence Taylor, Galamison's biographer, states that he arrived after the People's Board takeover (182–183).

24. Podair, 77.

25. Berube and Gittell, 17–18 (quotation 17); and Podair, 77, 79.

26. My summary of the OHB conflict draws on contemporaneous journalism and the following sources: Maurice Berube and Marilyn Gittel, eds. *Confrontation at Ocean Hill-Brownsville* (New York: Praeger, 1969), which contains documents from that time and the editors' comments; Martin Mayer, "The Full and Sometimes Very Surprising Story of Ocean Hill, the Teacher' Union and the Teachers Strikes of 1968," *New York Times* 2 February 1969; Martin Mayer, *The Teachers Strike—New York 1968* (New York: Harper & Row, 1969); Naomi Levine, *Ocean Hill-Brownsville Schools in Crisis: A Case History* (New York: Popular Press, 1969); Diane Ravitch, *The Great School Wars—New York, 1805–1973* (New York: Basic Books, 1973); Gordon, *Why They Couldn't Wait*; Podair, *Strike That Changed New York*; and Kahlenberg, *Tough Liberal*. I limit my citations to quotations, paraphrases, and particular information such as statistics.

27. "Draft Guidelines for a Demonstration Project," 26 March 1968, in Berube and Gittell, *Confrontation at Ocean Hill-Brownsville*, 19–24; and "Excerpts from the Niemeyer Report," 30 July 1968, in Berube and Gittell, 24–32.

28. Jonathan Kaufman's chapter-long biography of McCoy is at once realistic, sympathetic, and experientially textured. See Kaufman, *Broken Alliance: The Turbulent Times Between Blacks and Jews in America* (New York: Scribner's, 1988), 127–164.

29. Podair, 87–94 (quotation 90); and Kahlenberg, *Tough Liberal*, 80.

30. Kahlenberg, 77–78.

31. "Negroes Disrupt School Meeting," *New York Times*, 28 September 1967.

32. Kahlenberg, 82.

33. "Letter of Transfer," 8 May 1968, in Berube and Gittell, 33; Podair, *Strike That Changed New York*, 109 (teacher walk-out); and Berube and Gittell, 155–162 (transfer policy, 156–157).

34. Podair, 105, 107; and Francis E. Rivers, "Board of Education of the City of New York, Administrative Hearing into Complaints of Rhody A. McCoy, Unit Administrator of Ocean Hill-Brownsville, Requesting Transfer of Teachers: Report and Recommendation," 26 August 1968, in Berube and Gittell, 83–101.

35. Podair, 114.

36. Kahlenberg's account of the strikes is more sympathetic to Shanker and places more emphasis on the alleged Black anti-Semitism (93–111).

37. "Anti-Semitism Held an Artificial Issue," *New York Times*, 22 October 1968.

38. Emergency Citizens Committee to Save School Decentralization and Community Control, "Three Strikes—and the Children Are Out," *New York Times*, 16 October 1968.

39. "Anti-Semitism? A Statement by the Teachers of Ocean Hill-Brownsville to the People of New York," *New York Times*, 11 November 1968.

40. Kaufman, *Broken Alliance*, 155.

41. Kaufman, 155–156 (first quotation), 155 (second quotation). In *Tough Liberal*, Kahlenberg acknowledges that even Shanker's supporters felt he acted imprudently in duplicating the pamphlets and intensifying the discourse of Black anti-Semitism that galvanized Jewish opposition (107–110).

42. Kaufman, 155 (all quotations). On the leaflet campaign and Jewish organizations circulating Black anti-Semitism discourse, see Fred Ferretti, "New York's Black Anti-Semitism Scare," in *Strangers and Neighbors: Relations between Blacks and Jews in the United States*, ed. Maurianne Adams and John Bracey (Amherst: University of Massachusetts Press, 1999), 645–659; and Walter Karp and H. R. Shapiro, "Exploding the Myth of Black Anti-Semitism," in Adams and Bracey, 660–668.

43. Podair, *Strike That Changed New York*, 112.

44. Murray Illson, "Negroes Will Run N.Y.U King Center," *New York Times*, 2 November 1968.

45. "15 Jews Protest Action by N.Y.U.," *New York Times*, 6 August 1968; and McCandish Phillips, "Jewish Militants Step Up Activity," *New York Times*, 25 June 1969 (background information on JDL).

46. "Hester Is Urged to Oust Hatchett," *New York Times*, 10 October 1968.

47. "Mayor Jeered at Jewish Center As He Speaks on School Crisis," *New York Times*, 16 October 1968. Another account, somewhat less detailed, appears in Kovach.

48. Martin Tolchin, "Lindsay Backlash Confronts Javits," *New York Times*, 17 October 1968.

49. Leonard Buder, "2 Teachers' Cases Sent to Donovan," *New York Times*, 23 January 1969; Thomas F. Brady, "Outcry Growing Against Bigotry," *New York Times*, 25 July 1969; and Margaret Fox, "Julius Lester, Chronicler of Black America, Is Dead at 78," *New York Times*, 19 January 2018. Although much maligned in 1968–1969, Lester went on to have a distinguished career as a writer and academic historian. Ironically, he had a Jewish ancestor on his mother's side of the family and converted to Judaism in 1996.

50. Peter Kihss, "Museum Withdraws Catalogue Attacked as a Slur on Jews," *New York Times*, 31 January 1969. Information also from Martin Arnold, "The Metropolitan Yields on 'Racism' in Show Catalogue," *New York Times*, 18 January 1969; Martin Arnold, "Hoving Accepts Onus for Furor," *New York Times*, 22 January 1969; and "Irony Over Anti-Semitism Issue Seen in Harlem Art Catalogue," *New York Times*, 29 January 1969.

51. "Defense League Scored by Rabbi," *New York Times*, 18 May 1969.

52. Phillips, "Jewish Militants Step Up Activity"; and Irving Spiegel, "Judaism, Council Denounces a 'Call to Violence,'" *New York Times*, 18 July 1969. The criticisms of the JDL were, unfortunately, prescient. That summer the group began training members in military tactics at a camp in the Catskills and, over many succeeding years, would engage in many acts of murder and mayhem.

53. Paul Ritterband, "Ethnic Power and the Public Schools: The New York City School Strike of 1968," *Sociology of Education* 47, no. 2 (Spring 1974): 251.

54. Linda Charlton, "Jews Fear Anti-Zionism of New Left," *New York Times*, 14 August 1970.

55. Nathan Abrams, "Speaking to Power," *Jewish Quarterly* 53, no. 1 (2006): 47–50.

56. Abrams, 47 (quotation), 49 (other information]. Murray Friedman similarly portrays *Commentary* during Podhoretz's tenure and also discusses the conservatism of the *New Republic* after Marty Peretz, another neocon, purchased this formerly liberal magazine. See Friedman, *What Went Wrong? The Creation and Collapse of the Black-Jewish Alliance* (New York: Free Press, 1995), 266–269.

57. Norman Podhoretz, "My Negro Problem—And Ours," *Commentary* 35, no. 2 (February 1963): 95–101 (first and second quotation 98; long quotation 99–100).

58. Earl Raab, "The Black Revolution & the Jewish Question," *Commentary* 47, no. 1 (January 1969): 30 (all quotations).

59. Henry Raymont, "Jews Debating Black Anti-Semitism," *New York Times*, 26 January 1969.

60. Nathan Glazer, "Blacks, Jews & the Intellectuals," *Commentary* 47, no. 4 (April 1969): 35 (both quotations).

61. See Kovach, "Racist and Anti-Semitic Charges"; Irving Spiegel, "Jews Are Advised Not to Exaggerate Animosity of Negro," *New York Times*, 10 September 1968, 73; Raymont, "Jews Debating Black Anti-Semitism"; and Maurice Carroll, "Reform Leader Fears Some Jews Are Overreacting to Slurs by 'Hate-Mongers,'" *New York Times*, 3 February 1969.

62. Spiegel, "Jews Advised Not to Exaggerate."

63. "Dore Schary Tells Panel on Violence Racism Is Divisive," *New York Times*, 4 October 1968.

64. Carroll, "Reform Leader Fears Some Jews Are Overreacting."

65. Robert D. McFadden, "B'nai B'rith Says State U. Discriminates," *New York Times*, 3 May 1972 (SUNY Albany); "'Reverse Discrimination,'" *Chicago Tribune*, 23 November 1972 (OCR complaints); and Irving Spiegel, "Job Rights Role of U.S. Disputed," *New York Times*, 18 November 1972 (ADL annual meeting).

66. Murray Illson, "6 Jewish Groups Charge Colleges With Reverse Bias," *New York Times*, 14 January 1973; and Irving Spiegel, "Job Drive Backed By H.E.W.'s Chief," *New York Times*, 17 November 1973, 18 (ADL dinner).

67. Judith Cummings, "State Clears City College Of Racial-Quota Charges," *New York Times*, 30 August 1974; Iver Peterson, "3 Charging Bias Rejected Again for City College Medical Class," *New York Times*, 1 September 1975; Lawrence Van Gelder, "2 Suits Challenge Biomedical Unit," *New York Times*, 15 January 1975; and "Rejected Students Win in City College Suit," *New York Times*, 28 June 1977.

68. *Chance v. Board of Examiners* 458 F.2d 1167–1179 (1972).

69. *Kirkland v. New York State Department of Correctional Services*, 520 F.2d 420–431 (Second Circuit 1975). This class-action lawsuit, filed on 10 April 1973, challenged a civil service examination taken by correctional officers who wished to qualify for promotions. The plaintiffs claimed the test had a disproportional impact on Black and Hispanic officers (that is, they failed at a significantly higher rate than did white officers) and that it did not test for job-related knowledge and skills.

70. Murray Friedman's *What Went Wrong?*, 275–291, offers a nuanced account of Southern Jews who experienced pressure from both vigilante and "respectable" white supremacists. *Struggles in the Promised Land: Toward a History of Black-Jewish Relations in the United States*, edited by Jack Salzman and Cornel West (New York: Oxford, 1997), discusses Jewish opponents and supporters of affirmative action. Jerome A. Chanes's "Affirmative Action: Jewish Ideals, Jewish Interests" traces the organizational opposition to affirmative-action guidelines and programs from the early years through the Clinton administration (*Struggles in the Promised Land*, 295–321). Jack Greenberg's *Crusaders in the Courts: How a Dedicated Band of Lawyers Fought for the Civil Rights Revolution* (New York: Basic Books, 1994) provides a rich insider history of the NAACP Legal Defense and Education Fund.

71. Kaufman, *Broken Alliance*, 117–118.

CHAPTER 2. JUST WORDS?

1. Quoted in Seth S. King, "Agnew Denounces Universities Quotas to Help Minorities," *New York Times*, 13 February 1970.

2. "Text of Vice-President Agnew's Criticism of Lowered Entrance Standards," *Chronicle of Higher Education*, 20 April 1970.

3. For background on the mid-twentieth-century ideology and infrastructure of the conservative movement, see Paul Gottfried, *The Conservative Movement*, rev. ed. (New York: Twayne, 1993); Thomas Byrne Edsall and Mary D. Edsall, *Chain Reaction: The Impact of Race, Rights, and Taxes on American Politics* (New York: Norton, 1991); Sara Diamond, *Roads to Dominion: Right-Wing Movements and Political Power in the United States* (New York: Guilford, 1995); and James Allen Smith, *The Idea Brokers: Think Tanks and the Rise of the New Policy Elite* (New York: Free Press, 1991). In *From the New Deal to the New Right: Race and the Southern Origins of Modern Conservatism* (New Haven, CT: Yale University Press, 2008), Joseph E. Lowndes argues against the claim that modern conservatism arose from the backlash against the 1960s–1970s movements, especially the civil rights and Black Power movements. He remarks that backlash accounts often do not "interrogate the cross-cutting institutional, discursive, and cultural paths that made race an important aspect of political identification for an increasing segment of white voters in the post-war era"; nor do they "explain how that political identification became linked to others," such as economic and social issues (4). While the book provides a close examination of ideologies and strategies during the Goldwater, Wallace, and Nixon campaigns, with an emphasis on southern outreach and later the racialization of the "silent majority," it has limitations that, I think, reflect the emphasis of American political development on the institutional and ideational aspects of transformational political moments. The book does not engage the contemporaneous literatures on how diverse identities, cultures, and discourses work in both formal political and movement activities, particularly when they intersect.

4. Lino A. Graglia, "Special Admission of the 'Culturally Deprived' to Law School," *University of Pennsylvania Law Review* 119, no. 2 (December 1970), 351–63; and Robert M. O'Neil, "Preferential Admissions: Equalizing the Access of Minority Groups to Higher Education," *Yale Law Journal* 80, no. 4 (March 1971): 699–758 (cited hereafter as O'Neil, *Yale*).

As of January 2020, according to information posted for HeinOnline's U.S. Core Journals, Lino Graglia's article had received 962 citations; overall, it listed 76 articles authored by Graglia, which include 23 on affirmative action or race-conscious admissions; several on judicial review, and a few each on LGBT issues, busing, and immigration. He is also the author of three books. Educated at City College of New York and Columbia University School of Law, he served in the US Department of Justice and private practices before joining the University of Texas School of Law in 1966, where he occupies the A. W. Walker Centennial Chair in Law (his curriculum vitae is posted on the university website, accessed 16 January 2020, https://law.utexas.edu/faculty/lino-a-graglia.

As of January 2020, according to information posted for HeinOnline's U.S. Core Journals, Robert M. O'Neil's article had received 966 citations; overall, it listed 85 articles authored by O'Neil, 17 on affirmative action or race-conscious admissions, 35 on speech issues, five on academic freedom, and over a dozen on the rights of labor, consumers, and welfare recipients. He is also the author of a dozen books. O'Neil (1934–2018) received undergraduate, master's, and law degrees from Harvard University. After clerking for Justice William J. Brennan Jr., he joined the faculty at the University of California, Berkeley, and then held leadership positions including provost at the University of Cincinnati (1972–1975); vice president of Indiana University (1975–1980), president of the University of Wisconsin System (1980–1985), president of the University of Virginia (1986–1990), and founding director of its Thomas Jefferson Center for the Protection of Free Speech (1990–2010). Information from "In Memoriam: Robert M. O'Neil," American Law Institute, accessed 15 January 2020, https://www.ali.org/news/articles/memoriam-robert-m-oneil/; Emily Langer, "Robert O'Neil, Former U-Va. President and Scholar of First Amendment, Dies at 83," *Washington Post*, 3 October 2018; and James D. McComus (president, University of Toledo), forward to Honors Day Address by Robert M. O'Neil, University of Toledo, 13 May 1987, accessed 15 January 2020, https://files.eric.ed.gov/fulltext/ED287333.pdf.

5. In a 2017 telephone conversation, O'Neil told me that the law review editors recognized the Graglia article would be controversial and published it for that reason. Some years later, Professor Graglia told him that since it was the only reputable journal to accept the article, he felt shunned (Robert M. O'Neil, phone conversation with the author, 11 January 2017). The editors might also have accepted the article to balance the views in Jack Greenberg's "Integration or Segregation?" (*University of Pennsylvania Law Review* 118 [1969–70]: 939–943), which was his March 1970 speech at the journal's annual banquet. My survey of the *University of Pennsylvania Law Review* from volume 116 (1967–1968) through volume 128 (1979–1980) revealed that the majority of articles dealt with technical issues of law; only a few addressed such flash-point public issues as the Pentagon Papers, wartime speech, welfare, and rape.

6. Derrick A. Bell Jr., "In Defense of Minority Admissions Programs: A Response to Professor Graglia," *University of Pennsylvania Law Review* 119, no. 2 (December 1970): 364 (first quotation), 365 (second, third, and fourth quotations).

7. Graglia's use of "Negro" throughout the article is telling. By 1970 "African-American," "Afro-American," and "Black" were common usage in academic scholarship, on campuses, in Black communities, and in the New Left, Black Power, antiwar, and emerging Second Wave women's movements.

8. Graglia, 351 (all quotations).

9. Graglia, 352 (both quotations).

10. Graglia, 361. Many such passages dot the article.

11. In the years before the *University of Pennsylvania Law Review* published Graglia's article, literary critics, such as Wayne Booth in *The Rhetoric of Fiction* (Chicago: University of Chicago Press, 1961) and W. Walker Gibson in *Tough, Sweet, and Stuffy* (Bloomington: Indiana University Press, 1966), were analyzing how narratives fictionalized their narrators and readers as well as their characters. In "The Writer's Audience Is Always a Fiction" (1975), Walter J. Ong explained that the writer uses narrative techniques to cast the readers

"in some sort of role—entertainment seekers, reflective sharers of experience (as those who listen to Conrad's Marlow), inhabitants of a lost and remembered world of prepubertal latency (readers of Tolkien's hobbit stories)." In turn, readers must agree to step into the fictionalized role, which seldom coincides with the roles they play in their actual lives (*PMLA* 90, no. 1 [January 1975]: 12).

12. Here and elsewhere, Graglia derogates minority students, minority lawyers, and liberal faculty members to persuade readers to step into the peer role he offers them. In one instance, he depicts liberal faculty members as a moaning chorus in a Greek tragedy. The dialogue reads: "Unjust cultural and economic disadvantages should be removed, but we cannot do that. Educational facilities from nursery school through graduate school should be improved, but we cannot do that. What we can do is ignore the inevitable effects of these disadvantages and deprivations and admit the deprived to our law schools. It at least shows where our hearts are" (353). In another instance, they foolishly devastate academe: "If the underrepresentation of certain groups is to be remedied by lowered admissions standards, why not [do so] directly and completely? . . . If lowered admissions standards are appropriate, is the inevitable demand for lowered performance standards improper? If certain courses are not suited to this approach, they can be made optional, changed, or eliminated" (361). These derisive passages, which contrast with the "rational and resolute" narrator, cultivate reader self-esteem. For high self-esteem, I am indebted to Ong's analysis of the opening passage in Ernest Hemingway's *A Call to Arms*. This passage reads, "In the late summer of that year we lived in a house in a village that looked across the river and the plain to the mountains." After dissecting Hemingway's use of "we" in conjunction with the lack of specifics (which year, house, village, river, plain, and mountains?), Ong remarks, "The reader here has a well-marked role assigned him. He is a companion-in-arms, somewhat later become a confident. It is a flattering role. Hemingway readers are encouraged to cultivate high self-esteem" (13).

13. After the *Brown* decisions in 1954 and 1955, New Orleans school integration was stalled by lawsuits, politics, and street riots until a court finally ordered the admission of six Black children to white schools. During my sophomore year at Tulane University (1960–1961), I watched marshals escort six-year-old Ruby Bridges to a white elementary school while a crowd of housewives, many holding infants and toddlers, screamed obscenities. Shocked by the rage, I wrote about this event for my creative writing class and observed a Ku Klux Klan rally held out by a bayou. After days of street rioting and a Klan synagogue bombing, I fled back home to Cincinnati, graduating from college, dipping into the student movement, attending activist training workshops offered by Saul Alinsky's Industrial Areas Foundation, and, in graduate school, helping to organize women on my campus. For accounts of that tumultuous period, see Juan Williams, *Eyes on the Prize: America's Civil Rights Years, 1954–1965* (New York: Penguin, 1987); Todd Gitlin, *The Sixties: Years of Hope, Days of Rage* (New York: Bantam, 1987); James Miller, *Democracy Is in the Streets: From Port Huron to the Siege of Chicago* (New York: Simon & Schuster, 1987); and Maurice Isserman and Michael Kazin, *America Divided: The Civil War of the*

1960s (New York: Oxford University Press, 2000). For campus conflict escalation, see Max Heirich, *The Spiral of Conflict: Berkeley 1964* (New York: Columbia University Press, 1971); and for campus struggles over affirmative action, see Paul M. Gaston, "Reflections on Affirmative Action: Its Origins, Virtues, Enemies, Champions, and Prospects," in *Diversity Challenged: Evidence on the Impact of Affirmative Action*, ed. Gary Orfield with Michael Kurlaender (Cambridge, MA: Harvard Education Publishing Group, 2001), 277–293.

14. Graglia, 359 (first quotation quoting Ernest Gellhorn, "The Law Schools and the Negro," *Duke Law Journal* [1968]: 1089), 360 (second quotation), 356 (third quotation).

15. Graglia, 355–356.

16. On stereotyping, Luke Charles Harris and Uma Narayan similarly observe that "an individual woman or minority person's inadequacies can be generalized and seen as signs of the incompetence of whole groups, whereas the failures of white men remain personal limitations. Furthermore, success stories involving women or minorities often tend to be interpreted as exceptions, and not as examples of the capabilities of women or people of color generally" ("Affirmative Action and the Myth of Preferential Treatment: A Transformative Critique of the Terms of the Affirmative Action Debate," *Harvard Blackletter Law Journal* 11 [1994]: 31). Sometimes Graglia's attempt to retain his reasonable man persona while engaging in racist stereotyping results in very strange logic, as in this example: "When my child's new teacher turns out to be a Negro, I am very pleased; it permits me to think that the world, or at least the country, is on its way to being well. (This pleasure would not be possible, or would be much diminished, if I had reason to believe the Negro teacher less qualified than his or her white counterpart.)" (354). Readers should recognize the invidious logic wrapped in saccharine prose. When Graglia's child has an African American teacher, he is pleased only if this teacher is qualified, and he adduces from this one qualified teacher that the country is on its way to eliminating racism. He doesn't entertain the possibility that his child might have an underqualified white teacher, nor would he attribute any national significance to a qualified or underqualified white teacher.

17. Graglia, 352.

18. For a history of the "nation of minorities" trope, see Ian F. Haney López, "'A Nation of Minorities': Race, Ethnicity, and Reactionary Colorblindness," *Stanford Law Review* 59, no. 4 (February 2007): 985–1063.

19. Graglia, 362.

20. See Jerome Karabel, "How Affirmative Action Took Hold at Harvard, Yale, and Princeton," *Journal of Blacks in Higher Education* 48 (Summer 2005): 58–77 (quotation 59); and Laura Kalman, *Yale Law School and the Sixties: Revolt and Reverberations* (New York: Oxford University Press, 2005). For a detailed history of discrimination and affirmative action at three elite universities, see Jerome Karabel, *The Chosen: The Hidden History of Admission and Exclusion at Harvard, Yale, and Princeton* (New York: Houghton Mifflin, 2005). For information about the Black Student Alliance, see its website: http://bsayale.squarespace.com/.

21. "Notes: The Affirmative Duty to Ingrate in Higher Education," *Yale Law Journal* 79, no. 4 (March 1970): 666–697.

22. Robert M. O'Neil, "Preferential Admissions: Equalizing Access to Legal Education," *University of Toledo Law Review* 2, no. 2–3 (1970): 281–320. Cited hereafter as O'Neil, *Toledo*.

23. Alfred W. Blumrosen, "Legal Education for Black Students: A Remedy for Class Discrimination," *University of Law Review* 2, nos. 2–3 (Spring–Summer 1970): 799 (first and second quotations), 800 (third quotation).

24. No phrasing is free from complications. "Preferential admissions" invokes more negative responses than "race-conscious admissions," which in turn evokes more negative responses than "equalizing measures." "Affirmative action" covers many more measures than does race-conscious admissions, such as outreach, recruitment, and training of excluded or underrepresented groups in the education, employment, and contracting sectors.

25. O'Neil, *Yale*, 700, note 3.

26. A similar observation appears in "Brief of Amicus Curiae, Young Lawyers Section, Seattle-King County Bar Association," *DeFunis v. Odegaard*, Washington State Supreme Court: "Although the terms 'preferential treatment' and 'reverse discrimination' may have some efficacy in other contexts, the use of such terms to characterize the . . . [University of Washington] Law School's admissions policy is inappropriate, unfair and misleading. . . . The very nature of the words prejudges the issue; for if any racial 'preference' is found, the necessary conclusion is that such 'preference' is discriminatory and unconstitutional because it violates the Fourteenth Amendment's Equal Protection Clause . . . it is regrettable that these terms have been fashioned to describe a policy which seeks to achieve equality for minorities in a real, not 'paper,' sense" (18). From a bound volume of briefs supplied by the Washington State Law Library.

27. O'Neil, *Yale*, 699.

28. O'Neil, *Yale*, 700; emphases mine.

29. O'Neil, *Yale*, 702–703.

30. These sorts of nonmerit preferences continue, as suggested by a stunning instance in 2009. The University of Illinois had, it seems, maintained a "clout system" whereby applicants with ties to university trustees and other influential people were designated as Category I priorities for admission. A review panel, appointed by Illinois governor Pat Quinn "recommended a complete overhaul of the admissions process," urged "the resignation of all members of the Board of Trustees," and implicated both the Urbana-Champaign campus chancellor Richard Herman and the system president B. Joseph White in this preferential policy. Under pressure from the new trustees, the system president tendered his resignation (Kathryn Masterson, "U. of Illinois President Resigns in Wake of Admissions Scandal," *Chronicle of Higher Education*, 23 September 2009). Further investigative journalism discovered that Illinois legislators had exercised blatant preferences regarding scholarships. Every year each legislator received two four-year scholarships covering tuition and fees at the state's public universities. The legislator could award the scholarships in whole or carve them up into eight one-year awards. An article in the *Chicago*

Tribune reported that legislators gave most of these scholarships to family, friends, political supporters, and campaign workers, adding, "In 2008, the lawmakers awarded 1,509 scholarships totaling $12.5 million. The awards—which average $8,300 a piece—come as state lawmakers slashed funding for other college grants" that mainly helped poor and low-income students (Stacy St. Clair, Tara Malone, and Jodi S. Cohen, "Illinois Lawmakers' Handouts," *Chicago Tribune*, 27 September 2009). More recently the Varsity Blues scandal revealed that preferential treatment was given to underqualified or unqualified students whose wealthy and prominent parents paid large sums of money to sources that misrepresented the students' test scores, school achievements, athletic abilities, and other qualifications.

31. O'Neil, *Yale*, 705.

32. O'Neil, *Yale*, 706.

33. O'Neil, *Yale*, 710 (all quotations).

34. O'Neil, *Yale*, 750 (both quotations).

35. See James S. Coleman et al., *Equality of Educational Opportunity* (Washington, DC: US Department of Health, Education, and Welfare and Office of Education, 1966), 3. The Coleman report, named after Johns Hopkins University sociologist James S. Coleman, who chaired the committee that issued it, is a survey mandated under the Civil Rights Act of 1964. Covering preschool through higher education, it showed that severe racial segregation and inequality existed nationwide. As for teacher and peer treatment of minority students, a robust debate continues today as to whether these attitudes, sometimes called "microaggressions," constitute subtle discrimination or simply bad manners.

36. O'Neil, *Yale*, 743 (first quotation), 744 (second quotation).

37. O'Neil, *Yale*, 746.

38. Quoted in O'Neil, *Yale*, 718.

39. See O'Neil, *Yale*, 719–725. The studies he consulted and cited include those by the American Council on Education, Association of American Universities, Carnegie Commission on Higher Education, National Association of State Universities and Land Grant Colleges, Association of American Law Schools, Association of American Medical Colleges, US Department of Health, Education, and Welfare, and more than a dozen authored by scholars.

40. O'Neil, *Yale*, 726 (Mississippi and Georgia); 727 (California, New Mexico, and Arizona). The problem with such ratios, as scholars would point out, is that the population counts are overinclusive. A more accurate ratio of Black lawyers to Black population would count the adults and the far fewer children in need of legal services, and it would also emphasize that some populations (both white and minority) more frequently need legal services than others. Nevertheless, the differentials between white and minority ratios are undeniably stunning.

41. O'Neil, *Yale*, 727–728.

42. Thomas W. Christopher and Frederick M. Hart, "Indian Law Scholarship Program at the University of New Mexico," *University of Toledo Law Review* 2, nos. 2–3 (Spring–Summer 1970): 692.

43. O'Neil, *Yale*, 732.

44. O'Neil, *Yale*, 732 (both quotation); his full discussion of testing occurs on 731–737. For a later history and critique of standardized testing, see Nicholas Lemann, *The Big Test: The Secret History of American Meritocracy*, rev. ed. (New York: Farrar, Straus and Giroux, 2000); and David Owen with Marilyn Doerr, *None of the Above: The Truth behind the SATs*, rev. ed. (Lanham MD: Rowman & Littlefield, 1999).

45. O'Neil, *Yale*, 737.

46. In "Equalizing Access to Legal Education: Special Programs for Law Students Who Are Not Admissible by Traditional Criteria," Sanford Jay Rosen wrote that special admissions students "are usually drawn from subcultural groups that are quite different from those of the typical white middle class law student. Further, their educational backgrounds tend to be markedly inferior to those of their white counterparts. . . . Yet, traditional admissions criteria tend to accentuate linguistic, verbal, logical and other such skills which are extracted from the predominantly white middle class culture to the virtual exclusion of those found in minority subcultures" (*University of Toledo Law Review* 2, nos. 2–3 [Spring–Summer 1970]: 329). Other articles explained that the tests' standard English dialect disadvantaged test-takers whose native language or dialect was not standard English. Interestingly, Franklin R. Evans and Richard R. Reilly's "A Study of Speededness as a Source of Test Bias" reported that timed tests of reading comprehension had a racially disparate impact on test-takers who were attempting to answer questions near the end of the test period. When the test period was lengthened, minority test-takers showed more improvement in reaching and answering these questions than did white test-takers. The authors concluded that the amount of time allotted to test-taking was a potential source of bias (*Journal of Educational Measurement* 9, no. 2 [Summer 1972]: 123–131).

47. Clyde W. Summers, "Preferential Admissions: An Unreal Solution to a Real Problem," *University of Toledo Law Review* 2, nos. 2–3 (Spring–Summer 1970): 391.

48. Rosen, "Equalizing Access," 332 (first quotation), 333 (second quotation).

49. Haywood Burns, "Racism and American Law: A New Course in Legal History," *University of Toledo Law Review* 2, nos. 2–3 (Spring–Summer 1970): 905. In 2015 and 2016, almost five decades after Burns wrote this article, media coverage of police brutality targeting African Americans and others of color, legal proceedings on these episodes, and the Black Lives Matter movement suddenly made most of white America aware of racism in law.

50. O'Neil, *Yale*, 766.

CHAPTER 3. THE STORIES THEY TELL

1. Jim Chen, "*DeFunis*, Defunct," *Constitutional Comment* 16, no. 1 (1999): 94 (on Kama Sutra, quoting Jim Chen, "Embryonic Thoughts on Racial Identity as New Property," *University of Colorado Law Review* 68 [1997]: 1123, 1127).

2. Case texts were published in *DeFunis v. Odegaard and the University*

of Washington, ed. Ann Fagan Ginger (Dobbs Ferry, NY: Oceana, 1974). Robert M. O'Neil's *Discriminating against Discrimination: Preferential Admissions and the DeFunis Case* (Bloomington: Indiana University Press, 1975) focuses exclusively on the case and the larger questions of affirmative action in admissions. Allan P. Sindler's *Bakke, DeFunis, and Minority Admissions: The Quest for Equal Opportunity* (New York: Longman, 1978) deals equally with the two cases. Several books on *Bakke* also discuss *DeFunis*, for instance Bernard Schwartz's *Before Bakke: Affirmative Action and the Supreme Court* (New York: New York University Press, 1988); Howard Ball's *The Bakke Case: Race, Education, and Affirmative Action* (Lawrence: University of Kansas Press, 2000); Terry Eastland and William J. Bennett, *Counting by Race: Equality from the Founding Fathers to Bakke and Weber* (New York: Basic Books, 1979); and Harvie J. Wilkinson, *From Brown to Bakke: The Supreme Court and School Integration* (New York: Oxford University Press, 1979). Journals publishing special issues, symposia, or clusters of articles in subsequent years on *DeFunis* include the *Black Law Journal* (1973, 1974, 1975), *Columbia Law Review* (1975), *Duquesne Law Review* (1973–1974), *University of Florida Law Review* (1974–1975), *Journal of Law and Education* (1974, 1975), *Washington Law Review* (1974–1975), and *Virginia Law Review* (1974).

3. Quintard Taylor, "Black Urban Development—Another View: Seattle's Central District, 1910–1940," *Pacific Historical Review* 38, no. 4 (November 1989): 429–448 (population statistics 434). Also see Q. Taylor, *The Forging of a Black Community: Seattle's Central District from 1870 through the Civil Rights Era* (Seattle: University of Washington Press, 1994). During the 1960s, according to the Seattle Civil Rights Labor Project, King County had 27,805 African Americans, 10,789 Japanese Americans, 4,434 Filipinos, and 4,324 Chinese Americans. The project report provides maps of Blacks ghettos from the early to late twentieth century. See "Seattle Segregation Maps, 1920–2010," Seattle Civil Rights Labor History, n.d., 35 pp. (data 10), accessed 16 January 2020, https://depts.washington.edu/civilr/segregation_maps.htm. I am grateful to Robert M. O'Neil for reminding me that the state was not always liberal; he referred me to the Legislative Joint Fact-Finding Committee on Un-American Activities in Washington State, chaired by Albert F. Canwell (Republican representing Spokane) and modelled on Congress's House Un-American Activities Committee (HUAC). It sought to expose (alleged) Communists and specifically targeted the University of Washington. See https://www.historylink.org/File/1484.

4. Quintard Taylor, "The Civil Rights Movement in the American West: Black Protest in Seattle, 1960–1970," *Journal of Negro History* 80, no. 1 (Winter 1995): 3; and Taylor, *The Forging of a Black Community*, 190–233.

5. Taylor, "Civil Rights Movement in the American West," 5–7 (quotations 5); and Taylor, *The Forging of a Black Community*, 201–209.

6. See Taylor, "The Civil Rights Movement in the American West," 8–9 (quotations 8); and Taylor, *The Forging of a Black Community*, 209–216. For other accounts of the struggle over the schools, I draw from Doris H. Pieroth, "With All Deliberate Caution: School Integration in Seattle, 1954–1968,"

Pacific Northwest Quarterly 73, no. 2 (April 1982): 49–61; and Brooke Clark, "The Seattle School Boycott of 1966," Seattle Civil Rights and Labor History Project, 2005, accessed 19 February 2009, http://depts.washington.edu/civilr/school_boycott.htm.

7. See Clark, "Seattle School Boycott of 1966." In "Civil Rights Movement of the American West," Taylor claims that nearly 4,000 students, representing 55 percent of the Black student enrollment in the district, boycotted the schools, as did a considerable number of Asian students (9). Also Taylor, *The Forging of a Black Community*, 209–216.

8. Pieroth and Taylor tell essentially the same story. Pieroth, "With All Deliberate Caution," 57 (Central District crowding and citizens committee), 58 (auditorium permit); Taylor, "The Civil Rights Movement in the American West," 9–10 (first quotation), 9 (second quotation). Taylor quotes Carmichael's remarks as quoted in *Seattle Post-Intelligencer*, 20 April 1967.

9. Pieroth, 59–61.

10. Taylor, *Forging of a Black Community*, 192–201(198 [retail protests], 192–194 [retail protests], 193 [Boeing quotation and unemployment data]).

11. Taylor, *Forging of a Black Community*, 193. Also see Trevor Griffey, "History," Seattle Civil Rights and Labor History Project, accessed 19 February 2009, https://depts.washington.edu/civilr/ucwa_history.htm. Griffey's history focuses on construction industry discrimination, protest, and litigation.

12. Taylor, "Civil Rights Movement in the American West," 2–3 (Taylor takes the statistics from the Urban League report).

13. See William B. Gould, "The Seattle Building Trades Order: The First Comprehensive Relief against Employment Discrimination in the Construction Industry," *Stanford Law Review* 26, no. 4 (April 1974): 781–784. In 1970 and 1971, I attended weekend retreats sponsored by Saul Alinsky's Chicago-based Industrial Areas Foundation, which was just beginning to train women as change agents. We learned about Alinsky's famous Back of the Yards project in Chicago and the Kodak Company project in Rochester. Seattle activists used several Alinsky tactics including buy-ins to tie up retail operations, blockades at Sea-Tac Airport, and shut-downs of construction sites.

14. Gould, "Seattle Building Trades Order," 785–787. The union practices Gould cites were included in the findings of fact for *United States v. Local 86, Ironworkers*, 315 F. Supp. 1202 (W.D. Wash. 1970), the case brought against five unions in Seattle. In a long footnote, Gould mentions that the ironworkers' union compelled Howard Lewis, a Black welder with thirty years of experience, to take a knot-tying test as a condition of union membership. He was not informed that knot-tying would be included in the examination and consequently failed this part twice. On his third try, he successfully tied the seven knots but then was asked to tie an eighth knot he didn't know existed. The board found that knot-tying was not required of white welders and was not a skill needed in welding (Gould 785–786). The union's knot-tying test mirrors the tests used in the South to disqualify Blacks from voting.

15. Gould, 788–792.

16. In "The BSU Takes on BYU and the UW Athletics Program 1970," Craig Collison describes direct action during the 1970 winter and spring terms—marches, protests, and building occupations as the Athletics Department studied whether it could break its athletics contract with Brigham Young University which, among other things, circulated the Mormon doctrine that Blacks were spawn of the devil. The article appears on the Seattle Civil Rights and Labor History website, accessed 2 January 2019, https://depts.washington.edu/civilr/BSU_BYU.htm.

17. The Seattle Civil Rights and Labor History website contains articles and interviews on campus groups. My specific information comes from Gould, 792–799; and Griffey, "History," Seattle Civil Rights and Labor History Project, accessed 19 February 2009, http://depts.washington.edu/civilr/ucwa_history.htm.

18. In his "Profile—Josef Diamond," Tom Chambers wrote, "Joe was a rainmaker. He represented 90 percent of the construction firms in the city as well as the Associated General Contractors, Seattle Construction Council, Seattle Master Builders and Home Builders," *Bar Bulletin* 20, no. 7 (March 2002): 1. Chambers, who began law practice in Diamond's firm during the late 1960s, was elected as a Washington State Supreme Court justice in 2000.

19. See James B. Wilson, "Municipal Ordinances, Mississippi Style," in *Southern Justice*, ed. Leon Friedman (New York: Pantheon, 1965), 35–42; and Carole Beers, "James B. Wilson, Dies at 70; Retired UW Chief Counsel," *Seattle Times*, 16 October 1996.

20. Marco DeFunis, Trial Transcript, *DeFunis v. Odegaard*, King County Superior Court, 11. I thank Craig S. Sternberg for sending me a copy of the typed transcript that is more complete (one page missing) than the excerpted version published in Ginger. Cited hereafter as Trial Transcript.

21. "Letter from BSU to Odegaard," 6 May 1968, quoted in Marc Robinson, "The Early History of the UW Black Student Union," Seattle Civil Rights and Labor History Project, accessed 19 February 2009, http://depts.washington.edu/civilr/BSU_beginnings.htm. Unless otherwise noted, all information on the Black Student Union is from Robinson.

22. Marsha King, "I-200—Equality on Campus: Are We There Yet?—Efforts to Diversify State Colleges Show Mixed Results after 30 Years," *Seattle Times*, 18 October 1998.

23. Robinson, "Early History."

24. Trial Transcript, 221–222 (quotations 222).

25. Trial Transcript, 223–224.

26. Trial Transcript, 226–230, 232.

27. Trial Transcript, 233 (quotation), and also 227.

28. To reconstruct the official story, I drew chiefly on the following texts: (1) Josef Diamond for the DeFunises, "Complaint for Mandamus, Injunction and Damages," *DeFunis v. Odegaard*, King County Superior Court, in Ginger, *DeFunis versus Odegaard*, vol. 1, 1–10; (2) James B. Wilson for the University, "Answer to Complaint for Mandamus, Injunction and Damages," in Ginger, vol. 2, 15–20; (3) University of Washington, "Answers to Interrogatories Propounded

by Plaintiffs," in Ginger, vol. 2, 21–48; (4) Judge Lloyd Shorett, "Oral Decision of Washington Superior Court for King County," in Ginger, vol. 2, 113–118; (5) Judge Lloyd Shorett, "Findings of Fact and Conclusions of Law," in Ginger, vol. 2, 119–130; (6) Slade Gorton and James B. Wilson, "Brief of Appellants," *DeFunis v. Odegaard*, 507 P.2d 1169 (Wash. 1973): in bound volume of briefs supplied by the Washington State Law Library; (7) Josef Diamond, Lyle L. Iverson, and Craig S. Sternberg, "Brief of Respondents," briefs supplied by the Washington State Law Library; (8) Gorton and Wilson, "Reply Brief of Appellants," briefs supplied by the Washington State Law Library; (9) Justice Marshall A. Neill, Opinion of the Court, *DeFunis v. Odegaard*, Washington State Supreme Court, 507 P.2d 1169, 1171–1176; (10) Chief Justice Frank Hale, Dissent, Washington State Supreme Court, 507 P.2d 1169, 1190–1192; and (11) *DeFunis v. Odegaard* 416 U.S. 312 (1974). Most of the summaries provided by scholars in articles and books on *DeFunis* follow, with little variation, the official story.

29. I thank Lynda Reese (Director of Psychometric Research) and Stephen Luebke (Principal Test Specialist) Law School Admissions Council for sending me documents on test scores (email and attached documents to author, 5 June 2018). My data on DeFunis's percentiles are based on one of their attachments, "Percent of Candidate Scores Below, Selected LSAT Scaled Scores (1969–1980)," which provides nationwide data on score ranges and corresponding percentiles for LSAT test-takers during each academic year from 1969–1970 through 1979–1980.

30. University of Washington, "Answers to Interrogatories Propounded by Plaintiffs," in Ginger, vol. 1, 35–36. The quoted phrase came from a law school guide sent to all applicants.

31. University of Washington, "Answers to Interrogatories," 29–32.

32. Court documents describe the admissions process in 1971 but not in 1970. Unless otherwise noted, my information is from Slade Gorton and James B. Wilson, "Brief of Respondents," *DeFunis v. Odegaard* 416 U.S. 312 (1974), in *Landmark Briefs and Arguments of the Supreme Court of the United States: Constitutional Law*, ed. Philip B. Kurland and Gerhard Casper, vol. 80 (Arlington, VA: University Publications of America, 1975), 130 (quotations 130) (hereafter Kurland and Casper, *Landmark Briefs*); and from Trial Transcript, 325–412.

33. Brief of Respondents, *DeFunis v. Odegaard* 416 U.S. 312 (1974) in Kurland and Casper, *Landmark Briefs*, 132.

34. Josef Diamond, "Complaint for Mandamus, Injunction and Damages," 5–6 (first quotation); vol. 1, 6 (second quotation).

35. Chronology from King County Superior Court Docket Entries, Single Appendix, *DeFunis v. Odegaard* 416 U.S. 312 (1974), file date 2 January 1974, U.S. Supreme Court Records and Briefs, 1832–1978, 2–3.

36. Trial Transcript, 21, 28–29.

37. Trial Transcript, 21–22 (quotation 21).

38. Trial Transcript, 280–281.

39. Nina Totenberg, "Discriminating to End Discrimination: The Painful DeFunis Case Raises the Specters of Racism and Anti-Semitism," *New York Times*, 14 April 1974.

40. "Questions for Craig Sternberg: Email Interview concerning *DeFunis v.*

Odegaard" (1971–1974), 18 September 2016 (responses received), p. 1 of 8 (long quotation), 8 (first short quotation), 2 (second short quotation).

41. Totenberg, "Discriminating to End Discrimination."

42. Sternberg, "Questions."

43. Transcript of Oral Argument, *DeFunis v. Odegaard* 416 U.S. 312 (1974), rpt. in *Black Law Journal* 3, no. 3 (1973): 251, (first quotation), 256 (second quotation). For reasons I cannot ascertain, Oral Argument occurred on February 26, 1974, yet the journal issue was dated 1973. Cited hereafter as Transcript of Oral Argument.

44. Sternberg.

45. Sternberg.

46. Sternberg on getting DeFunis into law school, 2, 3, 5 (twice), 8; and on policies and procedures, 3, 4 (twice), 5.

47. Chambers, "Profile—Josef Diamond," 1.

48. Trial Transcript, 14, 17, 20.

49. Trial Transcript, 23, 30–31. DeFunis said he spoke with the two admissions deans several times, but his testimony as to when the conversations occurred is confusing and contradictory.

50. Trial Transcript, 47, 51; and Trial Transcript, 355–356.

51. University of Washington, "Answer to Interrogatories," 36.

52. Trial Transcript, 33.

53. See Trial Transcript, 52–54 (quotation from Wilson while examining letter, 54).

54. Trial Transcript, 33–34.

55. "Oral Argument of Josef Diamond, Esq. on Behalf of the Petitioners," Supreme Court of the United States, February 26, 1974, Transcript of Oral Argument, 251.

56. Trial Transcript, 113–114 (quotations 114).

57. Trial Transcript, 115–116.

58. Chronology provided by the university in its "Answers to Interrogatories," 28. The date of complaint filing is on page 2 of the King County Superior Court Docket Entries.

59. University of Washington, "Answer to Interrogatories," 36–37.

60. Trial Transcript, 356.

61. Trial Transcript, 183 (first quotation), 183–184 (second quotation).

62. Trial Transcript, 198–200.

63. Trial Transcript, 181.

64. The law school's formula for calculating the PSFA was: 3.4751 x junior-senior GPA; 0.0159 x LSAT score; and 0.0456 x Writing Test score (a component of the LSAT), the total x 51.3. Using only his third taking of the LSAT, DeFunis's calculation would have been: 3.4751 x 3.71 (GPA) = 12.8926, 0.0159 x 668 (LSAT) = 10.6212, and 0.0456 x 64 (writing) = 2.9189 for a total of 25.4327 x 51.3 for a PSFA of 77.73. Law school formula in the University of Washington's "Answer to Interrogatories," 25.

65. "Brief of the National Council of Jewish Women et al." (filed 1 February 1974), *DeFunis v. Odegaard*, 11.

66. Trial Transcript, 44 (DeFunis Sr.'s occupation). While sources agree that Diamond and his clients met with four (or five) regents, not all of them mention a prior meeting with the law school dean. In his oral argument before the Supreme Court, Diamond stated, "We first met with the dean of the law school, and inquired: what was the basis of the denial? He had the chairman of the Admissions Committee [with him]. . . . We next appeared and met with the Board of Regents. Took his parents with us. I don't think we took the boy" (Transcript of Oral Arguments, 251). Diamond did not clarify who arranged these meetings and who "we" denoted. In *Bakke, Defunis, and Minority Admissions: The Quest for Equal Opportunity* (New York: Longman, 1978), Allan P. Sindler writes, "With Defunis's active cooperation, the senior lawyer [i.e., Diamond] arranged for meetings with the UWLS dean, the admissions committee, and the regents, all in an effort to have DeFunis's application reconsidered favorably" (39).

67. Dan Richman, "Josef Diamond, 1907–2007: Parking Magnate Built Business in 8 States and Canada," *Seattle Post-Intelligencer*, 5 March 2007.

68. Chambers, "Profile—Josef Diamond."

69. Quoted in Richman, "Josef Diamond, 1907–2007."

70. Judge Lloyd Shorett's "Findings of Fact and Conclusions of Law" lists seven regents: James R. Ellis, Robert L. Flennaugh, Mort Frayn, Jack G. Newpert, Robert F. Philip, George V. Powell, and Harold S. Shefelman. My search of the University of Washington website, Seattle newspapers, and Google turned up professional information on regents who met with Diamond and his clients: Ellis (a lawyer), Flennaugh (a dentist), Powell (a lawyer), Shefelman (a lawyer), and Frayn (a lawyer) (These regents are named by Powell in the Trial Transcript, 114).

71. Trial Transcript, 101.

72. Trial Transcript, 102.

73. Trial Transcript, 112 and 113 (Powell).

74. When I served as assistant to University of Cincinnati (UC) president Warren Bennis from 1975 through 1977, the other assistant and I took calls from influential parents who protested decisions affecting their children, usually low grades in undergraduate courses and rejection by the medical or law schools. Our policy, which we dubbed "re-directional therapy," was to direct the parent to the line administrator who could then consider the complaint without any presidential pressure. Even less likely to inject themselves into such matters, the University Trustees maintained a cool distance from complaining individuals inside and outside of the university—sometimes frustratingly so as when, for instance, for the women's studies community board tried to raise the issue of sexual harassment.

75. Robert M. O'Neil, "Preferential Admissions: Equalizing Access to Legal Education," *University of Toledo Law Review* 2, nos. 2–3 (Spring–Summer 1970): 310.

76. The shade of entitlement appeared again at oral argument before the US Supreme Court. Josef Diamond stated, "It was inconceivable to us that an honor student, with the grades that he had, Phi Beta Kappa, Magna Cum

Laude, from the same university, would not be qualified and would be denied admission to the university law school. To us it wasn't possible that all those who were being admitted were better qualified than DeFunis" (Transcript of Oral Arguments, 251). Washington state attorney general Slade Gorton said, "Obviously neither Mr. DeFunis nor any other individual had a constitutional right to enter the University of Washington Law School" (Transcript of Oral Arguments, 260). Later, Gorton explained that everyone is entitled to attend school when a state provides public schools, but "no one is entitled to a law education at the expense of the State" (263).

CHAPTER 4. COLORING THE CASE

1. Josef Diamond, "Complaint for Mandamus, Injunction and Damages," in *DeFunis v. Odegaard and the University of Washington*, ed. Ann Fagan Ginger (Dobbs Ferry, NY: Oceana, 1974), vol. 1, 3–9. Cited hereafter as Diamond, "Complaint" and Ginger.

2. A 1995 obituary described Lloyd W. Shorett as "one of King County's toughest vice fighters," who as a prosecutor went after dozens of racketeers and scam artists. A graduate of the UW Law School, he served in private practice and then in public office as a state assistant attorney general, King County prosecutor, and Superior Court judge (Carole Beers, "Lloyd W. Shorett, 86, Prosecutor, Judge," *Seattle Times*, 13 August 1995).

3. See Walter J. Leonard, "*DeFunis v. Odegaard:* An Invitation to Look Backward," *Black Law Journal* 3, no. 3 (1973): 224–231; Mary K. Hammond, "May the Constitution Be Color Conscious to Remain Color-Blind?," *Ohio Northern University Law Review* 1, no. 1 (1973): 81–96; "Ameliorative Racial Classifications under the Equal Protection Clause: DeFunis v. Odegaard," *Duke Law Journal* 1, no. 5 (December 1973): 1126–1152; John Hart Ely, "The Constitutionality of Reverse Racial Discrimination," *University of Chicago Law Review* 41, no. 4 (Summer 1974): 723–741; Monroe G. Paulson, "*DeFunis:* The Road Not Taken," *Virginia Law Review* 60, no. 6 (October 1974): 917–924 (introduction to a special issue on *DeFunis*); and Richard A. Posner, "The DeFunis Case and the Constitutionality of Preferential Treatment of Racial Minorities," *Supreme Court Review* (1974): 1–32.

4. On racial systems and racialized discourse, see Michael Omi and Howard Winant, *Racial Formation in the United States: From the 1960s to the 1990s*, 2nd ed. (New York: Routledge, 1994); David Theo Goldberg, *Racist Culture: Philosophy and the Politics of Meaning* (Malden, MA: Blackwell, 1993); Rohit Barot and John Bird, "Racialization: The Genealogy and Critique of a Concept," *Ethnic and Racial Studies* 24, no. 4 (2001): 601–618; Eduardo Bonilla-Silva, *Racism without Racists: Color-Blind Racism and the Persistence of Racial Inequality in the United States* (Lanham, MD: Rowman & Littlefield, 2003); Herbert Gans, "Racialization and Racialization Research," *Ethnic and Racial Studies* 40, no. 3 (2017): 341–352; Robin DiAngelo, *White Fragility: Why It's So Hard for White People to Talk about Racism* (Boston: Beacon, 2018); Karim Murji, *Racism, Policy, and Politics* (Bristol, UK: Policy Press, 2018), 37–56;

and John F. Davidio, Adam R. Pearson, and Louis A. Penner, "Aversive Racism, Implicit Bias, and Microagressions," in *Microagression Theory: Influence and Implications*, ed. Gina C. Torino et al. (Hoboken, NJ: Wiley, 2019), 16–31.

5. Craig D. Sternberg, "Questions for Craig Sternberg: email concerning *DeFunis v. Odegaard*," 17 September 2016.

6. Henry Campbell Black, *Black's Law Dictionary*, ed. Bryan A. Garner, 2nd pocket ed. (St. Paul, MN: West Group, 2001), 307 (good faith), 56 (bad faith).

7. Trial Transcript of *DeFunis v. Odegaard* in King County Superior Court, 14 October 1971, 211 (Diamond quotes the Washington State Constitution, Article IX, Section 1). Craig D. Sternberg sent me a typescript copy of the trial transcript in October 2012. Cited hereafter as Trial Transcript.

8. Trial Transcript, 212–216.

9. Trial Transcript, 219–220. Before the early 1960s, many schools accepted applicants with GPAs of B and a few did not even require college completion. In 1961 the University of California Law School at Berkeley accepted 517 of its 708 applicants. By the end of the decade, as Baby Boomers flooded into applicant pools, schools raised their standards. See Susan Welch and John Gruhl, *Affirmative Action and Minority Enrollments in Medical and Law Schools* (Ann Arbor: University of Michigan Press, 1998), 52–53.

10. Trial Transcript, 6–7.

11. Trial Transcript, 349 (rule 1), 350 (rule 2), 376–378 (veteran numbers).

12. Diamond, "Complaint," 5.

13. From the 1964 Gulf of Tonkin incident through the 1968 Tet Offensive, President Lyndon B. Johnson escalated the war through Operation Rolling Thunder bombings, Agent Orange defoliations, napalm strikes, and search-and-destroy missions. Starting in 1969, President Richard Nixon's Vietnamization policy combined the bombings with negotiations and troop drawdowns. Sensational media coverage of the ravages—an estimated 1.3 million total deaths including troops, massacred civilians, raped and murdered women, and napalm-incinerated children—fueled antiwar movements at home and abroad. People staged draft card burnings, draft office raids, teach-ins, building occupations, and massive protests at the Pentagon, the Washington Mall, the United Nations, and US embassies around the world. See David Halberstam, *The Best and the Brightest* (New York: Random House, 1972); Stanley Karnow, *Vietnam: A History*, rev. ed. (New York: Penguin, 1997); Marvin E. Gettleman, Jane Franklin, Marilyn B. Young, and H. Bruce Franklin, *Vietnam and America: The Most Comprehensive Documented History of the Vietnam War*, 2nd ed. (New York: Grove Press, 1995); Pete Hamill, *Vietnam: The Real War: A Photographic History by the Associated Press* (New York: Harry N. Abrams, 2013); and Kenneth J. Heineman, *Campus Wars: The Peace Movement at American State Universities in the Vietnam Era* (New York: New York University Press, 1994).

14. Mel and Johanna Steil, entry in *The Book of Memories*, n.d., n.p., accessed 19 February 2009, http://www.visq.com/legacy/jd/bookmemo.htm.

15. Shorett, "Findings of Fact and Conclusions of Law," in Ginger, vol. 1, 128.

16. Trial Transcript, 248–288.

17. Trial Transcript, 264. An article posted on the Sampson Family website, written by a female member of the UW Law School Class of 1974, reported that a classmate, Neola Heidegger, discovered that the school had been admitting only two women per year. The author credits Rochelle Kleinberg and Tamara Zorn for the admission of thirty-five women (who were 25 percent of the entering class) in 1971. "The Different Class of '74," *Sampson Family*, 4 June 2012, 8 pp., accessed 1 June 2018 at http://theoregonsampsons.blogspot.com/2012/06:uw-law.html.

18. Trial Transcript, 311–318. Diamond's questioning of Kleinberg filled less than these eight pages because Wilson and the judge interjected comments.

19. Trial Transcript, 292–310. For examples of power-imbued racialized conversations, see Beverly Daniel Tatum, *Why Are All the Black Kids Sitting Together in the Cafeteria?*, new ed. (New York: Basic Books, 2017 [1999]). For discussions of disequilibrium in the context or racial, gendered, and classed hierarchies, see DiAngelo, *White Fragility*.

20. Tom Chambers, "Profile—Josef Diamond," *Bar Bulletin* 20, no. 7 (March 2002); Dan Richman, "Josef Diamond, 1907–2007: Parking Magnate Built Business in 8 States, Canada," *Seattle Post-Intelligencer*, 5 March 2007; and Stuart Eskenazi, "Josef 'Joe' Diamond, Father of Self-Serve Parking Lots, Remembered as Tough, Genuine," *Seattle Times*, 5 March 2007.

21. I first learned that Sternberg and DeFunis were fraternity brothers by reading David J. Balint, "In Memoriam—Marco DeFunis," 21 June 2006. This document, available on the Balint law firm website in June 2007, was subsequently removed. Balint was a member of Sigma Alpha Mu when DeFunis joined during his freshman year at the University of Washington. In 1978, after DeFunis had worked at Jennings Bryant, he and Balint formed their own law firm (Sara Jean Green, "Marco DeFunis, Student in 1971 UW Bias Suit, Dies at 52," *Seattle Times*, 18 January 2002). Craig Sternberg confirmed that he and DeFunis were fraternity brothers ("Questions for Craig Sternberg," 1).

22. Trial Transcript, 25.

23. Marco DeFunis, *The Book of Memories*, n.d., n.p.

24. Trial Transcript, 21.

25. Transcript of Oral Argument, *DeFunis v. Odegaard* 416 U.S. 312 (1974), reported in *Black Law Journal* 3, no. 3 (1973): 249–268 (first quotation 251), (second quotation 253). For reasons I can't ascertain, this issue of the journal is dated 1973, but the oral argument actually occurred on February 26, 1974. Cited hereafter as Transcript of Oral Argument.

26. Erwin N. Griswold, "Some Observations on the *DeFunis* Case," *Columbia Law Review* 75, no. 3 (April 1975): 512–519 (quotation 513).

27. "Questions for Craig Sternberg," 7.

28. In "Panel. DeFunis and Its Impact" (*Black Law Journal* 4, no. 2 [1975]: 268–290), the panelists spoke about anti-Semitism in US higher education. Rabbi Arthur Hertzberg, president of the American Jewish Congress, which had submitted an amicus brief supporting Marco DeFunis, spoke at length about anti-Jewish quotas; Robert M. O'Neil attempted to assuage fears that

Jews would suffer from affirmative action; and Albert J. Rosenthal, a Columbia Law School professor, argued that racism was far worse than anti-Semitism in terms of its prevalence and severity in the US.

29. The phrase "discrete and insular minorities" appeared in footnote 4 of Justice Harlan Fiske Stone's opinion in *United States v. Carolene Products Co.*, 304 (1937), 152–153 (phrase 153). *Carolene Products* concerned the constitutionality of government regulation of adulterated milk that was distributed through interstate shipment. According to Aviam Soifer, the Supreme Court was trending toward placing limitations on judicial intervention, particularly in economic matters, and Stone carved out an exception in the third paragraph of the footnote—namely that alleged discrimination against discrete and insular minorities, particularly religious minorities, would receive judicial scrutiny. See Aviam Soifer, "On Being Overly Discrete and Insular: Involuntary Groups and the Anglo-American Judicial Tradition," *Washington and Lee Law Review* 48, no. 2 (Spring 1991): 381–418 (especially 389–390).

30. Griswold, "Some Observations on the *DeFunis* Case," 512.

31. "Questions for Craig Sternberg," 3.

32. Trial Transcript, 70–71.

33. Trial Transcript, 73–74.

34. Trial Transcript, 5–6.

35. Trial Transcript, 6.

36. Trial Transcript, 231.

37. Trial Transcript, 149–150.

38. The university provided statistics on averaged grades and test scores for some groups but not for applicants who did and did not attend CLEO institutes. To ascertain the college grades of CLEO and non-CLEO students, one would have to read all 1,601 applicant files.

39. Trial Transcript, 153.

40. The reading of and questioning of Ruud on Graglia's article fills five pages of the Trial Transcript (154–158).

41. Trial Transcript, 168.

42. See Trial Transcript, 420–422 for introduction of O'Neil's article and the banter among the judge and lawyers.

43. Trial Transcript, 230–231.

44. At oral argument before the US Supreme Court, this exchange occurred:

Mr. Diamond: But you were requested to fill that out, and you could do so or not, as you pleased, and you made your own self determination as to where you belonged.

Question: Well, since there were no personal interviews, I suppose if Mr. DeFunis had circled one of those, he would have given—

Mr. Diamond: We wouldn't be here today.

Question: He would have been admitted.

Mr. Diamond: We wouldn't have a problem. (Laughter)

Question: Right.

Mr. Diamond: None.

This burlesque exchange turns on the invidious assumption that minority admittees were academically inferior to the white plaintiff (Oral Argument of Josef Diamond Esq. on behalf of the petitioners, Supreme Court of the United States, February 26, 1974, transcript in *The Black Law Journal* 3, no. 3 [1973]: 253).

45. When Diamond asked Kummert why three minority applicants were admitted on August 31, he replied that their applications "were not received . . . until the completion of the various CLEO institutes," adding that although directors notified law schools of promising students early in the program they sent recommendations only if students had successfully completed it (Trial Transcript, 397). The 15 March 1971 application deadline appears in Trial Transcript, 342.

46. Trial Transcript, 80–81, 152–153. Diamond insinuated that it was inappropriate for Crooks to vote on CLEO students he had recommended. Trial testimony did not clarify whether Crooks took on both roles—acting as a CLEO faculty member who recommended CLEO students and acting a committee member who evaluated them.

47. From the late 1960s onward, women's commissions in the professional associations published status of women studies that combined quantitative and qualitative evidence of sex discrimination against female applicants, students, and faculty. For discussion, see chapter 2, "Constructing Sex Discrimination" in my *Disciplining Feminism: From Social Activism to Academic Discourse* (Durham, NC: Duke University Press, 2002), 48–79 and 298–308 (citations). For sex discrimination cases contemporaneous with *DeFunis* and *Bakke*, see George R. LaNouie and Barbara A. Lee, *Academics in Court: The Consequences of Faculty Discrimination Litigation* (Ann Arbor: University of Michigan Press, 1987).

48. Trial Transcript, 340–342, 350–353.

49. Trial Transcript, 359.

50. Trial Transcript, 399 (first three quotes); Trial Transcript, 402 (exchange).

51. Trial Transcript, 399 (first three quotes); Trial Transcript, 402.

52. Trial Transcript, 70–71.

53. Trial Transcript, 128.

54. Trial Transcript, 128–131. After explaining the distribution of LSAT scores on the nonminority bell-shaped curve and the flatter minority curve, Ruud alluded to the thirty-point margin of error. In his article, Erwin Griswold explained more clearly that "standard statistical theory shows that there is a large margin of error in any test score. For example, if the test score is 500, the standard error is thirty points, which means there is one chance in three that the 'true' score is either above 530 or below 470. Moreover, even if the score was precise, the correlation between the test score and success in law school is not high. It usually ranges from 0.30 to 0.50, which means that the conformity is half or less" ("Some Observations on the *DeFunis* Case," 514).

55. Trial Transcript, 179–183 (rambling answers), 184–85 (quotation).

56. Trial Transcript, 265–266 (first quotation), 267 (second quotation).

57. Trial Transcript, 268 (first quotation), 269 (second quotation).

58. Trial Transcript, 274.

59. Trial Transcript, 284 (both quotations).

60. When the Washington State Supreme Court ruled in favor of the university, Chief Justice Frank Hale wrote a blistering dissent in favor of DeFunis that presented nonfactual statements as if they were facts and accused student committee members of harboring political biases (see chapter 5).

61. Judge Lloyd Shorett, "Oral Decision," *DeFunis v. Odegaard*, Superior Court of the State of Washington in and for the County of King, in Ginger, vol. 1, 115–116.

62. Shorett, "Findings of Fact and Conclusions of Law," in Ginger, vol. 1, 122 (first quotation), 124 (second quotation. An exchange at trial showed that Shorett knew the correct GPA:

> Q [Diamond]: Professor Kummert, you used the average of 76.3 as DeFunis' Predicted First Year Average. Now, if his Predicted First Year Average is, in fact, 76.56, then there would be considerably a greater number of students that had a Predicted First Year Grade Average [*sic*] below his, more than 85.
>
> THE COURT: This 76.36 . . . is predicted [*sic*] upon accepting the nine hours of Latin.
>
> MR. DIAMOND: That's correct (Trial Transcript, 385).

63. Shorett, "Findings of Fact and Conclusions of Law," in Ginger, vol. 1, 124.

64. The exact numbers of minority applicants, offers, and enrollments are difficult to ascertain because the university's trial documents reported forty-four minority offers, but its state Supreme Court brief reported seventy minority applicants, thirty-seven offers, and eighteen enrollments (Gorton and Wilson, "Brief of Appellants," in Ginger, vol. 1, 9.)

65. Shorett, "Findings of Fact and Conclusions of Law," 127 (all quotations).

66. Shorett, "Findings of Fact and Conclusions of Law," 128.

67. Shorett, "Oral Decision," 116 (all quotations).

68. Judge Shorett's color-blind interpretation of equal protection goes back to Justice John Marshall Harlan's dissent in *Plessy v. Ferguson* (1896). Objecting to the majority's statement of what became known as the "separate but equal" doctrine, he wrote that the Constitution is color-blind and does not tolerate classes of citizens. Following the *Brown* decision, two interpretations hardened: the color-blind interpretation declared all racial classifications to be unconstitutional, and the color-conscious interpretation declared remedial racial classifications to be constitutional. It is instructive to read Justice Shorett's comments on *Brown* through the lens of *What Brown v. Board of Education Should Have Said*, ed. Jack M. Balkin (New York: New York University Press, 2002); in particular, see Balkin's "*Brown* as Icon" and "Rewriting *Brown*: A Guide to the Opinions," 3–28 and 44–74.

69. Shorett, "Oral Decision," 116 (first quotation), 117 (second quotation).

70. Robert M. O'Neil, *Discriminating against Discrimination: Preferential Admissions and the DeFunis Case* (Bloomington: Indiana University Press, 1975), 15.

CHAPTER 5. PLYING FACT AND LAW

1. Thomas Slade Gorton III was born and reared in Evanston, Illinois, graduated from Dartmouth College, and earned a law degree from Columbia University in 1953. After a second tour in the armed forces, he settled in Seattle, joining a private law firm and, as a Republican candidate, winning a seat in the Washington House of Representatives. From 1968 to January 1981, he served as Washington state's attorney general and then as its US senator for two terms. As attorney general, he gained a reputation for being a tough opponent of both organized crime and Native American fishing rights. Tribe members regarded the fishing cases as examples of white government failing to live up to treaties with indigenous peoples. See Jim Kershner, "Slade Gorton (b. 1928)," HistoryLink.org Essay, 26 November 2014; and "Slade Gorton: Former United States Senator Returns from Washington," Miller Center, n.d.

2. Briefs submitted for local organizations are the City of Seattle, Seattle-King County Bar Association, and Young Lawyers Section of the Seattle-King County Bar Association (all supporting the university and minorities). Those submitted for national organizations are a joint brief of American Bar Association, Association of American Law Schools, Council on Legal Education Opportunity, and Law School Admission Council (supporting the university and minorities); American Indian Law Students, Inc.; American Civil Liberties Union (supporting the university and minorities); Anti-Defamation League (supporting DeFunis); Mexican American Legal Defense and Education Fund; and National Jewish Rights Council (supporting DeFunis). Briefs submitted by local lawyers in their own behalf are Philip L. Burton (supporting minorities), George Constable (supporting DeFunis), and Ralph B. Potts (supporting DeFunis). Arval Morris originally wished to submit a brief on behalf of the American Association of University Professors but was denied and submitted it on his own behalf. G. Robert Brain et al. submitted a brief as members of the American Bar Association members objecting to the joint brief of the ABA, AALS, CLEO, and LSAC. Finally, I have a copy of a draft brief by Frank Askin, David Lubell, Alfred Slocum (Rutgers University Law School), and Mary O'Melveny (Lubell, Lubell, Fine and Shapp) that was not filed. The law review articles by Lino Graglia and Robert M. O'Neil continued to be influential. On DeFunis's side, those by Baronsky and Constable echoed Graglia without attribution; Felix cited him three times; and Chief Justice Hale relied on his rhetoric. On the sides of the university or minorities, the Seattle-King County Bar Association, the Young Lawyers Section, Burton, Rosen and Rosen, and Gordon and Armstrong all cited or drew from O'Neil's article. Justice Neill, writing for the majority, cited O'Neil's work no less than seven times.

3. The chronology appears in Single Appendix, A. Docket Entries, *DeFunis v. Odegaard*, 416 U.S.312 (1974) (No. 73–235). Scholars who discuss the case report it as a 6–2 ruling. Although I follow their characterization, I want to point out that the ruling seems to have been 7–2 because after Justice Neill wrote the opinion of the court, which was joined by five of his colleagues, he retired and Justice Tuttle, who then served pro tem, endorsed the opinion.

See the list of judges, *DeFunis v. Odegaard*, 507 P.2d 1170. Interestingly, the authors of the short opinions, Justices Wright and Hunter, did not attend law school but took the Washington State clerkship program. The program, at least in its 1990s form, required study with tutors, examinations, supervised legal work, and passage of the bar exam (Peter Lewis, "Becoming A Lawyer without Law School," *Seattle Times* 25 November 1991).

4. Mary K. Hammond, "May the Constitution Be Color Conscious to Remain Color-Blind?," *Ohio Northern Law Review* 1, no. 1 (1973–1974): 81.

5. Kim Lane Scheppele, "Facing Facts in Legal Interpretation: Questions of Law and Questions of Fact," *Representations* 30 (Spring 1990): 42 (first and second quotations), 43 (third and fourth quotations).

6. Scheppele, "Facing Facts in Legal Interpretation," 44.

7. Nonlinguistic evidence, such as a table of applicant GPA and LSAT scores, is also an interpretative construct because its compiler will select the applicant categories, score representations (such as mean or high-low range), and table format. In turn, the table will be differently interpreted by a dean who wants to recruit top-notch applicants and a lawyer who wants to argue about admissions preferences.

8. Emmet T. Flood, "Fact Construction and Judgment in Constitutional Adjudication," *Yale Law Journal* 100, no. 6 (April 1991): 1795–1814 (first quotation 1808, second quotation 1807).

9. Gary Minda, *Postmodern Legal Movements: Law and Jurisprudence at the Century's End* (New York: New York University Press, 1995), 13 (short quotation), 13–14 (long quotation).

10. Rene Wellek and Austin Warren, *Theory of Literature* (New York: Harcourt Brace, 1942). For retrospectives on New Criticism and Chicago School Neo-Aristotelianism, see Michael Sprinker, "What Is Living and What Is Dead in Chicago Criticism," *Boundary 2* 13, nos. 2–3 (Winter–Spring 1985): 189–212); W. J. T. Mitchell, "The Commitment to Form: Or, Still Crazy after All These Years," *PMLA* 118, no. 2 (March 2003): 321–325; and Wayne Booth, "Between Two Generations: The Heritage of the Chicago School," *Profession* (1982): 19–26. My own graduate training occurred at a turning point; while most of my professors hewed to New Criticism, a few younger faculty members and most graduate students read Marxism, semiotics, and the nascent feminist work.

11. Minda's *Postmodern Legal Movements: Law and Jurisprudence at the Century's End* reviews critical legal studies, law and literature, feminist legal theory, critical race theory, and their reception in the legal academy. Work on law and literature typically analyzes law in literature or law as literature; see Julie Stone Peters's "Law, Literature, and the Vanishing Real: On the Future of an Interdisciplinary Illusion" (*PMLA* 120, no. 2 [March 2005: 442–453]) and Peter Brooks's "Narrativity of the Law" (*Law and Literature* 14, no. 1 [2002]: 1–10). Cheryl I. Harris's "Critical Race Studies: An Introduction" (*UCLA Law Review* 49, no. 5 [2002]:1215–1239) and Richard Delgado's "Liberal McCarthyism and the Origins of Critical Race Theory" (*Iowa Law Review* 94, no. 5 [2009]: 1505–1545) combine intellectual history, sociology of movements, and institutional analysis. Feminist legal scholarship appears in an array of

disciplinary venues. See D. Kelly Weisberg, ed., *Feminist Legal Theory: Foundations* (Philadelphia: Temple University Press, 1993), which attempts to map the field; Laura A. Rosenbury's "Feminist Legal Scholarship: Charting Topics and Authors, 1978–2002" (*Columbia Journal of Gender and Law* 12, no. 3 [2003]: 446–460), which reviews nearly 1,500 articles published in 18 women/gender and law journals; and Katherine T. Bartlett's "Feminist Legal Scholarship: A History through the Lens of the 'California Law Review'" (*California Law Review* 100, no. 2 [April 2012]: 381–429), which discusses feminist legal studies articles published in this journal.

12. Lawrence B. Solum, "On the Indeterminacy Crisis: Critiquing Critical Dogma" *University of Chicago Law Review* 54, no. 2 (Spring 1987): 462–503 (quotations 503).

13. Lawrence B. Solum, "The Interpretation-Construction Distinction," *Constitutional Commentary* 27, no. 1 (Fall 2010): 96.

14. Solum, "The Interpretation-Construction Distinction," 99. Later in this article, Solum recognizes that even readers working within the strict confines of Originalism produce different meanings of the same constitutional passage:

> Original-Intentions Originalists may believe that the semantic content of the Constitution was fixed by the intentions of the framers or ratifiers. Original-public-meaning Originalists may believe that the linguistic meaning of the Constitution is the meaning that the constitutional text had to the competent speakers of American English at the time the Constitution was framed and ratified. Some Living Constitutionalists may believe that the meaning of the Constitution is fixed by contemporary usage at the time interpretation occurs (101).

This explanation shows that Originalists differently interpret a constitutional passage depending on whether they locate its meaning with nineteenth-century framers, ratifiers, or English speakers or with twentieth-century readers. But it omits the interpretive palimpsest created over time: when an Originalist locates a passage's meaning with ratifiers, she must interpret writings by and/or about the ratifiers, who in turn interpreted the passage and other texts to articulate the passage's meanings.

15. *Black's Law Dictionary* defines "fact" as "1. Something that actually exists; an aspect of reality. 2. An actual or alleged event or circumstance, as distinguished from its legal effect, consequence, or interpretation. 3. An evil deed, a crime" (Henry Campbell Black, *Black's Law Dictionary*, ed. Bryan A. Garner, 2nd Pocket Edition [St. Paul, MN: West, 2001], 268). Facts do not exist as unmediated events; they are discursive constructs conveyed by meaningful statements, statistics, images, and other mediums. The dictionary is ontologically inconsistent because, in using "actual or alleged" to modify "event," it regards a fact as both an unmediated event and as a linguistic construct (an allegation is a statement). The ontological materialism of *Black's* facts dovetails nicely with formalism's epistemological "truths." For a detailed account of how discourses order what we take as reality, see Michel Foucault, *The Order*

of Things: An Archaeology of the Human Sciences (New York: Vintage, 1994); the first edition, published by Gallimard in 1966, was titled *Les Mots et les Choses*. This French title better conveys its focus on the relations of words and things in discourses of different epistemic eras.

16. Kenneth Culp Davis, "Judicial Notice," *Columbia Law Review* 55, no. 7 (November 1955): 946–984 (quotation 952); also see Davis, "Judicial Notice," *Law and the Social Order* (1969): 513–532. The journal is now titled *Arizona State Law Journal*.

17. For histories and critiques of judicial notice, see Josh Camson, "History of the Federal Rules of Evidence," *Litigation News*, American Bar Association (2012); Davis, "Judicial Notice," *Columbia Law Review*; Davis, "Judicial Notice," *Law and the Social Order*; and James William Moore and Helen I. Bendix, "Congress, Evidence and Rulemaking," *Yale Law Journal* 84, no. 1 (November 1974): 9–38.

18. Rule 201. Judicial Notice of Adjudicative Facts, *Federal Rules of Evidence* (Effective 1 December 2011), accessed 24 June 2014, http://www.law.cornell.edu/rules/fre/rule_201. This version is somewhat amended from the 1975 version. Although Washington state did not adopt the Federal Rules of Evidence until 1979, state lawyers were familiar with its provisions and with the state's Rules of Evidence, which required courts to "take judicial notice of the Constitution, common law, civil law, and statutes of every state, territory, and other jurisdiction of the United States." Quotation from RCW 5.24.010 Judicial Notice of Constitution and Laws (1941), Revised Code of Washington, accessed 15 March 2017, https://app.leg.wa.gov/rcw/default.aspx?cite=5.24.010. For the adoption of the judicial notice rule, see Rule ER 201 Judicial Notice of Adjudicative Facts (1979), Rules of Evidence, Washington Courts, accessed 15 March 2017, https://www.courts.wa.gov/court_rules/?a=court_rules.display&group=ga&set=ER&ruleid=gaer0201.

19. Caitlin E. Borgmann, "Appellate Review of Social Facts in Constitutional Rights Cases," *California Law Review* 101, no. 5 (October 2013): 1193.

20. Rule 52(a)(6) states in part, "Findings of fact, whether based on oral or other evidence, must not be set aside unless clearly erroneous" (Rule 52. Findings and Conclusions by the Court; Judgment on Partial Findings, Federal Rules of Civil Procedure, accessed 28 February 2017, https://www.law.cornell.edu/rules/frcp/rule_52). Although legal scholars note that Rule 52(a)(6) applies to case-specific facts, not to social facts, Borgmann argues that it should also apply to constitutional rights cases when social facts would help to protect individuals from majoritarian power (Borgman, 1185–1248). Also see David L. Faigman's "'Normative Constitutional Fact-Finding': Exploring the Empirical Component of Constitutional Interpretation," *University of Pennsylvania Law Review* 139, no. 3 (January 1991): 541–614; and "Evidentiary Incommensurability: A Preliminary Exploration of the Problem of Reasoning from General Scientific Data to Individualized Legal Decision-Making," *Court Review* 50, no. 2 (2014): 52–61. Faigman notes that courts find it difficult to reconcile social-science findings with case findings because the former often uses quantitative methods to investigate large-scale social populations or processes

while the latter uses qualitative methods to adjudicate individual actions. In "Cultures of Facts," Kim Lane Scheppele notes that social scientists tolerate more uncertainty than courts do because in studying complex matters they seek "both evidence and counterevidence for the theory being tested" (Scheppele, "Cultures of Facts," *Perspectives on Politics* 1, no. 2 [June 2003]: 365). In *Scientific Evidence and Equal Protection of the Law* (New Brunswick, NJ: Rutgers University Press, 2006), Angelo N. Ancheta discusses these and other difficulties when scientific evidence is used in equal protection cases. I want to point out that some fields do better than the law at making large-scale findings relevant to the individual case. In life-or-death contexts, doctors meld statistical research with individual patient diagnosis to make decisions about patient treatment and prognosis.

21. William A. Gamson and Andre Modigliani, "The Changing Culture of Affirmative Action," *Research in Political Sociology* 3 (1987): 143 (long quotation), 145–150 (types of affirmative-action frames). Also see Stanley Fish, "The Nifty Nine Arguments against Affirmative Action in Higher Education," *Journal of Blacks in Higher Education* 27 (Spring 2000): 79–81. Although Fish doesn't use the term "narrative frames," one can easily see them in the nine arguments he deconstructs.

22. Mark Kelman, "Interpretive Construction in the Substantive Criminal Law," *Stanford Law Review* 33, no. 4 (April 1981): 593.

23. On boundary-work and disciplines, see Thomas F. Gieryn, "Boundary-Work and the Demarcation of Science from Non-Science: Strains and Interests in Professional Ideologies of Scientists," *American Sociological Review* 48, no. 6 (1983): 781–795; Tony Becher, *Academic Tribes and Territories: Intellectual Enquiry and the Culture of Disciplines* (Milton Keynes, UK: Open University Press, 1989); Mattei Dogan and Robert Pahre, *Creative Marginality: Innovations at the Intersections of Social Sciences* (Boulder, CO: Westview, 1990); David Shumway and Ellen Messer-Davidow, "Disciplinarity: An Introduction," *Poetics Today* 12, no. 2 (Summer 1991): 201–225; Ellen Messer-Davidow, David R. Shumway, and David J. Sylvan, eds., *Knowledges: Historical and Critical Studies in Disciplinarity*, (Charlottesville: University Press of Virginia, 1991); and Julie Thompson Klein, *Crossing Boundaries: Knowledge, Disciplinarities, and Interdisciplinarities* (Charlottesville: University Press of Virginia, 1996).

24. Some scholars have argued that Diamond and Wilson had converging interests in omitting facts about racism that would make the plaintiff and the university look like racists. Legal scholars have applied the theory of interest convergence developed by Derrick A. Bell Jr., who argued that Blacks tend to secure legal and legislative victories when their interests coincide with elite white interests. See Bell's "*Brown v. Board of Education* and the Interest-Convergence Dilemma," *Harvard Law Review* 93, no. 3 (January 1980): 518–533; "*Brown v. Board of Education*: Reliving and Learning from Our Racial History," *University of Pittsburgh Law Review* 66, no. 1 (Fall 2004): 21–34; and "The Unintended Lessons of *Brown v. Board of Education*" (*New York Law School Law Review* 49, no. 4 (2004–2005): 1053–1068. Justin Driver has criticized interest convergence theory for painting within-group interests as monolithic and the

agency of Black people as negligible ("Rethinking the Interest-Convergence Thesis," *Northwestern University Law Review* 105, no. 1 [Winter 2011]: 149–198). To the contrary, I would argue that both the literature on social movements and the cross-sector amici coalition in *Gratz v. Bollinger* and *Grutter v. Bollinger* show how interest convergence can build cross-identity movements, intermovement coalitions, and public support.

25. The motions to strike appear in Single Appendix, A.2 Washington Supreme Court Docket Entries, 7–9. See also Josef Diamond, Lyle L. Iverson, and Craig S. Sternberg, "Brief of Respondents," *DeFunis v. Odegaard,* Washington State Supreme Court, 34, at *DeFunis v. Odegaard,* 507 P.2d.1169 (1973 Wash) (No. 42198). Cited hereafter as Diamond, Iverson, and Sternberg, "Brief of Respondents."

26. Diamond, Iversen, and Sternberg, "Brief of Respondents," 34.

27. Documents available at the website of the Seattle Civil Rights and Labor Project reveal the breadth of communications about racism in the community. Brooke Clark's "The Seattle School Boycott of 1966" lists about two-dozen stories in the *Seattle Times*, a half-dozen in the *Post-Intelligencer*, several in minority newspapers, along with several fliers and posters. Accessed August 17, 2016, http://depts.washington.edu/civilr/school_boycot.htm. Articles on the project website also describe protests at construction sites and Sea-Tac airport, meetings with public officials, litigation, and widespread media coverage. See http://depts.washington.edu/civilr.

28. Article III, Section 2, of the Constitution describes the jurisdiction of the federal courts as extending to several types of cases and controversies; the case or controversy must be a live dispute and the parties to it must have standing. Several amici argued that once the trial court ordered DeFunis's admission to the law school, he no longer had standing and thus the case was no longer a live dispute; others argued that the importance of the core issue, the constitutional status of race-conscious admissions, kept the case alive.

29. Slade Gorton and James B. Wilson, "Brief of Appellants," *DeFunis v. Odegaard,* Washington State Supreme Court, 3: at *DeFunis v. Odegaard,* 507 P.2d.1169 (1973 Wash) (No. 42198). Cited hereafter as Gorton and Wilson, "Brief of Appellants."

30. Gorton and Wilson, "Brief of Appellants," 5–6.

31. Gorton and Wilson, "Brief of Appellants," 12–13.

32. We have several explanations for semantic shift. In "Ideological Drift and the Struggle over Meaning" (*Connecticut Law Review* 25, no. 3 [1992–1993]: 871), Jack M. Balkin discusses ideological drift which seems to be a subtype of semantic shift. One example of drift concerns the migration of color-blindness from *Plessy v. Ferguson* to other cases. Justice Harlan's meaning of "color-blind" to repudiate his colleague's idea that the law requires formal but not actual equality, shifts with the post-*Brown* courts that ordered race-conscious measures to achieve school integration and shifts again with the reverse-discrimination plaintiffs who invoke color-blindness to protect themselves against race-conscious remedies. In *Class, Codes, and Control,* a four-volume study of knowledge production and transmission, Basil Bernstein argues that

the language, actions, and social relations of a discourse shift when it moves from one site to another. The calculations and interactions used by Brazilian children who hawk goods in the streets are quite different from those they use in math classes at school. For a brief summary, see Parlo Singh, "Pedagogising Knowledge: Bernstein's Theory of the Pedagogic Device," *British Journal of Sociology of Education* 23, no. 4 (December 2002): 571–582. In "Semantic Drift in Conversations" (*Human Studies* 35, no. 2 [Summer 2012]: 263–277), Kenneth Liberman offers an ethnomethodology of similar shifts in cross-cultural conversations.

33. Gorton and Wilson, "Brief of the Appellants," 24.

34. Gorton and Wilson, "Brief of Appellants," 24.

35. Diamond, Iverson, and Sternberg, "Brief of Respondents," 37. Today we have a large literature in the social sciences, humanities, and law showing how the effects of discriminatory policies and practices accumulate over the individual life course and transfer down generations. See, for example, Gary A. Dymski, "Racial Exclusion and the Political Economy of the Subprime Crisis," *Historical Materialism* 17, no. 2 (2009): 149–179, a fine analysis of the pass-along effects of discrimination in housing policy, practice, and finance.

36. Diamond, Iverson, and Sternberg, "Brief of Respondents," 43.

37. Diamond, Iverson, and Sternberg, "Brief of Respondents," 19 (first quotation), 20 (second quotation), 21 (third quotation).

38. Diamond, Iverson, and Sternberg, "Brief of Respondents," 11 (first quotation), 13 (second quotation), and 12 (third quotation).

39. Single Appendix, A.2 Washington Supreme Court Docket Entries, 4–5. The court did not similarly caution the amici supporting DeFunis.

40. Phillip Burton (1915–1995) came to Seattle in 1915, opened a law practice in the Central District, and took on leadership roles as president and board member of the local NAACP chapter, which was deeply involved in the struggles against residential apartheid, school segregation, and employment discrimination. See Mary T. Henry, "Burton, Phillip (1915–1995)," HistoryLink .org, n.d. Some years later, the Loren Miller Law Club established an award in his honor.

41. Philip L. Burton, "Brief of *Amicus Curia, DeFunis v. Odegaard*," Washington State Supreme Court, at *DeFunis v. Odegaard*, 507 P.2d 1169 (Wash. 1973) (No. 42198), 1–2.

42. In an article on the US Supreme Court's antidiscrimination doctrine, Alan Freeman explains, "The concept of 'racial discrimination' may be approached from the perspective of either its victim or its perpetrator." The victim perspective focuses on the material, social, legal, and symbolic conditions experienced by the group(s) subjected to discrimination, while the perpetrator perspective focuses on the actions allegedly performed by an individual (or individuals) against the victim(s). The one describes discrimination as the social structuring of lived experience, the other as a discrete act of misconduct. See Alan Freeman, "Legitimizing Racial Discrimination through Antidiscrimination Law: A Critical Review of Supreme Court Doctrine," *Minnesota Law Review* 62, no. 6 (July 1978): 1049–1119 (quotation 1052; other claims 1054); and

Freeman, "Antidiscrimination Law: The View from 1989," *Tulane Law Review* 64, no. 6 (June 1990): 1407–1441 (discussion of perspectives, 1410–1413). Obviously, Burton introduces the victim perspective.

43. Haywood Burns, quoted in Burton, "Brief of *Amicus Curia*," 2.

44. Burton, "Brief of *Amicus Curia*," 3 (quotations), 3–4 (information).

45. Burton, "Brief of *Amicus Curia*," 4–5. Burton also provides facts showing that Hispanic Americans, Native Americans, and Eskimos are even more drastically underrepresented in the legal profession (6).

46. Burton, "Brief of *Amicus Curia*," 7 (first quotation), 8 (second quotation).

47. Burton, "Brief of *Amicus Curia*," 13.

48. Burton, "Brief of *Amicus Curia*," 21.

49. Burton, "Brief of *Amicus Curia*," 23 (internal quotation from *Reitman v. Mulkey*).

50. Jorgen G. Bader and Wilbert Maez, "Brief of *Amicus Curiae*, City of Seattle, *DeFunis v. Odegaard*," Washington State Supreme Court, at *DeFunis v. Odegaard*, 507 P.2d 1169 (Wash. 1973) (No. 42198). The impressive bibliography lists fifty-four cases, fifty-eight books, articles, and reports, and many federal and state statutes, codes, and regulations—almost all discussed in the brief.

51. Bader and Maez, "Brief of *Amicus Curiae*, City of Seattle," 1.

52. Bader and Maez, "Brief of *Amicus Curiae*," 20–21.

53. Bader and Maez, "Brief of *Amicus Curiae*," 20–27 (on testing statistics), 25 (quotation).

54. Bader and Maez, "Brief of *Amicus Curiae*," 19.

55. Bader and Maez, "Brief of *Amicus Curiae*," 27.

56. A. Ludlow Kramer, *Race and Violence in Washington State: Report of the Commission on the Causes and Prevention of Civil Disorder*, February 1969. The commission, established in 1968, included representatives from state and municipal government, law enforcement, state courts, universities, churches, businesses, advocacy groups, and community organizations as well as an advisory board with more of the same constituents. The sixty-three-page report, a shorter but no less shocking version of the Kerner Commission report, contains information on minority ghettoization, poverty, and other forms of discrimination as well as reviews of what is being done and what else should be done. Within a few years, the commission had distributed 20,000 copies and issued a third printing.

57. Bader and Maez's analysis of minority isolation, employment, and education spans more than twenty pages (27–49).

58. Charles F. Wilkinson and John H. Sennhauser, "Brief of the American Indian Law Students, Inc. et al.," Washington State Supreme Court, at *DeFunis v. Odegaard*, 507 P.2d 1169 (Wash. 1973) (No. 42198), 1. Wilkinson was president of the Native American Rights Fund (NARF), which had begun as a pilot project of the California Indian Legal Services and, with Ford Foundation funding, relocated to Boulder and became a national organization in 1970. He went on to become a distinguished professor of law at the University of Colorado and author or coauthor of more than a dozen books. See Charles

Wilkinson's biography, University of Colorado Law School, accessed 12 February 2017, http://lawweb.colorado.edu/profiles/profile.jsp?id=65. Sennhauser, an attorney with the Legal Services Center in Seattle, represented many tribes and, at that time, was representing the Muckleshoot tribe in *United States v. State of Washington* 384 F. Supp. 312 (1974).

59. Wilkinson and Sennhauser, "Brief of the American Indian Law Students, Inc. et al.," 10.

60. Wilkinson and Sennhauser, "Brief of the American Indian Law Students, Inc. et al.," 4–5.

61. Joseph Tussman and Jacobus tenBroek's "The Equal Protection of the Laws" (*California Law Review* 37, no. 3 [September 1949]: 341–381), cited by the Washington State Supreme Court's Opinion of the Court in *DeFunis v. Odegaard*, delved deeply into classificatory logic and its fallacies. In one section, the authors identify three features of discriminatory legislation: using suspect classifications such as race, ancestry, and religion; having a narrow purpose suggestive of partiality; and using an underinclusive category. Their example is a state statute, which specified that no female could serve as a bartender in a licensed liquor establishment, except for the wife or daughter of the male owner of said establishment. The state and Congressional legislation in *Simmons v. Eagle Seelatsee*, like their example, used suspect classifications (race and ancestry), had a narrow purpose (presumably preserving Yakima property ownership), and was underinclusive (inheritance by only close-to-full-blood tribe members). Obviously, the *Simmons* court did not see discrimination in the legislation.

62. United States Court of Appeals, Tenth Circuit, *Groundhog v. Keeler* 442 F.2d (1971), 676–677.

63. *Groundhog v. Keeler*, 692–683.

64. Wilkinson and Sennhauser, "Brief of the American Indian Law Students, Inc. et al.," 5–6.

65. *Morton v. Mancari*, 417 U.S. 535–555 (1974), 548 (first quotation), 550 (second quotation), and 553 (third quotation). The non-Indian plaintiffs claimed that the Indian preference violated the due process clause of the Fifth Amendment and Title VII of the Civil Rights Act of 1964, which they said voided a provision of the Indian Reorganization Act of 1934 that allowed Indian preferences to enhance tribal self-governance. The Court rejected the due process claim because the preference did not constitute invidious racial discrimination, and it rejected the Title VII claim by citing congressional bills passed before and after the Civil Rights Act that gave preferences to Indians for opportunities on and near reservations.

66. Jennings P. Felix, "Amicus Curiae Brief for Respondents," *DeFunis v. Odegaard*, Washington State Supreme Court, at *DeFunis v. Odegaard*, 507 P.2d 1169 (Wash. 1973) (No. 42198), 2 (all quotations).

67. Felix, "Amicus Curiae Brief for Respondents," 4. The percentage-of-blood examples are also called "quantum blood" theories, but actually should be recognized as identity attributions based on the races attributed to parents, grandparents, and great-grandparents. As such, they characterize races as hereditary.

68. Felix, "Amicus Curiae Brief for Respondents," 7 (short quotations), 7–8 (quoting Frankfurter).

69. In 1972, during Rabbi Seymour Siegel's presidency, the National Jewish Community Rights Council joined other politically conservative Jewish organizations to oppose the construction of low-income housing in Forest Hills, Queens. See Murray Schumach, "Six Jewish Groups Suggest a Meeting with Black Leadership," *New York Times*, 12 February 1972; and Murray Schumach, "Halt in Project Sought in Queens," *New York Times*, 24 May 1972. In a 1972 letter to the *New York Times*, Rabbi Siegel stated that Jewish voters should support Nixon for not only his Middle East policy but also his "promise of an open society without quotas" (Seymour Siegel, "Letter to the Editor," *New York Times*, 25 August 1972). The rabbi campaigned for Nixon, delivered a prayer at his second inauguration, and served on the Republican National Committee Advisory Board. See Ari L. Goldman, "Rabbi Scymour Siegel, 61, Leader in Conservative Judaism, Is Dead," *New York Times*, 25 February 1988; and Israel Shenker, "Rabbi to Give Nixon a Kingly Blessing," *New York Times*, 19 January 1973.

70. George Constable, "Brief of George Constable, Amicus Curiae," *DeFunis v. Odegaard*, Washington State Supreme Court, at *DeFunis v. Odegaard*, 507 P.2d 1169 (Wash. 1973) (No. 42198), 16–17 (first quotation), 16 (second quotation). No biographical information is available for Constable.

71. Constable, "Brief of George Constable," 16.

72. See Walter Goodman's "The Return of the Quota System" (*New York Times*, 10 September 1972), an article on the quota debate nationwide. He notes that Jewish organizations were well aware that Jews were overrepresented in the student bodies of public universities, in the New York school system, and in social service positions. Having benefited from the use of civil service tests, they were appalled by the critique of testing in academic research, lawsuits, and government agency regulations. Also see Sharae Wheeler, "DeFunis v. Odegaard: Another Kind of 'Jewish Problem,'" Seattle Civil Rights-Labor History Project (2006), accessed 19 February 2017, http://depts.washington.edu/civilr/DeFuins.htm.

73. Robert Baronsky, "Brief of Amicus Curiae," *DeFunis v. Odegaard*, Washington State Supreme Court, at *DeFunis v. Odegaard*, 507 P.2d 1169 (Wash. 1973) (No. 42198), 5. Baronsky, a 1961 graduate of the University of Washington Law School and attorney at Beresford & Booth, specialized in general civil and trial practice including business, construction, real-estate, probate, and adoption law; see short biography at prabook.com, accessed 19 February 2017, http://prabook.com/web/person-view.html?profileId=1229034.

74. Baronsky, "Brief of Amicus Curiae," 6 (first quotation), 7 (second and third quotations), 9 (fourth quotation), 13 (fifth quotation).

75. Baronsky, "Brief of Amicus Curiae," 13 (first quotation), 14 (*Shelley* quotation), 15 (third quotation).

76. Baronsky, "Brief of Amicus Curiae," 15.

77. Justice Marshall A. Neill, "Opinion of the Supreme Court of the State of Washington," *DeFunis v. Odegaard*, Washington State Supreme Court, at

DeFunis v. Odegaard, 507 P.2d 1169 (Wash. 1973) (No. 42198), reported in *DeFunis versus Odegaard and the University of Washington*, ed. Ann Fagan Ginger (Dobbs Ferry, NY: Oceana, 1974), vol. 1, 137.

78. Neill, "Opinion of the Supreme Court of the State of Washington," 143.

79. Neill, "Opinion," 140 (first quotation), 141 (second quotation), 145 (third quotation), 146 (fourth quotation), 139 (fifth quotation).

80. Joseph H. Gordon and Grant Armstrong, "Brief of *Amici Curiae, DeFunis v. Odegaard*," Washington State Supreme Court, at *DeFunis v. Odegaard*, 507 P.2d 1169 (Wash. 1973) (No. 42198). The brief lists Robert M. O'Neil as Of Counsel and frequently cites or echoes his work. In responses to my interview questions (9 February 2017 and 22 February 2017), O'Neil told me that Wex Malone, a professor of law at Louisiana State University and president of the American Association of Law Schools, enlisted him to draft an amicus brief for the AALS, which was joined by the American Bar Association, Council on Legal Education Opportunity, and Law School Admissions Council. Malone urged O'Neil to travel to Seattle where he met William Anderson. Together the two men drafted the brief, but, since they did not practice before the state supreme court, Gordon and Armstrong became the authors of record.

81. Neill, "Opinion," 149 (first quotation), 150–151 (second quotation).

82. Neill, "Opinion," 154 (first quotation), 153 (second quotation).

83. Neill, "Opinion," 157 (quotations from text and footnote 12).

84. Neill, "Opinion," 160 (both quotations).

85. Neill, "Opinion," 158, footnote 13.

86. Neill, "Opinion," 164.

87. Neill, "Opinion," 165.

88. Chief Justice Frank Hale, "Dissenting Opinion," *DeFunis v. Odegaard*, Washington State Supreme Court, in Ginger, vol. 1, 176 (all quotations above).

89. Hale, "Dissenting Opinion," 176 (first quotation), 177 (second quotation).

90. Hale, "Dissenting Opinion," 177.

91. Hale, "Dissenting Opinion," 189–90 (first reference to *Anderson*), 194–195 (second reference to *Anderson*), 195 (Hale quotation).

CHAPTER 6. THE MEANINGS OF *DEFUNIS*

1. The assurance that DeFunis would be permitted to continue his studies and upon satisfactory completion graduate with his class appeared in Slade Gorton and James B. Wilson, "Motion of Dismissal of Appeal, or, in the Alternative, Affirmance of the Judgment Below and Statement in Opposition to Certiorari," in *DeFunis versus Odegaard and the University of Washington: The University Admissions Case*, ed. Ann Fagin Ginger (Dobbs Ferry, NY: Oceana, 1974), vol. 1, 257–280 (cited hereafter as Ginger). The mootness briefings are Slade Gorton and James B. Wilson, "Appellees-Respondents' Memorandum on the Question of Mootness," in Ginger, vol. 1, 281–292; and Josef Diamond, Lyle L. Iversen, and Craig S. Sternberg, "Petitioner's Memorandum on Mootness," in Ginger, vol. 1, 293–302.

2. See Bob Woodward and Scott Armstrong, *The Brethren: Inside the Supreme*

Court (New York: Simon and Schuster, 1979), 282; and Bernard Schwartz, *Behind Bakke: Affirmative Action and the Supreme Court* (New York: New York University Press, 1988), 33–34.

3. See the complaints in Thomas C. Fischer, "*Defunis* in the Supreme Court: Is That All There Is?," *Journal of Law and Education* 4, no. 3 (1975): 487–509; Richard C. Posner, "The DeFunis Case and the Constitutionality of Preferential Treatment of Racial Minorities," *Supreme Court Review* (1974): 1–32; and Larry M. Lavinsky, "*DeFunis v. Odegaard*: The 'Non-Decision' with a Message," *Columbia Law Review* 75, no. 3 (1975): 520, 530, 532.

4. Josef Diamond, in "Oral Argument," *DeFunis v. Odegaard*, US Supreme Court, 26 February 1974, transcript published in *Black Law Journal* 3 (1973): 251 (first quotation), 252 (all other quotations). Cited hereafter as Oral Argument (regardless of speaker). Although the oral argument occurred in 1974, the journal is dated 1973. Its transcript and the one posted on Oyez (https://www.oyez.org/cases/1973/73-235) differ only occasionally in phrasing. The main difference is the latter identifies the justices asking questions.

5. Oral Argument, 262.

6. Oral Argument, 255 (Blackmun quotation) 256 (Diamond and Rehnquist quotations).

7. Oral Argument, 258 (correction on State Court decision), 260 (description of DeFunis as marginally qualified).

8. I am grateful to Lynda Reese (director of Psychometric Research) and Stephen Luebke (principal test specialist), both at the Law School Admissions Council, for answering my questions about LSAT scoring. They supplied a table showing score distributions each academic year from 1969–1970 through 1979–1980. Marco DeFunis's score of 582 (averaged from three test-takings yielding scores of 512, 566, and 668) would place him at about the seventy-fourth percentile mark of scores reported nationwide for 1969–1970.

9. Oral Argument, 260 (Burger), 262.

10. Oral Argument, 262.

11. See "Mootness," U.S. Constitution Annotated, Legal Information Institute, Cornell University Law School; and Dee V. Benson, "Constitutional Law—Mootness—DeFunis v. Odegaard," *Brigham University Law Review* 1, no. 1 (1975): 181–194.

12. Justice Potter Stewart, "Per Curiam Opinion," *DeFunis v. Odegaard*, 416 U.S. 312 (1973), 314 (quotation). On p. 316, Stewart begins his analysis of mootness by quoting from *North Carolina v. Rice*, 404 U.S. 244, 246 (1971); and *Liner v. Jafco*, 376 U.S. 301, 306 n. 3 (1964).

13. Stewart, "Per Curiam Opinion," 319–320 (short quotation). During oral argument, Diamond had stated, "And I think the brief of the respondents, they say that this question will arise again, and, as a matter of fact, I have in my office two clients, one girl and one man, waiting for the determination of this [case] to see whether they can get into law school" (Oral Argument, 256).

14. Stewart, "Per Curiam Opinion," 320.

15. Robert M. O'Neil argued that the justices should have dismissed the case and left the Washington State Supreme Court opinion standing, particularly

because the trial record was so deficient (*Discriminating against Discrimination: Preferential Admissions and the DeFunis Case* [Bloomington: Indian University Press, 1975], 35–37). Louis B. Pollak felt the justices should have dismissed the case because it did not measure up to the Article III exception that a federal court could adjudicate a case of great constitutional significance and wide public import. Yet he wrote, "I see in *DeFunis* about as inapt a vehicle for major constitutional pronouncements as has come before the Court in many years" and went on to detail a dozen or more questions that the deficient trial record could not answer ("*DeFunis* Non Est Disputandum," *Columbia Law Review* 75, no. 3 [1975]: 503).

16. Justice William J. Brennan, "Dissent," *DeFunis v. Odegaard*, 416 U.S. 312 (1973), 349 (first quotation), 348 (all other quotations).

17. The subject of course makeups arose during oral argument before the US Supreme Court when Slade Gorton was asked repeatedly whether DeFunis had registered for his final quarter and assured the Court that once he had registered by the deadline he would "then complete his law school studies, assuming he passes his courses. . . . The only discretion which would then remain in the law school would be if he failed the courses . . . and requested special permission to come back in fall to make up for it . . . (Oral Argument, 258).

18. Brennan, "Dissent," 350.

19. Stewart, "Per Curiam Opinion," 318; and Brennan, "Dissent," 350.

20. Stewart, "Per Curiam Opinion," 319; and Brennan, "Dissent," 350.

21. Lavinsky, "*DeFunis v. Odegaard*," 530.

22. Daniel Steiner, "DeFunis and Its Impact," *Black Law Journal* 4, no. 2 (1975): 269; O'Neil, *Discriminating against Discrimination*, 275.

23. Some scholars, instead of cherry-picking quotations from the dissent, selected issues that would allow them to make novel arguments. In "The DeFunis Case and the Constitutionality of Preferential Treatment of Racial Minorities," Richard A. Posner argued that the law school used race as a proxy for differences in socioeconomic status, prior education, life experience, and motivation that would not necessarily enhance legal education (*Supreme Court Review* 2 [1974]: 1–32). In "The Constitutionality of Reverse Racial Discrimination," John Hart Ely argued that "when White people have decided to favor Black people at the expense of White people," these racial preferences are "not 'suspect' in a constitutional sense" because the majority is discriminating against itself (*University of Chicago Law Review* 41, no. 4 [1973–1974]: 727).

24. Jim Chen, "*DeFunis,* Defunct," *Constitutional Commentary* 16, no. 1 (1999): 96 (first quotation), 97 (second quotation), 96–97 (third quotation). Copies of some conference memoranda, vote tallies, clerk memoranda, newspaper articles, and drafts of the per curiam opinion and dissent are held in the Justice Lewis Powell Archive, Washington and Lee University Law School. See *DeFunis v. Odegaard*, Supreme Court Case Files Collection, Box 17, Powell Papers, Lewis F. Powell Jr. Archives, Washington & Lee University School of Law, Virginia, accessed 6 December 2018, https://scholarlycommons.law.wlu.edu/casefiles/43.

25. Annette Kolodny, "Dancing through the Minefield: Some Observations

on the Theory, Practice, and Politics of a Feminist Literary Criticism," *Feminist Studies* 6, no. 1 (Spring 1980): 11. In "Hiding the Ball," Pierre Schlag provides an entertaining account of how the Socratic method used in law classes trains students to interpret case law without critically analyzing the ontological and epistemological assumptions that make the interpretations possible (*New York University Law Review* 71, no. 6 [December 1996]: 1683–1688).

26. William O. Douglas, "Dissent," *DeFunis v. Odegaard,* 416 U.S. 320–341 (1974), 324.

27. Douglas, "Dissent," 325.

28. Douglas, "Dissent," 325–326.

29. Douglas, "Dissent," 326–27.

30. Douglas, "Dissent," 328 (quoting Banash Hoffmann, *The Tyranny of Testing* [New York: Crowell-Collier, 1962], 91–92).

31. Isabel Wilkerson, "Bancsh Hoffmann, An Author and Collaborator of Einstein," *New York Times,* 6 August 1986. Hoffmann's book, which a reviewer praises for its empirical and scholarly work, reveals that multiple-choice tests do not provide test-takers with subject-matter context, question-and-answer reasoning, or the opportunity to explain their answers (see A. Gordon Wilcox, "The Tyranny of Testing by Banesh Hoffmann and Jacques Barzun," *Journal of General Education* 15, no. 4 [January 1964]: 301–304; Barzun wrote a foreword, but did not coauthor the book).

32. Douglas, "Dissent," 329.

33. Douglas, "Dissent," 329–330.

34. Justice Douglas quotes from the testimony of John A. Winterbottom that is published as "Excerpts from Trial Transcript in King County Superior Court," in Ginger, vol. 1, 73.

35. Justice Douglas devotes a paragraph to a critique of the grade point average (GPA), which states in part: "Grades have their own problems; one school's A is another school's C. . . . The law student with lower grades may in the long pull of a legal career surprise those at the top of the class. . . . '[t]here is no clear evidence that the LSAT and GPA provide particularly good evaluations of the intrinsic or enriched ability of an individual to perform as a law student or lawyer in a functioning society undergoing change'" (Douglas, 330). Douglas quotes from Sanford Rosen, "Equalizing Access to Legal Education: Special Programs for Law Students Who Are Not Admissible by Traditional Criteria," *University of Toledo Law Review* 2, nos. 2–3 (Spring–Summer 1970): 321–376 (Douglas, "Dissent," quotation from 333).

36. See Michel Foucault, *Discipline and Punish: The Birth of the Prison,* trans. Alan Sheridan, 2nd ed. (New York: Vintage, 1995), 181–194.

37. Douglas, "Dissent," 330 (first quotation), 331 (second quotation).

38. Most commentators—such as Ely in "The Constitutionality of Reverse Racial Discrimination" and Posner in "The DeFunis Case and the Constitutionality of Preferential Treatment of Racial Minorities"—focused on the significance of *DeFunis* for constitutional jurisprudence and mentioned Justice Douglas's dissent in passing. Among those who read his statements as signifying his embrace of color-blindness and/or his potential conclusion that the

admissions program was unconstitutional are Monrad G. Paulson, "*DeFunis*: The Road Not Taken," *Virginia Law Review* 60, no. 6 (October 1974): 922; Robert M. O'Neil, "After *DeFunis:* Filling the Constitutional Vacuum," *University of Florida Law Review* 27, no. 2 (Winter 1975): 319; and Fletcher N. Baldwin Jr., "*DeFunis v. Odegaard*, the Supreme Court and Preferential Law School Admissions: Discretion Is Sometimes Not the Better Part of Valor," *University of Florida Law Review* 27, no. 2 (1975): 347. Among those who mentioned racially neutral individualized review are Arval A. Morris, "Equal Educational Opportunity, Constitutional Uniformity and the *DeFunis* Remand," *Washington Law Review* 50, no. 3 (1975): 586–588; Pollak, "*DeFunis* Non Est Disputandum," 504–505; Fischer, "*DeFunis* in the Supreme Court," 502–503; and Lavinsky, "'Non-Decision' with a Message," 530–532 (as chair of the Anti-Defamation League's law committee, Lavinsky was involved in both *DeFunis v. Odegaard* and *Regents of the University of California v. Bakke*).

39. Douglas, "Dissent," 333–334 (first quotation), 336 (second quotation), 342 (third quotation), and 343–344 (fourth quotation).

40. Douglas, "Dissent," 331.

41. Douglas, "Dissent," 332.

42. *DeFunis*, 334 (all three quotations).

43. Douglas, "Dissent," 332 (first quotation), 333 (second quotation).

44. Douglas, "Dissent," 334 (both quotations). His quotation comes from page 10 of *Loving v. Virginia* 388 U.S. 1–14 (1967).

45. Douglas, "Dissent," 334.

46. Douglas, "Dissent," 335.

47. Robert H. Keller Jr., "William O. Douglas, the Supreme Court, and American Indians," *American Indian Law Review* 3, no. 2 (1975): 333–360.

48. Douglas, "Dissent," 335 (both quotations).

49. Douglas, "Dissent," 335–336.

50. For those interested in the aporias of racial discourse, see Steven D. Farough, "Structural Aporia and White Masculinities: White Men Respond to the White Male Privilege Critique," *Race, Gender & Class* 10, no. 4 (2003): 38–53; and Beth H. Piatote, "The Indian/Agent Aporia," *American Indian Quarterly* 37, no. 3 (Summer 2013): 45–62. Farough's article is based on interviews of white men whose discussions of race and affirmative action were littered with contradictions and ambiguities. Piatote's article goes back in time to explore the contradictions between tribes as independent nations and US wards, tribe members and government-appointed Indian agents, and so forth.

51. Douglas, "Dissent," 344.

52. In "The Jurisprudence of Race and Meritocracy: Standardized Testing and 'Race-Neutral' Racism in the Workplace" (*Law and Human Behavior* 18, no. 3 [June 1994]: 223–248), Craig Haney and Aida Hurtado argue that the law's ideologies of individualism and meritocracy prevent the courts from comprehending, let along remedying, employment discrimination with group impacts. While they provide a convincing analysis of employment cases brought under Title VII of the Civil Rights Act, they do not compare them to higher-education cases brought under the equal protection clause. I would argue that the concept

of innate abilities, derived from historical racial taxonomies and hereditarian "science," was more entrenched in the higher-education cases than in the employment cases for the obvious reason that the latter involved intellectual competition. For a short review of findings that support Justice Douglas's view of standardized testing, see Peter Sacks, "Standardized Testing: Meritocracy's Crooked Yardstick," *Change* 29, no. 2 (March–April 1997): 24–31.

CHAPTER 7. SLANTING THE STORY

1. Unless otherwise noted, the information in this section is taken from several sources: Allan Bakke, "Plaintiff's Answers to Defendant's First Set of Interrogatories," Yolo County Superior Court of California, in *Allan Bakke v. Regents of the University of California*, ed. Alfred Slocum (Dobbs Ferry, NY: Oceana, 1978), vol. 1, 79–86 (cited hereafter as Slocum); *Allan Bakke v. Regents of the University of California* (1976), 18 Cal. 3d 34–92; *Regents of the University of California v. Bakke* (1978), 98 S. Ct. 2738 (cited hereafter as *Bakke*); Howard Ball, *The Bakke Case: Race, Education, and Affirmative Action* (Lawrence: University Press of Kansas, 2000); "Chronology of Reverse Bias Lawsuit," *Chicago Tribune*, 29 June 1978; Robert Lindsey, "White/Caucasian—and Rejected," *New York Times Magazine*, 3 April 1977, 41–47; and Bernard Schwartz, *Behind Bakke: Affirmative Action and the Supreme Court* (New York: New York University Press, 1988).

2. "Brief for the United States" (filed 19 September 1977), in *Bakke*, 3–4.

3. See "Letter to the Editor," *Sacramento Bee*, 4 January 1977, appended to "Brief of the National Urban League et al." (filed 14 January 1977), 9a–10a.

4. "Brief of the National Conference of Black Lawyers" (filed 7 June 1977 with the US Supreme Court), in *Bakke*, 16 (acceptance numbers).

5. Quoted in Schwartz, *Behind Bakke*, 7–8.

6. "Deposition of George H. Lowrey, M.D.," in Slocum, vol. 1, 70; and Reynold Colvin, "Petitioner's Reply Memorandum," in Slocum, vol. 1, 131–132. According to this memorandum, five of the six scores assigned to Bakke were 92, 94, 94, 96, and 87; the memorandum does not report the sixth score, which was 86.

7. *Bakke v. The Regents of the University of California* (1976), 553 P.2d, 1165 (UCD goals), 1172 (holdings).

8. Schwartz, 25.

9. *Bakke*, 2743.

10. "Plaintiff's Answers to Defendant's First Set of Interrogatories," in Slocum, vol. 1, 83–84 (quotation 84).

11. Schwartz, 3 (quotations are Schwartz quoting from Bakke's application).

12. "Plaintiff's Answers to Defendant's First Set of Interrogatories," 81–82. Ball states incorrectly that for all eleven schools "Bakke's age was given as the major factor in their decisions not to admit him" (Ball, *Bakke Case*, 54).

13. Ball, 47. Ball does not indicate the source of his admissions committee quotation, though he mentions that it appeared in a reply to a query made by Bakke.

14. Quoted in Allan P. Sindler, *Bakke, DeFunis, and Minority Admissions: The Quest for Equal Opportunity* (New York: Longman, 1978), 67–68.

15. "Deposition of George H. Lowrey, M.D.," 29–77 (first exchange 71; second exchange 77).

16. "Brief of Columbia University, Harvard University, Stanford University, and the University of Pennsylvania" (filed 7 June 1977), 19.

17. "Brief of the Mexican American Legal Defense and Education Fund et al." (filed 7 June 1977), 20. This brief and another brief submitted by the UCLA Black Law Students Association, the UCLA Black Law Alumni Association, and the Union Women's Alliance to Gain Equality (filed 7 June 1977) also provide data that show glaring disparities between whites and racial minorities in family income, types of jobs, part-/full-time employment, unemployment rates, and other socioeconomic factors.

18. Feminists at the University of Cincinnati, my graduate school, learned about age discrimination in 1973 when the Campus Coalition of Women presented the administration with over one hundred demands that included the increased admission of women to the medical and law schools. The data we obtained showed that less than 10 percent of the medical school classes consisted of both white women and racial minorities; the numbers of white women declined as those for minorities rose and vice versa.

19. *Cannon v. University of Chicago* (1979), 441 U.S., 1946–1985 (quotation 1949). The first half-dozen law review articles on this case focused not on age or sex discrimination but on the issue of a Title IX private right of action. See, for instance, Madeleine Weldon-Linne, "Title IX: No Longer an Empty Promise—*Cannon v. University of Chicago*," *DePaul Law Review* 29, no. 1 (Fall 1979): 263–286; and Diane L. Burkhardt, "A Private Right of Action under Title IX: *Cannon v. University of Chicago*," *Denver Law Journal* 57, no. 3 (1980): 437–452.

20. George R. LaNoue, "The Future of Antidiscrimination Enforcement," *Change* 6, no. 5 (June 1974): 44–45; Jennie Farley, "Women versus Academe: Who's Winning," *Journal of Social Issues* 41, no. 4 (1985): 112; and Athena Theodore, *The Campus Troublemakers: Academic Women in Protest* (Houston: Cap and Gown, 1986), 83–90.

21. The Age Discrimination in Employment Act of 1967, United States Equal Employment Opportunity Commission, accessed 12 June 2011, http://www.eeoc.gov/laws/statutes/adea.cfm.

22. Age Discrimination Act of 1975, United States Department of Labor, accessed 12 June 2011, http://dol.gov/oasam/regs/statutes/age_act.htm.

23. Thomas J. Flygare, "The Proposed HEW Regulations on Age Discrimination: One Rule with Many Exceptions," *Phi Delta Kappan* 61 (January 1980): 353–354.

24. "Declaration of George H. Lowrey, M.D.," in Slocum, vol. 1, 90.

25. "Deposition of George H. Lowrey, M.D.," 68 (quotation), but also see Slocum, vol. 1, 90.

26. "Deposition of George H. Lowrey, M.D.," 40.

27. Quoted in Sindler, *Bakke, DeFunis, and Minority Admissions*, 67–68.

28. See Ball, 46–47; and Schwartz, 2.

29. To understand the prevalence of gender stereotypes in academe during the 1960s and 1970s, see my *Disciplining Feminism: From Social Activism to Academic Discourse* (Durham, NC: Duke University Press, 2002), 19–79. The personal stories of female graduate students in physics, sociology, literary studies, and art history will shock today's readers.

30. Sindler, 69.

31. Quoted in Sindler, 69–70.

32. Quoted in Sindler, 75.

33. Colvin, "Petitioner's Reply Memorandum," 132–133.

34. On ideological downgrading at the National Endowment for the Humanities (NEH), see Ellen Messer-Davidow, "Dollars for Scholars: The Real Politics of Humanities Research and Programs," in *The Politics of Research*, ed. E. Ann Kaplan and George Levine (New Brunswick, NJ: Rutgers University Press, 1997), 103–233; and Anne Marie Borrego, "Humanities Endowment Returns to 'Flagging' Nontraditional Projects," *Chronicle of Higher Education*, 16 January 2004.

35. "Brief for the Respondent in Opposition," in Slocum, vol. 1, 7 (committee members' individual scores).

36. Quoted in Sindler, 78.

37. See Reynold H. Colvin, "Memorandum of Points and Authorities in Support of Order to Show Cause and Alternative Writ of Mandate," in Slocum, vol. 1, 21–28.

38. See Donald Reidhaar, "Memorandum of Points and Authorities in Opposition to Issuance of Preliminary Injunction or Writ of Mandate," in Slocum, vol. 1, 99–120.

39. "Deposition of Dr. George M. Lowrey, M.D.," 67–68.

40. William Trombley, "Medical Dean Aids 'Special Interest' Applicants," *Los Angeles Times*, 5 July 1976.

41. Trombley , "Medical Dean."

42. William Trombley, "Bending of Medical School Admission Rules Rapped," *Los Angeles Times*, 14 July 1976.

43. Lou Cannon, "Bakke Also Vied with the Well-to-Do," *Washington Post*, 2 October 1977.

44. Peter C. Storandt, letter to Allan Bakke, 18 July 1973, 1a–3a; Allan Bakke, letter to Peter C. Storandt, 7 August 1973, 4a–6a; and Peter C. Storandt, letter to Allan Bakke, 15 August 1973, 7a–8a—all appended to National Urban League et al., "Brief of *Amici Curiae*" (filed 14 January 1977 on petition), *Regents of the University of California v. Bakke*, U.S. Supreme Court. The other amici were the National Organization for Women; United Automobile, Aerospace, and Agricultural Implement Workers of America; National Conference of Black Lawyers; La Raza National Lawyers Association; Mexican American Legal Defense and Educational Fund; California Rural Legal Assistance; National Bar Association; UCLA Black Alumni Association; National Federation of Women's Organizations; UC Davis Law School; Chicano Alumni Association; Charles Houston Bar Association; National Lawyers Guild; La Raza

National Law Students Association; and Black American Law Student Association. The correspondence between the two men is trenchantly criticized in the "Brief of the National Conference of Black Conference of Black Lawyers" (filed 7 June 1977), in *Bakke*, 3–6.

45. See Peter C. Storandt, letter to Allan P. Bakke, 18 July 1973, appended to National Urban League et al., "Brief of Amici Curiae" (filed 14 January 1977), 1a–3a.

46. Storandt, letter to Bakke, 18 July 1973, 2a.

47. Storandt, letter to Bakke, 18 July 1973, 2a.

48. Joel Dreyfuss and Charles Lawrence III, *The Bakke Case: The Politics of Inequality* (New York: Harcourt Brace Jovanovich, 1979), 3 (date of meeting), 23 (quotation). Their account of the evening meeting, although not backed by citations, includes details that could only have been obtained by interviewing Storandt and perhaps Bakke.

49. Dreyfuss and Lawrence, *The Bakke Case*, 23 (first and second quotations), 12–13 (third and long quotation).

50. Bakke to Storandt, 7 August 1973, 4a.

51. Bakke to Storandt, 7 August 1973, 5a (all quotations).

52. Bakke to Storandt, 7 August 1973, 5a–6a.

53. Storandt to Bakke, 15 August 1973, 7a–8a (long quote), 7a (short quotes).

54. Sindler, 80.

55. Urban League et al., "Brief of Amici Curiae," 16, fn. 10.

56. National Conference of Black Lawyers, "Brief of the *Amicus Curiae*" (filed with US Supreme Court, 7 June 1977), 2.

57. National Conference of Black Lawyers, "Brief of the *Amicus Curiae*," 5. A long footnote on page 5 quotes passages from Speich's story to this effect.

58. Don Speich, "Former UC Davis Official Backed 'Reverse Bias' Suit," *Los Angeles Times*, 4 February 1977.

59. Speich, "Former UC Davis Official."

CHAPTER 8. TEXTUALIZING *BAKKE*

1. Kim Lane Scheppele, "Facing Facts in Legal Interpretation," *Representations* 30 (Spring 1990): 42.

2. Angelo N. Ancheta, *Scientific Evidence and Equal Protection of the Law* (New Brunswick, NJ: Rutgers University Press, 2006), 130 (short quotation), 133 (long quotation).

3. *Anderson v. San Francisco Unified School District*, 357 F. Sup. 248 (N.D. Cal. 1972).

4. For the *Bakke* case chronology, see Howard Ball, *The Bakke Case: Race, Education, and Affirmative Action* (Lawrence: University of Kansas, 2000), 207–211. For Colvin, see Ball, 53; Bernard Schwartz, *Behind Bakke: Affirmative Action and the Supreme Court* (New York: New York University Press, 1988), 9 (quotation 9); and Joel Dreyfuss and Charles Lawrence III, *The Bakke Case: The Politics of Inequality* (New York: Harcourt Brace Jovanovich, 1979), 32–35.

5. Dreyfuss and Lawrence, *The Bakke Case*, 36.

6. Schwartz, *Behind Bakke*, 14–16; Dreyfuss and Lawrence, 36–37.

7. Dreyfuss and Lawrence, 57.

8. See "Donald L. Reidhaar, Chief UC System Legal Counsel," *Los Angeles Times*, 12 December 1985; Schwartz, 16 (quotation 16); Ball, 53–54; and Dreyfuss and Lawrence, 38–39. On 12 December 1985, Reidhaar, who was fifty-two, leaped to his death from the Golden Gate bridge; a note left for his wife alluded to torment he could no longer bear.

9. Dreyfuss and Lawrence, 40.

10. Dreyfuss and Lawrence, 40–42.

11. Dreyfuss and Lawrence, 44 (short quotation) 48 (long quotation).

12. Dreyfuss and Lawrence, 49.

13. Dreyfuss and Lawrence, 59–60 (quotations 59).

14. Courts have not warmly embraced social-science and statistical information. Kim Lane Scheppele explains that social-science findings "are almost always of the 'on the one hand, on the other hand' sort. Particularly good social science . . . presents both evidence and counterevidence for the theory being tested" ("Cultures of Facts," *Perspectives on Politics* 1, no. 2 [June 2003]: 365). Angelo N. Ancheta comments frankly that "scientific evidence and expert witnesses are thus employed largely to serve instrumental ends, advancing the interests of the party that introduces the evidence" (*Scientific Evidence*, 133); elsewhere he notes that the parties may selectively include and omit published studies, commission their own studies, and rhetoricize their presentations.

15. Edward Chen, "The Case for Minority Participation in Reverse Discrimination Litigation," *California Law Review* 67, no. 1 (January 1979): 195–196.

16. Chen, "Case for Minority Participation," 196–204.

17. Chen points out that to be effective an intervenor must participate in the early stages of the case, such as pretrial discovery and trial examination, but potential intervenors often do not know about a case even after the complaint is filed because the litigants seldom alert them. Chen suggests that interest advocacy organizations might be more vigilant in monitoring filings, but this suggestion presumes that jurisdictions will provide easily accessible filing records and organizations will have the resources to monitor hundreds of jurisdictions (see Chen, 222–223).

18. See California Evidence Code, General Provisions, 300–413, California Legislative Information, accessed 11 June 2017, http://leginfo.legislature.ca.gov/face/codes_displayText.xhtml?lawCode=EVID&division=3.&title=&part=&chapter=4.&article=2.

19. In "The Discourse on Language," Foucault states, "Within its own limits, every discipline recognizes true and false propositions, but it repulses a whole teratology of learning. The exterior of a science is both more, and less, populated than one might think" (Michel Foucault, in *The Archaeology of Knowledge and the Discourse on Language*, trans. A. M. Sheridan Smith [New York: Pantheon, 1972], 223). He describes several rules of exclusion: prohibitions concerning who may speak about what; the logic of division and rejection (such as reason/folly and truth/falsity), and the preliminary condition that

statements must be uttered "within the true" of the discourse. As an example, Foucault explains that although Mendel spoke the truth about hereditary traits, the biology of his time did not recognize his objects and methods of investigation or his theoretical perspective (123–124). Analogously, I would argue that in speaking of systemic racism the pro-minority amici in *DeFunis* and *Bakke* did not meet the conditions imposed by judicial discourse (e.g., narrow time and action framing, individualized intentionality and harm, tight cause and effect) and thus fell "outside of the true" customarily recognized by courts.

20. Colvin, "Complaint for Mandatory, Injunctive, and Declaratory Relief," in Alfred Slocum, ed., *Allan Bakke v. Regents of the University of California* (Dobbs Ferry, NY: Oceana, 1978), vol. 1, 5 (first quotation), 6 (second quotation). Cited hereafter as Slocum.

21. Donald L. Reidhaar, "First Amended Answer" (31 July 1974, Yolo County Superior Court of California), in Slocum, vol. 1, 8 (first quotation), 9 (second and third quotations).

22. Donald L. Reidhaar, "First Amended Cross-Complaint for Declaratory Relief" (31 July 1974, Yolo County Superior Court of California), in Slocum, vol. 1, 12.

23. *Brown v. Board of Education* 347 U.S. 483 (1954) (quotation 493).

24. Jack M. Balkin, "Rewriting *Brown:* A Guide to the Opinions," in *What "Brown v. Board of Education" Should Have Said*, ed. Jack M. Balkin (New York: New York University Press, 2001), 57.

25. *Green v. County School Board of New Kent Co., Va.*, 391 U.S. 430 (1968); *Swann v. Charlotte-Mecklenburg Board of Education*, 402 U.S. 1 (1971); and *San Antonio Independent School District v. Rodrigues*, 411 U.S. 1 (1973) (quotation 33).

26. "Declaration of George H. Lowrey, M.D." (29 August 1974), in Slocum, vol. 1, 91.

27. "Deposition of George H. Lowrey, M.D.," in Slocum, vol. 1, 33.

28. "Deposition of George H. Lowrey, M.D.," 54–55.

29. See Exhibits B and C, in Slocum, vol. 1, 141–163.

30. Dreyfuss and Lawrence, 41, 85.

31. Sarah Gray, "Letter to the Editor," *Sacramento Bee*, 4 January 1977, appended to National Urban League et al., "Brief of Amici Curiae, Appendix B" (filed 14 January 1977 in the Supreme Court of the United States), in Slocum, vol. 2, 277–278.

32. Colvin, "Complaint for Mandatory, Injunctive, and Declaratory Relief," 4.

33. Reynold H. Colvin, "Memorandum of Points and Authorities in Support of Order to Show Cause and Alternative Writ of Mandate" (5 August 1974), in Slocum, vol. 1, 24–25.

34. *Sweatt v. Painter*, 339 U.S. 629–636 (1950).

35. "Declaration of George H. Lowrey, M.D.," 88.

36. See "Declaration of George H. Lowrey, M.D.," 91–93; last quotation from Colvin, "Memorandum of Points and Authorities in Support of Order to Show Cause and Alternative Writ of Mandate," 22.

37. Reidhaar, "Memorandum of Points and Authorities in Opposition to the Issuance of Preliminary Injunction or Writ of Mandate," in Slocum, vol. 1, 112 (first quotation); 113 (second and third quotations).

38. See Exhibit C, in Slocum, vol. 1, 144–147; and "Deposition of George H. Lowrey, M.D.," 59 and 62.

39. In "Affirmative Action and Equal Protection," Kenneth L. Karst and Harold W. Horowitz state that the concept of merit has two implications for judicial analysis: first, that "an individual's claim to equality is necessarily made as a member of a group"; and second that "the content of 'merit' is necessarily defined by reference to community needs" (*Virginia Law Review* 60, no. 6 [1974]: 955–974 [quotation 956]). My point, however, is that excellence requires the material and social means of cultivation. In "Unraveling the Myth of Meritocracy within the Context of US Higher Education," Amy Liu examines such assumptions as innate abilities, hard work, and moral grounding that prop up meritocratic ideology (*Higher Education* 62, no. 4 [October 2011]: 383–397).

40. "Deposition of George H. Lowrey, M.D.," 60.

41. In "The Causation Fallacy: Bakke and the Basic Arithmetic of Selective Admissions," Goodwin Liu makes a statistically cogent argument for his position that race-conscious admissions programs at professional schools have a tiny negative impact on nonminority applicants and a significantly positive one for minority applicants. Strangely he takes the numbers on the *Bakke* table at face value and does not specifically mention that the comparison of Bakke's individual scores to regular and special admittee mean scores is fallacious (*Michigan Law Review* 100, no. 5 [March 2002]: 1053–1054).

42. Reidhaar, "Memorandum of Points and Authorities in Opposition to Issuance of Preliminary Injunction or Writ of Mandate," 101–102.

43. Reidhaar, "Memorandum on Points and Authorities," 100–106 (trial quotation 105; injunction quotation, 106).

44. Judge F. Leslie Manker, "Addendum to Notice of Intended Decision," in Slocum, vol. 1, 195 (first quotation); and Manker, "Findings of Fact and Conclusions of Law," in Slocum, vol. 1, 202 (second quotation).

45. Speech act theory was developed in the 1960s by British linguists and philosophers of language including J. L. Austin who, in *How To Do Things with Words*, 2nd ed. (Cambridge, MA: Harvard University Press 1975), wrote about constative and performative utterances and locutionary and illocutionary acts. Here I rely on three texts: John R. Searle, "Austin on Locutionary and Illocutionary Acts," *Philosophical Review* 77, no. 4 (October 1968): 405–424; John R. Searle, "How Performatives Work," *Tennessee Law Review* 58, no. 3 (1990–1991): 371–392; and Pintip Hompluem Dunn, "How Judges Overrule: Speech Act Theory and the Doctrine of *Stare Decisis*," *Yale Law Journal* 113, no. 2 (November 2003): 493–531. Oddly, Searle's article, though published in a law journal, does not provide examples of performatives in legal-judicial discourse; Dunn's article is one of the few that applies speech act theory to legal-judicial discourse.

46. Searle uses the terms "linguistic act" and "extra-linguistic act" rather than "social act." He notes that the speakers of both utterances—"I promise

to visit you" and "I adjourn the meeting"—perform linguistic acts simply by uttering these statements, but the *facts* they create—a promise and an end to the meeting—are respectively linguistic and social. He further explains that creating the adjournment of a meeting requires an institution (that is, a set of rules on meetings that give the meeting chair authority to perform certain acts), but he waffles between whether creating a promise does or does not need an institution, suggesting with respect to the promise to visit that language itself is an institution. I disagree that language is an institution, and another example, "I order you to leave the room," demonstrates why. If I lack the institutional authority to order you to leave the room, you might refuse to leave or you might leave if you perceive me as personally threatening. (See "How Performatives Work," 384.)

47. Searle, "How Performatives Work," 383.

48. Dunn, "How Judges Overrule," 514.

49. Judge F. Leslie Manker, "Notice of Intended Decision" (22 November 1974), in Slocum, vol. 1, 167 (first and second quotes), 166 (third quote).

50. Manker, "Notice of Intended Decision," 170. The cause of action, which must appear in the initial complaint, consists of the facts that give the would-be plaintiff the right to seek reliefs from another party's actions ("Cause of action," Legal Dictionary, accessed 15 June 2017, http://legal-dictionary.thefreedictionary.om/cause+of+action. In "Civil Procedure—What Identifies a 'Cause of Action'; Joinders," Timothy P. Kerry asks whether civil cases involving two or more actions that cause harm to the plaintiff should be heard as separate or joined cases (*Marquette Law Review* 50, no. 1 [August 1966]: 101–111). Given that Bakke was disadvantaged by age bias, interviewer animus, date of application, and preferences for applicants with prominent parents or enrolled spouses, one might ponder how a factually robust case would have been decided.

51. Manker, "Notice of Intended Decision," 170–171.

52. Manker, "Notice of Intended Decision," 178.

53. Manker, "Notice of Intended Decision," 178.

54. Manker, "Notice of Intended Decision," 190–191.

55. Manker, "Notice of Intended Decision," 191.

56. Reidhaar, "Memorandum of Points and Authorities," 101–102.

57. Manker, "Notice of Intended Decision," 174 (first quotation), 174 (second quotation), 176 (third quotation).

58. Manker, "Notice of Intended Decision," 176.

59. Manker, "Notice of Intended Decision," 177.

60. Statistics, Admissions Office, May 8, 1973, Exhibit B, in Slocum, vol. 1, 143–144.

CHAPTER 9. THE DISAPPEARANCE OF RACISM

1. Donald L. Reidhaar, "Petition for Transfer," 27 May 1975, in Alfred Slocum, ed., *Allan Bakke v. Regents of the University of California* (Dobbs Ferry, NY: Oceana, 1978), vol. 1, 215–221 (216 importance and urgency) (cited hereafter as Slocum).

2. Commentators do not agree on precisely how many amicus briefs were submitted to the California Supreme Court. Howard Ball stated that nine were filed, six siding with UCD and three with Bakke (*The Bakke Case: Race, Education, and Affirmative Action* [Lawrence: University Press of Kansas, 2000], 58); Allan P. Sindler wrote that eight briefs were filed, six siding with UCD and two with Bakke (the ADL and AFT) (*Bakke, DeFunis, and Minority Admissions: The Quest for Equal Opportunity* [New York and London: Longman, 1978], 223). Nine briefs are reprinted in Slocum—for Bakke the Anti-Defamation League and for UCD or minority interests the Association of American Law Schools, American Medical Student Association, Association of American Medical Colleges, Charles Houston Bar Association and National Conference of Black Lawyers, Mexican American Legal Defense and Education Fund, National Association for the Advancement of Colored People, National Lawyers Guild, and Society of American Law Teachers. In fact, two of these briefs were submitted after the court announced its decision: the NAACP pressed for a retrial with a minority intervenor who would present a full range of evidence; the Charles Houston Bar Association and National Conference of Black Lawyers also wanted a retrial and objected to the retroactive application of a state constitution amendment to this case.

3. Justice Stanley Mosk, "Opinion, *Regents of the University of California v. Bakke,* California Supreme Court," in Slocum, vol. 2, 55. Joel Dreyfus and Charles Lawrence III implicitly attribute the placement of the holding to Mosk's antipathy to quotas and affirmative action generally (*The Bakke Case: The Politics of Inequality* [New York: Harcourt Brace Jovanovich, 1979]), 70–84).

4. Mosk, "Opinion," 69.

5. Mosk, "Opinion," 70.

6. Justice Matthew O. Tobriner was a labor lawyer before serving on the Washington State Supreme Court (1962–1982). Described as a liberal, he wrote opinions that upheld busing to desegregate schools, affirmed the division of property by unmarried partners, and illegalized the refusal to hire homosexuals at public utilities corporations ("California Supreme Court Justice Matthew Tobriner Dead at 78," United Press International Archives, 7 April 1982, accessed 30 April 2017, http://www.upi.com/Archives/1982/04/07/California-Supreme-Court-Justice-Matthew-Tobriner-dead-at-78/6232387003600). Dreyfuss and Lawrence noted that Tobriner, originally a registered Republican, later became a Democrat and acquired the reputation of a liberal jurist concerned by racism (*The Bakke Case*, 72–73, 88–89).

7. Justice Matthew O. Tobriner, "Dissent, *Regents of the University of California v. Bakke,* California Supreme Court," in Slocum, vol. 2, 109.

8. While searching HeinOnline's Core U.S. Journals for articles on *Bakke* published in 1978 and 1979, I wondered whether citation counts reflected other patterns. Among the many articles that focused on the Supreme Court opinions and gave little attention to the lower courts were the following: Earl M. Maltz's "Commentary: A *Bakke* Primer" (*Oklahoma Law Review* 32, no. 1 [Winter 1979]: 119–137), cited 1,597 times; Richard A. Posner's "The *Bakke*

Case and the Future of 'Affirmative Action'" (*California Law Review* 67, no. 1 [January 1979]: 171–190), cited 22,540 times; and Kenneth L. Karst and Harold W. Horowitz's "The *Bakke* Opinions and Equal Protection Doctrine" (*Harvard Civil Rights-Civil Liberties Law Review* 14, no.1 [Spring 1979]: 7–30), cited 4,998 times. Among the few articles containing detailed discussion of the case from beginning to end were these: Ralph R. Smith's "Reflections on a Landmark: Some Preliminary Observations on the Development and Significance of Regents of the University of California v. Allan Bakke" (*Howard Law Journal* 21, no. 1 [1978]: 72–127), cited fifty times; and Adolphus Levi Williams Jr.'s "A Critical Analysis of the Bakke Case" (*Southern University Law Review* 6, no. 1 [1979–80]: 41–142), cited twelve times. The citations counts seem to reflect the prominence of the author, the prestige of the journal, and the interest in high-level constitutional debates.

9. The ontological crisis, as it is sometimes dubbed, may have been anticipated by Karl Marx's satirical critique of the old and young Hegelians in "The German Ideology" (in *The Marx-Engels Reader*, ed. Robert C. Tucker, 2nd ed. [New York: Norton, 1978], 146–200). But the modern version seems to have been propelled by incommensurabilities among schools of thought (e.g., Marxian materialism and poststructuralist indeterminacy in literary and cultural theory, realism and conceptualism in art and architecture, and sociolinguistics and generative grammar in language study), by several aspects of digital technology, and by the long trajectory from material commodities to money to electronic finance. To erode the hard and fast divide between the material and symbolic, some scholars have focused on the material production of the symbolic while others have focused on the symbolic production of the material.

10. Jeffrey C. Dobbins, "New Evidence on Appeal," *Minnesota Law Review* 96, no. 6 (June 2012): 2029–2030 (first quotation), 2021 (second, third, and fourth quotations).

11. Dobbins, "New Evidence," 2029 (first and second quotations), 2051 (third quotation).

12. Dobbins, 2049–2051 (quotation 2050).

13. "Brief of the American Medical Student Association," in Slocum, vol. 1, 383 (Howard, Meharry, and Rush).

14. "Brief of the Mexican American Legal Defense and Education Fund," in Slocum, vol. 1, 463.

15. "Brief of the National Lawyers Guild," in Slocum, vol. 1, 538.

16. "Brief of the American Medical Student Association," 383–384 (numbers admitted to UCD).

17. "Brief of the Association of American Medical Colleges," in Slocum, vol. 1, 425.

18. "Brief of the Association of American Medical Colleges," 427.

19. "Brief of the Association of American Medical Colleges," 424.

20. Reynold H. Colvin and Arthur D. Links, "Reply Brief as to Appeal and Opening Brief as to Cross-Appeal," in Slocum, vol. 1, 318–319, 348–355 (cited hereafter as Colvin and Links, "Reply Brief as to Appeal and Opening Brief as to Cross-Appeal").

21. Donald L. Reidhaar, John F. Lundberg, and Gary Morrison, "Opening Brief of Appellant and Cross-Respondent," in Slocum, vol. 1, 255–256. He borrowed the dictum on evil from *Oregon v. Mitchell* (400 U.S. 112–296 [1970]). This case, which seems irrelevant to *Bakke*, challenged provisions of the 1970 Amendment of the Voting Rights Act concerning voter age, literacy tests, and resident status; the quotation comes from an opinion, dissenting in part and concurring in part, by Justices Brennan, White, and Marshall. If Reidhaar had wanted to support the claim that racial discrimination was an evil manifested in all parts of the country, he could have cited rulings in the university, school, employment, and housing cases.

22. "Brief of the National Lawyers Guild," 524–525.

23. *Lau v. Nichols*, 414 U.S. 563–572 (1974).

24. "Brief of the Mexican American Legal Defense and Education Fund," 479–480.

25. "Brief of the National Lawyers Guild," 526.

26. "Brief of the Association of American Medical Colleges," 426.

27. "Brief of the American Medical Student Association," 385–386.

28. "Brief of the American Medical Student Association," 382.

29. "Brief of the American Medical Student Association," 384 (data and quotation).

30. "Brief of the National Lawyers Guild," 536–537 (physician-population numbers).

31. "Brief of the Mexican American Legal Defense and Education Fund," 461–462 (Chicano data), 461 (bilingual issue).

32. "Brief of the National Lawyers Guild," 538–540.

33. Colvin and Links, "Reply Brief as to Appeal and Opening Brief as to Cross-Appeal," 332 (first quotation), 345 (second quotation), 347 (third quotation).

34. Donald L. Reidhaar, John F. Lundberg, and Gary Morrison, "Stipulation," in Slocum, vol. 2, 53–54.

35. Mosk, "Opinion," 57, fn. 5 (first quotation), 59, fn. 7 (second quotation).

36. Mosk, "Opinion," 71 (first quotation), 76 (second quotation), 76–77 (third quotation), 77, fn. 29 (fourth quotation).

37. *Serrano v. Priest*, 5 Cal.3d 584–619 (1971). This case, which returned to the California Supreme Court in 1976 after the US Supreme Court had ruled on a similar case, was a class-action lawsuit challenging the state's school financial scheme that relied on local property revenues to provide most of each district's funding. The minority plaintiffs claimed that the state denied low-income children—disproportionately Black, Hispanic, and other minority students—equal educational opportunity. Justice Raymond L. Sullivan's opinion does not mention the racial component, but Justice McComb's dissent quotes the racial component of the plaintiff's complaint (619).

38. For contrasting articles reviewing the literature on analogical reasoning, see Cass R. Sunstein, "On Analogical Reasoning," *Harvard Law Review* 106, no. 3 (January 1993): 741–791; and Emily Sherwin, "A Defense of Analogical Reasoning in Law," *University of Chicago Law Review* 66, no. 4 (Autumn 1999): 1179–1197.

39. Frederick Schauer, "Why Precedent in Law (And Elsewhere) is Not Totally (Or Even Substantially) about Analogy," *Perspectives on Psychological Science* 3, no. 6 (November 2006): 456 (stages of analogical reasoning), 455 (obligation and Supreme Court quotation).

40. Dan Hunter, "Reason Is Too Large: Analogy and Precedent in Law," *Emory Law Journal* 50, no. 4 (2001): 1206.

41. Frederick Schauer, "Precedent," *Stanford Law Review* 39, no. 3 (1986–1987): 577. Acknowledging that no cases have identical facts, he also recognizes "that the relevance of an earlier precedent depends upon how we characterize the facts arising in the earlier case" (577).

42. Jacob M. Carpenter, "Persuading with Precedent: Understanding and Improving Analogies in Legal Argument," *Capital University Law Review* 44, no. 3 (Summer 2016): 473.

43. Carpenter, "Persuading with Precedent," 467 (quotation). On relational features, see Hunter, "Reason Is Too Large," 1220–1224; Schauer, "Precedent," 577; and Carpenter, 481–85.

44. Sunstein, 745. The two cases he contrasts are *National Socialist Party of America v. Village of Skokie*, 432 U.S. 43 (1977), and *Brandenburg v. Ohio*, 395 U.S. 494 (1969).

45. For fascinating histories, see Mark V. Tushnet, *The NAACP's Legal Strategy against Segregated Education, 1925–1950* (Chapel Hill, NC: University of North Carolina Press, 1987); Leland B. Ware, "Setting the Stage for *Brown*: The Development and Implementation of the NAACP's School Desegregation Campaign, 1930–1950," *Mercer Law Review* 52, no. 2 (Winter 2001): 631–674; and Genna Rae McNeil, "Before *Brown*: Reflections on Historical Context and Vision," *American University Law Review* 52, no. 6 (August 2003): 1431–1460. In *Murray v. Pearson* 169 Md. 478, 182 A. 590 (1936), Donald Gaines Murray applied to the University of Maryland Law School, a white institution, and was rejected on the basis of his race. Maryland, a segregated state, had no law school for African Americans and provided small grants for Blacks to attend out-of-state law schools. The Maryland Court of Appeals affirmed the trial court in ordering the law school to admit Murray. In *Missouri Ex Rel. Gaines v. Canada* (1938) 305 U.S. 337–354, Lloyd Gaines applied to the University of Missouri Law School, a white institution, and was rejected on the basis of his race. Missouri, a segregated state that had no law school for Blacks at the historically Black Lincoln University, provided small grants for Black students to attend out-of-state law schools. The Supreme Court held it unconstitutional for the state to base access to legal education on race and reversed the lower court's ruling to the contrary. In *Sipuel v. Board of Regents of the University of Oklahoma* (1948) 332 U.S. 631–633, Ada Lois Sipuel was the first African American to apply to the University of Oklahoma Law School. Reversing the lower court, the Supreme Court found that she was rejected solely on the basis of race and remanded to the lower court for proceedings consistent with the opinion in *Gaines*. In *Sweatt v. Painter* (1950) 339 U.S. 629–636, Heman Sweatt was offered admission to a clearly substandard law school that Texas hastily established for African Americans; instead, he applied to the University of Texas Law School, which rejected him on the basis of

race. Quite apart from the question of whether the white and Black law schools were equal in terms of faculty and facilities, the Supreme Court held that the equal protection clause required the University of Texas to admit the plaintiff and remanded to the lower court for proceedings consistent with the opinions in prior cases. In *McLaurin v. Oklahoma State Regents for Higher Education* (1950) 339 U.S. 637–642, George McLaurin applied to the University of Oklahoma's doctoral program in education and was rejected on the basis of his race; when litigation ensued, the state amended its segregation laws to permit the admission of African Americans to programs not available at Black institutions. After admitting him, however, the university required him to sit in separate classrooms, on a separate floor of the library, and at a separate cafeteria table. Although the university argued that McLaurin was able to use the same facilities as white students, the Supreme Court held that McLaurin, having been admitted to the graduate school, must be treated the same as other students.

46. Colvin and Links, "Reply Brief as to Appeal and Opening Brief as to Cross-Appeal," 330. Actually, Reidhaar, Lundberg, and Morrison argued that the court should acknowledge the broad discretion of professional schools in the University of California system to determine admissions goals, criteria, and decisions. They noted that the California Constitution gave the regents broad power over the university and that federal and state court rulings typically deferred to universities when lacking proof that their actions were arbitrary or capricious ("Opening Brief of Appellant and Cross-Respondent," in Slocum, vol. 1, 236–244).

47. Colvin and Links, "Reply Brief as to Appeal and Opening Brief as to Cross-Appeal," 330–331.

48. Reidhaar, Lundberg, and Morrison, "Opening Brief of the Appellant and Cross-Respondent," in Slocum, vol. 1, 251.

49. Mosk, "Opinion," 67–68.

50. Tobriner, "Dissent," 84 (long quotation), 85 (short quotations).

51. See John Hart Ely, "The Constitutionality of Reverse Racial Discrimination," *University of Chicago Law Review* 41, no. 4 (Summer 1974): 723–741. The article, discussing the *DeFunis* case just after the Court issued its opinions, has been cited 5,749 times (according to HeinOnline).

52. Colvin and Links, "Reply Brief as to Appeal and Opening Brief as to Cross-Appeal," 339.

53. Colvin and Links, "Reply Brief as to Appeal and Opening Brief as to Cross-Appeal," 340.

54. See Mark Strasser, "The Invidiousness of Invidiousness: On the Supreme Court's Affirmative Action Jurisprudence," *Hastings Constitutional Law Quarterly* 21, no. 2 (Winter 1994): 323–404. Strasser argues that the Court's invidiousness discourse is muddled. Sometimes the Court looks for a policy's intended goal (e.g., to segregate or integrate), sometimes for the policymakers' motivation (e.g., malice or benevolence), and sometimes for adverse effects on fundamental interests (332–339).

55. *Burton v. Wilmington Parking Authority*, 365 U.S. 715–730 (1961).

56. *Palmer v. Thompson*, 403 U.S. 217–273 (1971), 225 (quotation on motivation), 226 (quotation on Blacks and whites alike).

57. *Wright v. Council of the City of Emporia*, 407 U.S. 451–483 (1972), 462.

58. *Swann v. Charlotte-Mecklenburg Board of Education*, 402 U.S. 1–32 (1971), 22.

59. *Swann v. Charlotte-Mecklenburg Board of Education*, 25.

60. Reidhaar, Lundberg, and Morrison, "Opening Brief of Appellant and Cross-Respondent," 251–252 (first quotation), 261–262 (second quotation).

61. In a landmark article, Joseph Tussman and Jacobus tenBroek examined underinclusivity, overinclusivity, and other classificatory problems with respect to statutory and constitutional law ("The Equal Protection of the Laws," *California Law Review* 37, no. 3 [September 1949]: 348–353).

62. Colvin and Links, "Reply Brief as to Appeal and Opening Brief as to Cross-Appeal," 336–37.

63. Colvin and Links, "Reply Brief as to Appeal and Opening Brief as to Cross-Appeal," 337.

64. The Constitution of Virginia, Article VIII. Education, Section 1 required the Assembly to maintain free public elementary and secondary schools and ensure that they had high quality programs. Accessed 7 September 2018, https://law.lis.virginia.gov/constitution/article8/section1/. The California Constitution's Article IX defined its public-school system as consisting of free kindergarten, elementary, secondary, and technical schools; it specifically exempted public universities from free access and compulsory attendance. See Article IX, Sections 6, 9–13, accessed 5 July 2017, https://leginfo.legislature.ca.gov/faces/codes_displayText.xhtml?lawCode=CONS&division=&title=&part=&chapter=&article=IX.

65. Donald L. Reidhaar, John F. Lundberg, and Gary Morrison, "Reply Brief of Appellant and Cross-Respondent," in Slocum, vol. 1, 294.

66. Mosk, "Opinion," 63–64.

67. Tobriner, "Dissent," 90–91.

68. Tobriner, "Dissent," 92.

69. Mosk, "Opinion," 61–62.

70. Colvin and Links, "Reply Brief as to Appeal and Opening Brief as to Cross-Appeal," 334 (discussion), 335 (quotation).

71. Reidhaar, Lundberg, and Morrison, "Opening Brief of the Appellant and Cross-Respondent," 258 (short quotation), 258–259 (long quotation).

72. Reidhaar, Lundberg, and Morrison, "Opening Brief of the Appellant and Cross-Respondent," 259.

73. Mosk, "Opinion," 65–66, fn. 12 (admissions program not benign), 72, footnote 23 (no constitutional right).

74. Mosk, "Opinion," vol. 2, 70.

75. *Griggs v. Duke Power Co.* 401 U.S. 428–436.

76. "Brief of the National Lawyers Guild," 521–522 (1971) (Douglas), 522–527 (MCAT studies).

77. "Brief of the National Lawyers Guild," 541.

78. "Brief of the American Medical Student Association," 385 (short and long quotations).

79. "Brief of the American Medical Student Association," 391 (first quotation), 387 (second quotation).

80. Mosk, "Opinion," 71.

81. Mosk, "Opinion," 76.

82. Mosk, "Opinion," 76–77 (long quotation), 77, fn. 29.

83. "Brief of the American Medical Student Association," 387. The National Lawyers Guild asked the court to reverse the trial court or, "in the alternative, reverse and remand to the trial court an order that appropriate intervenors may participate in a hearing or issues relating to the discriminatory effect of traditional medical school entrance criteria" ("Brief of the National Lawyers Guild," 542). Also asking for a retrial, the Charles Houston Bar Association and the National Conference of Black Lawyers objected, among other things, to the lack of proof for Bakke's claims ("Brief Amici Curiae of the Charles Houston Bar Association and the National Conference of Black Lawyers in Support of the Regents of the University of California," in Slocum, vol. 1, 435–447).

84. Charles R. Lawrence III and Nathaniel S. Colley, "Petition of the National Association for the Advancement of Colored People for Leave to File Amicus Curiae on Petition for Rehearing," in Slocum, vol. 1, 484–485 (first quotation), 488 (second, third, and fourth quotations).

85. Edward Chen, "The Case for Minority Participation in Reverse Discrimination Litigation," *California Law Review* 67, no. 1 (January 1979): 191–229; and Emma Coleman Jones, "Litigation without Representation: The Need for Intervention to Affirm Affirmative Action," *Harvard Civil Rights/ Liberties Law Review* 14, no. 1 (Spring 1979): 31–87 (discussion of interest impairment, 56–69. Also see Michael Selmi, "The Life of *Bakke:* An Affirmative Action Retrospective," *Georgetown Law Review* 87, no. 4 (April 1999): 981–1022; and Allison Orr Larsen, "The Trouble with Amicus Facts," *Virginia Law Review* 100, no. 8 (December 2014): 1757–1818.

CHAPTER 10. PLACES

1. Joel Dreyfuss and Charles Lawrence III, *The Bakke Case: The Politics of Inequality* (New York: Harcourt Brace Jovanovich, 1979), 177 (Cox, Mishkin, and Owens).

2. Dreyfuss and Lawrence, *The Bakke Case*, 33–34 (Colvin).

3. Bernard Schwartz, *Behind Bakke: Affirmative Action and the Supreme Court* (New York: New York University Press, 1988), 41–42 (Brennan's objections); and Lee Epstein and Jack Knight, "Piercing the Veil: William J. Brennan's Account of *Regents of the University of California v. Bakke*," *Yale Law and Policy Review* 19, no. 2 (2001): 346–357 (tallies of voting). Schwartz explains that although Justice Brennan had chastised his colleagues for ducking the constitutional issue in *DeFunis v. Odegaard*, he lobbied against a review of *Bakke* because he feared that his colleagues would regard the special admissions places as a quota and strike down all race-conscious admissions programs (40–41).

4. Michael Selmi, "The Life of *Bakke:* An Affirmative Action Retrospective," *Georgetown Law Review* 87, no. 4 (April 1999): 987–988.

5. For the list of attorneys, see the syllabus of *Regents of the University of California v. Bakke* 438 U.S. 265–421 (1978), 268–270. Charles E. Odegaard had just published *Minorities in Medicine: From Receptive Passivity to Positive Action, 1966–1976* (Washington, DC: Josiah Macy Jr. Foundation, 1977).

6. Ralph R. Smith, "Reflections on a Landmark: Preliminary Observations on the Development and Significance of Regents of the University of California v. Allan Bakke," *Howard Law Journal* 21, no. 1 (1978): 72–127 (quotation 91). The National Conference of Black Lawyers quotation appears in the same article on p. 91, fn. 58. Smith's article, published a few months before the Supreme Court announced its opinions, provides a damning critique that should be required reading.

7. Emma Coleman Jones and Peter D. Roose, "Brief of Amici Curiae" (14 January 1977), *Regents of the University of California v. Bakke* 438 U.S. 265–421 (1978), 19, 20, 21, 23–27 (facts not in the record) (cited hereafter as *Bakke*). They represented the National Urban League, National Organization for Women, United Automobile, Aerospace, and Agricultural Implement Workers (UAW), National Conference of Black Lawyers, La Raza National Lawyers Association, Mexican American Legal Defense and Education Fund, Puerto Rican Legal Defense and Education Fund, California Rural Legal Assistance, National Bar Association, UCLA Black Alumni Association, National Federation of Women's Organizations, UC Davis Law School, Chicano Alumni Association, Charles Houston Bar Association, National Lawyers Guild, La Raza National Law Students Association, and Black American Law Students Association.

8. Reidhaar, Morrison, and Mishkin, "Reply to Brief of Amici Curiae in Opposition to Certiorari," in *Bakke*, 6 (first quotation), 3 (second quotation).

9. See Nancy Hicks, "Califano Says Quotas Are Necessary to Reduce Bias in Jobs and Schools," *New York Times*, 18 March 1977; David Bird, "Califano Concedes Error in Advocating Job Quotas," *New York Times*, 1 April 1977; Peter Kihss, "Califano Asks 'Goals' on Minority Students in Colleges," *New York Times*, 6 June 1977; and Gene L. Maeroff, "Minority Goals in Education," *New York Times*, 9 June 1977.

10. Herbert O. Reid Sr. and Arthur Kindy, "Brief in Reply of Members of the Congressional Black Caucus, Members of the Congress of the United States, to Brief of the United States, Amici Curiae" (1 June 1977), in *Bakke*, 5 (first quotation), 4 (second and third quotations), 11 (fourth quotation). Caucus members signing the brief were William Clay, Cardiss Collins, John Conyers, Ronald Dellums, Charles C. Diggs, Jr., Walter E. Fauntroy, Augustus F. Hawkins, Barbara Jordan, Ralph H. Metcalf, Robert N. C. Nix, and Charles B. Rangel.

11. Ralph R. Smith, Anslyene A. Abraham, and Vance Fort, "Brief of Amicus Curiae the National Conference of Black Lawyers" (7 June 1977), in *Bakke*, vii (first quotation), 38 (second quotation).

12. Dreyfuss and Lawrence, 166–167.

13. The pressure campaigns are described in Dreyfuss and Lawrence, 162–171; Schwartz, *Behind Bakke*, 45–47 (quotation on justices, 46); Howard Ball,

The Bakke Case: Race, Education, and Affirmative Action (Lawrence: University Press of Kansas, 2000), 70–77; Lee Lescaze, "Blacks Decry 'Neglect' by White House," *Washington Post*, 29 August 1977; Bill Peterson, "Proposed Justice Dept. Brief Draws Fire of Rights Groups," *Washington Post*, 9 September 1977; Bill Peterson, "Justice Dep. Brief Irks Black Caucus, Civil Rights Groups," *Washington Post*, 9 September 1977; "Blacks Urge Carter to Back 'Affirmative Action,'" *New York Times*, 10 September 1977; William Claiborne, "Hill Black Caucus Warns Carter on Stand on Quotas," *Washington Post*, 13 September 1977; Simon Anekwe, "NAACP Seeks Meeting with Carter on Administration Stand on Bakke," *New York Amsterdam News*, 24 September 1977; and Bill Neikirk, "Blacks Score Points with Carter," *Chicago Tribune*, 25 September 1977.

14. Epstein and Knight, "Piercing the Veil," 359. Also see Bernard Schwartz, *Behind Bakke*, 42–141.

15. "Opinion of Justice John Paul Stevens, Chief Justice Warren E. Berger, Justice Potter Stewart, and Justice William H. Rehnquist," in *Bakke*, 421. Cited hereafter as Stevens.

16. "Opinion of Justices William J. Brennan, Byron R. White, Thurgood Marshall, and Harry A. Blackmun," in *Bakke*, 379. Cited hereafter as Brennan.

17. "Opinion of Justice Lewis F. Powell," in *Bakke*, 271–272. Cited hereafter as Powell.

18. A search of HeinOnline Core U.S. Journals reveals the publication of 514 articles, comments, and notes on *Regents of the University of California v. Bakke* in 1978–1979 alone. The majority focused on the Supreme Court opinions—explicating opinions, debating issues, and speculating on the implications for affirmative action. Examples include Kent D. Lollis, "Right to Education: *University of California v. Bakke*," *Black Law Journal* 6, nos. 2–3 (1978), 265–275 (20 citations); Earl M. Matz, "A Bakke Primer," *Oklahoma Law Review* 32, no. 1 (1979): 119–137 (1,603 citations); Robert M. O'Neil, "Bakke in the Balance: Some Preliminary Thoughts," *California Law Review* 67, no. 1 (1979): 143–170 (946 citations); and David F. Schwartz, "Discriminatory Intent and Disproportionate Impact: A Postmortem of Regents of the University of California v. Bakke," *California Western Law Review* 15, no. 2 (1979): 179–218 (26 citations). Very few articles offered a critical perspective on the whole case from beginning to end. One of the best was Smith's "Reflections on a Landmark" (50 citations). Only a few discussed systemic racism and its ideological underpinnings. For instance, Guido Calabrisi's "Bakke as Pseudo-Tragedy" discussed the clash between meritocratic ideology and reparative justice in cases involving scarce resources (*Catholic University Law Journal* 28, no. 3 [1978] 427–444 [6,165 citations]); and Alan David Freeman's "Legitimizing Racial Discrimination through Antidiscrimination Law: A Critical Review of Supreme Court Doctrine" (*Minnesota Law Review* 62, no. 6 [July 1978]: 1049–1120 [802 citations]) analyzed legal individualism's erasure of group subjugation. Finally, citation counts for the 1978–1979 articles reveal that articles published in mainstream law journals or authored by prominent law scholars received more attention than those published in minority law journals or

authored by minority scholars. Thus reputation and race intersected to marginalize minority scholarship—with rare exceptions like Derrick Bell, whose articles routinely received over 2,000 citations.

19. Paul J. Mishkin, Jack B. Owens, and Donald L. Reidhaar, "Brief for Petitioner" (7 June 1977), in *Bakke*, 2.

20. Mishkin, Owens, and Reidhaar, "Brief for Petitioner," 19.

21. Mishkin, Owens, and Reidhaar, "Brief for Petitioner," 21.

22. Mishkin, Owens, and Reidhaar, "Brief for Petitioner," 23.

23. Mishkin, Owens, and Reidhaar, "Brief for Petitioner," 25.

24. Mishkin, Owens, and Reidhaar, "Brief for Petitioner," 29 (first quotation), 30 (second quotation).

25. Norman Dorsen, Ruth Bader Ginsburg, and Frank Askin, "Brief of the American Civil Liberties Union, the ACLU of Northern California, the ACLU of Southern California, *Amici Curiae*" (7 June 1977), in *Bakke*, 17.

26. Dorsen, Ginsburg, and Askin, "Brief of the American Civil Liberties Union," 2 (first quotation), 8 (second and third quotation), 11 (fourth quotation).

27. Dorsen, Ginsburg, and Askin, "Brief of the American Civil Liberties Union," 12.

28. Warren E. Burger, "Memorandum to the Conference" (21 October 1977), reproduced in Schwartz, *Behind Bakke*, 169.

29. Lewis F. Powell Jr., "Memorandum to the Conference" (22 November 1977), reproduced in Schwartz, *Behind Bakke*, 215 (quotation).

30. William H. Rehnquist, "Memorandum to the Conference" (10 November 1977), reproduced in Schwartz, *Behind Bakke*, 189 (both quotations).

31. Rehnquist, "Memorandum to the Conference," 191

32. Joseph Tussman and Jacobus tenBroek, "The Equal Protection of the Laws," *California Law Review* 37, no. 3 (September 1949): 344 (first quotation), 345 (second quotation).

33. In the eighteenth century, the two major taxonomies for classifying plants—the Linnaean system (Carolus Linnaeus) and the Buffonian system (Georges-Louis Leclerc, Comte de Buffon)—used different traits and relations to construct their classes. Although both systems had difficulty accommodating anomalies, Buffon's addition of time to taxonomic thinking led to theories about species modification that prompted taxonomic revisions. See Randall T. Schuh, "The Linnaean System and Its 250-Year Persistence," *Botanical Review* 69, no. 1 (January-March 2003): 59–78; and Paul L. Farber, "Buffon and the Concept of Species," *Journal of the History of Biology* 5, no. 2 (Autumn 1972): 259–284. John Money and Anke Ehrhardt's work with "hermaphroditic" patients (*Man & Woman, Boy & Girl: The Differentiated and Dimorphism of Gender Identity from Conception to Maturity* [Baltimore: Johns Hopkins University Press, 1972]) challenged the male/female binary; feminist scientists then produced a large literature on the diversity of sex chromosomes, physical features, and sex/gender identities. Where Justice Rehnquist believed that the existence of anomalies should invalidate classification, I believe they indicate that we should question the belief that classification can freeze what is gradated and fluctuating.

34. Thomas S. Kuhn, *The Structure of Scientific Revolutions* (Chicago: University of Chicago Press, 1962), 10–11 (paradigm), 66–76 (coproduction of facts, theories, and paradigms), 76–90 (responses to anomalies and paradigms).

35. Alan Lightman and Owen Gingerich, "When Do Anomalies Begin?," *Science* 255, no. 5045 (7 February 1992); 690 (first quotation), 693 (second quotation).

36. The logic of discipline is described by Michel Foucault in *Discipline and Punish: The Birth of the Prison*, trans. Alan Sheridan (New York: Vintage, 1979). By the early nineteenth century, disciplinary techniques, many originating with the Jesuits, included the seriation of time, partitioning of space, disaggregation of the mass into individuals, continual observation, and normalizing judgment. They structured schools, factories, clinics, military camps, and prisons.

37. Vilma S. Martinez, Peter D. Roos, Linda Hanten, Tomas Olmos, Albert Meyerhoff, and Ralph Santiago Abascal, "Brief of Amici Curia: Mexican American Legal Defense and Educational Fund, American G. I. Forum, League of United Latin American Citizens, National Council of La Raza, Association of Mexican American Educators, La Raza National Lawyers Association, IMAGE, Los Angeles MECHA Central, Country of Santa Clara, National Association for Equal Educational Opportunities, John Vasconcellos, and UNITAS" (7 June 1977), in *Bakke*, 5 (quotation), 6–19 (social and legal history), 19–27 (data). Cited hereafter as Martinez et al.

38. Martinez et al., "Brief of Amici Curia," 27.

39. Martinez et al., "Brief of Amici Curia," 39 (quotation), 28–45 (medical students, physicians, and community healthcare).

40. Harry B. Reese, "Brief Amicus Curiae of the Law School Admissions Council in Support of Petitioner the Regents of the University of California" (7 June 1977), in *Bakke*, 10.

41. Reese, "Brief Amicus Curiae," 11 (all data).

42. Reese, "Brief Amicus Curiae," 13.

43. Reese, "Brief Amicus Curiae," 18.

44. Reese, "Brief Amicus Curiae," 19 (both quotations).

45. Ephraim Margolin, "Brief of the Black Law Students Association at the University of California, Berkeley School of Law as Amicus Curiae" (2 June 1977), in *Bakke*, 3 (short quotation), 8 (long quotation).

46. Margolin, "Brief of Black Law Students Association," 9 (first quotation), 13 (second quotation).

47. Margolin, "Brief of Black Law Students Association," 14–15 (long quotation), 15 (short quotation).

48. Margolin, "Brief of Black Law Students Association," 16.

49. Reynold H. Colvin and Robert D. Links, "Brief for Respondent" (5 August 1977), in *Bakke*, 2.

50. Justice Rehnquist wrote, "Because the Regents' policy is to deliberately prefer minorities for sixteen of the seats in the medical school," evidence of minority underrepresentation "in the absence of a showing of intent" cannot "sustain the policy" (Justice William H. Rehnquist, "Memorandum to the

Conference," 10 November 1977, reproduced in Schwartz, *Behind Bakke*, 177). He uses intent as a wedge strategy to undermine the medical school: it had a policy of intentionally preferring minority applicants, but it provided no evidence that the policy remedied its intentional past discrimination against such applicants.

51. Colvin and Links, "Brief for Respondent," 27–28.

52. The scores appear in several documents including Colvin and Links, "Brief for Respondent," 8–9. Emma Coleman Jones and Peter D. Roos's brief explains that as applications arrived in batches, the admissions committee made offers to the top applicants in each batch. When Bakke applied belatedly for the first time, the committee was not accepting applicants at or above his benchmark score; when he applied early in the process for the second time, the committee waitlisted twenty applicants with higher scores than he had. They conclude that he would not have been among the sixteen regular applicants admitted in the absence of the special admissions places (Emma Coleman Jones and Peter D. Roos, "Brief of Amici Curiae" [14 January 1977], in *Bakke*, 10).

53. Benjamin Vinar, "Brief of the Queens Jewish Community Council and The Jewish Rights Council as *Amici Curiae* in Opposition to Petitioner" (21 June 1977), in *Bakke*, 2.

54. Jennings P. Felix and Marco DeFunis, "Brief of Amicus Curiae Young Americans for Freedom" (4 August 1977), in *Bakke*, 4. Clearly smarting from DeFunis's own litigation, they filled nine pages with references to Justice Douglas's dissent, Lino Graglia's *Pennsylvania Law Review* article, and another article sympathetic to DeFunis. Recalling the claim that DeFunis was denied a (nonexistent) resident preference, they claimed that Bakke's rejection by his home state medical school virtually foreclosed his opportunity to obtain a medical education (21–25 and 30 on Douglas and sympathetic articles; 5–8 on resident argument).

55. Judith R. Cohn and Robert L. Blacksberg, "Brief Amicus Curiae for the Order Sons of Italy in America in Support of Respondent" (4 August 1977), in *Bakke*, 9.

56. Robert D. McFadden, "B'nai B'rith Says State U. Discriminates," *New York Times*, 3 March 1972; "'Reverse Discrimination' U.S. Probes White Male Bias Cases," *Chicago Tribune*, 23 November 1972; and Murray Illson, "6 Jewish Groups Charge Colleges with Reverse Bias," *New York Times*, 14 January 1973. The white plaintiffs in *Alevy v. Downstate Medical Center* (39 N.Y. 2d 325 [1976]) did not prevail.

57. Philip B. Kurland et al., "Brief of Amici Curiae" (4 August 1977), in *Bakke*, 5–6. The lawyers were Philip B. Kurland, Daniel D. Polsby, Larry M. Lavinsky, and Arnold Forster for the Anti-Defamation League, Leonard Greenwald for the New York City Council of Supervisors and Administrators, Dennis Raft for the National Jewish Commission on Law and Public Affairs, David J. Ashe for the Jewish Labor Committee, and Renato R. Biribin and Anthony J. Fornelli for UNICO National. Cited hereafter as Kurland.

58. Kurland, "Brief of Amici Curiae," 13 (first header), 15 (second header), 19 (third header).

59. Kurland, "Brief of Amici Curiae," 15–16.

60. Kurland, "Brief of Amici Curiae," 5; Cohn and Blacksberg, "Brief of Amicus Curiae for the Order Sons of Italy," 3; Vinar, "Brief," 9; and Justice Harry A. Blackmun, "Memorandum to the Conference," 1 May 1978, in Schwartz, *Behind Bakke*, 257–258.

61. Justice Lewis F. Powell Jr., "Regents of the University of California v. Bakke Oral Argument—October 12, 1977," *Oyez*, 6. Justice John Paul Stevens and Archibald Cox, "Oral Argument," 7, https://www.oyez.org/cases/1979/76-811.

62. Reynold H. Colvin and Justice William H. Rehnquist, "Oral Argument," 44 (Colvin quotation), 45 (Rehnquist quotation).

63. Justice Lewis F. Powell Jr., "Memorandum to the Conference" (22 November 1977), in Schwartz, *Behind Bakke*,199–200.

64. Reynold H. Colvin, "Oral Argument," 40.

65. "Hearsay," *Black's Law Dictionary*, ed. Bryan A. Garner, 2nd pocket ed. (St. Paul, MN: West, 2001), 118. For a fuller description of hearsay rules and exceptions, see Article VIII. Hearsay, Federal Rules of Evidence, Legal Information Institute, Cornell University Law School. Accessed 16 January 2018, https://www.law.cornell.edu/rules/fre/article_VIII.

66. Colvin and Links, "Brief for Respondent," 31.

67. Colvin and Links, "Brief for Respondent," 32–34 (quotation 33–34)

68. The lawyers were Howard L. Greenberger and Samuel Rabinove (American Jewish Committee), Abraham S. Goldstein and Nathan Z. Dershowitz (American Jewish Congress), Themis N. Anastos and Philip S. Makin (Hellenic Bar Association of Illinois), Arthur J. Gajarsa (Italian-American Foundation), Anthony J. Fornelli (Unico National), Anthony P. Krzywicki (Polish American Affairs Council), Thaddeus L. Kowalski (Polish American Educators Association), and Julian E. Kulas (Ukrainian Congress Committee), with Alan M. Dershowitz of counsel. See "Brief of . . . Amici Curiae" (5 August 1977), in *Bakke*, 21–22. Cited hereafter as Greenberger et al.

69. Greenberger et al., "Brief of . . . Amici Curiae," 2, (first quotation) 12 (second quotation), 21–22 (third quotation).

70. Justice Felix Frankfurter, "Opinion of the Court," *Hughes v. Superior Court of California*, 339 U.S. 460–469 (1950), 464.

71. Greenberger et al., "Brief of . . . *Amici Curiae*," 32.

72. Greenberger et al., "Brief of . . . *Amici Curiae*," 34.

73. Greenberger et al., "Brief of . . . *Amici Curiae*," 35–36.

74. Ronald A. Zumbrun, John H. Findley, and William P. Harvey, "Brief of Amicus Curiae for Pacific Legal Foundation in Support of Respondent," 5 August 1977, in *Bakke*, 14.

75. *On Equality of Educational Opportunity*, ed. Frederick Mosteller and Daniel P. Moynihan (New York: Random House, 1972.

76. Zumbrun, Findley, and Harvey, "Brief of Amicus Curiae," 16 (all quotations).

77. Zumbrun, Findley, and Harvey, "Brief of Amicus Curiae," 17 (all quotations).

78. Diane Ravitch, "On Equality of Educational Opportunity. By Frederick Mosteller and Daniel P. Moynihan," *Change* 4, no. 4 (May 1972): 62.

79. Arthur R. Jensen, "Social Class, Race, and Genetics: Implications for Education," *American Educational Research Journal* 5, no. 1 (January 1968): 1–42; and Arthur R. Jensen, "Selection of Minority Students in Higher Education," *University of Toledo Law Review* 2, no. 2–3 (Spring–Summer 1970): 403–457. Jensen divides the determinants of lower Black scores on standardized tests into extrinsic factors, such as economic disadvantage, racial discrimination, and educational inequality, and intrinsic factors, mainly genetically determined intelligence and abilities. He argues that mean scores on IQ tests and college entrance tests, differentiated by race and sex, show that whites are more intelligent than Black women who are more intelligent than Black men. He concludes that better K-12 education of Black students will not improve their performance in higher education.

80. Reese, "Brief Amicus Curiae," 23.

81. Kenneth K. Wong and Anna C. Nicotera, "'Brown v. Board of Education' and the Coleman Report: Social Science Research and the Debate on Educational Equality," *Peabody Journal of Education* 79, no. 2 (2004): 122–135 (large research project, 128); and Karl Alexander and Stephen L. Morgan, "The Coleman Report at Fifty: The Legacy and Implications for Future Research on Equality of Opportunity," *Russell Sage Foundation Journal of the Social Sciences* 2, no. 5 (September 2016): 1–16 (fallible student reports, 2).

82. Anthony E. Boardman, "On Equality of Educational Opportunity, by Frederick Mosteller and Daniel P. Moynihan," *Journal of the American Statistical Association* 68, no. 342 (June 1973): 489–491 (quotation 491).

83. Ronald F. Carver, "The Coleman Report: Using Inappropriately Designed Achievement Tests," *American Educational Research Journal* 12, no. 1 (Winter 1975): 77–86.

84. Vinar, "Brief," 5–6 (first quotation), 6–7 (second quotation).

85. Vinar, "Brief," 8 (all quotations).

86. Vinar, "Brief," 9.

87. Vinar, "Brief," 12.

88. Theodore M. Shaw (associate director and counsel), interview with the author, NAACP Legal Defense and Education Fund, New York, 23 October 2002, 24 pp. in typescript (quotation, 3).

CONCLUSION

1. Ernesto Laclau and Chantal Mouffe, "Post-Marxism without Apologies," *New Left Review* 166 (November–December 1982): 82.

2. Michel Foucault, "Two Lectures," in *Power/Knowledge: Selected Interviews and Other Writings 1972–1977*, ed. Colin Gordon, trans. Colin Gordon, Leo Marshall, John Mepham, and Kate Soper (New York: Pantheon, 1980), 79–108 (quotation 88).

3. Foucault, "Two Lectures," 93 (first quotation), 96 (second quotation), 99 (third quotation).

4. On professionalization, see Magali Sarfatti Larson, *The Rise of Professionalism: A Sociological Analysis* (Berkeley: University of California Press, 1977); Burton J. Bledstein, *The Culture of Professionalism: The Middle Class and the Development of Higher Education in America* (New York: Norton, 1976); Andrew Abbott, *The System of Professions: An Essay on the Division of Expert Labor* (Chicago: University of Chicago Press, 1988); Hugh Davis Graham and Nancy Diamond, *The Rise of American Research Universities Elites and Challengers in the Postwar Era* (Baltimore: Johns Hopkins University Press, 1997); and Sheila Slaughter and Gary Rhoades, *Academic Capitalism and the New Economy* (Baltimore: Johns Hopkins University Press, 2004).

5. James Allen Smith, *The Idea Brokers: Think Tanks and the Rise of the New Policy Elite* (New York: Free Press, 1991); and John L. Campbell and Ove K. Pedersen, *The National Origins of Policy Ideas: Knowledge Regimes in the United States, France, Germany, and Denmark* (Princeton, NJ: Princcton University Press, 2014), 22 (first quotation), 23 (second quotation). For an overview of old and new conservatism, see Valerie L. Scatamburlo, *Soldiers of Misfortune: The New Right's Culture War and the Politics of Political Correctness* (Bern: Peter Lang, 1998), chapter 1, "Backlash: Old Strategies, New Times," 25–73. Chapter 9 of Smith's book is titled "The Marketplace of Ideas," a phrase often uttered by officials I interviewed at the Heritage Foundation and other conservative organizations.

6. See my discussion of conservative organizations in "Manufacturing the Attack on Liberalized Higher Education," *Social Text* 36 (Fall 1993): 40–80. Classic works on think tanks—such as Smith's *The Idea Brokers* and Gregg Easterbrook's "'Ideas Move Nations': How Conservative Think Tanks Have Helped to Transform the Terms of Political Debate" (*Atlantic* 257, no. 1 [January 1986])—focus on their policy output but not their operations in larger networks that produce and circulate discourse.

7. *Cultural Conservatism: Toward a New National Agenda* (Washington, DC: Institute for Cultural Conservatism/Free Congress Foundation, 1987), 5 (quotation).

8. William S. Lind and William H.Marshner, eds., *Cultural Conservatism: Theory and Practice* (Washington, DC: Free Congress Foundation/Center for Cultural Conservatism, 1991).

9. See James Davison Hunter, *Culture Wars: The Struggle to Define America* (New York: Basic Books, 1991); John K. Wilson, *The Myth of Political Correctness: The Conservative Attack on Higher Education* (Durham, NC: Duke University Press, 1995); Michael Berube and Cary Nelson, eds., *Higher Education Under Fire: Politics, Economics, and the Crisis of the Humanities* (New York: Routledge, 1995); Jeffrey Williams, ed., *PC Wars: Politics and Theory in the Academy* (New York: Routledge, 1995); and Chris Mooney, *The Republican War on Science*, rev. ed. (New York: Basic Books, 2005).

10. Charles L. Heatherly, ed., *Mandate for Leadership: Policy Management in a Conservative Administration* (Washington, DC: Heritage Foundation, 1981) presented a comprehensive agenda for the Reagan administration. For Heritage's academic initiatives, see my "Manufacturing the Attack on Liberalized

Higher Education" and "Dollars for Scholars: The Real Politics of Humanities Scholarship and Programs," in *The Politics of Research*, ed. E. Ann Kaplan and George Levine (New Brunswick, NJ: Rutgers University Press, 1997), 193–233.

11. Author interview with Curt A. Levey (director of Legal and Public Affairs), Center for Individual Rights, Washington, DC, 4 June 2001, 23 pp. in typescript (quotation, 3).

12. Levey Interview, 2001, 5.

13. Levey Interview, 2001, 9–10.

14. Author interview with Roger Clegg (vice president and general counsel), Center for Equal Opportunity, Washington, DC, 5 June 2001, 23 pp. in typescript; and author interview with Roger Clegg, Topaz Hotel, Washington, DC, 25 June 2002, 16 pp. in typescript.

15. Jamie Halper, "Meet the Man behind the Harvard Admissions Lawsuit," *Boston Globe*, 15 June 2018; and Anemona Hartocollis, "A One-Man Legal Factory Fights Harvard over Affirmative Action," *New York Times*, 20 November 2017.

16. Clegg Interview, 2001, 7 (quotation).

17. Clegg Interview, 2001, 13–14.

18. Author interview with Kevin Nguyen (executive director), American Civil Rights Institute, Hotel Monaco, San Francisco, CA, 21 July 2002, 22 pp. in typescript.

19. Proposition 54 (2003). Text of Proposed Law, California Statewide Special Election Official Voter Information Guide, Secretary of State website, California, accessed 4 March 2019, at http://vigarchive.sos.ca.gov /2003/special /propositions/2-3-4-text.html.

20. Nguyen Interview, 2002, 14.

21. Nguyen Interview, 2002, 16.

22. Nguyen Interview, 2002, 18.

23. Nguyen Interview, 2002, 7–8.

24. Nguyen Interview, 2002, 6–8 (quotations and summary).

25. "Appendix: SP-1: Resolution of the University of California Board of Regents Adopting a Policy 'Ensuring Equal Treatment' of Admissions," 20 July 1995, *Representations* 55 (Summer 1996): 184–186.

26. Proposition 209: Text of Proposed Law, California Secretary of State website, accessed 4 March 2019, http://vigarchive.sos.ca.gov/1996/general /pamphlet/209text.htm. For background, see Ula Taylor, "Proposition 209 and the Affirmative Action Debate on the University of California Campus," *Feminist Studies* 25, no. 1 (Spring 1999): 95–103. Passed by voters in November 1996, Proposition 209 was a joint project of Governor Pete Wilson and UC Regent Ward Connerly. At a twelve-hour meeting on the Berkeley campus, they persuaded the regents to abolish "preferential treatment" and then raised $5.2 million to support the ballot initiative campaign.

27. Theodore Cross and Robert Bruce Slater, "How Bans on Race-Sensitive Admissions Severely Cut Black Enrollments at Flagship State Universities," *Journal of Blacks in Higher Education* 38 (Winter 2002–2003): 95.

28. Jennifer M. Chacon, "Race as a Diagnostic Tool: Latinas/os and Higher

Education in California Post-209," *California Law Review* 96, no. 5 (October 2008):1224–1226. University of California enrollment data for all campuses, broken out by seven racial groups, are available in Cecilia A. Conrad, "Affirmative Action and Admission to the University of California," in *Impacts of Affirmative Action: Policies and Consequences in California*, ed. Paul Ong (Walnut Creek, CA: Sage, 1999), 171–196. As a result of the ban, system-wide enrollments dropped by 131 percent for Blacks, 148 percent for Chicanos/Latinos, and 39 percent for Native Americans; enrollments increased by 11 percent for Filipinos, 115 percent for whites, and 451 percent for Asian Americans (180).

29. Grant H. Blume and Mark C. Long, "Changes to Levels of Affirmative Action in College Admissions in Response to State-Wide Bans and Judicial Rulings," *Educational Evaluation and Policy Analysis* 36, no. 2 (June 2014): 231.

30. Catherine L. Horn and Stella M. Flores, "Percent Plans in College Admissions: A Comparative Analysis of Three States' Experiences," The Civil Rights Project (now at UCLA, but originally at Harvard University), 2003. A brief submitted to the US Supreme Court in *Gratz v. Bollinger*, 539 U.S. 244–305 (2003) reports that after the affirmative-action ban the UC system admitted 1,600 fewer African Americans, 4,000 fewer Latinos, and 675 fewer Native Americans at a time when the numbers of high-school graduates in each group increased. See Christopher A. Hansen and E. Vincent Warren (ACLU) and Elaine R. Jones et al. (NAACP LDF), "Brief for the Patterson Respondents," *Gratz v. Bollinger*, 539 U.S. 244–305 (2003), posted on the ACLU website. For charts showing Black and Hispanic declines at UC Berkeley and UCLA for 1990 through 2011, see "How Minorities Have Fared in States with Affirmative Action Bans," which accompanies Tamar Lewin and Richard Pérez-Peña, "Colleges Brace for Supreme Court Review of Race-Based Admissions," *New York Times*, 30 June 2015._

31. Chacon, "Race as a Diagnostic Tool," 1217 (first and second quotations), 1218 (third quotation). For one of the most thorough studies of percent plans in California, Texas, and Florida, see Horn and Flores, "Percent Plans."

32. "Poor School Conditions Prompt Lawsuit on Behalf of Students: How Does Your School Compare?," *Education World*, 18 May 2000; and Jeannie Oakes and Martin Lipton, "Schools That Shock the Conscience: Williams v. California and the Struggle for Education on Equal Terms Fifty Years after Brown," *Berkeley Journal of African-American Law & Policy* 6, no. 2 (2004): 152–177. When Governor Arnold Schwarzenegger took office, he settled the case out of court in 2004.

33. Stella M. Flores and Catherine L. Horn, "Texas Top Ten Percent Plan: How It Works, What Are Its Limits, and Recommendations to Consider," Educational Testing Service Report (Princeton, NJ: ETS, 2015), 5–6 (information on California Plan); and Chacon, 1228 (quotation), 1231–1232 (high-school courses). An ACLU report published nine years after the 2004 settlement showed that California had failed to make many of the obligatory improvements in facilities, teachers, and textbooks (Sally Chung, *Williams v. California: Lessons Learned from Nine Years of Implementation* [Los Angeles: ACLU Foundation of Southern California, 29 September 2013]).

34. Author interview with Theodore M. Shaw (associate director and counsel), NAACP Legal Defense and Education Fund, New York, 23 October 2002, 25 pp. in typescript (quotation 4).

35. *Cheryl J. Hopwood v. State of Texas*, 78 F.3d 932–968 (5th Cir. 1996), 949–951. To limit race-conscious remedies to the smallest possible unit, the Fifth Circuit argued that the law school, which was operationally autonomous within the university and separated from the public school system, could not remedy the effects of past college or school discrimination (959–961).

36. "Texas after Hopwood: Revisiting Affirmative Action," House Research Organization, Texas House of Representatives, 22 April 1997, 8 pp. (discussion of Morales opinion, 3–6).

37. "Texas after Hopwood: Revisiting Affirmative Action," 5–6 (percentage data); Cross and Slater, "Bans on Race-Sensitive Admissions," 95 (numerical data).

38. "Texas after Hopwood: Revisiting Affirmative Action," 5–8.

39. Data from Nicholas Webster, "Analysis of the Texas Ten Percent Plan," Kirwan Institute Research Paper (Columbus: Ohio State University, 2007), 4.

40. Flores and Horn, "Texas Top Ten Percent," 7.

41. For the Texas Ten Percent Plan, see Flores and Horn, 7–15 (review of the research), 11 (race-conscious admissions compared to percent plans); Cross and Slater, 95–96, 98–99; and Angela M. Hough, "All Deliberate Ambiguity: The Question of Diversity, College Admissions, and the Future of the Texas Top-Ten-Percent Plan," *Texas Tech Law Review* 39, no. 1 (Fall 2006): 203–205, 211–228 (TTPP and new proposals). The most sophisticated analysis of minority applications, admissions, and enrollments is Angel Harris and Marta Tienda, "Minority Higher Education Pipeline Consequences of Changes in College Admissions Policy in Texas," *Annals of the American Academy of Political and Social Sciences* 627, no. 1 (January 2010): 60–81. For trends through 2011, see Ford Fessenden and Josh Kelly, "How Minorities Have Fared in States with Affirmative Action Bans," (charts),in Lewin and Pérez-Peña, "Colleges Brace for Supreme Court Review."

42. Shaw Interview, 2002, 1.

43. Author interview with Diane L. Gross (public policy counsel), Lawyers Committee for Civil Rights Under the Law, Washington, DC, 8 June 2001, 15 pp. in typescript (national and local groups, 9–10); and author interview with Julian Bond (chair of the NAACP Board), Washington, DC, 26 June 2002, 14 pp. in typescript (Florida voter turn-out and quotation, 7). After the 2000 election, I interviewed the chair of the NAACP's Florida Conference; the director of the People for the American Way's Florida voting project; the organizer of the Miami LGBT and Cuban communities; and the senior attorney for the Advancement Project. We discussed the get-out-the-vote campaign: the march on Tallahassee, the "Arrive with Five" project to bring voters to the polls, and the "Election Protection" assistance on election day. The interviewees told me that police stopped and ticketed African Americans who carpooled to polling places; that the names of fully eligible voters appeared on the felon list (among them, the NAACP state chair and her minister); and that polling

places lacked interpreters and bilingual ballots in Haitian districts, access for wheelchair occupants, and large print ballots for visually impaired voters. In addition, campaign staff handed prepunched Republican ballots to some Cuban voters in Miami, and dated photographs showed chained ballot boxes left in a school stairwell while votes were counted. Subsequently the NAACP (joined by the Advancement Project, Lawyers' Committee for Civil Rights Under the Law, NAACP Legal Defense and Education Fund, and People for the American Way) filed *NAACP v. Harris* (January 2001), which was settled in 2002. Many of these practices are mentioned in "ACLU, National Civil Rights Groups File Florida Voting Rights Lawsuit to Eliminate Unfair Voting Practices," American Civil Liberties Union, 10 January 2001. See Rick Bragg, "Affirmative Action Ban Meets a Wall in Florida," *New York Times*, 7 June 1999; Sarah Lueck, "Thanks, Brother: Bush Faces Hot Debate in Florida over Affirmative Action," *Wall Street Journal*, 6 March 2000; Ron Daniels, "Black Vote Disrespected, Disregarded in Election 2000," *Pittsburgh Courier*, 23 December 2000; F. Finley McRae, "Town Hall Meeting Set on Election Fraud; U.S. to Sue Florida Counties," *Los Angeles Sentinel*, 6 June 2002; and Neely Tucker, "He Got His Way. Then He Got a Mess," *Washington Post*, 7 January 2016.

44. "Look What Happens When Affirmative Action Is Banned: Black Students Are Pushed Down into Second- and Third-Tier Institutions of Higher Education," *Journal of Blacks in Higher Education* 34 (Winter 2001–2002): 86 (2000–2001 numbers); and "Let's Hear the Truth about How Blacks Are Faring under Jeb Bush's One Florida Plan," *Journal of Blacks in Higher Education* 45 (Autumn 2004): 56 (2002–2004 numbers), 57 (state university demographics).

45. Scott Powers and Louis Zaragoza, "10 Years in, 'One Florida' Posts Mixed Results for Minorities at Universities," *Orlando Sentinel*, 10 April 2010.

46. *Katuria E. Smith et al. v. University of Washington Law School et al.*, United States District Court, W.D. Wash, 2F.Supp.2d, 1324 (1998). The district court certified the class for purposes of injunctive and declaratory relief but not for damages. As the case progressed, Smith and Rock attended other law schools and Pyle attended the UW Law School.

47. American Civil Rights Institute, "Background on I-200," n.d., I-200 read, "Shall government be prohibited from discriminating or granting preferential treatment based on race, sex, color, ethnicity, or national origin in public employment, education and contracting?" Quoted in Paul Guppy, "A Citizen's Guide to Initiative 200: The Washington State Civil Rights Initiative," Policy Center, 1 September 1998.

48. Tom Brune and Joe Heim, "Initiative 200—New Battle Begins Interpreting Law," *Seattle Times*, 4 November 1998; and Tom Brune, "Locke Keeps Diversity as Goal," *Seattle Times*, 1 December 1998.

49. *Katuria E. Smith et al. v. University of Washington Law School et al.*, United States Court of Appeals, Ninth Circuit, 233 F.3d, 1188 (2000).

50. On the University of Washington, see "Look What Happens When Affirmative Action Is Banned," 83–85. On 1990–2011 trends, see Fessenden and Kelly, "How Minorities Have Fared in States with Affirmative Action Bans."

51. See *Gratz v. Bollinger*, 539 U.S. 244–305 (2003).

52. See *Grutter v. Bollinger*, 539 U.S. 306–395 (2003).

53. NAACP Legal Defense and Education Fund, "Case: University of Michigan Race-Conscious Admissions," 18 February 2003, accessed 16 February 2019, https://www.naacpldf.org/case-issue/university-michigan-race-conscious-admissions/; Jeremy Berkowitz, "Student Intervenors Denied Time to Give Oral Arguments to Court," *Michigan Daily* 11 March 2003, accessed 16 February 2019, https://www.michigandaily.com/content/student-intervenors-denied-time-give-oral-arguments-court; and Miranda Massie, "A Student Voice and a Student Struggle: The Intervention in the University of Michigan Law School Case," *Berkeley La Raza Law Journal* 12, no. 2 (2001): 231–234 (quotations 233).

54. As Jennifer Gratz continued to lead the effort to ban affirmative action, it was not smooth sailing. A 2011 letter written by her attorney to the ACRI and its affiliates announced that she was resigning her position as the ACRI's director of Research. She accused the organization and CEO Ward Connerly of inadequate stewardship of donor money, payroll irregularities, nondisclosure of personal relationships with employees and contractors, use of funds for unrelated personal matters, and failure to file organizational tax returns. See Robert N. Driscoll, letter to Board of Directors of ACRI, ACRC, ACRF, 22 September 2011, accessed 16 February 2019, https://www.documentcloud.org/documents/284163-gratz-driscoll-letter.html. A year later in 2012, Gratz cofounded the XIV Foundation to champion the cause of eliminating affirmative action; see her page on the foundation website at https://www.scribd.com/doc/217511782/Jennifer-Gratz-Bio; and her "Discriminating Toward Equality: Affirmative Action and the Diversity Charade," Heritage Foundation, 7 February 2014, accessed 16 February 2019, https://www.heritage.org/node/11456/print-display.

55. The language of Prop 2 went beyond previous bans, reading in part: "(1) The University of Michigan, Michigan State University, Wayne State University, and any other public college or university, community college, or school district shall not discriminate against, or grant preferential treatment to, any individual or group on the basis of race, sex, color, ethnicity, or national origin in the operation of public employment, public education, or public contracting. (2) The state shall not discriminate against, or grant preferential treatment to, any individual or group on the basis of race, sex, color, ethnicity, or national origin in the operation of public employment, public education, or public contracting." Quoted from 2006 Proposal 2 Amendment Language, Office of Diversity, Equity, and Inclusion, University of Michigan, n.d., accessed 16 February 2019, https://diversity.umich.edu/about/history/legal-matters/2006-proposal-2/.

56. Center for Individual Rights, "*Gratz* & *Grutter*: Michigan Civil Rights Initiative," n.d., accessed 16 February 2019, https://www.cir-usa.org/cases/gratz-v-bollinger-grutter-v-bollinger/gratz-grutter-michigan-bans-racial-preferences/; and *Schuette v. Coalition to Defend Affirmative Action . . . (BAMN)*, 572 U.S. 291–392 (2014).

57. For the Harvard case, most of the documents are available at Supporting Documents, The Harvard Case, Harvard University website, accessed 2 July

2019, https://admissionscase.harvard.edu/supporting-documents. As of this writing, the University of North Carolina has not posted its case documents, but the SFFA complaint is available on the Project for Fair Representation website (SFFA is an affiliate) at https://www.projectonfairrepresentation.org/case/students-for-fair-admissions-v-university-of-north-carolina-chapel-hill/. For an analysis of strategy in the two SFFA cases, see Liliana M. Garces and OiYan Poon, "Asian Americans and Race-Conscious Admissions: Understanding the Conservative Opposition's Strategy of Misinformation, Intimidation & Racial Division" (Los Angeles," Civil Rights Project Report, 1 November 2018, accessed 14 February 2019, https://www.civilrightsproject.ucla.edu/research/college-access/affirmative-action/asian-americans-and-race-conscious-admissions-understanding-the-conservative-opposition2019s-strategy-of-misinformation-intimidation-racial-division. For a critique of the SFFA study, see Harvard's Response to SFFA's Proposed *Findings of Fact and Conclusions of Law, Students for Fair Admissions, Inc. v. President and Fellows of Harvard College*, United States District Court for the District of Massachusetts, Boston Division (Civil Action No. 1:14-cv-14176-ADB), 23 January 2019, accessed 7 July 2019, https://admissionscase.harvard.edu/supporting-documents. Also see Iris M. Lewis and Sanjana L. Narayanan, "Data Could Decide the Harvard Admissions Trial. Here's How and Why," *Harvard Crimson*, 13 November 2018, accessed 7 July 2019, https://www.thecrimson.com/article/2018/11/13/admissions-data/.

58. Levey Interview, 2001, 10–11; and Nugyen Interview, 2002, 18.

59. Lewis F. Powell Jr., "Confidential Memorandum: Attack on American Free Enterprise System," to Eugene B. Sydnor, Jr. (chairman, Education Committee, US Chamber of Commerce), 23 August 1971. The document is available at the Washington and Lee School of Law Scholarly Commons. For discussion of the memo, see Lawrence B. Glickman, *Free Enterprise: An American History* (New Haven: Yale University Press, 2019), chapter 1, "A Memo That Changed the Course of History," 22–54.

60. Powell, "Confidential Memorandum," 2 (first quotation), 12–13 (second quotation), 13 (third and fourth quotations).

61. Powell, 11 (first and second quotations), 15 (third quotation).

62. Powell, 26 (first quotation), 27 (second quotation).

63. Steven M. Teles, *The Rise of the Conservative Legal Movement: The Battle for Control of the Law* (Princeton, NJ: Princeton University Press, 2010), 58–89. Only a few first-generation organizations submitted briefs in *Bakke*—the Pacific Legal Foundation, Young Americans for Freedom, and Committee on Academic Nondiscrimination and Integrity (the predecessor of the National Association of Scholars).

64. Oliver A. Houck, "With Charity for All," *Yale Law Journal* 93, no. 8 (July 1984): 1415–1564 (quotation 1514).

65. Teles, *Rise of the Conservative Legal Movement*, 67–70.

66. Author interview with Wade J. Henderson (executive director), Leadership Conference on Civil Rights, Washington, DC, 8 June 2001, 13 pp. in typescript. The organization changed its name to the Leadership Conference

on Civil and Human Rights. Current information can be found at https://civil rights.org/.

67. Adam Meyerson, "Building the New Establishment," *Policy Review* 58 (Fall 1991): 6–17, (quotation 6).

68. For a detailed summary of the 1992 Resource Bank meeting, see Ellen Messer-Davidow, *Disciplining Feminism: From Social Activism to Academic Discourse* (Durham, NC: Duke University Press, 2002), 224–228. I attended the Thirteenth Annual Resource Bank Meeting, Ideas Have Consequences: A Conservative Battleplan for the 1990s, Chicago, 21–24 April 1992.

69. See Teles, chapter 5, "The Federalist Society: Counter-Networking," 135–180 (quotations 138).

70. Amanda Hollis-Brusky, *Ideas with Consequences: The Federalist Society and the Constitutional Counterrevolution* (New York: Oxford University Press, 2015), 13, 15 (quotation).

71. See Hollis-Brusky, chapter 6, "Saying What the Law Is," 148–164.

72. Messer-Davidow, "Manufacturing the Attack on Liberalized Higher Education,",52–53. In June 1992, I spent a good bit of time at the Heritage Foundation, interviewing officials, attending events, and reading organizational material (all cited in this *Social Text* article).

73. For the full analysis, see Walter Nicholls, "Networks, Space: Theorizing the Geographies of Social Movements," *Transactions of the Institute of British Geographers* 34, no. 1 (January 2009): 78–93.

74. Ellen Messer-Davidow, "Why Democracy Will Be Hard To Do," *Social Text* 86 (Spring 2006): 1–35.

75. Sally Covington, *Moving a Public Policy Agenda: The Strategic Philanthropy of Conservative Foundations* (Washington, DC: National Committee for Responsive Philanthropy, July 1997), 42–43 (chart) and elsewhere scattered through the report.

76. On dark money, see Jeffrey Toobin's "Money Unlimited: How Chief Justice John Roberts Orchestrated the Citizens United Decision," *New Yorker*, 21 May 2012; Jane Mayer's *Dark Money: The Hidden History of the Billionaires behind the Rise of the Racial Right* (New York: Random House, 2017); and Nancy McLean's *Democracy in Chains: The Deep History of the Radical Right's Stealth Plan for America* (New York: Viking, 2017). On gerrymandering, see Anthony J. McGann's *Gerrymandering in America: The House of Representatives, the Supreme Court, and the Future of Popular Sovereignty* (Cambridge, UK: Cambridge University Press, 2016). On legislation written by special interests, see Rob O'Dell and Nick Penzenstadler, "You Elected Them to Write New Laws. They're Letting Corporations Do It Instead," *USA Today* 4 April 2019. This report is also available at the Center for Public Integrity.

77. Shaw Interview, 2002, 20.

BIBLIOGRAPHY

CASES

Anderson v. San Francisco Unified School District, 357 F. Supp. 248–255 (N.D. Cal. 1972).

Bakke v. Regents of the University of California, 18 Cal.3d 34 (1976).

Barrows v. Jackson, 346 U.S. 249–269 (1953).

Board of Trustees of the University of Alabama v. Garrett, 531 U.S. 356–424 (2001).

Brown v. Board of Education of Topeka, Shawnee County, Kan., 347 U.S. 483–496 (1954).

Burton v. Wilmington Parking Authority, 365 U.S. 715–730 (1961).

Cannon v. University of Chicago, 441 U.S. 677–749 (1979).

Chance v. Board of Examiners, 458 F.2d 1167–1179 (1972).

Cheryl J. Hopwood v. State of Texas, 78 F.3d 932–968 (5th Cir. 1996).

Citizens United v. Federal Elections Committee, 558 U.S. 310–485 (2010).

DeFunis v. Odegaard, 507 P.2d 1169 (Wash. 1973).

DeFunis v. Odegaard, 416 U.S. 312–349 (1974).

Douglas v. People of the State of California, 372 U.S. 353–367 (1963).

Fisher v. University of Texas at Austin, 570 U.S. 297–337 (2013).

Fisher v. University of Texas at Austin, 136 S.Ct. 2198–2243 (2016).

Gratz v. Bollinger, 539 U.S. 244–304 (2003).

Green v. County School Board of New Kent Co., Va., 391 U.S. 430–442 (1968).

Griggs v. Duke Power Co. 401 U.S. 428–436 (1971).

Groundhog v. Keeler, 442 F.2d 674–687 (US Court of Appeals, Tenth Circuit, 1971).

Grutter v. Bollinger, 539 U.S. 306–395 (2003).

Hughes v. Superior Court of California, 339 U.S. 460–469 (1954).

Katuria E. Smith et al. v. University of Washington Law School et al., 2F.Supp.2d, 1324 (United States District Court, W.D. Wash., 1998).

Kirkland v. New York State Department of Correctional Services, 520 F.2d 420–431 (Second Circuit, 1975).

Lau v. Nichols, 414 U.S. 563–572 (1974).

Liner v. Jafco, Inc., 375 U.S. 301–310 (1964).
Loving v. Virginia, 388 U.S. 1–13 (1967).
McLaurin v. Oklahoma State Regents for Higher Ed., 339 U.S. 637–642 (1950).
Missouri Ex Rel. Gaines v. Canada, 305 U.S. 337–354 (1938).
Morton v. Mancari, 417 U.S. 535–555 (1974).
Muller v. State of Oregon, 208 U.S. 412–423 (1908).
NAACP v. Harris, No. 01-CIV-120-GOLD (S.D. Fla. filed 10 Jan. 2001).
North Carolina v. Rice, 404 U.S. 244–248 (1971).
Oregon v. Mitchell, Attorney General 400 U.S. 112–296 (1970).
Oyama v. California, 332 U.S. 633–689 (1948).
Palmer v. Thompson, 403 U.S. 217–273 (1971).
Pearson v. Murray, 169 Md. 478 (Court of Appeals of Maryland, 1936).
Plessy v. Ferguson, 163 U.S. 537–564 (1896).
Regents of the University of California v. Bakke, 438 U.S. 265–421 (1978).
Reitman v. Mulkey, 387 U.S. 369–396 (1967).
San Antonio Independent School District v. Rodriguez, 411 U.S. 1–137 (1973).
Schuette v. Coalition to Defend Affirmative Action, Integration and Immigrant Rights and Fight for Equality by Any Means Necessary (BAMN), 572 U.S. 291–392 (2014).
Serrano v. Priest, 5 Cal. 3d 584–619 (1971).
Shelby County v. Holder, 570 U.S. 529–593 (2013).
Shelley v. Kraemer, 334 U.S. 1–23 (1948).
Simmons v. Eagle Seelatsee, 244 F. Supp. 808 (E.D. Wash., Southern Division, 1965).
Sipuel v. Board of Regents of the University of Oklahoma, 332 U. S. 631–633 (1948).
Students for Fair Admissions, Inc. v. President and Fellows of Harvard College, United States District Court for the District of Massachusetts, Boston Division (Civil Action No. 1:14-cv-14176-ADB). 23 January 2019 (now as 397 F.Supp.3d 126–206 (2019).
Swann v. Charlotte-Mecklenburg Board of Education, 402 U.S. 1–32 (1971).
Sweatt v. Painter, 339 U.S. 629–636 (1950).
United Jewish Organizations of Williamsburg, Inc. v. Carey 430 U.S. 144–187 (1976).
United States v. Carolene Products Co., 304 U.S. 144–155 (1937).
United States v. Local 86, Ironworkers, 315 F. Supp. 1202 (W.D. Wash. 1970).
Williams v. State of California, No. 312236 Cal. Sup. Ct. S.F. County (filed 17 May 2000).
Wright v. Council of the City of Emporia, 407 U.S. 451–483 (1972).
Wright v. Rockefeller, 376 U.S. 52–72 (1964).
Yick Wo v. Hopkins, 118 U.S. 356–374 (1886).

INTERVIEWS AND FIELDWORK

Bond, Julian (chair, NAACP Board). Interview with the author. Washington, DC. 26 June 2002 (in person).

Clegg, Roger (vice president and general counsel, Center for Equal Opportunity). Interviews with the author. Washington, DC. 5 June 2001 and 25 June 2002 (both in person).

Gross, Diane L. (public policy counsel, Lawyers Committee for Civil Rights Under the Law). Interview with the author. Washington, DC. 8 June 2001 (in person).

Henderson, Wade (executive director, Leadership Conference on Civil Rights). Interview with the author. Washington, DC. 8 June 2001 (in person).

Heritage Foundation. Thirteenth Annual Resource Bank Meeting, Ideas Have Consequences: A Conservative Battleplan for the 1990s. Chicago, IL. 21–24 April 1992 (attendance by the author).

Levey, Curt A. (director, Legal and Public Affairs, Center for Individual Rights). Interview with the author. Washington, DC. 4 June 2001 (in person).

Nguyen, Kevin (executive director, American Civil Rights Institute). Interview with the author. San Francisco, CA. 21 July 2002 (in person).

O'Neil, Robert M. Interviews with the author. 13 December 2016, 3 January 2017, 4 January 2017, and 9 January 2017 (email); 11 January 2017 (phone); and 23 March 2017 (in person).

Shaw, Theodore M. (associate director and counsel, NAACP Legal Defense and Education Fund). Interview with the author. New York City. 23 October 2002 (in person).

Sternberg, Craig D. Interviews with the author. 24 August 2016 (phone) and 17 September 2016 (email questionnaire).

SCHOLARSHIP AND JOURNALISM

"15 Jews Protest Action by N.Y.U." *New York Times*, 6 August 1968.

"2006 Proposal 2 Amendment Language," Office of Diversity, Equity, and Inclusion, University of Michigan, n.d., 2 pp. Accessed 16 February 2019. https://diversity.umich.edu/about/history/legal-matters/2006 -proposal-2/.

Abbott, Andrew. *The System of Professions: An Essay on the Division of Expert Labor*. Chicago: University of Chicago Press, 1988.

Abrams, Nathan. "Speaking to Power." *Jewish Quarterly* 53, no. 1 (Spring 2006): 47–50.

"ACLU, National Civil Rights Groups File Florida Voting Rights Lawsuit to Eliminate Unfair Voting Practices." American Civil Liberties Union, 10 January 2001.

Adams, Maurianne, and John Bracey, eds. *Strangers and Neighbors: Relations between Blacks and Jews in the United States*. Amherst: University of Massachusetts Press, 1999.

Age Discrimination Act of 1975, United States Department of Labor. Accessed 12 June 2011. http://dol.gov/oasam/regs/statutes/age_act.htm.

The Age Discrimination in Employment Act of 1967, United States Equal Employment Opportunity Commission. Accessed 12 June 2011. www.eeoc.gov /laws/statutes/adea.cfm.

Alexander, Karl, and Stephen L. Morgan. "The Coleman Report at Fifty: The

Legacy and Implications for Future Research on Equality of Opportunity." *Russell Sage Foundation Journal of the Social Sciences* 2, no. 5 (September 2016): 1–16.

Althusser, Louis. "Ideology and Ideological State Apparatuses (Notes toward an Investigation)." In *Lenin and Philosophy and Other Essays*, translated by Ben Brewster, 127–186. New York: Monthly Review Press, 1971.

"Ameliorative Racial Classifications under the Equal Protection Clause: DeFunis v. Odegaard." *Duke Law Journal* 1, no. 5 (December 1973): 1126–1152.

Ancheta, Angelo N. *Scientific Evidence and Equal Protection of the Law*. New Brunswick, NJ: Rutgers University Press, 2006.

Anekwe, Simon. "NAACP Seeks Meeting with Carter on Administration Stand on Bakke." *New York Amsterdam News*, 24 September 1977.

"Anti-Semitism? A Statement by the Teachers of Ocean Hill-Brownsville to the People of New York." *New York Times*, 11 November 1968.

"Anti-Semitism Held an Artificial Issue." *New York Times*, 22 October 1968.

"Appendix: SP-1: Resolution of the University of California Board of Regents Adopting a Policy 'Ensuring Equal Treatment' of Admissions, 20 July 1995." *Representations* 55 (Summer 1996): 184–186.

Arnold, Martin. "Hoving Accepts Onus for Furor." *New York Times*, 22 January 1969.

———. "The Metropolitan Yields on 'Racism' in Show Catalogue." *New York Times*, 18 January 1969.

Austin, J. L. *How to Do Things with Words*. 2nd ed. Cambridge, MA: Harvard University Press, 1975.

Babb, Sarah. "The Social Consequences of Structural Adjustment: Recent Evidence and Current Debates." *Annual Review of Sociology* 31 (2005): 199–222.

Baldwin, Fletcher N., Jr. "*DeFunis v. Odegaard*, the Supreme Court and Preferential Law School Admissions: Discretion Is Sometimes Not the Better Part of Valor." *University of Florida Law Review* 27, no. 2 (1975): 343–360.

Balint, David J. "In Memoriam—Marco DeFunis." 21 June 2006, paper copy (originally at http://www.balintlaw.com, but taken down).

Balkin, Jack M. "Ideological Drift and the Struggle Over Meaning." *Connecticut Law Review* 25, no. 3 (1992–1993): 869–892.

———. "Rewriting *Brown*: A Guide to the Opinions." In *What "Brown v. Board of Education" Should Have Said*, edited by Jack M. Balkin, New York: New York University Press, 2001: 44–76.

Ball, Howard. *The Bakke Case: Race, Education, and Affirmative Action*. Lawrence: University Press of Kansas, 2000.

Barak, Aharon. *Purposive Interpretation in Law*. Princeton, NJ: Princeton University Press, 2005.

Barber, Sotirious A., and James E. Fleming. *Constitutional Interpretation: The Basic Questions*. New York: Oxford University Pres, 2007.

Barot, Rohit, and John Bird. "Racialization: The Genealogy and Critique of a Concept." *Ethnic and Racial Studies* 24, no. 4 (2001): 601–618.

Bartlett, Katherine T. "Feminist Legal Scholarship: A History through the Lens of the 'California Law Review.'" *California Law Review* 100, no. 2 (April 2012): 381–429.

Becher, Tony. *Academic Tribes and Territories: Intellectual Enquiry and the Culture of Disciplines*. Milton Keynes, UK: Open University Press, 1989.

Beers, Carole. "James B. Wilson, Dies at 70; Retired UW Chief Counsel." *Seattle Times*, 16 October 1996.

Bell, Derrick A., Jr. "*Brown v. Board of Education* and the Interest-Convergence Dilemma." *Harvard Law Review* 93, no. 3 (January 1980): 518–533.

———. "*Brown v. Board of Education:* Reliving and Learning from Our Racial History." *University of Pittsburgh Law Review* 66, no. 1 (Fall 2004): 21–34.

———. "In Defense of Minority Admissions Programs: A Response to Professor Graglia." *University of Pennsylvania Law Review* 119, no. 2 (December 1970): 241–244.

———. "The Unintended Lessons of *Brown v. Board of Education*." *New York Law School Law Review* 49, no. 4 (2004–2005): 1053–1068.

Benson, Dee V. "Constitutional Law—Mootness—DeFunis v. Odegaard." *Brigham University Law Review* 1, no. 1 (1975): 181–194.

Berkowitz, Jeremy. "Student Intervenors Denied Time to Give Oral Arguments to Court." *Michigan Daily*, 11 March 2003.

Bernstein, Basil. *Class, Codes and Control*. 4 vols. London: Routledge, 1971–1990.

Berube, Maurice R., and Marilyn Gittell, eds. *Confrontation at Ocean Hill-Brownsville: The New York School Strikes of 1968*. New York: Praeger, 1969.

Berube, Michael, and Cary Nelson, eds. *Higher Education Under Fire: Politics, Economics, and the Crisis of the Humanities*. New York: Routledge, 1995.

Bird, David. "Califano Concedes Error in Advocating Job Quotas." *New York Times*, 1 April 1977.

Black, Henry Campbell. *Black's Law Dictionary*. 2nd pocket ed. Edited by Bryan A. Garner. St. Paul, MN: West Group, 2001.

"Blacks Urge Carter to Back 'Affirmative Action.'" *New York Times*, 10 September 1977.

Blalock, Corinne. "Neoliberalism and the Crisis of Legal Theory." *Law and Contemporary Problems* 77, no. 4 (2014): 71–104

Bledstein, Burton J. *The Culture of Professionalism: The Middle Class and the Development of Higher Education in America*. New York: Norton, 1976.

Bloom, Alexander, and Wini Breines, eds. *"Takin' It to the Streets": A Sixties Reader*. New York: Oxford University Press, 1995.

Blume, Grant H., and Mark C. Long. "Changes to Levels of Affirmative Action in College Admissions in Response to State-wide Bans and Judicial Rulings." *Educational Evaluation and Policy Analysis* 36, no. 2 (June 2014): 228–252.

Blumrosen, Alfred W. "Legal Education for Black Students: A Remedy for Class Discrimination." *University of Toledo Law Review* 2, nos. 2–3 (Spring–Summer 1970): 799–808.

Boardman, Anthony E. "On Equality of Educational Opportunity, by Frederick Mosteller and Daniel P. Moynihan." *Journal of the American Statistical Association* 68, no. 342 (June 1973): 489–491.

Bonilla-Silva, Eduardo. *Racism without Racists: Color-Blind Racism and the*

Persistence of Racial Inequality in the United States. Lanham, MD: Rowman & Litlefield, 2003.

Booth, Wayne. "Between Two Generations: The Heritage of the Chicago School." *Profession* (1982): 19–26.

———. *The Rhetoric of Fiction*. Chicago: University of Chicago Press, 1961.

Borgmann, Caitlin E. "Appellate Review of Social Facts in Constitutional Rights Cases." *California Law Review* 101, no. 5 (October 2013): 1185–1248.

Borrego, Anne Marie. "Humanities Endowment Returns to 'Flagging' Nontraditional Projects," *Chronicle of Higher Education* 50, no. 19 (16 January 2004).

Brady, Thomas F. "Outcry Growing against Bigotry." *New York Times*, 25 July 1969.

Bragg, Rick. "Affirmative Action Ban Meets a Wall in Florida." *New York Times*, 7 June 1999.

Brandwein, Pamela. "Constitutional Doctrine as Paring Tool: The Struggle for Relevant Evidence in University of Alabama v. Garrett." *University of Michigan Journal of Law Reform* 35, nos. 1–2 (Fall 2001/Winter 2002): 37–80.

Breyer, Stephen. *Active Liberty: Interpreting Our Democratic Consitution*. New York: Vintage, 2003.

Brooks, Peter. "Narrativity of the Law." *Law and Literature* 14, no. 1 (2002): 1–10.

Brune, Tom. "Locke Keeps Diversity as Goal." *Seattle Times*, 1 December 1998.

Brune, Tom, and Joe Heim. "Initiative 200—New Battle Begins Interpreting Law." *Seattle Times*, 4 November 1998.

Buder, Leonard. "2 Teachers' Cases Sent to Donovan." *New York Times*, 23 January 1969.

Burkhardt, Diane L. "A Private Right of Action under Title IX: *Cannon v. University of Chicago*." *Denver Law Journal* 57, no. 3 (1980): 437–452.

Burns, Haywood. "Racism and American Law: A New Course in Legal History." *University of Toledo Law Review* 2, nos. 2–3 (Spring–Summer 1970): 903–912.

Butler, Melissa A. "Early Liberal Roots of Feminism: John Locke and the Attack on Patriarchy." *American Political Science Review* 72, no. 1 (March 1978): 135–150.

Calabrisi, Guido. "Bakke as Pseudo-Tragedy." *Catholic University Law Journal* 28, no. 3 (1979) 427–444.

California Evidence Code, General Provisions, California Legislative Information, 300–413. Accessed 11 June 2017. http://leginfo.legislature.ca.gov/faces/codes_displayText.xhtml?lawCode=EIVD&division=2.&title=&part=&chapter=4.&article=2.

Campbell, John L., and Ove K. Pedersen. *The National Origins of Policy Ideas: Knowledge Regimes in the United States, France, Germany, and Denmark*. Princeton, NJ: Princeton University Press, 2014.

Camson, Josh. "History of the Federal Rules of Evidence." *Litigation News*, American Bar Association, 2012.

Cannon, Lou. "Bakke Also Vied with the Well-to-Do." *Washington Post*, 2 October 1977.

Carpenter, Jacob M. "Persuading with Precedent: Understanding and Improving Analogies in Legal Argument." *Capital University Law Review* 44, no. 3 (Summer 2016): 461–506.

Carroll, Maurice. "Reform Leader Fears Some Jews Are Overreacting to Slurs by 'Hate-Mongers.'" *New York Times*, 3 February 1969.

Carver, Ronald F. "The Coleman Report: Using Inappropriately Designed Achievement Tests." *American Educational Research Journal* 12, no. 1 (Winter 1975): 77–86.

"Cause of Action." *Legal Dictionary*. Accessed 15 June 2017. http://legal-dictionary.thefreedictionary.com/cause+of+action.

Center for Individual Rights. "*Gratz & Grutter:* Michigan Civil Rights Initiative." n.d., 2 pp. Accessed 16 February 2019. https://www.cir-usa.org/cases/gratz-v-bollinger-grutter-v-bollinger/gratz-grutter-michigan-bans-racial-preferences/.

Chacon, Jennifer M. "Race as a Diagnostic Tool: Latinas/os and Higher Education in California Post-209." *California Law Review* 96, no. 5 (October 2008): 1215–1258.

Chambers, Tom. "Profile—Josef Diamond." *Bar Bulletin* 20, no. 7 (March 2002).

Chanes, Jerome A. "Affirmative Action: Jewish Ideals, Jewish Interests." In *Struggles in the Promised Land: Toward a History of Black-Jewish Relations in the United States*, edited by Jack Salzman and Cornel West, New York: Oxford, 1997: 295–321.

Charlton, Linda. "Jews Fear Anti-Zionism of New Left." *New York Times*, 14 August 1970.

Chen, Edward. "The Case for Minority Participation in Reverse Discrimination Litigation." *California Law Review* 67, no. 1 (January 1979): 191–230.

Chen, Jim. "*DeFunis*, Defunct." *Constitutional Comment* 16, no. 1 (1999): 91–100.

Christopher, Thomas W., and Frederick M. Hart. "Indian Law Scholarship Program at the University of New Mexico." *University of Toledo Law Review* 2, nos. 2–3 (Spring–Summer 1970): 691–700.

"Chronology of Reverse Bias Lawsuit." *Chicago Tribune*, 29 June 1978.

Chung, Sally. *Williams v. California: Lessons Learned from Nine Years of Implementation*. Los Angeles: ACLU Foundation of Southern California, 29 September 2013.

Claiborne, William. "Hill Black Caucus Warns Carter on Stand on Quotas." *Washington Post*, 13 September 1977.

Clark, Brooke. "The Seattle School Boycott of 1966." Seattle Civil Rights and Labor History Project, 2005. http://depts.washington.edu/civilr/school_boycott.htm.

Clark, Burton T. *The Higher Education System: Academic Organization in Cross-National Perspective*. Berkeley: University of California Press, 1983.

Coleman, James S., et al. *Equality of Educational Opportunity*. Washington, DC: US Department of Health, Education, and Welfare and Office of Education, 1966.

Coleman Jones, Emma. "Litigation without Representation: The Need for Intervention to Affirm Affirmative Action." *Harvard Civil Rights/ Liberties Law Review* 14, no. 1 (Spring 1979): 31–87.

Collison, Craig. "The BSU Takes on BYU and the UW Athletics Program 1970." Seattle Civil Rights and Labor History Project. Accessed February 4, 2021. https://depts.washington.edu/civilr/BSU_BYU.htm.

Conrad, Cecilia A. "Affirmative Action and Admission to the University of California." In *Impacts of Affirmative Action: Policies and Consequences in California*, ed. Paul Ong, Walnut Creek, CA: Sage, 1999: 171–196.

Covington, Sally. *Moving a Public Policy Agenda: The Strategic Philanthropy of Conservative Foundations*. Washington, DC: National Committee for Responsive Philanthropy, July 1997.

Cross, Theodore, and Robert Bruce Slater. "How Bans on Race-Sensitive Admissions Severely Cut Black Enrollments at Flagship State Universities." *Journal of Blacks in Higher Education* 38 (Winter 2002–2003): 93–99.

Cultural Conservatism: Toward a New National Agenda. Washington, DC: Institute for Cultural Conservatism/Free Congress Foundation, 1987.

Cummings, Judith. "State Clears City College of Racial-Quota Charges." *New York Times*, 30 August 1974.

Daniels, Ron. "Black Vote Disrespected, Disregarded in Election 2000." *Pittsburgh Courier*, 23 December 2000, 5.

Dardot, Pierre, and Christian Laval. *The New Way of the World: On Neoliberal Society*. Translated by Gregory Elliott. London: Verso, 2013.

Davidio, John F., Adam R. Pearson, and Louis A. Penner. "Aversive Racism, Implicit Bias, and Microagressions." In *Microagression Theory: Influence and Implications*, edited by Gina C. Torino et al., Hoboken, NJ: Wiley, 2019: 16–31.

Davis, Kenneth Culp. "Judicial Notice." *Columbia Law Review* 55, no. 7 (November 1955): 946–984.

———. "Judicial Notice." *Law and the Social Order* (1969): 513–532.

"Defense League Scored by Rabbi." *New York Times*, 18 May 1969.

DeFunis v. Odegaard. Supreme Court Case Files Collection, Box 17, Powell Papers, Lewis F. Powell Jr. Archives, Washington & Lee University School of Law, Virginia. Accessed 6 December 2018. https://scholarlycommons.law.wlu.edu/casefiles/43/.

Delgado, Richard. "Liberal McCarthyism and the Origins of Critical Race Theory." *Iowa Law Review* 94, no. 5 (2009): 1505–1545.

Diamond, Sara. *Roads to Dominion: Right-Wing Movements and Political Power in the United States*. New York: Guilford, 1995.

DiAngelo, Robin. *White Fragility: Why It's So Hard for White People to Talk about Racism*. Boston: Beacon, 2018.

"The Different Class of '74." *Sampson Family*, 4 June 2012. http://theoregonsampsons.blogspot.com/2012/06/uw-law.html.

Dobbins, Jeffrey C. "New Evidence on Appeal." *Minnesota Law Review* 96, no. 6 (June 2012): 2029–2030.

Dogan, Mattei, and Robert Pahre. *Creative Marginality: Innovations at the Intersections of Social Sciences*. Boulder, CO: Westview, 1990.

"Donald L. Reidhaar, Chief UC System Legal Counsel." *Los Angeles Times*, 12 December 1985.

"Dore Schary Tells Panel on Violence Racism Is Divisive." *New York Times*, 4 October 1968.

Dreyfuss, Joel, and Charles Lawrence III. *The Bakke Case: The Politics of Inequality*. New York: Harcourt Brace Jovanovich, 1979.

Driscoll, Robert N. Letter to Board of Directors of ACRI, ACRC, ACRF, 22 September 2011, 5 pp. Accessed 16 February 2019. https://www.documentcould.org/documents/284163-gratz-driscoll-letter.html.

Driver, Justin. "Rethinking the Interest-Convergence Thesis." *Northwestern University Law Review* 105, no. 1 (Winter 2011): 149–198.

Dunn, Pintip Hompluem. "How Judges Overrule: Speech Act Theory and the Doctrine of *Stare Decisis*." *Yale Law Journal* 113, no. 2 (November 2003): 493–531.

Dymski, Gary A. "Racial Exclusion and the Political Economy of the Subprime Crisis." *Historical Materialism* 17, no. 2 (2009): 149–179.

Easterbrook, Gregg. "'Ideas Move Nations': How Conservative Think Tanks Have Helped to Transform the Terms of Political Debate." *Atlantic* 257, no. 1 (January 1986).

Eastland, Terry, and William J. Bennett. *Counting by Race: Equality from the Founding Fathers to Bakke and Weber*. New York: Basic Books, 1979.

Edsall, Thomas Byrne, and Mary D. Edsall. *Chain Reaction: The Impact of Race, Rights, and Taxes on American Politics*. New York: W. W. Norton, 1991.

Ely, John Hart. "The Constitutionality of Reverse Racial Discrimination." *University of Chicago Law Review* 41, no. 4 (Summer 1974): 723–741.

Emergency Citizens Committee to Save School Decentralization and Community Control. "Three Strikes—and the Children Are Out." *New York Times*, 16 October 1968.

Epstein, Lee, and Jack Knight. "Piercing the Veil: William J. Brennan's Account of *Regents of the University of California v. Bakke*." *Yale Law and Policy Review* 19, no. 2 (2001): 341–380.

Eskenazi, Stuart. "Josef 'Joe' Diamond, Father of Self-Serve Parking Lots, Remembered as Tough, Genuine." *Seattle Times*, 5 March 2007.

Eskridge, William N., Jr., Philip P. Frickey, and Elizabeth Garret. *Legislation and Statutory Interpretation*. St. Paul, MN: West/Foundation Press, 2000.

Evans, Franklin R., and Richard R. Reilly. "A Study of Speededness as a Source of Test Bias." *Journal of Educational Measurement* 9, no. 2 (Summer 1972): 123–131.

Faigman, David L. "Evidentiary Incommensurability: A Preliminary Exploration of the Problem of Reasoning from General Scientific Data to Individualized Legal Decision-Making." *Court Review* 50, no. 2 (2014): 52–61.

———. "'Normative Constitutional Fact-Finding': Exploring the Empirical Component of Constitutional Interpretation." *University of Pennsylvania Law Review* 139, no. 3 (January 1991): 541–614.

Farber, M. A. "Brooklyn Sit-In Bars 2nd Hearing by School Board." *New York Times*, 21 December 1966.

Farber, Paul L. "Buffon and the Concept of Species." *Journal of the History of Biology* 5, no. 2 (Autumn 1972): 259–284.

Farley, Jennie. "Women versus Academe: Who's Winning." *Journal of Social Issues* 41, no. 4 (1985): 111–119.

Farough, Steven D. "Structural Aporia and White Masculinities: White Men Respond to the White Male Privilege Critique." *Race, Gender & Class* 10, no. 4 (2003): 38–53.

Ferretti, Fred. "New York's Black Anti-Semitism Scare." In *Strangers and Neighbors: Relations between Blacks and Jews in the United States*, edited by Maurianne Adams and Joh Bracey. Amherst, University of Massachusetts Press, 1999.

Fessenden, Ford, and Josh Kelly. "How Minorities Have Fared in States with Affirmative Action Bans" (charts). In Lewin and Richard Pérez-Peña, "Colleges Brace for Supreme Court Review of Race-Based Admissions."

Fischer, Thomas C. "*DeFunis* in the Supreme Court: Is That All There Is?" *Journal of Law and Education* 4, no. 3 (1975): 487–509.

Fish, Stanley. "The Nifty Nine Arguments against Affirmative Action in Higher Education." *Journal of Blacks in Higher Education* 27 (Spring 2000): 79–81.

Flood, Emmet T. "Fact Construction and Judgment in Constitutional Adjudication." *Yale Law Journal* 100, no. 6 (April 1991): 1795–1814.

Flores, Stella M., and Catherine L. Horn. "Texas Top Ten Percent Plan: How It Works, What Are Its Limits, and Recommendations to Consider." Educational Testing Service Report. Princeton, NJ: ETS, 2015.

Flygare, Thomas J. "The Proposed HEW Regulations on Age Discrimination: One Rule with Many Exceptions." *Phi Delta Kappan* 61 (January 1980): 353–354.

Foucault, Michael. *The Archaeology of Knowledge and the Discourse on Language*. Translated by A. M. Sheridan Smith. New York: Pantheon, 1972.

———. *Discipline and Punish: The Birth of the Prison*. Translated by Alan Sheridan, 2nd ed. New York: Vintage, 1995.

———. *The Order of Things: An Archaeology of the Human Sciences*. New York: Vintage, 1994.

———. "Two Lectures." In *Power/Knowledge: Selected Interviews and Other Writings 1972–1977*, edited by Colin Gordon, translated by Colin Gordon, Leo Marshall, John Mepham, and Kate Soper, New York: Pantheon, 1980: 78–108.

Fox, Margaret. "Julius Lester, Chronicler of Black America, Is Dead at 78." *New York Times*, 19 January 2018 (blog).

Freeman, Alan. "Antidiscrimination Law: The View from 1989." *Tulane Law Review* 64, no. 6 (June 1990): 1407–1441.

———. "Legitimizing Racial Discrimination through Antidiscrimination Law: A Critical Review of Supreme Court Doctrine." *Minnesota Law Review* 62, no. 6 (July 1978): 1049–1119.

Friedman, Murray. *What Went Wrong? The Creation and Collapse of the Black-Jewish Alliance*. New York: Free Press, 1995.

Frymer, Paul. *Black and Blue: African Americans, the Labor Movement, and the Decline of the Democratic Party*. Princeton, NJ: Princeton University Press, 2011.

Gamson, William A., and Andre Modigliani. "The Changing Culture of Affirmative Action." In *Research in Political Sociology (A Research Annual)*, vol. 3, edited by Richard G. Braungart and Margaret M. Braungart, 137–177. Greenwich, CT: JAI Press, 1987.

Gans, Herbert. "Racialization and Racialization Research." *Ethnic and Racial Studies* 40, no. 3 (2017): 341–352.

Garces, Liliana M., and OiYan Poon. "Asian Americans and Race-Conscious Admissions: Understanding the Conservative Opposition's Strategy of Misinformation, Intimidation & Racial Division." Los Angeles Civil Rights Project Report. November 1, 2018.

Gaston, Paul M. "Reflections on Affirmative Action: Its Origins, Virtues, Enemies, Champions, and Prospects." In *Diversity Challenged: Evidence on the Impact of Affirmative Action*, edited by Gary Orfield with Michael Kurlaender, 277–293. Cambridge, MA: Harvard Education Publishing Group, 2001.

Gettleman, Marvin E., Jane Franklin, Marilyn B. Young, and H. Bruce Franklin. *Vietnam and America: The Most Comprehensive Documented History of the Vietnam War*. 2nd ed. New York: Grove Press, 1995.

Gibson, W. Walker. *Tough, Sweet, and Stuffy*. Bloomington: Indiana University Press, 1966.

Giddens, Anthony. *The Constitution of Society: Outline of a Theory of Structuration*. Berkeley: University of California Press, 1984.

Gieryn, Thomas F. "Boundary-Work and the Demarcation of Science from Non-Science: Strains and Interests in Professional Ideologies of Scientists." *American Sociological Review* 48, no. 6 (1983): 781–95.

Ginger, Ann Fagan, ed. *DeFunis versus Odegaard and the University of Washington: The University Admissions Case*. 3 vols. Dobbs Ferry NY: Oceana, 1974.

Gitlin, Todd. *The Sixties: Years of Hope, Days of Rage*. New York: Bantam, 1987.

Glazer, Nathan. "Blacks, Jews and the Intellectuals." *Commentary* 47, no. 4 (April 1969): 33–39.

Glickman, Lawrence B. *Free Enterprise: An American History*. New Haven, CT: Yale University Press, 2019.

Goldberg, David Theo. *Racist Culture: Philosophy and the Politics of Meaning*. Malden, MA: Blackwell, 1993.

Goldman, Ari L. "Rabbi Seymour Siegel, 61, Leader in Conservative Judaism, Is Dead." *New York Times*, 25 February 1988.

Goodman, Walter. "The Return of the Quota System." *New York Times*, 10 September 1972.

Gordon, Jane Anna. *Why They Couldn't Wait: A Critique of the Black-Jewish Conflict over Community Control in Ocean Hill-Brownsville (1967–1971)*. New York: Routledge, 2001.

Gottfried, Paul. *The Conservative Movement*, rev. ed. New York: Twayne, 1993.

Gould, William B. "The Seattle Building Trades Order: The First Comprehensive Relief against Employment Discrimination in the Construction Industry." *Stanford Law Review* 26, no. 4 (April 1974): 773–814.

Graglia, Lino A. "Special Admission of the 'Culturally Deprived' to Law School." *University of Pennsylvania Law Review* 119, no. 2 (December 1970): 232–240.

Graham, Hugh Davis. *The Civil Rights Era: Origins and Development of National Policy, 1960–1972*. New York: Oxford University Press, 1990.

Graham, Hugh Davis, and Nancy Diamond. *The Rise of American Research Universities Elites and Challengers in the Postwar Era*. Baltimore: Johns Hopkins University Press, 1997.

Gratz, Jennifer. "Discriminating toward Equality: Affirmative Action and the Diversity Charade." Heritage Foundation, 7 February 2014.

Gray, Sarah. "Letter to the Editor." *Sacramento Bee*, 4 January 1977.

Green, Jean. "Marco DeFunis, Student in 1971 UW Bias Suit, Dies at 52." *Seattle Times*, 18 January 2002.

Greenberg, Jack. *Crusaders in the Courts: How a Dedicated Band of Lawyers Fought for the Civil Rights Revolution*. New York: Basic Books, 1994.

———. "Integration or Segregation?" *University of Pennsylvania Law Review* 118 (1969–70): 939–943.

Griffey, Trevor. "History." Seattle Civil Rights and Labor History Project. Accessed 4 February 2021. http://depts.washington.edu/civilr/ucwa_history.htm.

Griswold, Erwin N. "Some Observations on the *DeFunis* Case." *Columbia Law Review* 75, no. 3 (April 1975): 512–519.

Guppy, Paul. "A Citizen's Guide to Initiative 200: The Washington State Civil Rights Initiative." Washington Policy Center, 1 September 1998. https://www.washingtonpolicy.org/publications/detail/a-citizens-guide-to-initiative-200-the-washington-state-civil-rights-initiative.

Gutting, Gary. *Michel Foucault's Archaeology of Scientific Reason*. Cambridge, UK: Cambridge University Press, 1989.

Halberstam, David. *The Best and the Brightest*. New York: Random House, 1972.

Halper, Jamie. "Meet the Man behind the Harvard Admissions Lawsuit." *Boston Globe*, 15 June 2018.

Hamill, Pete. *Vietnam: The Real War: A Photographic History by the Associated Press*. New York: Harry N. Abrams, 2013.

Hammond, Mary K. "May the Constitution Be Color Conscious to Remain Color-Blind?" *Ohio Northern University Law Review* 1, no. 1 (1973): 81–96.

Haney, Craig, and Aida Hurtado. "The Jurisprudence of Race and Meritocracy: Standardized Testing and 'Race-Neutral' Racism in the Workplace." *Law and Human Behavior* 18, no. 3 (June 1994): 223–248.

Haney López, Ian F. "'A Nation of Minorities': Race, Ethnicity, and Reactionary Colorblindness." *Stanford Law Review* 59, no. 4 (2007): 985–1063.

Harris, Angel, and Marta Tienda. "Minority Higher Education Pipeline Consequences of Changes in College Admissions Policy in Texas." *Annals of the American Academy of Political and Social Sciences* 627, no. 1 (January 2010): 60–81.

Harris, Cheryl I. "Critical Race Studies: An Introduction." *UCLA Law Review* 49, no. 5 (2002): 1215–1239.

Harris, Luke Charles, and Uma Narayan. "Affirmative Action and the Myth of Preferential Treatment: A Transformative Critique of the Terms of the Affirmative Action Debate." *Harvard Blackletter Law Journal* 11 (1994): 1–36.

Hartocollis, Anemona. "A One-Man Legal Factory Fights Harvard over Affirmative Action." *New York Times*, 20 November 2017.

Harvey, David. *A Brief History of Neoliberalism*. Oxford, UK: Oxford University Press, 2005.

Heatherly, Charles L., ed. *Mandate for Leadership: Policy Management in a Conservative Administration*. Washington, DC: Heritage Foundation, 1981.

Heineman, Kenneth J. *Campus Wars: The Peace Movement at American State Universities in the Vietnam Era*. New York: New York University Press, 1994.

Heirich, Max. *The Spiral of Conflict: Berkeley 1964*. New York: Columbia University Press, 1971.

Henry, John F. "The Historic Roots of the Neoliberal Program." *Journal of Economic Issues* 44, no. 3 (June 2010): 543–550.

Henry, Mary T. "Burton, Phillip (1915–1995)." HistoryLink.org.

"Hester Is Urged to Oust Hatchett." *New York Times*, 10 October 1968.

Hicks, Nancy. "Califano Says Quotas Are Necessary to Reduce Bias in Jobs and Schools." *New York Times*, 18 March 1977.

Hill, Herbert. "Racism within Organized Labor: A Report of Five Years of the AFL-CIO, 1955–1960." *Journal of Negro Education* 3, no. 2 (Spring 1961): 109–118.

Hoffmann, Banash. *The Tyranny of Testing*. New York: Crowell-Collier, 1962.

Hollis-Brusky, Amanda. *Ideas with Consequences: The Federalist Society and the Constitutional Counterrevolution*. New York: Oxford University Press, 2015.

Horn, Catherine L., and Stella M. Flores. "Percent Plans in College Admissions: A Comparative Analysis of Three States' Experiences." The Civil Rights Project, Harvard University, January 2003. https://www.researchgate.net/publication/234563152_Percent_Plans_in_College_Admissions_A_Comparative_Analysis_of_Three_States%27_Experience.

Houck, Oliver A. "With Charity for All." *Yale Law Journal* 93, no. 8 (July 1984): 1415–1564.

Hough, Angela M. "All Deliberate Ambiguity: The Question of Diversity,

College Admissions, and the Future of the Texas Top-Ten-Percent Plan." *Texas Tech Law Review* 39, no. 1 (Fall 2006): 197–228.

Hunter, Dan. "Reason Is Too Large: Analogy and Precedent in Law." *Emory Law Journal* 50, no. 4 (2001): 1197–1264.

Hunter, James Davison. *Culture Wars: The Struggle to Define America*. New York: Basic Books, 1991.

Illson, Murray. "6 Jewish Groups Charge Colleges with Reverse Bias." *New York Times*, 14 January 1973.

———. "Negroes Will Run N.Y.U King Center." *New York Times*, 2 November 1968.

"In Memoriam: Robert M. O'Neil." American Law Institute. Accessed 15 January 2020. https://www.ali.org/news/articls/memoriam-robert-m-oneil/.

"Irony over Anti-Semitism Issue Seen in Harlem Art Catalogue." *New York Times*, 29 January 1969.

Isserman, Maurice, and Michael Kazin. *America Divided: The Civil War of the 1960s*. New York: Oxford University Press, 2000.

Jensen, Arthur R. "Selection of Minority Students in Higher Education." *University of Toledo Law Review* 2, nos. 2–3 (Spring–Summer 1970): 403–457.

———. "Social Class, Race, and Genetics: Implications for Education." *American Educational Research Journal* 5, no. 1 (January 1968): 1–42.

Kahlenberg, Richard D. *Tough Liberal: Albert Shanker and the Battles over Schools, Unions, Race, and Democracy*. New York: Columbia University Press, 2007.

Kalman, Laura. *Yale Law School and the Sixties: Revolt and Reverberations*. New York: Oxford University Press, 2005.

Karabel, Jerome. *The Chosen: The Hidden History of Admission and Exclusion at Harvard, Yale, and Princeton*. New York: Houghton Mifflin, 2005.

———. "How Affirmative Action Took Hold at Harvard, Yale, and Princeton." *Journal of Blacks in Higher Education* 48 (Summer 2005): 58–77.

Karnow, Stanley. *Vietnam: A History* Rev. ed. New York: Penguin, 1997.

Karst, Kenneth L., and Harold W. Horowitz. "Affirmative Action and Equal Protection." *Virginia Law Review* 60, no. 6 (1974): 955–974.

———. "The *Bakke* Opinions and Equal Protection Doctrine." *Harvard Civil Rights-Civil Liberties Law Review* 14, no.1 (Spring 1979): 7–30.

Kaufman, Jonathan. *Broken Alliance: The Turbulent Times between Blacks and Jews in America*. New York: Scribner's, 1988.

Keller, Robert H., Jr. "William O. Douglas, the Supreme Court, and American Indians." *American Indian Law Review* 3, no. 2 (1975): 333–360.

Kelman, Mark. "Interpretive Construction in the Substantive Criminal Law." *Stanford Law Review* 33, no. 4 (April 1981): 591–674.

"Kerner, Cook Will Be Cited by B'nai B'rith." *Chicago Tribune*, 21 April 1968.

Kerry, Timothy P. "Civil Procedure—What Identifies a 'Cause of Action'; Joinders." *Marquette Law Review* 50, no. 1 (August 1966): 101–111.

Kershner, Jim. "Slade Gorton (b. 1928)." HistoryLink.org Essay, 26 November 2014.

Kifner, John. "Blacks vs. Jews." *New York Times*, 26 January 1969.

Kihss, Peter. "Califano Asks 'Goals' on Minority Students in Colleges." *New York Times*, 6 June 1977.

———. "Museum Withdraws Catalogue Attacked as a Slur on Jews." *New York Times*, 31 January 1969.

King, Marsha. "I-200—Equality on Campus: Are We There Yet?—Efforts to Diversify State Colleges Show Mixed Results after 30 Years." *Seattle Times*, 18 October 1998.

King, Seth S. "Agnew Denounces Universities Quotas to Help Minorities." *New York Times*, 13 February 1970.

Klein, Julie Thompson. *Crossing Boundaries: Knowledge, Disciplinarities, and Interdisciplinarities*. Charlottesville: University Press of Virginia, 1996.

Klein, Naomi. *The Shock Doctrine: The Rise of Disaster Capitalism*. New York: Metropolitan Books/Henry Holt, 2007.

Kolodny, Annette. "Dancing through the Minefield: Some Observations on the Theory, Practice, and Politics of a Feminist Literary Criticism." *Feminist Studies* 6, no. 1 (Spring 1980): 1–25.

Kovach, Bill. "Racist and Anti-Semite Charges Strain Old Negro-Jewish Ties." *New York Times*, 23 October 1968.

Kramer, A. Ludlow. *Race and Violence in Washington State: Report of the Commission on the Causes and Prevention of Civil Disorder*. Washington (State): Urban Affairs Council, February 1969.

Kuhn, Thomas S. *The Structure of Scientific Revolutions*. Chicago: University of Chicago Press, 1962.

Kurland, Philip B., and Gerhard Casper, eds. *Landmark Briefs and Arguments of the Supreme Court of the United States: Constitutional Law*, vol. 80. Arlington, VA: University Publications of America, 1975.

Laclau, Ernesto, and Chantal Mouffe. "Post-Marxism without Apologies." *New Left Review* 166 (November–December 1982): 79–106.

Langer, Emily. "Robert O'Neil, Former U-Va. President and Scholar of First Amendment, Dies at 83." *Washington Post*, 3 October 2018.

LaNouie, George R. "The Future of Antidiscrimination Enforcement." *Change* 6, no. 5 (June 1974): 44–45.

LaNouie, George R., and Barbara A. Lee. *Academics in Court: The Consequences of Faculty Discrimination Litigation*. Ann Arbor: University of Michigan Press, 1987.

Larsen, Allison Orr. "The Trouble with Amicus Facts." *Virginia Law Review* 100, no. 8 (December 2014): 1757–1818.

Larson, Magali Sarfatti. *The Rise of Professionalism: A Sociological Analysis*. Berkeley: University of California Press, 1977.

Lavinsky, Larry M. "*DeFunis v. Odegaard:* The 'Non-Decision' with a Message." *Columbia Law Review* 75, no. 3 (1975): 520–533.

Lazzarato, Maurizio. *The Making of the Indebted Man: An Essay on the Neoliberal Condition*. Translated by Joshua David Jordan. Amsterdam: Semiotext[e], 2011.

Lemann, Nicholas. *The Big Test: The Secret History of American Meritocracy*. Rev. ed. New York: Farrar, Straus and Giroux, 2000.

Leonard, Walter J. "*DeFunis v. Odegaard:* An Invitation to Look Backward." *Black Law Journal* 3, no. 3 (1973): 224–231.

Lescaze, Lee. "Blacks Decry 'Neglect' by White House." *Washington Post*, 29 August 1977.

"Let's Hear the Truth about How Blacks Are Faring under Jeb Bush's One Florida Plan." *Journal of Blacks in Higher Education* 45 (Autumn 2004): 56–57.

Levine, Naomi. *Ocean Hill-Brownsville Schools in Crisis: A Case History.* New York: Popular Press, 1969.

Levitch, Diane. "On Equality of Educational Opportunity. By Frederick Mosteller and Daniel P. Moynihan." *Change* 4, no. 4 (May 1972): 62–64.

Lewin, Tamar, and Richard Pérez-Peña. "Colleges Brace for Supreme Court Review of Race-Based Admissions." *New York Times*, 30 June 2015.

Lewis, Iris M., and Sanjana L. Narayanan. "Data Could Decide the Harvard Admissions Trial. Here's How and Why." *Harvard Crimson*, 13 November 2018.

Lewis, Peter. "Becoming a Lawyer without Law School." *Seattle Times*, 25 November 1991.

Liberman, Kenneth. "Semantic Drift in Conversations." *Human Studies* 35, no. 2 (Summer 2012): 263–277.

Lightman, Alan, and Owen Gingerich. "When Do Anomalies Begin?" *Science* 255, no. 5045 (7 February 1992): 690–695.

Lind, William S., and William H. Marshner, eds. *Cultural Conservatism: Theory and Practice.* Washington, DC: Free Congress Foundation/Center for Cultural Conservatism, 1991.

Lindsay, Peter. "Possessive Individualism at 50: Retrieving Macpherson's Lost Legacy." *Good Society* 21, no. 1 (2012): 132–150.

Lindsey, Robert. "White/Caucasian—and Rejected." *New York Times Magazine*, 3 April 1977, 41–47.

Liu, Amy. "Unraveling the Myth of Meritocracy within the Context of US Higher Education." *Higher Education* 62, no. 4 (October 2011): 383–397.

Liu, Goodwin. "The Causation Fallacy: Bakke and the Basic Arithmetic of Selective Admissions." *Michigan Law Review* 100, no. 5 (March 2002): 1045–1107.

Locke, John, *Two Treatises of Government: A Critical Edition.* Edited by Peter Laslett. Cambridge, UK: Cambridge University Press, 1966.

Lollis, Kent D. "Right to Education: *University of California v. Bakke.*" *Black Law Journal* 6, no. 2 (1978): 265–275.

"Look What Happens When Affirmative Action Is Banned: Black Students Are Pushed Down into Second- and Third-Tier Institutions of Higher Education." *Journal of Blacks in Higher Education* 34 (Winter 2001–2002): 82–94.

Lowndes, Joseph E. *From the New Deal to the New Right: Race and the Southern Origins of Modern Conservatism.* New Haven: Yale University Press, 2008.

Lueck, Sarah. "Thanks, Brother: Bush Faces Hot Debate in Florida over Affirmative Action." *Wall Street Journal*, 6 March 2000.

Luxemburg, Rosa. "The Accumulation of Capital—An Anti-Critique" (1913).

In *Rosa Luxemburg: Reflections and Writings*, edited by Paul LeBlanc, 175–197. Amherst, NY: Humanities Books, 1999.

MacLean, Nancy. *Democracy in Chains: The Deep History of the Radical Right's Stealth Plan for America*. New York: Viking, 2017.

Macpherson, C. B. *The Political Theory of Possessive Individualism: Hobbes to Locke*. New York: Oxford University Press, 1962.

Maeroff, Gene L. "Minority Goals in Education." *New York Times*, 9 June 1977.

Maltz, Earl M. "Commentary: A *Bakke* Primer." *Oklahoma Law Review* 32, no. 1 (Winter 1979): 119–137.

Marcantel, Jonathan A. "The Corporation as a Real Constitutional Person." *University of California Davis Business Law Review* 11, no. 2 (Spring 2011): 221–266.

Marshall, Ray. "Unions and the Negro Community." *ILR Review* 17, no. 2 (January 1964): 179–202.

Marx, Karl. "The German Ideology." In *The Marx-Engels Reader*, ed. Robert C. Tucker, 2nd ed., edited by Robert C. Tucker, 146–200. New York: Norton, 1978.

———. "Theses on Feuerbach" (1888). In Tucker, *The Marx-Engels Reader*, 143–145.

Massie, Miranda. "A Student Voice and a Student Struggle: The Intervention in the University of Michigan Law School Case." *Berkeley La Raza Law Journal* 12, no. 2 (2001): 231–234.

Masterson, Kathryn. "U. of Illinois President Resigns in Wake of Admissions Scandal." *Chronicle of Higher Education*, 23 September 2009.

Mayer, Jane. *Dark Money: The Hidden History of the Billionaires behind the Rise of the Radical Right*. New York: Doubleday, 2016.

Mayer, Martin. "The Full and Sometimes Very Surprising Story of Ocean Hill, the Teachers' Union and the Teachers' Strikes of 1968." *New York Times*, 2 February 1969.

———. *The Teachers Strike—New York 1968*. New York: Harper & Row, 1969.

"Mayor Jeered at Jewish Center As He Speaks on School Crisis." *New York Times*, 16 October 1968.

McComus, James D. "Forward to Honors Day Address by Robert M. O'Neil." University of Toledo, Toledo, Ohio, 13 May 1987.

McFadden, Robert D. "B'nai B'rith Says State U. Discriminates." *New York Times*, 3 May 1972.

McGann, Anthony J. *Gerrymandering in America: The House of Representatives, the Supreme Court, and the Future of Popular Sovereignty*. Cambridge, UK: Cambridge University Press, 2016.

McNeil, Genna Rae. "Before *Brown:* Reflections on Historical Context and Vision." *American University Law Review* 52, no. 6 (August 2003): 1431–1460.

McRae, F. Finley. "Town Hall Meeting Set on Election Fraud; U.S. to Sue Florida Counties." *Los Angeles Sentinel*, 6 June 2002.

Messer-Davidow, Ellen. "Caught in the Crunch." In "Academic Freedom and Intellectual Activism in the Post-9/11 University," edited by Edward J. Carvalho. Special issue, *Works and Days* 26, nos. 1–2 (2008–2009): 399–419.

———. *Disciplining Feminism: From Social Activism to Academic Discourse*. Durham, NC: Duke University Press, 2002.

———. "Dollars for Scholars: The Real Politics of Humanities Scholarship and Programs." In *The Politics of Research*, edited by E. Ann Kaplan and George Levine, 193–233. New Brunswick, NJ: Rutgers University Press, 1997.

———. "Investing in Higher Education: Debtors, Bettors, Lenders, Brokers." In "Saving the Humanities from the Neoliberal University," edited by Ronald Strickland. Special issue, *Humanities* 6, no. 2 (March 2017): 18 pages.

———. "Manufacturing the Attack on Liberalized Higher Education." *Social Text* 36 (Fall 1993): 40–80.

———. "The Struggle for the Academy." In *Encyclopedia of American Cultural and Intellectual History*, edited by Mary Kupiec Cayton and Peter W. Williams, vol. 2, 237–251. New York: Scribner's, 1999.

———. "Why Democracy Will Be Hard to Do." *Social Text* 86 (Spring 2006): 1–35.

Messer-Davidow, Ellen, David R. Shumway, and David J. Sylvan, eds. *Knowledges: Historical and Critical Studies in Disciplinarity*. Charlottesville: University Press of Virginia, 1991.

Meyerson, Adam. "Building the New Establishment." *Policy Review* 58 (Fall 1991): 6–17.

Miller, James. *Democracy Is in the Streets: From Port Huron to the Siege of Chicago*. New York: Simon & Schuster, 1987.

Minda, Gary. *Postmodern Legal Movements: Law and Jurisprudence at the Century's End*. New York: New York University Press, 1995.

Mitchell, W. J. T. "The Commitment to Form: Or, Still Crazy after All These Years." *PMLA* 118, no. 2 (March 2003): 321–325.

Money, John, and Anke Ehrhardt. *Man & Woman, Boy & Girl: The Differentiated and Dimorphism of Gender Identity from Conception to Maturity*. Baltimore: Johns Hopkins University Press, 1972.

Mooney, Chris. *The Republican War on Science*. Rev. ed. New York: Basic Books, 2005.

Moore, James William, and Helen I. Bendix. "Congress, Evidence and Rulemaking." *Yale Law Journal* 84, no. 1 (November 1974): 9–38.

"Mootness." U.S. Constitution Annotated, Legal Information Institute, Cornell University Law School.

Morris, Arval A. "Equal Educational Opportunity, Constitutional Uniformity and the *DeFunis* Remand." *Washington Law Review* 50, no. 3 (1975): 586–588.

Morrison, Patt. "Legislator Asks Investigation of Mosk's Conduct." *Los Angeles Times*, 19 November 1981.

Mosteller, Frederick, and Daniel P. Moynihan, eds. *On Equality of Educational Opportunity*. New York: Random House, 1972.

Murji, Karim. *Racism, Policy, and Politics*. Bristol, UK: Policy Press, 2018.

NAACP Legal Defense and Education Fund. "Case: University of Michigan Race-Conscious Admissions." 18 February 2003. Accessed 16 February 2019.

https://www.naacpldf.org/case-issue/university-michigan-race-conscious-admissions.

"Negroes Disrupt School Meeting." *New York Times*, 28 September 1967.

Neikirk, Bill. "Blacks Score Points with Carter." *Chicago Tribune*, 25 September 1977.

Nicholls, Walter. "Networks, Space: Theorizing the Geographies of Social Movements." *Transactions of the Institute of British Geographers* 34, no. 1 (January 2009): 78–93.

"Notes: The Affirmative Duty to Ingrate in Higher Education." *Yale Law Journal* 79, no. 4 (March 1970): 666–697.

Oakes, Jeannie, and Martin Lipton. "Schools That Shock the Conscience: Williams v. California and the Struggle for Education on Equal Terms Fifty Years after Brown." *Berkeley Journal of African-American Law & Policy* 6, no. 2 (2004): 152–177.

Odegaard, Charles E. *Minorities in Medicine: From Receptive Passivity to Positive Action, 1966–1976*. Washington, DC: Josiah Macy Jr. Foundation, 1977.

O'Dell, Rob, and Nick Penzenstadler. "You Elected Them to Write New Laws. They're Letting Corporations Do It Instead." *USA Today*, 4 April 2019.

Omi, Michael, and Howard Winant. *Racial Formation in the United States: From the 1960s to the 1990s*. 2nd ed. New York: Routledge, 1994.

O'Neil, Robert M. "After *DeFunis:* Filling the Constitutional Vacuum." *University of Florida Law Review* 27, no. 2 (Winter 1975): 315–342.

———. "Bakke in the Balance: Some Preliminary Thoughts." *California Law Review* 67, no. 1 (1979): 143–170.

———. *Discriminating against Discrimination: Preferential Admissions and the DeFunis Case*. Bloomington: Indiana University Press, 1975.

———. "Preferential Admissions: Equalizing Access to Legal Education." *University of Toledo Law Review* 2, nos. 2–3 (1970): 281–320.

———. "Preferential Admissions: Equalizing the Access of Minority Groups to Higher Education." *Yale Law Journal* 80, no. 4 (March 1971): 699–758.

Ong, Walter J. "The Writer's Audience Is Always a Fiction." *PMLA* 90, no. 1 (January 1975): 9–21.

Owen, David, with Marilyn Doerr. *None of the Above: The Truth behind the SATs*. Rev. ed. Lanham, MD: Rowman & Littlefield, 1999.

"Panel. DeFunis and Its Impact." *Black Law Journal* 4, no. 2 (1975): 268–290.

Paulson, Monroe G. "*DeFunis:* The Road Not Taken." *Virginia Law Review* 60, no. 6 (October 1974): 917–924.

Pedriana, Nicholas, and Robin Stryker. "Political Culture Wars 1960s Style: Equal Employment Opportunity-Affirmative Action Law and the Philadelphia Plan." *American Journal of Sociology* 103, no. 3 (November 1997): 633–691.

Peters, Julie Stone. "Law, Literature, and the Vanishing Real: On the Future of an Interdisciplinary Illusion." *PMLA* 120, no. 2 (March 2005): 442–453.

Peterson, Bill. "Justice Dep. Brief Irks Black Caucus, Civil Rights Groups." *Washington Post*, 9 September 1977.

———. "Proposed Justice Dept. Brief Draws Fire of Rights Groups." *Washington Post*, 9 September 1977.

Peterson, Iver. "3 Charging Bias Rejected Again for City College Medical Class." *New York Times*, 1 September 1975.

Phillips, McCandish. "Jewish Militants Step Up Activity." *New York Times*, 25 June 1969.

Piatote, Beth H. "The Indian/Agent Aporia." *American Indian Quarterly* 37, no. 3 (Summer 2013): 45–62.

Pieroth, Doris H. "With All Deliberate Caution: School Integration in Seattle, 1954–1968." *Pacific Northwest Quarterly* 73, no. 2 (April 1982): 49–61.

Podair, Jerald E. *The Strike That Changed New York: Blacks, Whites, and the Ocean Hill-Brownsville Crisis*. New Haven: Yale University Press, 2002.

Podhoretz, Norman. "My Negro Problem—And Ours." *Commentary* 35, no. 2 (February 1963): 95–101.

Pollak, Louis B. "*DeFunis* Non Est Disputandum." *Columbia Law Review* 75, no. 3 [1975]: 495–511.

"Poor School Conditions Prompt Lawsuit on Behalf of Students: How Does Your School Compare?" *Education World*, 18 May 2000.

Posner, Richard A. "The *Bakke* Case and the Future of 'Affirmative Action.'" *California Law Review* 67, no. 1 (January 1979): 171–190.

———. "The DeFunis Case and the Constitutionality of Preferential Treatment of Racial Minorities." *Supreme Court Review* (1974): 1–32.

Powell, Lewis F., Jr. "Confidential Memorandum: Attack on American Free Enterprise System," to Eugene B. Sydnor Jr. (chair, Education Committee, U.S. Chamber of Commerce), 23 August 1971.

Powers, Scott, and Louis Zaragoza. "10 Years In, 'One Florida' Posts Mixed Results for Minorities at Universities." *Orlando Sentinel*, 10 April 2010.

Proposition 54 (2003). Text of Proposed Law, California Statewide Special Election Official Voter Information Guide, California Secretary of State website. Accessed 4 March 2019. http://vigarchive.sos.ca.gov/2003/special/propositions/2–3-4-text.html.

Proposition 209 (1996). Text of Proposed Law, California Secretary of State website. Accessed 4 March 2019. http://vigarchive.sos.ca.gov/1996/general/pamphlet/209text.htm.

Raab, Earl. "The Black Revolution & the Jewish Question." *Commentary* 47, no. 1 (January 1969): 23–33.

"Race, Empire, and the Crisis of the Subprime." In "Race, Empire, and the Crisis of the Subprime," edited by Paula Chakaravartty and Diane Ferreira da Silva. Special issue, *American Quarterly* 64, no. 3 (September 2012).

Ravitch, Diane. "On Equality of Educational Opportunity. By Frederick Mosteller and Daniel P. Moynihan." *Change* 4, no. 4 (May 1972): 62–64.

———. *The Great School Wars—New York, 1805–1973*. New York: Basic Books, 1973.

Raymont, Henry. "Jews Debating Black Anti-Semitism." *New York Times*, 26 January 1969.

RCW 5.24.010 Judicial Notice of Constitution and Laws (1941). Revised Code of Washington. Accessed 15 March 2017. https://app.leg.wa.gov/rcw/default.aspx?cite=5.24.010.

Reese, Lynda (director of Psychometric Research) and Stephen Luebke (principal test specialist), Law School Admissions Council, "Percent of Candidate Scores Below, Selected LSAT Scaled Scores (1969–1980)," document attached in email exchange with author, 5 June 2018.

"Rejected Students Win in City College Suit." *New York Times*, 28 June 1977.

Report of the National Advisory Commission on Civil Disorders. Washington, DC: US Government Printing Office, 1 March 1968.

Resnick, Stephen, and Richard Wolff. "Althusser's Liberation of Marxian Theory." In the *Althusserian Legacy*, edited by E. Ann Kaplan and Michael Sprinker, 59–72. London: Verso, 1993.

"Reverse Discrimination' U.S. Probes White Male Bias Cases." *Chicago Tribune*, 23 November 1972.

Riches, William T. Martin. *The Civil Rights Movement: Struggle and Resistance*. New York: St. Martin's Press, 1997.

Richman, Dan. "Josef Diamond, 1907–2007: Parking Magnate Built Business in 8 States and Canada." *Seattle Post-Intelligencer*, 5 March 2007.

Ritterband, Paul. "Ethnic Power and the Public Schools: The New York City School Strike of 1968." *Sociology of Education* 47, no. 2 (Spring 1974): 251–267.

Robinson, Marc. "The Early History of the UW Black Student Union." Seattle Civil Rights and Labor History Project. Accessed 4 February 2021. http://depts.washington.edu/civilr/BSU_beginnings.htm.

Rose, Peter I. "Blacks and Jews: The Strained Alliance." *Annals of the American Academy of Political and Social Science* 454 (March 1981): 55–69.

Rosen, Sanford Jay. "Equalizing Access to Legal Education: Special Programs for Law Students Who Are Not Admissible by Traditional Criteria." *University of Toledo Law Review* 2, nos. 2–3 (Spring–Summer 1970): 321–376.

Rosenbury, Laura A. "Feminist Legal Scholarship: Charting Topics and Authors, 1978–2002." *Columbia Journal of Gender and Law* 12, no. 3 (2003): 446–460.

Rule 52. Findings and Conclusions by the Court; Judgment on Partial Findings, Federal Rules of Civil Procedure. Accessed 28 February 2017. https://www/law.cornell.edu/rules/frcp/rule_52.

Rumsfield, Donald. NATO Press Conference, Brussels, 6 June 2002. https://www.nato.int/docu/speech/2002/s020606g.htm.

Sacks, Peter. "Standardized Testing: Meritocracy's Crooked Yardstick." *Change* 29, no. 2 (March–April 1997): 24–31.

Salzman, Jack, and Cornel West, eds. *Struggles in the Promised Land: Toward a History of Black-Jewish Relations in the United States*. New York: Oxford, 1997.

Scalia, Antonin. *A Matter of Interpretation: Federal Courts and the Law*. Princeton, NJ: Princeton University Press, 1997.

Scatamburlo, Valerie L. *Soldiers of Misfortune: The New Right's Culture War and the Politics of Political Correctness*. Bern: Peter Lang, 1998.

Schane, Sanford A. "Corporation Is a Person: The Language of a Legal Fiction." *Tulane Law Review* 61, no. 3 (1986–1987): 563–610.

Schauer, Frederick. "Precedent." *Stanford Law Review* 39, no. 3 (1986–1987): 571–606.

———. "Why Precedent in Law (And Elsewhere) Is Not Totally (Or Even Substantially) about Analogy." *Perspectives on Psychological Science* 3, no. 6 (November 2006): 454–460.

Scheppele, Kim Lane. "Cultures of Facts." *Perspectives on Politics* 1, no. 2 (June 2003): 363–368.

———. "Facing Facts in Legal Interpretation: Questions of Law and Questions of Fact." *Representations* 30 (Spring 1990): 42–77.

Schlag, Pierre. "Hiding the Ball." *New York University Law Review* 71, no. 6 (December 1996): 1683–1688.

Schuh, Randall T. "The Linnaean System and Its 250-Year Persistence." *Botanical Review* 69, no. 1 (January–March 2003): 59–78.

Schumach, Murray. "Halt in Project Sought in Queens." *New York Times*, May 24, 1972.

———. "Six Jewish Groups Suggest a Meeting with Black Leadership." *New York Times*, 12 February 1972.

Schwartz, Bernard. *Behind Bakke: Affirmative Action and the Supreme Court.* New York: New York University Press, 1988.

Schwartz, David F. "Discriminatory Intent and Disproportionate Impact: A Postmortem of Regents of the University of California v. Bakke." *California Western Law Review* 15, no. 2 (1979): 179–218.

Searle, John R. "Austin on Locutionary and Illocutionary Acts." *Philosophical Review* 77, no. 4 (October 1968): 405–424.

———. "How Performatives Work." *Tennessee Law Review* 58, no. 3 (1990–1991): 371–392.

"Seattle Segregation Maps, 1920–2010." Seattle Civil Rights Labor History, n.d., 35 pp. Accessed 4 February 2021. https:/depts.washington.edu/civilr/segregation_maps.htm.

Selmi, Michael. "The Life of *Bakke:* An Affirmative Action Retrospective." *Georgetown Law Review* 87, no. 4 (April 1999): 981–1022.

Shenker, Israel. "Rabbi to Give Nixon a Kingly Blessing." *New York Times*, 19 January 1973.

Sherwin, Emily. "A Defense of Analogical Reasoning in Law." *University of Chicago Law Review* 66, no. 4 (Autumn 1999): 1179–1197.

Shumway, David, and Ellen Messer-Davidow. "Disciplinarity: An Introduction." *Poetics Today* 12, no. 2 (Summer 1991): 201–225.

Siegel, Seymour. "Letter to the Editor." *New York Times*, 25 August 1972.

Sindler, Allan P. *Bakke, DeFunis, and Minority Admissions: The Quest for Equal Opportunity*. New York: Longman, 1978.

Singh, Parlo. "Pedagogising Knowledge: Bernstein's Theory of the Pedagogic Device." *British Journal of Sociology of Education* 23, no. 4 (December 2002): 571–582.

Skrentny, John David. *The Ironies of Affirmative Action: Politics, Culture, and Justice in America*. Chicago: University of Chicago Press, 1996.

"Slade Gorton: Former United States Senator Returns from Washington." Miller Center, n.d.

Slaughter, Sheila, and Gary Rhoades. *Academic Capitalism and the New Economy*. Baltimore: Johns Hopkins University Press, 2004.

Slocum, Alfred, ed. *Allan Bakke v. Regents of the University of California*. 7 vols. Dobbs Ferry, NY: Oceana, 1978.

Smith, James Allen. *The Idea Brokers: Think Tanks and the Rise of the New Policy Elite*. New York: Free Press, 1991.

Smith, Ralph R. "Reflections on a Landmark: Preliminary Observations on the Development and Significance of Regents of the University of California v. Allan Bakke." *Howard Law Journal* 21, no. 1 (1978): 72–127.

"The Society for Critical Exchange, Phase I: 1975–1988." Edited by Patricia Harkin. Special issue, *Works and Days* 25, nos. 1–2 (2007).

Soifer, Aviam. "On Being Overly Discrete and Insular: Involuntary Groups and the Anglo-American Judicial Tradition." *Washington and Lee Law Review* 48, no. 2 (Spring 1991): 381–418.

Solum, Lawrence B. "On the Indeterminacy Crisis: Critiquing Critical Dogma." *University of Chicago Law Review* 54, no. 2 (Spring 1987): 462–503.

———. "The Interpretation-Construction Distinction." *Constitutional Commentary* 27, no. 1 (Fall 2010): 95–118.

Speich, Don. "Former UC Davis Official Backed 'Reverse Bias' Suit." *Los Angeles Times*, 4 February 1977.

Spiegel, Irving. "Jews Are Advised Not to Exaggerate Animosity of Negro." *New York Times*, 10 September 1968.

———. "Jews Troubled over Negro Ties: Long Civil Rights Support Strained by Antagonisms." *New York Times*, 8 July 1968.

———. "Job Drive Backed by H.E.W.'s Chief." *New York Times*, 17 November 1973.

———. "Job Rights Role of U.S. Disputed." *New York Times*, 18 November 1972.

———. "Judaism, Council Denounces a 'Call to Violence.'" *New York Times*, 18 July 1969.

Sprinker, Michael. "What Is Living and What is Dead in Chicago Criticism." *Boundary 2* 13, nos. 2–3 (Winter–Spring 1985): 189–212.

"Stanley Mosk, 88, Long a California Supreme Court Justice." *New York Times*, 21 June 2001.

St. Clair, Stacy, Tara Malone, and Jodi S. Cohen. "Illinois Lawmakers' Handouts." *Chicago Tribune*, 27 September 2009.

Steil, Mel, and Johanna. Entry in *The Book of Memories*, n.d., n.p. Accessed 19 February 2009. www.vsiq.com/legacy/jd/bookmemo.htm.

Steiner, Daniel. "DeFunis and Its Impact." *Black Law Journal* 4, no. 2 (1975): 268–290.

Strasser, Mark. "The Invidiousness of Invidiousness: On the Supreme Court's

Affirmative Action Jurisprudence." *Hastings Constitutional Law Quarterly* 21, no. 2 (Winter 1994): 323–404.

"Students for Fair Admission v. University of North Carolina." Project for Fair Representation. Accessed 4 February 2021. https://www.projectonfairrepresentation.org/case/students-for-fair-admissions-v-university-of-north-carolina-chapel-hill/.

Summers, Clyde W. "Preferential Admissions: An Unreal Solution to a Real Problem." *University of Toledo Law Review* 2, nos. 2–3 (Spring–Summer 1970): 377–402.

Sunstein, Cass R. "On Analogical Reasoning." *Harvard Law Review* 106, no. 3 (January 1993): 741–791.

Tatum, Beverly Daniel. *Why Are All the Black Kids Sitting Together in the Cafeteria?* Rev. ed. New York: Basic Books, 2017.

Taylor, Clarence. *Knocking at Our Own Door: Milton A. Galamison and the Struggle to Integrate New York City Schools*. New York: Columbia University Press, 1997.

Taylor, Quintard. "Black Urban Development—Another View: Seattle's Central District, 1910–1940." *Pacific Historical Review* 38, no. 4 (November 1989): 429–448.

———. "The Civil Rights Movement in the American West: Black Protest in Seattle, 1960–1970." *Journal of Negro History* 80, no. 1 (Winter 1995): 1–14.

———. *The Forging of a Black Community: Seattle's Central District from 1870 through the Civil Rights Era*. Seattle: University of Washington Press, 1994.

Taylor, Ula. "Proposition 209 and the Affirmative Action Debate on the University of California Campus." *Feminist Studies* 25, no. 1 (Spring 1999): 95–103.

Teles, Steven M. *The Rise of the Conservative Legal Movement: The Battle for Control of the Law*. Princeton, NJ: Princeton University Press, 2010.

"Texas after Hopwood: Revisiting Affirmative Action." House Research Organization, Texas House of Representatives, 22 April 1997.

"Text of Vice-President Agnew's Criticism of Lowered Entrance Standards." *Chronicle of Higher Education*, 20 April 1970.

Theodore, Athena. *The Campus Troublemakers: Academic Women in Protest*. Houston: Cap and Gown, 1986.

Tolchin, Martin. "Lindsay Backlash Confronts Javits." *New York Times*, 17 October 1968.

Toobin, Jeffrey. "Money Unlimited: How Chief Justice John Roberts Orchestrated the Citizens United Decision." *New Yorker*, 21 May 2012.

Totenberg, Nina. "Discriminating to End Discrimination: The Painful DeFunis Case Raises the Specters of Racism and Anti-Semitism." *New York Times*, 14 April 1974.

"Transcript of Oral Argument." *DeFunis v. Odegaard* 416 U.S. 312 (1974), rpt. in *Black Law Journal* 3, no. 3 (1973): 249–268.

"Trial Transcript: DeFunis v. Odegaard, in King County Superior Court, 14

October 1971." Typed transcript mailed to author by Craig D. Sternberg, 2012.

Trombley, William. "Bending of Medical School Admission Rules Rapped." *Los Angeles Times*, 14 July 1976.

———. "Medical Dean Aids 'Special Interest' Applicants." *Los Angeles Times*, 5 July 1976.

Tucker, Neely. "He Got His Way. Then He Got a Mess." *Washington Post*, 7 January 2016.

Tushnet, Mark V. *The NAACP's Legal Strategy against Segregated Education, 1925–1950*. Chapel Hill: University of North Carolina Press, 1987.

Tussman, Joseph, and Jacobus tenBroek. "The Equal Protection of the Laws." *California Law Review* 37, no. 3 (September 1949): 341–381.

Van Gelder, Lawrence. "2 Suits Challenge Biomedical Unit." *New York Times*, 15 January 1975.

Ware, Leland B. "Setting the Stage for *Brown:* The Development and Implementation of the NAACP's School Desegregation Campaign, 1930–1950." *Mercer Law Review* 52, no. 2 (Winter 2001): 631–674

Webster, Nicholas. "Analysis of the Texas Ten Percent Plan." Kirwan Institute Research Paper. Columbus: Ohio State University, 2007.

Weeden, L. Darnell. "In *Fisher v. University of Texas* Derrick Bell's Interest Convergence Theory Is on a Collision Course with the Viewpoint Diversity Rationale in Higher Education." *Utah Law Review on Law* (2016): 101–119.

Weisberg, D. Kelly, ed. *Feminist Legal Theory: Foundations*. Philadelphia: Temple University Press, 1993.

Welch, Susan, and John Gruhl. *Affirmative Action and Minority Enrollments in Medical and Law Schools*. Ann Arbor: University of Michigan Press, 1998.

Weldon-Linne, Madeleine. "Title IX: No Longer an Empty Promise—*Cannon v. University of Chicago*." *DePaul Law Review* 29, no. 1 (Fall 1979): 263–286.

Wellek, Rene, and Austin Warren. *Theory of Literature*. New York: Harcourt Brace, 1948

Wheeler, Sharae. "DeFunis v. Odegaard: Another Kind of 'Jewish Problem.'" Seattle Civil Rights-Labor History Project, 2006. http://depts.washington.edu/civilr/DeFunis.htm.

Wilcox, A. Gordon. "The Tyranny of Testing by Banesh Hoffmann and Jacques Barzun." *Journal of General Education* 15, no. 4 (January 1964): 301–304.

Wilkerson, Isabel. "Banesh Hoffmann, an Author and Collaborator of Einstein." *New York Times*, 6 August 1986.

Wilkinson, J. Harvie. *From Brown to Bakke: The Supreme Court and School Integration*. New York: Oxford University Press, 1979.

Williams, Adolphus Levi, Jr. "A Critical Analysis of the Bakke Case." *Southern University Law Review* 6, no. 1 (1979–80): 41–142.

Williams, Jeffrey, ed. *PC Wars: Politics and Theory in the Academy*. New York: Routledge, 1995.

Williams, Juan. *Eyes on the Prize: America's Civil Rights Years, 1954–1965*. New York: Penguin, 1987.

Wilson, James B. "Municipal Ordinances, Mississippi Style." In *Southern Justice*, edited by Leon Friedman, 35–42. New York: Pantheon, 1965.

Wilson, John K. *The Myth of Political Correctness: The Conservative Attack on Higher Education*. Durham, NC: Duke University Press, 1995.

Wong, Kenneth K., and Anna C. Nicotera. "'Brown v. Board of Education' and the Coleman Report: Social Science Research and the Debate on Educational Equality." *Peabody Journal of Education* 79, no. 2 (2004): 122–135.

Woodward, Bob, and Scott Armstrong. *The Brethren: Inside the Supreme Court*. New York: Simon and Schuster, 1979.

INDEX